THE AUTHOR Barnaby Rogerson fir̲ ̲ ̲ ̲ ̲̲ ̲̲̲̲ ̲North Africa at the age of 16 and regularly conducts lecture tours through the area. He read History at St Andrew's University and has written several books on the area including the *Cadogan Guide to Morocco*, with Rose Baring the *Cadogan Guide to Tunisia* and is at work on the *Cadogan Guide to Libya*.

SERIES EDITOR Professor Denis Judd is a graduate of Oxford, a Fellow of the Royal Historical Society and Professor of History at the University of North London. He has published over 20 books including the biographies of Joseph Chamberlain, Prince Philip, George VI and Alison Uttley, historical and military subjects, stories for children and two novels. His most recent book is the highly praised *Empire: The British Imperial Experience from 1765 to the Present*. He has reviewed and written extensively in the national press and in journals, has written several radio programmes and is a regular contributor to British and overseas radio and television.

Cover illustration: *Arabs Skirmishing in the Mountains,* by Eugène Delacroix *c.* 1863. Chester Dale Fund, © 1997 Board of Trustees, National Gallery of Art, Washington.

Other Titles in the Series

THE TRAVELLER'S HISTORY SERIES

'**Ideal before-you-go reading**' *The Daily Telegraph*

'**An excellent series of brief histories**' *New York Times*

'**I want to compliment you . . . on the brilliantly concise contents of your books**' *Shirley Conran*

Reviews of Individual Titles

A Traveller's History of France
'**Undoubtedly the best way to prepare for a trip to France is to bone up on some history.** *The Traveller's History of France* **by Robert Cole is concise and gives the essential facts in a very readable form.**' *The Independent*

A Traveller's History of China
'**The author manages to get 2 million years into 300 pages. An excellent addition to a series which is already invaluable, whether you're travelling or not.**' *The Guardian*

A Traveller's History of India
'**For anyone . . . planning a trip to India, the latest in the excellent Traveller's History series . . . provides a useful grounding for those whose curiosity exceeds the time available for research.**' *The London Evening Standard*

A Traveller's History of Japan
'**It succeeds admirably in its goal of making the present country comprehensible through a narrative of its past, with asides on everything from bonsai to** *zazen,* **in a brisk, highly readable style . . . you could easily read it on the flight over, if you skip the movie**' *The Washington Post*

A Traveller's History of Ireland
'**For independent, inquisitive travellers traversing the green roads of Ireland, there is no better guide than** *A Traveller's History of Ireland.*' *Small Press*

A Traveller's History of
North Africa

Dedication

For Rose Baring,
Molly Rogerson and Hannah Rogerson
with love and squalor

Author's Acknowledgements
Amongst the hundreds of friends and guests that I have walked and talked my
way across North Africa in the last twenty years my most steadfast
companions have been a well thumbed copy of Abun Nasr's *History of the
Maghreb in the Islamic period* and Susan Raven's *Rome in Africa*. To quote
Richard Bury, a medieval bishop of Durham, 'If you approach them, they are
not asleep: if in the course of your enquiries you interrogate them, they do
not hide themselves; they do not grumble if you make mistakes, they do not
laugh if you are ignorant.' Without descending into the full academic
apparatus of footnotes and bibliography (which would be inappropriate to this
history designed for a general audience) I would also happily like to
acknowledge my pillaging of the works of such scholars as Roger Le
Tourneau, Charles-Robert Ageron, Michael Brett, David Mattingley and
Elizabeth Savage. My parents have been no less inspiring and it was only due to
the accident of my father's naval posting to Gibraltar and shared interests that first
exposed me at the tender age of 17 to the enduring fascination of the Maghreb.

In the process of writing I have only my partner Rose Baring to thank who has
not only shamed the slow gestation of this book by giving birth to two
daughters in the same period but also found time to give the chapters a critical
first read. With irrelevant discursions removed and grammar much repaired it
was dispatched to be further sifted and sorted by the attentive eye of Windrush's
editor Gillian Delaforce. It only remains for me to thank Ingrid Locke for the
index, Victoria Huxley for the initial commission and to enthusiastically claim all
the remaining errors as my own.

Publisher's note: Spellings of names and places have altered over the centuries
and Arabic script has been interpreted differently by non-Arab-writers; this
may lead to variations in the spelling of this book.

A Traveller's History
of North Africa

BARNABY ROGERSON

Series Editor   DENIS JUDD
Line Drawings   JOHN HOSTE

INTERLINK BOOKS
An Imprint of Interlink Publishing Group, Inc.
NEW YORK

First American edition published in 1998 by

INTERLINK BOOKS
An imprint of Interlink Publishing Group, Inc.
99 Seventh Avenue • Brooklyn, New York 11215 and
46 Crosby Street • Northampton, Massachusetts 01060

Library of Congress Cataloging-in-Publication Data available
1-56656-252-X

Typeset by Archetype IT Ltd, website: www.archetype-it.com
Printed and bound in Great Britain

Contents

Preface

This is a remarkably accomplished and enlightening book. It is also urgently needed, not least because North Africa is becoming so popular a destination for hundreds of thousands of visitors each year. But although the journey to these fascinating countries of the Maghreb – Morocco, Tunisia, Algeria, Mauretania and Libya – is only a short hop by jet plane, the sense of arriving in a very different world is immediate and profound.

My own experience of landing in Tunisia for the first time nearly twenty years ago was extraordinary: it was not merely the fact that even in early Spring real oranges were ripening on real orange trees, or that bougainvillaeas were in full and exotic bloom, or that the sun shone warmly upon a blue sea. It was the sheer contrast, the difference of culture in terms of architecture, dress, religion, body language, landscape, ways of buying and selling, the deportment of the elderly, and much else besides that was so striking. Donkeys carried sheep to market; many women were veiled; children often scampered barefoot; stalls in markets were either heaped with desirable commodities – decorated leatherwork, sweetmeats, carpets and spices, or sometimes seemed to offer goods so shabby that they would not have appeared at even the most down-at-heel car-boot sale in Britain.

Many first time travellers to North Africa probably carry a mixed bag of perceptions and prejudices to the lands of the Maghreb. This is, after all, often seen as the land of Beau Geste and the French Foreign Legion, of the Atlas Mountains, of Joe Orton disreputably at large in Morocco, of Bogart and Bacall loving and parting in *Casablanca*, of Rommel and Montgomery slugging it out in the desert battlefields, of the setting of some of the most moving scenes from *The English Patient*.

These images are, however, highly selective and almost entirely based upon modern European perceptions – many of them self-serving and ill-informed. They derive in part from the long-standing alienation, indeed the fear, which Christian Europe experienced as a result of the conquest of North Africa by Muslim Arabs during what is often known as the Dark Ages following the fall of the Roman Empire in the West. Thus, in order to render the region of the Maghreb 'safe', many of the most potent images available to the modern tourist are those which involve a European dimension. In other words, the region may be 'theirs' but it is also, somehow, 'ours'.

For many centuries, of course, European-based empires did indeed control the Maghreb: the Romans from 49BC to *c.*450AD, then, less directly and comprehensively, the Byzantine Emperors for a further century and a half, and finally the French during their imperial heyday – indeed Algeria only gained its independence as recently as 1962.

It is this rich cultural and historical mix, this plurality of identity and experience which makes North Africa so alluring and mysterious, as well as surprising – after all, few visitors would know that the Roman amphitheatre of El Jem in Tunisia is far better preserved and in many ways finer than the far more famous one in Rome, or that the great mosque in Kairouan is one of Islam's major sites of pilgrimage, or that Fez is one of the world's most important medieval monuments.

What they will know, having read this deeply researched, always relevant and endlessly intriguing book, is that the lands of North Africa are more complex and inviting than they could have imagined. The author puts this beautifully early in the text: 'A useful mental image to help understand the Maghreb is to imagine it as a mosaic. At a distance it produces a harmonious unified image but as you look closer you realise that it is composed of a mass of adamantine stones…. A second mental image… is that it should be imagined as an island quite distinct from its neighbours in continental Europe and Africa… The doorway into the Maghreb is from the east.'

No matter how these travellers arrive, this clear and authoritative book will have prepared them superbly for the pleasures which await them.
Denis Judd
London, 1998.

Introduction

North Africa is an elusive term. For the purpose of this book it is considered to coincide with the area collectively known to the Arab and French speaking world as the Maghreb, the land of the West, which comprises the modern nation states of Morocco, Algeria, Tunisia, Mauritania and Libya. The Maghreb is not an artificial construct, but a region that has thousands of years of culture, history, religion and language in common. It is also has a shared hope for the future, as expressed by UMA, the Maghreb Union Treaty, which was joyfully and freely undertaken by all five Maghrebi states in 1989. Whether Egypt is, should be, or is not, part of the Maghreb, is a source of lively contention which has recently been made into a live political issue by Egyptian overtures to join UMA. The trouble with including Egypt into either UMA or this book is that it tends to predominate. This is not just a question of Egypt's unique culture and breathless antiquity (or the existence of a separate *Traveller's History of Egypt*). Egypt's population has always been about equal in number to the rest of the Maghreb's put together. It has also always had a highly concentrated and settled population which has historically been easy to tax, while the population of the Maghreb is dispersed, was highly mobile and is notoriously difficult to tax. Another important difference is that Egypt's geographical position has always put it at the centre of the world's affairs while the Maghreb was for millenia considered to be on the western edge of the world. If the Nile can be considerd to unite Egypt, the Maghreb can just as usefully be considered to be divided by its mountains.

A useful mental image to help understand the Maghreb is to imagine it as a mosaic. At a distance it produces a harmonious unified image, but as you look closer you realize that it is composed of a mass of adamantine stones. For the Maghreb, despite its apparent uniformity to the outsider, is composed of hundreds of potentially, if not determinedly, independent regions. Any form of central government in the Maghreb is a heroic achievement that is constantly being tested against a natural inclination to return into its component regions. This is in part due to the genius of the inhabitants for conciliar government at a local level, but it is also an aspect determined by the particular geography of the region. The Maghreb is riven into regions by both its physical relief and a variety of climatic zones. The Atlas Mountains, a massive chain of interlinked mountain ranges that run east-west right across the length of the Maghreb, are the dominant relief feature. The mountains have always hindered communication, but this is perhaps less important than their role as refuges for dissidents and as nurseries for self-confident particularism. Climatically the Maghreb can be divided into at least four zones on a broad north to south division. Along the coastline and river valleys there stretches a relatively fertile zone that supports a typically Mediterranean flora with a continuous history of intensive agriculture and urban settlement. Inland there stretches an extensive semi-arid steppe, subdivided into regions by forests and mountain ranges. This area makes good grain country if there is sufficient rainfall in the spring, but is otherwise much better suited to pastoralism. As you progress further south you reach the arid fringes of the Sahara where the sparse grazing can only support transient herds, with settled agriculture restricted to isolated palm-fringed river valleys and oases. The Sahara Desert itself is a vast, near empty and lifeless zone, although a few tens of thousand herdsmen have eked out a living from travellers and grazing the central Saharan Mountains, such as Air or Tibesti. These climatic zones have of course dictated quite different diets, types of settlement, mental attitudes and communal loyalties.

A second mental image to help understand the Maghreb is that it should be imagined as an island quite distinct from its neighbours in continental Africa and Europe. For despite the evidence of the maps the region is isolated by three seas. To the north it is lapped by the waves of the Mediterranean, to the south by the sand sea of the Sahara, while to the west it is sealed by the vastness of the Atlantic. The doorway into the Maghreb is from the east. This is the direction from which all three of the great cultural transformations to have taken root in North Africa have arrived: the Neolithic Revolution, the Phoenician-borne Iron Age and the advent of Islam. Europe may now, after a period of colonial rule and a continuingly dominant role as a trading partner, claim some influence over the stomach of the Maghreb, but it would have to acknowledge that the heart, soul and mind of North Africa is still pledged to the Arabic and Islamic world to its east.

CHAPTER ONE

The Springboard of Mankind

If Africa is the mother of mankind, North Africa is the springboard from which the species spread throughout the globe. The first, savage, four million years of mankind's evolution all took place south of the Sahara. About a million years ago an heroic band of *homo erectus* achieved the crossing of the hitherto impassable desert onto the shores of the Mediterranean. *Homo erectus* could make fire, create symmetrical flint tools and could probably talk. Although he spread throughout the old world, most of the oldest evidence of his camps has been found in North Africa, particularly outside Casablanca and Rabat in Morocco and near the oasis of Kebili in Tunisia. Some of the earliest bone fragments (dated 200,000 BC) were found at El Kef in the centre of Tunisia.

At the peak of the last ice age, around 40,000 BC, North Africa was settled by a species of *homo sapiens* known as Neanderthal man. Neanderthal man had a heavy brow and stronger jaws than us, but his brain was just as big. There have been comparatively few of his bones found in North Africa, but ample evidence of his presence in the form of stone tools, labelled Mousterian in archaeological collections. In a process not yet fully understood, Neanderthal man was then replaced throughout the world by recognizably modern man who quickly divided into the various races that we know today.

As the last ice age ended, the waters of the Mediterranean rose and North Africa was decisively separated from Europe. Small communities of hunter-gatherers ranged over the forested hills of the Atlas Mountains and the seashore. Their culture, known as Ibero-Mauretanian, lasted for 10,000 years from 18,000 BC to 8,000 BC. They are identified by their particular stone tools and peculiar social customs, such as the practice of

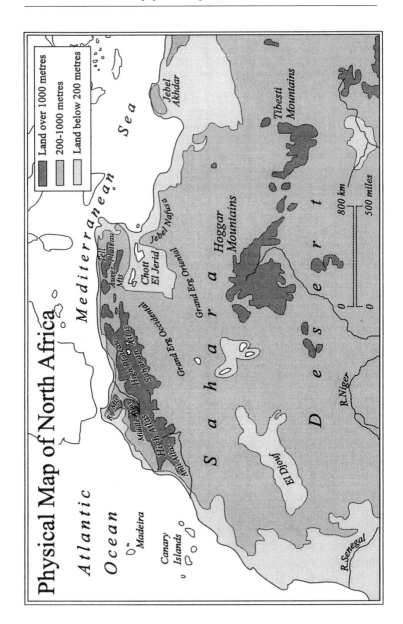

Physical Map of North Africa

plucking out the two front teeth of adult males. Their dead were buried reverently, in a crouched position, in graves marked by stones.

The Capsian Culture

At the end of the Ibero-Mauretanian period a distinct and rather advanced culture emerged from the southern plains of the interior. It is named after the first discoveries made at the Tunisian oasis town of Gafsa (Roman Capsa). Capsian man may have formed one of the first hunting communities to have switched to herding, following and controlling wild herds of native gazelle, which have recently been found to have been an important part of their diet. They may also have husbanded moufflon (also known as Barbary sheep), which are the indigenous wild sheep of the Mediterranean, a small animal just 26 inches high at the shoulder. This is corroborated mythologically by the Egyptian belief that the worship of Ammon, their ancient ram-headed god, was introduced to their country by herders from the west.

Capsian culture is remarkable for the elegance of its stone blades as well as for modelling tools and jewellery from bone and ostrich egg. A carved limestone head of a woman, her face veiled by two cones of hair, survives from the period to give a tantalizing glimpse of their creativity. From the evidence of their camps, they consumed copious quantities of snails and boiled food, which was prepared by dropping heated stones into animal skin tureens. Capsian dead were carefully prepared for the grave and, like a bloody child returning to the womb, they were anointed with red ochre.

The Neolithic Revolution

The advent of the Neolithic, or New Stone Age, was one of the most decisive transformations in mankind's history – nothing less than the invention of agriculture and stock-keeping. Hitherto man had lived in small itinerant groups, which could never grow beyond their ability to feed themselves on wild sources. Neolithic agriculture assured a year-round food supply, which allowed communities to grow rapidly in number and complexity.

The characteristic polished stone axes and hand mills of the Neolithic are easy to identify, but it is their new purpose, not so much their technical polish, which is so important. The new axes were used to clear the land, which was ploughed with sharpened, fire-hardened sticks and planted with wheat and barley. These crops, harvested with flint sickles, produced a quantity of dried seeds that could be stored underground in clay-sealed baskets for use throughout the year. The seeds could be boiled to make porridge, fermented into beer or crushed by primitive stone mills into flour for making bread. The change from hunting to stock-keeping also produced a dramatic increase in food supply. Quite apart from the yield of milk and tapped blood, a herd could afford to have half its newborn animals, the young males, slaughtered every year without diminishing its capacity for continued growth. The human population is estimated to have grown twenty-fold. Settled villages were established, pottery was invented, rectangular buildings began to replace round huts while boats and solid-wheeled ox-carts allowed for trade in flints, ivory, obsidian blades, amber and grinding stones. The management and disposal of the food surplus quickly resulted in social hierarchies and the development of specialized skills.

NEOLITHIC IN THE MAGHREB

This revolution first reached North Africa around 5,000 BC, where it took such spectacular root in the Nile Valley that within a thousand years the various agricultural communities there had coalesced into the world's first sizeable state.

Its techniques diffused quickly amongst the already advanced successors to the Capsian culture, who were well primed to pick up the improvements in herding and took quickly to the new, domesticated species of sheep and goat introduced from western Asia. Finds in the Haua Fteah cave in eastern Libya provide evidence of this peaceful transformation. Before 5,000 BC the cave floor was littered with layers of Barbary sheep bones. Without any sign of a break in the cave's use, later layers of the floor are covered with the bones of domesticated sheep and goats. The herders lived in light mobile huts, camping in the open but able to pen their animals in fenced enclosures or beside rock shelters.

SAHARAN ROCK PAINTINGS

From about 6,000 to 2,500 BC, the early Neolithic period, the Sahara was transformed, by one of its very infrequent wet periods, into a vast pastoral steppe, presenting uniquely favourable opportunities for the North African herdsmen. Only the vivid rock paintings of the period bear testimony to this vanished savannah. The paintings (especially those at Tassili-n-Ajer in Algeria) give us an extraordinary and vivid insight into this period of North African history. They are all painted on external rock faces, often protected by an overhang. The earliest were created by aboriginal hunter-gatherers of a negro-like appearance, and have been dated to between 6,000 and 4,000 BC. Although they are unconnected, either chronologically or culturally, with the famous Palaeolithic cave paintings of Europe (Altamira and Lascaux) they share the same earlier spiritual vision. The pictures are concerned with maintaining the harmony of existence of the hunter, so there are

Saharan rock art – The sable antelopes

depictions of masked shamans and scenes of human sexuality as well as pictures of animals drawn with a hunter's customary eye for movement and exaggeration. Scholars customarily subdivide this earliest period into three and place the crudest, ochre-red dominated paintings, which dwell obsessively on giants and monstrous spirits, into a decadent third stage. These categories probably say as much about the mind of scholars in the late 1950s as about the hunter-gatherers.

By about 4,000 BC the art of the hunter-gatherers is replaced by superbly executed paintings from the Neolithic period. These depict tall, angular, dread-locked Nilo-Saharan herdsmen with well-dressed women escorting great herds of horned cattle and goats. As well as the meticulously drawn cattle there are depictions of ostriches, giraffes and gazelle, domestic scenes, religious processions, fights and hunts. It is clear that from about 2,500 BC the Sahara began to dry up, for depictions of elephants, rhinoceros, hippopotamuses and the now extinct giant buffalo gradually fade from the artistic repertoire of Saharan mankind.

The last group of paintings, dated around 1,200 BC, record the conquest of this increasingly arid space by a white race of chariot-driving warriors. The charioteers are conspicuously well-armed, dressed in leather jerkins with their horses set at a perpetual gallop. Here art and historical record seem to be speaking with the same voice. We know that the horse was introduced to North Africa in about this period and that Berber tribes like the Garamantians controlled the Saharan trade routes. Their bellicosity, so prominently recorded in the rock paintings, is also testified by Rameses II, the Egyptian pharaoh, who had to defend his western frontier against charioteers from the Libyan desert in 1,280 BC. Even Herodotus, the Greek historian, writing seven centuries later, corroborates the genocidal story in his famous description of the Berber tribes of Libya. 'The Garamantes hunt the Ethiopian hole-men, or troglodytes, in four-horse chariots, for these troglodytes are exceedingly swift of foot – more so than any people of whom we have any information. They eat snakes and lizards and other reptiles and speak a language like no other, but squeak like bats.'

These Saharan herdsmen still foreswore the cultivation of crops although they did process local grains, perhaps in the same way that the contemporary Tuareg of the Sahara sow no grain but consume wild kreb grass in its season.

'WRITTEN STONES' OF THE ATLAS

Although the lessons of the Neolithic were quickly absorbed by the herdsmen of the fertile steppe lands, they infiltrated more slowly into the hunting communities that occupied the well-forested mountains of the central Maghreb. Although there is nothing that can be compared with the rock paintings of the Sahara, these communities have also left their own form of rock art, known as *hajra mektuba* ('written stones'). It is a crude but vigorous art, with images literally pecked, drilled or rubbed into flat boulders or living rock. It is emphatically not cave art, as it occurs in open spaces, often reclusive mountain combes above a stream. The best examples can be found in the Moroccan High Atlas, at Oukaimeden, Yagour and Tainant. Animals, such as elephants, lizards and oxen are depicted, as well as warriors and what are presumed to be

Saharan rock art – The hunters

deities. More common are well-executed depictions of flint knives and geometrically decorated circles. The rock carvings have been classified into two cultural groups. The first, found on the Atlas slopes and high plateaux, seem to have been carved by hunters on the cusp of the Neolithic. The second group tends to be found further north and closer to the coast, and is associated with Neolithic pottery. The rock carvings, therefore, seem to chronicle the gradual shift, at around 3,500 BC, from pure hunting in the hills to new agricultural communities sited in river valleys and on coastal plains. Pottery production in these communities changed so little that accurate dating of settlements from their sherds (the normal yardstick for archaeologists) is virtually useless. Throughout the more inaccessible areas of North Africa you can still buy attractive modelled pots, decorated with cross-hatched lozenges and diamonds, which would not look out of place in a museum collection.

The Imiazen: the Berbers of North Africa

With the arrival of the horse in 1,200 BC the indigenous people of coastal North Africa, now known as the Berbers, came of age. The name originates from the Greek for foreigner, *barbaroi*, although the Berbers' own definition of themselves is *imiazen*, the noble ones. Ethnically Caucasian, the Berbers are closely related to the Semites of the Middle East, but are quite distinct from the other indigenous races of Africa. Their language, however, subdivided into numerous dialects, is part of the larger Afro-Asiatic language group.

Armed with the horse the Berbers, hitherto restrained by the Atlas, began to push south into the fast-drying vastness of the Sahara. They gradually slaughtered, interbred with or enslaved the aboriginal black population, leaving only pockets to survive to this day – the Haratine cultivators of the Moroccan oases, the shrimp-gathering Dawada of southern Libya and the Tibu of the Tibesti Mountains, for example.

By about 1,100 BC, the Berbers numbered some one million and were the masters of North Africa. There are few populations in the world that can match their length of title to the land, for they were the direct descendants of the Capsian and Ibero-Mauretanian Stone-Age cultures and their own descendants farm the land to this day. They developed into the pre-eminent horsemen of the Mediterranean, and even today no festival is complete without a *fantasia*, a dramatic display of horsemanship which recalls their harassing fighting techniques. A Berber knight wore a long split robe gathered at the waist, was armed with several five-foot wooden javelins as well as a small, round shield, and sported one or two feathers stuck in his hair. He would gallop straight at the enemy line and when within javelin range would come to a dramatic halt, hurl his weapon with his right hand, at the same time rapidly turning to gallop back to the safety of his companions. As the famous Numidian cavalry of the classical world, they had taken to wearing reddish-brown trousers beneath a short white tunic, and were armed with a strong sword in addition to their javelins. They also used a bridle. Their shields were now stronger, carried on the left hand to parry sword blows from opposing cavalrymen. Aulus Gellius, the Latin grammarian (123-65), describes this age-old technique in his *Bellum Africanum*, 'they kept swooping down on us as soon as we started marching and then they would retreat when we resisted: however, they never engaged in hand to hand fighting and merely kept throwing their javelins at us'. Today, the javelin is replaced by the deafening bang of a gun.

CHAPTER TWO

Carthage: Empire and Culture
814–450 BC

The dark ships of the Phoenicians, with their distinctive figurehead of the dwarf-god Bes cresting the waves, must have been a familiar, but mysterious sight to those shepherds who chanced to be watching from the North African shore. The Berber tribes had remained completely outside the influence of the Bronze Age cultures of the Near East, but this isolation was gradually broken in the ninth century BC by Phoenician traders. The Phoenicians had the most technologically advanced culture of their time and they imported a whole cornucopia of skills, new crops and technologies to North Africa. They were numerically weak and had no interest in imperial conquest, but it was their interest in trade and industry that brought them west in their ships. At first the coast of North Africa simply presented a convenient trading route. Their eventual involvement with the area was an almost accidental process, strung out over centuries. By the end of the Phoenician period the North African coast was dotted with a sophisticated chain of trading cities whose advanced material culture was gradually disseminated to the tribes of the interior. Under the leadership of Carthage, the greatest of these cities, a far-flung Mediterranean Empire was created.

Who were the Phoenicians?

The Phoenician homeland was a loose confederation of five city states strung along the Syrian coast: Aradus, Byblos, Beirut, Sidon and Tyre. Their peculiar Phoenician identity was formed from a melting pot of peoples in around 1,200 BC: partly indigenous Canaanites, partly piratical 'Sea Peoples' and partly skilled refugees from the wreck of the great palace cultures of Mesopotamia, Egypt and Minoa. As well as preserving skills that elsewhere disappeared, the Phoenicians added their own distinct cultural innovations such as glass-working, the alphabet and, most famously, the dyeing of purple cloth. This expensive purple dye was made by crushing murex shells, cooking them in salt and then drying the extract in the sun. It was a laborious business, with at least 9,000 murex shells required to produce just a gram of dye. The dye stuck fast, for the very name 'Phoenician' can be translated as the 'purple ones'.

THE FIRST PHOENICIAN SETTLEMENTS IN NORTH AFRICA

The role of metal within the economy of the ancient world can only be compared with that of oil and uranium deposits today. The mines of southern Spain were some of the richest sources of raw material and early on the Phoenicians pioneered a trading route for themselves along the North African shore.

The journey, even for such a determinedly maritime people, was not a light undertaking. With a good wind and fair weather great distances could be covered under sail, but all that they could average reliably by rowing was 20 miles a day. The trading season was confined to summer, which was defined by the equinoctial storms of March and September. Even within this short sailing season the Mediterranean could throw up sudden and savage storms. Phoenician merchants developed a litany of useful harbours spaced about 20 miles apart, where they could shelter from a storm or stop to pick up fresh water, meat and firewood. Their eye for a good harbour, whether an offshore island, reef, sheltered beach, peninsula or river estuary was unerring. Most of the ports of North Africa today look back to a Phoenician origin. In Spain, the merchants were assured of a safe welcome in the Phoenician island city of Gades (Cadiz), which was founded in the thirteenth century BC. There was also need for a permanent settlement half way along the North African shore where the merchants could safely winter both on the journey out and the journey back. Utica in Tunisia appears to have been the first of these, founded in about 1,100 BC.

For the first centuries these Phoenician settlements were slight affairs. The sparse archaeological evidence suggests that the first permanent settlements were composed of moored boats joined by pontoons and old hulks, which must have looked like the sampan communities of China. Even in the first century AD the geographer Strabo wrote that the inhabitants of Gades lived on ships. The move to temporary buildings on dry land, to inter-marriage with the more civilized tribes and to a growing interest in the possibilities of trade with the interior first took place in the late ninth century. In these port-towns Phoenician craftsmen slowly began to introduce the high arts of the Near East. Ceramic production, utilizing the new pottery wheel, was one of the first innovations, but this was quickly followed by metallurgy, iron-working, stone carving, dyeing, skilled joinery and improved types of weaving on looms. Later, as the communities grew, they set about the construction of stone houses, temples, roads and harbours. These were matched by improvements in farming, particularly horticulture, as dozens of new crop species were introduced to suburban estates. The pomegranate, amongst the more notable of the Phoenician plant imports, is also known as *malum punicum*, the Punic apple.

The Foundation of Carthage

The foundation of Carthage in 814 BC by Elissa, known to the West as Dido, is a decisive historical event, a potent foundation myth and a celebrated incident of literature. For the latter we are indebted to the Roman poet Virgil's *Aeneid* (Book IV), which has itself fuelled an opera by Purcell, Turner's visionary landscapes and a gorgeous series of Renaissance tapestries. Even the early Christian bishop, St Augustine, was not immune to the power of the tale, for he later chides himself in the *Confessions* 'because I wept for Dido, who killed herself for love'.

The chain of events that led to the foundation of Carthage is known in surprising detail. Elissa was the daughter of the king of Tyre. When she reached her maturity she was duly married off to one of her princely uncles, Archabas the High Priest. Their happiness was shattered by Elissa's brother Pygmalion who not only usurped his father's throne, but also murdered Archabas in the process. Elissa, in the seventh year of her brother's reign, decided to flee Tyre and found a new city in the west. Her aristocratic party stopped at Cyprus, picking up more volunteers (including the priest of the Temple of Juno and his family) as well as abducting 80 maidens. From Cyprus they sailed directly to the future site of Carthage: three low hills and two small lagoons sitting in a broad isthmus flanked by two large salt lakes. There she bargained with Iarbas, king of the Berber Gaetulian tribe, for sufficient land for her new city. The two struck a deal, which gave Elissa as much land as could be covered by an ox hide. Elissa had a hide cut into the thinnest strips, with which she marked the boundaries of an ample city. The high citadel at the centre of Carthage, to this day retains the name Byrsa (from the Greek for ox hide). The increasingly fascinated Iarbas then began to press this crafty Tyrian princess to become his wife, but Elissa was concerned that marriage to a native king would sooner or later entail a move inland, away from the sea and Carthage's bright destiny. However, rather than endanger her fledgling city by refusing so powerful a suitor, she built a pyre of sandalwood outside her palace and took her life in its flames.

THE STORY EXAMINED

The foundation of Carthage was doubtless fired by less romantic political necessities than the myth suggests. First, Carthage was an excellent strategic site, well placed to secure both the North African trade route and the Sicilian straits. Secondly, the independence of the Phoenician homeland had slowly been undermined during the late ninth century BC by the gathering power of Assyria. The Assyrians had been quietly collecting tribute from the Phoenician cities since at least 876 BC, if we are to believe the claims of King Assurnasirpal's inscriptions. The crushing of the revolt of Aradus (the most northerly of the cities of Phoenicia) during the reign of the following Assyrian monarch, King Shalmaneser III (859–24 BC), must have filled its sister cities with acute alarm. Emigration from Tyre, the Manhattan of its day with its tall buildings packed tightly onto a small offshore island, must have appeared an attractive long-term proposition. Thirdly, emigration was a peaceful solution to civil strife. The rivalry between Pygmalion and Elissa can be read as a political conflict amongst the ruling class of

Reconstructed excavations at the *tophet* of Carthage: site of the *moloch* fire
sacrifices of children to Tanit and Bala Hammon

Tyre, brought to a head by the gathering Assyrian threat. Elissa
represented the traditionalist priestly party and her foundation of
Carthage (Kart Hadasht, 'the New City' or 'the New Capital') takes on
the light of a sacred mission to keep the ancient ways pure from
compromise. It is tempting to see the practice of child sacrifice, which
died out around this period in the Phoenician homeland but continued
to be enthusiastically observed at Carthage, as one of the key issues at
stake. Elissa's suicide can be taken not as the action of some foolish
love-plagued princess, but as a solemn dedicatory self-sacrifice by a
fervent exponent of the old ways.

The excavation of the *tophet* (the place of human sacrifice in
Carthage) has provided unexpected support for this view of Elissa. At
the centre and lowest level of the *tophet*, beneath layers of urns, ash,
dedicatory inscriptions and clay piled up over the centuries, archaeologists found the remnants of a small domed chapel, which had a single
urn at the centre of its stone paved floor. The chapel stands on bedrock
just 50 paces from the outer harbour and seems very similar to the
Phoenician royal tombs excavated at Sidon. It has been dated to the late

ninth century BC and identified as the shrine of Elissa, the royal founder of Carthage and the first of thousands who would pass through the fire sacrifice (the *moloch*) here, into the arms of the goddess Tanit.

On a lesser note, the tale of Elissa's ox hide is almost certainly a later addition. It had its purposes, for it not only alluded to the proverbial bargaining skill of the Carthaginians on the first day of their city, but also helped to cover up the unpalatable fact that for the first 350 years of its existence the city of Carthage continued to pay rent to the local Berber ruler for the land it occupied.

CARTHAGINIAN LEADERSHIP, 814–580 BC

The remarkable speed with which Carthage achieved dominance among the existing Phoenician settlements of the West may be explained by the sacred nature of its foundation. The greatest threat came from rival Greek traders, and as early as the mid-eighth century BC the settlements began to act together under Carthaginian leadership. From the mid-seventh century Carthage was developing its own fleet and armies to counteract the effect of new Greek trading stations in southern Italy, France and Sicily. The Carthaginian response was slow, cautious and unaggressive, but tactically sound for the numerically weaker party. In Sicily they abandoned two-thirds of the island to the Greeks and withdrew to their settlements in the western corner. Here, supported by an old understanding with the indigenous people, they founded the island fortress of Motya, which looked out over the narrowest section of the Sicilian straits within easy sailing distance of Carthage. The Sardinian coast, as yet unthreatened by the Greeks, was secured by the settlement of its southern harbours. In Spain, control of the vital metal trade was reinforced by the foundation of the cities of Sexi, Abdera and Malaga along the southern coast supported by Rachgoun on the Algerian shore opposite, and the Balearic islands were secured by the foundation of Ibiza in 654 BC. One of the last peaceful acts in this slow chess-like manoeuvring was the establishment by the Greeks of Cyrene on the eastern Libyan coast in 631 BC. Cyrene sat plumb astride the sea route between Carthage and its Near Eastern homeland and its establishment could have been considered a cause for war. Instead, the Phoenicians quietly isolated Cyrene by winning over

Punic carved ivory handle from the seventh century BC

the Berber tribes and developing an inland Saharan trade route to Egypt via the oasis communities of Augula and Ammon (modern Siwa). Cyrene, for its part, so dominated this fertile section of the coast that it is still known as Cyrenaica.

The first of the many wars between the Greeks and Carthaginian-led Phoenicians broke out in 580 BC in Sicily, which was destined to be their central battleground. The Sicilian Greeks, led by Pentathalus, attempted to establish a new city right in the heart of the Phoenician third of the island, but they were soundly repulsed by a Carthaginian general named Malchus. This first victory was followed by the long-expected, but still dreaded, news from Phoenicia. Tyre, after an epic 13-year resistance to the siege of King Nebuchadnezzar of Babylon (*c.* 604–562 BC), had finally fallen in 573 BC. The entire Phoenician homeland was now a subject province of a distant empire. Carthage stood alone as the heir of its great culture. It is now that we can begin to talk in terms of a Carthaginian Empire and its Punic culture. Punic, although it is derived from the Greek and Latin for a Phoenician (*poenos* and *punicus*) has come to refer specifically to Carthaginian.

CARTHAGE ESTABLISHES ITS EMPIRE: 550–480 BC

With a new vigour, confidence and authority Carthage, under the Magonid kings, established an empire that united the coast of North Africa, for the first time, into one cohesive unit. Mago, the eponymous founder of the dynasty, was ruling Carthage by 550 BC and is described by the historian Justin as 'the first, by regulating their military discipline, to lay the foundations of Punic power'. The core of the Carthaginian army, and its only standing regiment, was a 3,000-strong sacred battalion, recruited from among the noble families of the city. The battalion was both the lifeguard of the commanding general and a staff college for training young officers to command foreign regiments. For, in times of war the great armies of Carthage were almost entirely composed of a discordant array of foreign mercenaries. This was less chaotic than it sounds, for it allowed the Carthaginian army a broad range of talents that would have been impossible to expect from a single nation, let alone a city. A typical Carthaginian army might contain Numidian cavalry, Balearic slingers, Etruscan engineers and infantry recruited from the bellicose tribes of Iberia, Italy, North Africa and Gaul.

The military reforms of Mago were a response to the continuing threat of Greek expansion. In the last decades of the sixth century BC, Carthage was called upon to assist fellow Phoenician settlements at Leptis Magna, Malaga and even ancient Gades (Cadiz). Yet while Carthage controlled foreign policy and called for contributions from its sister cities in times of war, this was not an empire in the traditional hierarchical sense. The settlements were allowed to retain control of their own customs, internal government and trade routes.

By the end of the sixth century Carthage was taking an ever more active and aggressive role. Its influence was even felt in mainland Italy where there was a substantial Punic colony at the harbour town of Pyrgi-Caere, just 38 miles from Rome. Carthaginian diplomats were quick to spot further opportunities, for in 510 BC, the very year that the Tarquins (the Etruscan kings of Rome) were expelled, they signed a treaty with the new city-state. In this treaty Rome acknowledged Carthage's monopoly of trade in the western Mediterranean in return for a free hand in Latium. Despite his successes abroad, however, Mago's successor Hasdrubal was still unable to free the great imperial city of Carthage from paying rent to the nearby Berber king.

Rather than continue with the pragmatic defence of its league of trading cities, Carthage eventually fell for the temptation to adopt a more grandiose imperial foreign policy, with disastrous results. In 480 BC, the Carthaginian army under Hamilcar suffered a military defeat of sufficient magnitude to alter the whole course of Carthaginian history. Even before they had landed in Sicily, the army was crippled by a storm which sank all its horses and chariot transport. At the battle of Himera the Sicilian-Greeks, although greatly outnumbered in infantry, made decisive use of their advantage in cavalry. Hamilcar, known to be personally brave, stayed away from the fighting in order to fulfill the religious duties of kingship. He offered a ceaseless succession of burnt sacrifices to try to reverse the terrible auspices of the day. When he learned of the complete annihilation of his army, he threw himself into the flames as a last propitiation to the gods.

The Greeks throughout the Mediterranean were exultant. Not only had a Carthaginian attack in Spain been defeated, but also the fleet of Carthage's ally, King Xerxes of Persia, had been sunk at the battle of Salamis on the very same day as the battle of Himera.

CARTHAGE TURNS AFRICAN, 480–410 BC

After the humiliation of Himera, Carthage turned away from its Mediterranean possessions and concentrated on developing a North African empire. In the words of the historian Dio Chrysostom they transformed themselves 'from Tyrians into Africans'. Hamilcar's son Hanno instituted a stringent austerity regime, which virtually halted all luxury imports into Carthage and directed all resources to the conquest of the Tunisian hinterland. At the end of his single-minded campaign Carthage had carved out a greater agricultural hinterland for itself than any other city in the ancient world. The other Punic cities, especially Hadrumentum (Sousse), also extended their lands enormously. The indigenous Berber population worked the land, under the direction of

Punic glass head found in the cemetery of St Monica, Carthage

Punic overseers who began to lay out vineyards, olive groves and fruit orchards. The overseers supervised the harvest and dispatched the landlord's third to the cities, the oil and wine sent in amphorae with the owner's mark stamped into their shoulders. A ditch was dug to mark the eastern frontier of Carthaginian territory, and in the west fortresses at Sicca Veneria (El Kef, Tunisia) and Theveste (Tebessa, Algeria) kept an eye on the powerful Numidian tribes beyond.

LIKE A LEOPARD'S SKIN: THE BERBERS OF THE INTERIOR

Although the Carthaginian nobles had periodically married their daughters to important tribal leaders, it was only with this colonization of the interior that intermarriage became more common and a true cultural synthesis began. The interior was described by the Greek geographer, Strabo as 'like a leopard's skin, with spots of dense habitation surrounded by desert', and according to Herodotus these isolated and independent tribes differed widely in their religious practices, social habits and, notably, their hairstyles.

Ancient writers divided the tribes into three groups, Libyans, Numidians and Mauretanians, who were spread between the Nile and the Atlantic. The Libyans occupied the Tunisian and Libyan littoral and were the most heavily influenced by Punic culture. The Numidians were the independent nomadic tribes living on the high plateau of Tunisia and Algeria, whilst the Mauretanians inhabited western Algeria and Morocco. It was the Libyans who were forced into serfdom by Hanno's campaign, yet it was not long before they became willing allies of Carthage, playing important roles in the settlement of vital trading towns on the Atlantic coast of Morocco, for example.

The tribes were usually semi-nomadic, driving their herds between customary summer and winter pastures, planting crops when the weather or a reliable water source allowed. Leather was one of the principal items of trade, a ubiquitous material used for clothing, harnesses, prestigious tents, as well as storage flasks for water, grain and the various milk products of a herding people. Herodotus could almost be writing of today when he records that 'in the matter of oaths, their practice is to swear by those of their countrymen who had the best reputation for integrity and valour, laying their hands upon their tombs; and for purposes of divination they go to sleep, after praying, on the graves of their forebears, and take as significant any dream they may have.'

Further south, and way beyond the influence of Carthage, the Garamantian Berbers controlled the trans-Saharan trade route, known as the Garamantian Way. A millenium before the introduction of the camel to North Africa, caravans of pack-horses strapped with goatskin flasks of water made their slow, deliberate progress, marching for nine to twelve days, followed by an equal period of recuperation at an oasis. They returned from the Niger bend with cargoes of ivory, gold dust, rare woods, skins, essences, ostrich eggs, feathers and carbuncles (red garnets). The latter, highly regarded in the ancient world, were better known as 'Carthaginian stone'. For at some secret market-place on the edge of the desert the

Garamantian caravan was bought by Punic merchants who shipped the treasures to the outer world.

THE CARTHAGINIAN EXPLORATION OF THE ATLANTIC

Hanno next used the resources of Carthage to further its control over the metal trade routes. The first expedition, led by Hanno himself, attempted to corner the gold trade that the city of Gades had long exploited. A Carthaginian fleet of 60 ships headed south down the Atlantic coast of Morocco as far as the equatorial coast of West Africa. It was a heroic achievement and they brought back tales of strange music coming from the forests at night, of a volcano called 'the Chariot of the Gods' and of three skins of female gorillas, but they had been unable to penetrate inland to the source of the gold itself. However, on their return they established six colonies on the Moroccan coast, settled by tens of thousands of Libyan tribesmen, to confirm Carthage's control of the existing trade. The contemporary historian Herodotus has left an excellent description of this curious exchange:

> the Carthaginians also tell us that they trade with a race of men who live in a part of Libya beyond the pillars of Hercules. On reaching this country, they unload their goods, arrange them tidily along the beach, and then, returning to their boats, raise a smoke. Seeing the smoke the natives come down to the beach, place on the ground a certain quantity of gold in

Fourth century BC Punic coinage: Dido-Elissa in Phrygian headdress; on the obverse, lion before palm tree

exchange for the goods, and go off again to a distance. The Carthaginians then come ashore and take a look at the gold: and if they think it represents a fair price for their wares they collect it and go away; if on the other hand it seems too little they go back aboard and wait, and the natives come and add to the gold until they are satisfied. There is perfect honesty on both sides; the Carthaginians never touch the gold until it equals in value what they have offered for sale, and the natives never touch the goods until the gold has been taken away.

The second great Carthaginian exploratory expedition of this period was the navigator Himilco's four-month voyage into the North Atlantic. Himilco's aim was to secure the tin trade at its source and although he reached the Oestrymnian islands, which have variously been identified as Ireland, Cornwall, Brittany or Galicia, his encounters with fog, seaweed, tidal waters and sea monsters convinced him to leave the trade in the hands of the locals. He too established a string of colonies, this time along the Atlantic coast of Portugal, to secure the tin trade without endangering Punic ships any further north.

Cyrenaica: the Greek settlements of North Africa

Although rivalry between the Greeks and Carthaginians in the western Mediterranean led to violent wars, a strange truce held between the handful of Greek cities, headed by Cyrene, which were gradually established in eastern Libya on the otherwise Punic shore. It is less odd than at first it seems, for looking at isolated Cyrenaica on the globe you will see that it is Crete, not Carthage nor Cairo, that is by far its nearest neighbour.

Cyrene was founded in 631 BC by immigrants escaping a terrible, seven-year drought on Santorini. Much against their wishes they were directed to the Libyan coast by the Delphic oracle. A local Berber tribe took pity on the refugees and led them to a spring protected by the nymph Kurana. As the Berbers left they said 'Here, O Greeks, you may fitly dwell, for in this place there is a hole in the heavens'. The city was named after a Greek corruption of Kurana, who as well as looking after the spring also killed lions. The city of Cyrene prospered under a dynasty of kings that had been predicted by the Delphic oracle, 'Eight generations of men shall rule over Cyrene, four called Battus and four called Arcesilaus'. This statement seems to hint at the early marriage of Berber and Greek culture at Cyrene, for Battus is a Berber word for king.

By the fifth century BC, other Greek cities had been established on what is known as the Cyrenaican coast. Yet far from fighting over the sandy land between them, the Greeks and Carthaginians settled their frontier with an amicable running race. A Greek and a Punic team set off, at an agreed time, from their respective city walls and where they met along the desert coast would be accepted as the frontier. The Punic representatives, the Philaeni brothers, did so well that they were accused of cheating by the Greeks. However, when they offered to be buried alive on the spot as proof of their claim there could be no argument. Their graves, marked by great mounds of sand, became known as the Altars of the Philaeni, and have served as distinctive frontier posts ever since.

In 322 BC, the region was annexed by Ptolemy I, one of Alexander the Great's Macedonian generals, who had established dynastic rule over Egypt at this time. The rule of the Ptolemys was a comparatively prosperous and enlightened era. The governor, who was often a talented junior member of the royal family, allowed a fair measure of self-government. A surviving inscription records the carefully balanced Ptolemaic constitution by which Cyrene governed itself. In the best Aristotelian fashion power was divided between a 10,000-strong Popular Assembly of property owners, a Senate of 101 life members and a court of 500 elected councillors. Trade and silt replaced siege and civil war as the new arbiters of urban destiny. It was during this peaceful period that Cyrenaica became known as the Pentapolis, the land of five cities.

SYRACUSE, AGATHOCLES AND THE BURNED BOATS

While Cyrenaica was of little interest to Carthage, it had always known that its days would be numbered if it allowed Sicily to be united under one, potentially hostile, power. At the same time it was never strong enough to consider the permanent conquest and recolonization of the whole island. Its principle adversary was Syracuse, a

Greek harbour-city on the east coast protected by the near-invincible island fortress of Ortygia. In the fourth century BC the city was led by a series of charismatic men, all of whom were determined to throw Carthage out of its toe-hold in the west of the island.

Until 310 BC all the action had taken place in Sicily. The year began with Agathocles (361–288 BC) tightly besieged in his own city of Syracuse by a strong Carthaginian force. But deciding, audaciously, that the best method of defence was attack, he secretly equipped a fleet, divided his forces and slipped through the naval blockade to land at El Haouaria on the Cap Bon peninsula in mid-August. There, almost within view of Carthage, Agathocles burned his boats, committing his small force to offensive action and creating a colourful metaphor in the process. He defeated a large but ill-disciplined Carthaginian army, composed largely of untried conscript citizens. With Carthage in consternation Agathocles and his army roamed freely through the defenceless African countryside, sacking manors and pillaging the succession of rich, unfortified ports that dotted the coastline. Agathocles selected the hill of modern-day Tunis as a base from which to assault Carthage. However, despite a number of military expeditions deep into the interior, Agathocles failed to win over any substantial Berber tribe to his cause. Utica (the jealous neighbour and elder sister of Carthage) was the only town to abandon Carthage and ally itself to the Greeks. Despite brilliant tactical manoeuvering, Agathocles' long-term strategy was ruined by the lack of any substantial local allies. Increasingly hemmed in by three new Punic armies he decided to return to Syracuse secretly, where he ruled for another generation. His sons, stranded in North Africa, were not so fortunate. They were slaughtered by their outraged troops who quickly arranged a truce with the Carthaganian senate. Agathocles' unlikely failure against a defenceless Carthage exposed the city's strength and its lasting legacy to North Africa – its strong links with the African hinterland.

Carthaginian Culture

Political authority in fourth-century Carthage had devolved from the elected monarchy, which performed only religious and honorific roles, to an aristocratic Council of Elders headed by a Tribunal of 104. It governed through pentarchies, committees of five which watched over the various departments of state, and consulted with an Assembly of the People. It was a good constitution and one that was singled out for praise by Aristotle, the Greek philosopher, who admired its careful balance of monarchy, aristocracy and democracy.

Carthaginian craftsmen were known for their exotic scents, exquisitely worked furniture, beautifully woven cloth, dyed fabrics and embroidered cushions, none of which have survived to the present day. As a result, their material culture has been belittled by comparison with that of the Greeks, whose fine ceramics and sculpture have left a much more durable legacy. Nevertheless, surviving examples of Punic gold jewellery, glassware, carved gem stones and carved ivory testify to the exceptional creativity of its craftsmen.

In matters of religion, the Punic pantheon was headed by El, the ultimate source of all things, the beneficent all-father whose symbol was the sun. Yet Carthage is particularly associated with the worship of Baal and his sister goddess, Tanit. Baal was the young virile lover who fertilized the earth each year with rain and seed, and he who died each year with the annual harvest. The promise of a continued fecundity was assured each spring by his sister-lover, Tanit, who had been known variously as Astarte, Ishtar or Aphrodite in the Near East. The sacred precincts of Baal were usually located on mountain tops, the high places of the Bible, whilst those of Tanit tended to be sited in groves or near springs. However, the essential duality of Baal and Tanit (who was also known as 'the face of Baal') meant that wherever one was worshipped, so inevitably was the other. The most famous aspect of their cult was the practice of child sacrifice, which is passionately recalled in the Biblical episode of Abraham offering up Isaac to his God. Initially only children from priestly lineages were considered suitable offerings for the *moloch*, the fire sacrifice, although before the final fall of Carthage this privilege was shared by all its citizens. On a lower but very widespread level of spiritual activity there were also deities like Ptah Pteuk (known throughout the ancient world as the Punic dwarf) who shared many of the characteristics of Egyptian Bes. He was depicted with exaggerated genitals, a bulging stomach, bowed legs and a grotesque face crowned with a tall, ostrich-feather cap. He was an ubiquitous fellow, half comic, half vital who presided over the toilet table, drains and metalwork, kept poisonous animals at bay and was the figurehead washed by spray that guided every Punic ship safely to its destination.

CHAPTER THREE

The First and Second Punic Wars, 264–202 BC

The very name by which we know these wars says a great deal about the Roman roots of our own culture and the inevitable Eurocentric bias of so much of history. For it is from such historians as Polybius and Livy, writing for the Roman victors, that all our knowledge comes. From the point of view of the North African people, the lofty sounding Punic Wars were nothing more than the assault on the Carthaginian Empire by the ever expansive power of up-and-coming Rome. Viewed in this light the whole saga of the Punic Wars is a slow-moving tragedy in which the Carthaginians were able to defend themselves for well over a century against the inevitable conclusion. The effectiveness of such brilliant apologists as Livy has meant that few are aware that Rome was the aggressor. There is no doubt, however, that it is the Carthaginian general, Hannibal who is the hero of this epic conflict. He has caught and continues to hold the imagination of the world.

Carthage's Long Alliance with Rome

As we have seen, the first treaty between Carthage and Rome in 510 BC was a simple recognition of Rome's newfound independence from its Etruscan tutelage. Treaties in the fourth century BC further defined the mutual spheres of influence: Mediterranean trade for Carthage, Italy for Rome. This led in 306 BC to a Roman-Carthaginian alliance in the war with Agathocles and the Etruscans. With the death of Agathocles in 288 BC, when Rome had already made peace with the Etruscans, both Rome and Carthage found themselves able to extend their power rapidly. In the face of these encroaching empires, in 282 BC the Greek city of Tarentum in southern Italy appealed to King Pyrrhus of Illyria (297–272 BC) for aid. But Pyrrhus, kin to Alexander the Great, son-in-law of Agothocles and the so-called 'New Achilles', came with his own ambitious agenda. In a series of lightning campaigns he expelled Rome from southern Italy and almost managed to drive Carthage out of Sicily. In the end he was defeated as much by the treachery of his allies, who saw their liberator become their stern overlord, as by the strength of the watertight Romano-Carthaginian alliance. King Pyrrhus returned across the Adriatic and Tarentum, the last of the independent Greek cities in Italy, surrendered to Rome. The Roman republic was poised on the brink of imperial glory, and eight years later the Mediterranean world looked on in shock as it reversed an alliance of almost 250 years standing, and launched an unprovoked attack on Carthaginian territory.

The First Punic War, 264–241 BC

Once again, the battleground was Sicily. Invading the island on the slender pretext of aiding a group of southern Italian bandits, the Roman army proceeded swiftly from the straits of Messina to Syracuse, which sued for peace after only a year's resistance. This left the Roman army free to march on the Punic cities. The Carthaginians reinforced their possessions and tried to avoid pitched battles in Sicily by diverting attention with a diffuse, but highly profitable war of piracy and raiding on the long and vulnerable Italian coast. By 260 BC, Rome's lack of a navy became unsupportable and the city determined to equal the naval power of its enemy.

A famous Roman story tells how a single Carthaginian ship, which had been wrecked on the Latin shore, was used as a model by its industrious carpenters to create a whole navy. In fact Rome's new naval power came from the Greek cities of southern Italy, whose naval prowess had once been the equal of that of the Carthaginians. They had most to gain from the destruction of the Punic navy and it was they who financed the 'Roman' navy, built in the dockyards of Tarentum. The innovation of boarding bridges enabled the Roman soldiers to fight as if they were on land and resulted in a pair of naval

Check Out Receipt

West Bend Community Memorial Library
262-335-5151
www.west-bendlibrary.org

Tuesday, July 17, 2018 1:22:54 PM
24775

Item: 33357002024318
Title: A traveller's history of North Africa
Material: Book
Due: 08/14/2018

Total items: 1

Thank You!

victories: Mylae in 259 BC and Agrigentum in the spring of 256 BC.

These naval successes allowed the Romans to take the war into North Africa and in the summer of 256 BC the consul Regulus landed with an army at Cap Bon, just a few miles from where Agathocles had burned his boats a generation before. Like Agathocles he selected Kelibia as a base and proceeded to sack all the surrounding coastal towns. Regulus and his legions then advanced inland and won an initial victory beneath the walls of Adys (Oudna), after which they laid desultory siege to Carthage from the hill of Tunis. Later in the year he and his army were destroyed when Xanthippus (a Spartan soldier of fortune hired by the Carthaginians to give tactical advice) selected a flat battlefield which allowed the Carthaginian elephant corps and cavalry to be used to devastating effect.

Punic society at the time of this invasion is represented clearly by the ruins of the town of Kerkouane on Cap Bon, which never recovered from its devastation by Regulus. Undisturbed by any later building, excavations have revealed a sturdy hemisphere of walls protecting the town from the landward side. A large, but externally modest temple stood beside the central crossroads of this neat town, with its well-paved streets and immaculate drainage system. The houses are regular but not uniform, constructed around modest courtyards which house sturdy cisterns underfoot. The floors of many of the rooms are covered with a distinctive polished pink plaster, made from crushed fragments of terracotta, now and then flecked with *tesserae* of white marble. The large number of substantial basins found in the houses are thought either to have been hip-baths or dyeing vats.

After the invasion by Regulus, the heat went out of the conflict. Carthage was distracted by the need to discipline the various Berber tribes which had been stirred up by the invasion, and became increasingly interested in expanding its south-western frontier. Rome was similarly concerned by the home front in Etruria and the war in Sicily was increasingly left to the enterprise of local commanders. Twenty years into the war both Rome and Carthage had grown exhausted by the expense and losses of naval conflict and if it had not been for an unlucky last engagement, peace would probably have been made on the basis of the existing *status quo*. But in 241 BC the Punic fleet, escorting a relief convoy of merchantmen to one of their two naval bases in Sicily, was caught off guard by the entire Roman fleet of 200 galleys.

Carthage sued for terms and agreed to abandon its last two possessions in Sicily and pay a small war indemnity. It was an honourable peace, negotiated by the front line generals who knew the full fickleness of fortune. As the two undefeated Carthaginian garrisons marched out of Lilybaeum and Drepanum, they were given the honours of war by their Roman adversaries.

SOCIAL CRISIS AND THE MERCENARY WAR

The First Punic War can be compared to the First World War in many ways: in its waste, its strategic confusion, its vast expense and not least in the social chaos and revolution that it precipitated. Throughout the Mediterranean, the late third century saw a series of vicious conflicts between city and country and between rich and poor in the cities. It is a fascinating period, touched through and through with the enduringly controversial issues of class and race.

In North Africa the realities of this social crisis are masked by the alluring narrative of 'The Mercenary War' (241–237 BC), particularly the Orientalist version painted in Flaubert's historical novel, *Salammbô*. The immediate cause of the crisis was the penny-pinching Carthaginian government which, in need of money at the end of the long war in Sicily, decided to economize on the pay of the returning veterans. The army mutinied and 20,000 men besieged the city of Carthage from the hill of Tunis. However, this does nothing to explain the 70,000 Libyan peasants who rushed to their ranks, or the spontaneous risings amongst Carthaginian garrisons in Corsica and Sardinia in support. The Mercenary War appears to have been a genuine revolution, which pitted the over-exploited countryside against the exploitative city-dwellers. The Mercenary War differed from the normal run of doomed peasant revolts in that it was led, not suppressed, by a disenchanted army, largely recruited from landless peasants. Matho and Spendius, the leaders, had long experience of war and their polyglot identity – the former a Libyan of Punic culture, the latter a southern Italian of Greek culture – gave them a far-ranging appeal. They also exercised the

Libyan Berber head, blackstone Hermè

required ruthlessness, recruiting some murderous Gauls as their body-guard and regularly purging their ranks of potential enemies.

The size of the social threat they represented is revealed by the immediate unity they created amongst enemies. Heiron, king of Syracuse offered Carthage immediate material aid, whilst even the Roman Senate refused to trade with the rebels and instead authorized trade with Carthage. Within the walls of Carthage the urban populace grew in political confidence as their service in the army was desperately sought. By contrast, the aristocratic regime had been discredited by the treble humiliation of defeat by the Romans, the evacuation of Sicily and the mutiny. The old aristocratic committees were permitted to continue but ultimate power now rested with pairs of generals and suffetes (judges) who were annually elected by the popular assembly. These new constitutional arrangements created a genuinely democratic state whose citizens exercised much greater rights than their counterparts in Rome. The elected generals pursued a relentless campaign against the rebels, offering forgiveness to those ex-soldiers who surrendered but practising a vengeful 'white terror' on those who remained in revolt. Spendius was trapped with his army in the 'Defile of the Saw' and later crucified. The same fate awaited Matho, who fought on until 237 BC.

At about the same time Carthage began to gather up the reigns of its old empire and sent new officials out to Corsica and Sardinia. Rome, however, once again descended to an act of brutal cynicsm. The Senate tore up the recent peace treaty and declared war in 237 BC. Exhausted, Carthage had no choice but to hand over Sardinia, Corsica and an additional indemnity of 1,200 talents. Even the Greeks were shocked by this new example of Roman duplicity, while the Carthaginians, including Hannibal (247–182 BC), the nine-year-old son of one of the elected generals, swore silent revenge and eternal hatred for Rome.

A KINGDOM IN SPAIN

Hannibal's father, Hamilcar Barca, immediately set about restoring the power of Carthage. He headed west, beyond the pale of Roman influence, to rich and populous Spain. Punic influence had hitherto been restricted to a coastal strip, but Hamilcar Barca, having established his base on the venerable island city of Gades, advanced inland up the Guadalquivir valley and seized control of the silver mines. A third of the bullion went to Carthage, a third to Gades and the rest was reserved for Hamilcar Barca's war-chest. It was more than enough to finance the conquest of the disunited Iberian tribes by his professional army. By 235 BC Hamilcar Barca was confident enough to issue a silver coinage, of an exceptional purity, which bore his profile in the manner of Melqart (Hercules). It was a clear statement of royal intent which asserted that the new conquests in Iberia were to be the private fief of the Barcid family. These monarchical leanings were energetically followed by Hamilcar's successor, his brother-in-law, Hasdrubal, who married a Spanish princess, ruled from a palace at Cartagena and had himself portrayed on coins wearing a crown. In 221 BC the war-hardened, 25-year-old Hannibal succeeded to the Barcid throne after the assassination of his uncle. Rome grew ever more watchful of this vibrant offshoot of Carthage.

The Second Punic War Begins

The inevitable conflict broke out over Hannibal's conquest of the Greek city of Saguntum, on the Catalonian coast, in 218 BC. The balance of power was very different from what it had been in 264 BC. Rome had the largest navy in the Mediterranean and a professional army of 60,000, which could be expanded tenfold by calling up reserves. Throughout the war, Carthaginian policy was directed by Hannibal, who was semi-independent of Carthage itself, due to his Spanish coin and recruits, yet he never once lost the support of the people of Carthage. Although the city made an insignificant numerical contribution to Hannibal's armies, it was a vital arsenal and naval power that offered logistical support to Hannibal's military initiatives.

Hannibal knew that there was no benefit in delay and planned to forestall the war by making a quick strike into the heart of Italy to break up Rome's authority over its allies. In particular he wished to win over the wealthy Greek cities of southern Italy, which had provided so much of the financial, mercantile and naval basis for Rome's victory in the last war.

In the spring of 218 BC Hannibal left Cartagena with a 100,000-strong army. He fought his way through the tribes of northern Spain, but advanced comparatively easily through southern Gaul, an area antagonistic to Rome. Re-supplied by the Carthaginian navy Hannibal pressed on, and by October he was able to take his army across the Alps, probably via the St Bernard Pass. This legendary incident was not in fact a great challenge to an army used to campaigning amongst the Spanish mountains. The greatly reduced army with which he descended into Italy – 6,000 cavalry, 20,000 infantry and just 3 elephants – was due not to losses, but to the garrisons left behind to control the long road to Barcid Spain.

Hannibal's agents had been at work amongst the Gauls of northern Italy, who readily joined his attacks on the newly-established Roman colonies planted in the area. Hannibal destroyed a Roman army at the

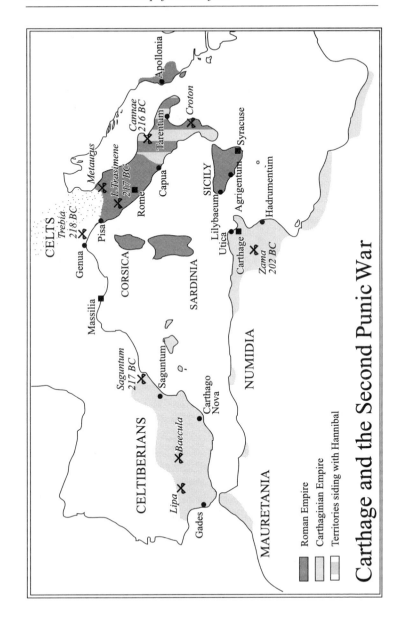

Carthage and the Second Punic War

battle of Trebia river in December, and a surprised Rome was forced to drop her plans for the invasion of Africa and Spain.

Hannibal's Italian Campaign, 218–204

For 14 years Hannibal waged war on enemy territory. Although he lost an eye due to swamp fever in the wet spring of 217 BC, at the battle of Lake Trasimene on 21 June he slaughtered the Roman army, which he had caught completely off guard, trapped in an impossible position beside the muddy banks of the lake. Deliberately bypassing Rome, Hannibal pressed on south to liberate the cities of southern Italy. Wherever possible Hannibal and his agents gave material backing to popular parties who were encouraged to overthrow the aristocratic regimes supported by Rome.

While one Roman army embarked across the sea to Catalonia, in the summer of 216 BC another marched south to its fate outside the little town of Cannae. Thanks to Hannibal's extraordinary tactical genius, the entire army was annihilated and Hannibal's grand strategy seemed complete. His youngest brother Mago rushed with the good news to Carthage, which immediately set about sending fleets to support local risings against Roman rule throughout the central Mediterranean. In the wake of Cannae, the greatest of the southern Italian Greek cities, Capua and Syracuse left the Roman fold and entered into alliance with Carthage, as did Philip V of Macedonia (220–179 BC).

Even in this year of near total victory there was a remarkable restraint in Carthaginian policy. They wanted Corsica, Sardinia and Sicily back, but nothing more. They had no interest in ruling over Italy and wanted Capua to become the president of the league of southern Italian cities, whose independence would be guaranteed by Macedonia and Carthage.

However five years of small-scale warfare in Italy, from 216–211 BC, slowly reversed the situation. A major flaw in Hannibal's strategy had been his early alliance with the Gauls of northern Italy. His employment of these fierce warriors reminded the people of Italy, again and again, of the need for Rome and the protection it could offer. A second weakness was Hannibal's reluctance to undertake sieges, at which the methodical Romans excelled. Rome, for its part, had proved unexpectantly resilient in coping with the demands of a total war fought on a number of fronts. In particular, the much-despised *publicani* (the tax farmers) filled the gap previously occupied by the Greeks of southern Italy. They financed numerous campaigns as well as the expense of the navy, imported basic goods into war-torn Italy, and managed to established factories and a new currency, the *denarius*, in the midst of the crisis.

After a period of stalemate, by 207 BC Rome was clearly in the ascendant. Hasdrubal, brother of Hannibal, who had followed his brother's famous march across the Alps to bring him a fresh army, was intercepted just a few days' march from Hannibal. The shattering news of the destruction of this, the last Punic hope, was broken when Hasdrubal's head was rolled into Hannibal's camp. The same year witnessed the destruction of the remaining Punic forces in Spain, so that aside from Hannibal bottled up in the southern toe of Italy there was only Mago, Hannibal's youngest brother, left to conduct a desultory guerilla war with his Gaulish auxiliaries in northern Italy. In 204 BC a Roman army, under the command of the same Scipio who had been victorious in Spain, was finally ready to launch its long-delayed assault on Africa.

Numidian Affairs: Syphax, Masinissa and Sophonisba

In the long prelude to the Roman invasion of Africa, Roman agents had been searching for a possible ally amongst the tribes of Numidia. As early as 213 BC Scipio, after much negotiation, dispatched a small Roman expeditionary force to the coast of Numidia to allow Syphax, chief of the Masaesyli, to free himself from Punic tutelage. In league with Masinissa (238–148 BC), heir to the rival Massyli tribe, Carthage reacted quickly to this threat to its dominion. But it was not until the Carthaginian general, Hasdrubal, (not Hannibal's brother) was forced out of Spain by the Romans in 207 BC that covert negotiations were able to achieve what no amount of raids could accomplish. Syphax was induced to betray his Roman allies and return to the Carthaginian alliance. To seal this compact Hasdrubal gave his noble daughter, the famously beautiful, cultured and intelligent Sophonisba, to Syphax as his wife. This in turn infuriated Masinissa's father, Gaia, who began toying with a Roman alliance. On his death however, Syphax swept in and annexed the entire kingdom of the Massyli. Masinissa was forced to flee for his life, pursued by Syphax's man-hunters. Initially he took refuge in the dense Khroumiri forests of northern Tunisia, but he was eventually forced to head south into the desert steppe.

SCIPIO'S INVASION, 204 BC

Scipio landed in Africa in the autumn of 204 BC with an army of 30,000. He established a fortified camp near Utica, on the site of present-day Kallat el Andalous, and over the winter conducted a number of raids. By spring, he seemed to have tired of these and opened negotiations with Carthage. Once these were well under way he launched a surprise assault on the Carthaginian forces that surrounded his camp, massacring them before marching quickly up the Mejerda valley and defeating a second Carthaginian force on the plains below Beja.

Here Masinissa was able to join the victorious Romans and continue the negotiations that his father had begun. Scipio, who had long known the importance of a Numidian alliance, sent a sizeable portion of his army to help Masinissa recover his ancestral domain and soon Masinissa was leading an army of Numidian horse to take his revenge on Syphax. By the winter of 203 BC, Syphax had fallen prisoner to Scipio and Masinissa enjoyed the surrender of Cirta, his old adversaries' capital, the following summer. Queen Sophonisba had lost none of her beauty nor her wit and was soon established as the consort of Masinissa. Fearing the effect of such a redoubtable Punic princess on his ally, Scipio demanded that she be handed into Roman captivity. But Masinissa had promised Sophonisba that she would never fall into the hands of her enemies and so presented her with a chalice of poison. In Livy's famous description she drank it saying 'I accept this bridal gift, a gift not unwelcome if my husband has been unable to offer a greater one to his wife'.

THE BATTLE OF ZAMA, 202 BC

The year 202 BC began peacefully enough with negotiations between the two sides, but these were dropped when news arrived of the destruction of the Roman squadron that protected Scipio's base at Utica. For the first time the army of Scipio looked vulnerable. Hannibal had forced his way through the Roman naval blockade and disembarked on the African coast near Hadrumentum (Sousse), thereby avoiding the politics which would have greeted and delayed him at Carthage. He marched rapidly inland to seize control of Masinissa's tribal heartland and to drive a wedge between the Roman army and their Numidian allies. By October his army of 50,000 had arrived within sight of the Numidian citadel of Zama. Disastrously, Scipio had arrived there before him, uniting with Masinissa on the way. As Hannibal surveyed the Siliana plain looking for his own Numidian ally, Prince Vermina, he knew that this was ideal terrain for cavalry and that, for the first time in his life, he was going into battle with the full weight of Numidian cavalry ranged against him rather than under his command.

The day before the battle a company of lifeguards rode out from both camps. The two converging squads of cavalry halted at prearranged stages, so that at last just the two generals, Hannibal and Scipio, were left to ride forward and meet alone. Nothing is known of this meeting except the tradition that Hannibal proposed a truce, doubtless playing for time so that Vermina could arrive on the western horizon. The generals returned to their armies and perfected their dispositions for the conflict on the morrow.

In order to neutralize his weakness in cavalry, Hannibal ordered his own force to engage Masinissa immediately, but then to flee in order to draw the cavalry away from the field of battle. Having achieved this, he sent his 80-strong elephant corps in to break up the Roman infantry, but Scipio had prepared for this by leaving gaps between his columns of soldiers. The unwieldy beasts, the tank corps of the ancient world, took the path of least resistance down these open spaces, assailed by javelins from both sides. Hannibal kept his experienced veterans in reserve, ordering wave after wave of mercenaries against the Roman front to tire the legions and blunt their weapons. When at last shattered survivors attempted to withdraw, Hannibal ordered his veterans to lower their lances. Faced with a certain dishonourable death if they retreated, the mercenaries were forced back once more against the legions. Only when the field of Zama grew slippery with blood and the

Roman legions wearied of the slaughter did Hannibal order his veterans, fresh and untired, into the assault. The Roman line held, then buckled, but just before Hannibal could deal the decisive stroke, Masinissa returned with his Numidian cavalry and fell upon the unprotected Carthaginian rear. The battle was instantly lost and by the end of the day 20,000 Carthaginian corpses littered the field. Hannibal, with his legendary energy, left the field of battle before dusk and rode night and day until he reached the safety of the coast. Prince Vermina and his tribal cavalry arrived at Zama a few days later, too late to do anything but observe the circling clouds of kites and vultures.

Zama was one of the most decisive battles of the ancient world. As the Greek historian Polybius records 'the Carthaginians were fighting for their very survival and the possession of Africa, the Romans for the Empire and sovereignty of the world'.

Hannibal's Peace Campaign

Once back within the walls of Carthage, Hannibal was enough of a patriot to champion peace, rather than take any personal satisfaction in a desperate, last-ditch struggle. Hannibal's popular party, which had hitherto been strongly identified with war, split in two over the issue, allowing the aristocratic opposition to assume control and negotiate the peace.

Scipio's terms, concluded in 202 BC, were tough but not vindictive. Carthage abandoned all its overseas possessions and had its North African territorial empire reduced to its 'Phoenician boundaries', defined by the *fossa regia*, the royal ditch, which ran south-east from Tabarka to Sfax. The vast steppe to the west was given to Scipio's ally Masinissa, now acknowledged as King of Numidia. In addition, the Carthaginian navy was limited to ten ships and it had to pay an indemnity of 10,000 talents, disband the elephant corps and agree not to wage war without the permission of Rome. The peace terms inevitably tainted the aristocratic government, whose fall was precipitated by the new taxes that they proposed in order to pay the indemnity. Hannibal, using his position as suffete (elected judge), began a wholescale inquiry into the national finances, which exposed a network of corruption and jobbery among the Carthaginian establishment. In confiscating the fortunes of the profiteers he was able simultaneously to ruin the aristocratic opposition and to pay off the indemnity. Prudent financial reforms and the grant of Carthaginian citizenship to the veterans of his army further confirmed Hannibal as the idol of the people.

The Flight and Death of a Hero

The extraordinary renewal of Carthage's energy, just ten years after her defeat, reawakened all the old Roman fears. Despite Scipio's opposition a Roman embassy was dispatched in 195 BC, ostensibly to judge a dispute over the *fossa regia,* but in fact to arrange the murder of Hannibal. He escaped east to a hero's welcome in the Phoenician mother-city of Tyre, but his life became increasingly desperate as he served as counsellor to the various Hellenistic monarchs. Pursued by enemy agents, he eventually ran out of patrons prepared to risk the anger of Rome, and rather than fall captive he took his own life in 182 BC.

To this day, Hannibal remains a hero to the people of North Africa, his name commemorated by innumerable streets and cafés. His face may be known to us from coins struck in Barcid Spain between 221 and 219 BC, but the three busts once thought to have been of him are now thought to portray Juba II of Mauretania (25 BC – AD 23). The coins depict a clean-shaven, handsome young man with high, jutting eyebrows, a long, arched nose with well-defined nostrils and a small mouth with full lips balanced by a strong chin. According to his Spartan tutor, Sosylus, he gave a great deal of private thought to his plans, which he would only reveal at the last moment. He could seize an opportunity with the same lightning speed as Alexander and was extremely good at adapting himself to different people and situations, behaving like a Gaul with Gauls and like a Greek with Greeks. Of his private life we know only that he married Imilke, a Spanish-born girl of Punic culture, who gave birth to a son before the wars separated her from her husband.

CHAPTER FOUR

The Roman Conquest of North Africa,
202 BC – AD 46

Scipio's victory over Hannibal at Zama had destroyed the Carthaginian Empire but the Romans had stopped short of occupying any territory in North Africa. Fifty years later Rome had recovered its strength sufficiently to renew the assault. The full awful extent of Roman ambition was exposed to the world by its destruction of Carthage in 146 BC. It would take another hundred years of border wars, annexations and the skilful use of client-kings before Roman dominion could be imposed over the North African shore from the Nile to the Atlantic.

The City and the King: Carthage and Masinissa

After the flight of Hannibal, the political momentum in North Africa passed to Masinissa. Having pacified the tribes within his enormous kingdom, he began to pursue an aggressive policy towards Carthage by exploiting a clause in the peace treaty which gave him the right to claim his ancestral heritage, even if it lay within the Punic frontier. Rome, distracted by war in Greece and still apprehensive of Carthage, tended to back its ally whatever the justice of the case. Masinissa's expansion reached a crescendo in 197 BC, when he seized the cities known as the 'Emporia', which controlled the lucrative trans-Saharan trade. A Roman commission of enquiry, faced with this cast-iron case of Numidian annexation of Carthaginian territory, decided to suspend its decision, but the trial was a turning point in Roman policy. The Romans began to realize that their old Numidian ally aspired to unite all North Africa under his control, with Carthage as his capital.

It was a potent vision, and one that would have taken the fusion of

Berber and Punic culture to a new level. Although foremost among the political allies of Rome, Masinissa was deeply Punic by culture. He employed Punic-speaking religious and technical officials to help administer and civilize the vast territories of his new Numidian Kingdom, where he was methodically encouraging agriculture. His commitment to the Punic religion even went to the extent of establishing a *tophet* at El Hofra outside Cirta, where child sacrifices to Tanit and Baal Hammon took place.

Masinissa's next policy was to sponsor a political party within Carthage, which called for peaceful union with Numidia. He also pursued a more traditional royal activity, bestowing dowry-laden daughters on various key Carthaginian nobles. But a violent swing to the left in Carthaginian politics in 155 BC turned Masinissa's friendly policy on its head. Supporters of the Numidian king were expelled from Carthage and Carthalo, the democratically elected general for that year, gave military backing to Agasis and Soubas, two Libyan Berbers who led a peasants' revolt against Masinissa. Their attack made little impact, however, except to provide an excuse for Masinissa to annex the rest of the emporia area and the two Carthaginian districts that were centred on Beja and Mactar. Masinissa, the great Berber king, the venerable veteran of a hundred battles, was 88 in 150 BC. It seemed that he was on the brink of achieving his life's ambition of presiding over a unified, Punic North Africa. Rome, however, had different plans.

The Third Punic War, 149–146 BC

Historians have spent much energy explaining why Rome needed to attack defenceless, democratic Carthage. Certainly, the prospect of Carthage unified with Masinissa's Numidia made for an even stronger North African adversary. But more than that, Rome's leaders at the time, a coterie of profiteering aristocrats who made vast fortunes from war and the brutal administration of conquered territories, feared for their own position. They were deeply suspicious of Carthage's popular democracy and disquieted by the number of slave revolts in the Italian countryside that had been led by ex-Carthaginian soldiers. Rome was also deeply embroiled in the eastern Mediterraean, where its legions

Punic terracotta mask recovered from Carthaginian tombs

alone seemed capable of maintaining the traditional social order and of keeping the lid on a bubbling cauldron of revolutionary and nationalist activity.

The real question (as in all wars) is not 'why?' but 'when?' and this is what the Roman senator Cato understood so well when he made the famous gesture of shaking out a rich cluster of Punic figs from the folds of his toga. Cato, who was rabidly pro-war and habitually finished each speech with the words '*delenda est Carthago*' (Carthage must be destroyed), sought to attract the special attention of his colleagues. The senators knew from boyhood how strong is the stalk of an unripe fig, but how when the fruit is ripe it drops effortlessly into the harvester's hand. Carthage, one of the juiciest prizes of the Mediterranean, was now considered ripe for the picking. The brutality and thoroughness of the destruction of Carthage by Rome is a bitter tale, and one that still has the power to send an involuntary shudder through the centuries.

THE SIEGE OF CARTHAGE

It was while fighting Masinissa in 150 BC that the Carthaginians first heard the news that Rome was mobilizing and they did everything they could to avoid this monstrous threat. Carthalo and Hasdrubal, the leaders of the popular party, were deposed and condemned to death, while an impeccably aristocratic embassy was dispatched to plea directly with the Roman Senate. The delegation was listened to, but only for the number of months it took Rome to complete its preparations.

By the spring of 149 BC the Roman army was ready. Led by the two consuls of state, the legions disembarked peacefully on to the North African shore at Utica, which had once again been quick to ally itself to the enemy of Carthage. As the Roman army advanced on Carthage, the Carthaginians agreed to their every new request. First, they gave over hostages, and then surrendered their military arsenal before finally, in desperation, placing the city's future in the hands of the Roman state. It was only when the Carthaginians heard the implacable intention of Rome to plunder and level the entire city, and to forbid them to establish a new one within ten miles of the sea, that they understood the awful logic of appeasement.

As one, they rose up to defend their homes, their temples, their livelihood and their honour. The surviving members of the democratic leadership were brought back into power by the Popular Assembly and any Roman found within the city was hounded to death. The entire population mobilized itself for war, labouring day and night to replace the arsenal that had been surrendered to the Roman army so naively just a few weeks before. The Carthaginian women cut off their long locks, which were woven to form catapult and bow strings while the city's forges achieved staggering heights of production: 100 shields, 500 javelins and 1,000 catapult darts every 24 hours.

The Roman legions delayed their first assault, and when at length they advanced, the city was ready and they were repulsed from the long line of walls, bordered by a 60-foot moat, which sealed off the landward approach to the peninsula of Carthage. The consuls made camp (on the site of today's airport) and settled down to the intricacies of a siege. For two years the Roman army became bogged down, literally, for the walls of Carthage were reinforced by pestilential marsh and salt lakes. They were also harrassed from behind by Punic forces operating from the hill country. In 147 BC, however, the precocious military talent of Scipio Aemilianus (*c.* 185–129 BC) (adopted grandson of the victor of Zama) was recognized and the legal constraints on his youth were waived. He

Numidian cavalryman depicted on a first century BC gravestone

was first elected consul and then, like some new Achilles, placed in command of the army. Carthage's fellow Punic cities, most of whom had sued for peace in 150 BC, watched in sympathetic horror as Scipio slowly tightened the noose. His army hunted out the last Punic bands from the hills, he established a naval blockade of the city and then launched a continuous series of marine assaults on the sea walls which protected the two harbours. Masinissa must have been equally appalled, but he kept up appearances by dispatching one of his sons, Gulusa, to command the Numidian cavalry in the service of his old Roman allies.

It was during the spring of 146 BC that Scipio finally broke through the battered sea walls. He rushed troops into the breach and seized control of the nearby Agora, the public heart of Carthage. His troops immediately began to loot the surrounding temples of their glittering treasures, collected over 700 years. The Carthaginians, starved and

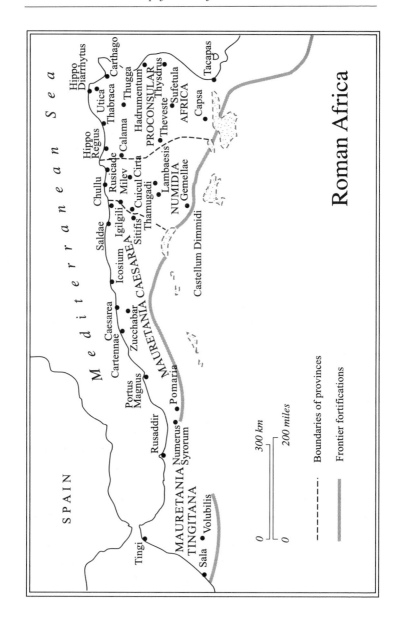

Roman Africa

- - - - - - - Boundaries of provinces

━━━━━━━ Frontier fortifications

exhausted by three years of continous fighting, continued to defend their falling city, contesting each street, each alley, each house. The citadel on Byrsa hill, now occupied by the colonial Cathedral of St Louis, held out for another six days. Here Scipio at last showed some compassion, accepting the surrender of the 50,000 starved and embattled citizens who had defended this hill against his legions. He spared their lives but that was the full extent of his mercy. They were sold into a lifetime of slavery. The Temple of Eshmoun (on the hill later to be occupied by the Roman theatre) was the last stronghold to fall, defended by Hasdrubal the Democrat with 900 zealots. Having exhausted every last resource of war, they turned the Temple of Eshmoun into a furnace, a last *moloch*, and sacrificed their lives amongst its flames. Hasdrubal alone implored for mercy at the knee of Scipio, while his wife, disgusted at his craven behaviour, hurled insults at his stooped back. She returned to the roaring sanctuary and, grasping her young children to her breast, she hurled herself into the flames, a second Dido.

The historian Polybius, the old tutor of Scipio Aemilianus, saw the young general weeping in the aftermath of victory. For in the flames of Carthage's destruction he forsaw that one day Rome, too, would fall, and quoted the *Iliad*: 'Holy Troy will perish also, and Priam and the people of Priam.'

RULE OF THE ROMAN REPUBLIC, 149–139 BC

Not even the smoking walls of Carthage, saturated with the blood of the slaughtered, were permitted to stand. The first task of the enslaved citizens was to level their city under the direction of Roman military engineers. The ruins were solemnly cursed and the administration moved to Utica. The boundary of the new province of Africa remained the old Carthaginian frontier, the *fossa regia*. The other Punic cities, such as Hadrumentum, which had surrendered to Rome at the start of the war, were confirmed in their status as self-governing city-states (*civitates liberae et immunes*) and remained free from tax and judicial oversight. The land holdings of all the Carthaginians and those towns and villages that were judged to have fought for Carthage in the war were surveyed, confiscated and the population enslaved. A small portion was set aside

The mausoleum of Ateban at Dougga: the sole surviving example of Punic
architecture in North Africa

to reward various local allies, but the majority of this vast land holding
was sold at public auction to a carpet-bagging confederacy of Roman
senators and speculators. The administration of the conquered province,
which was essentially confined to the supervising of the annual tribute
due to the Roman state, was bestowed upon a senator for just one year
at a time. It was a licence to extort money from a defenceless province,
given to reward a man after he had held some public office in Rome.
He brought with him his personal staff, but was inevitably dependent
on the local tax farmers, usually resident Italian merchants and
settlers. This republican period of Roman rule was a pitiless epoch
in North Africa, of which no trace of constructive building or
concerted policy survives. The one recorded act, the roasting alive
of the Roman governor by the irate citizens of Utica, casts a single
ghastly glow.

★ ★ ★

Numidia and the Jugurthine War

With Carthage reduced to vassal status, the Romans had still to decide what to do with their allies, the kings of Numidia. After the death of Masinissa in 148 BC during the siege of Carthage, the Numidian kingdom was divided between three of his heirs. Thus weakened this client kingdom could pose little threat to Rome until it was reunited under the leadership of Jugurtha (118–105 BC), Masinissa's grandson. In 112 BC, during his conquest of the old capital of Cirta, Jugurtha slaughtered all its male inhabitants, including a number of Italian corn merchants. This action, for all its brutality, took place deep within Numidian territory, but was nevertheless turned into an excuse for war by Rome. Rome was determined to prevent the creation of a united Numidia and the establishment of a strong North African power. A new generation of Roman nobles also wished to test their fortunes in the warm North African sun. This time however, the fig was far from ripe.

The six-year Jugurthine War (112–106 BC) tested Roman military capabilities to the full. The Romans found it comparatively easy to occupy the few Numidian towns and seize the hill-top citadels, but thereafter found themselves tied up with garrison duties and could not make contact with the enemy. The Numidians, still essentially a nomadic people, fought a fast-hitting war of raids and rapid retreats, living off the land. The Roman historian Sallust's history of the conflict records two characteristic episodes: the massacre of the Roman garrison by the citizens of Beja and a Roman surprise attack on the oasis town of Gafsa. In both accounts it is clear that there was no distinction between the population and the military. It is a classic example of a guerilla war of attrition, of which the twentieth century has furnished so many equivalents. Jugurtha was eventually defeated, but his army and his popularity were never destroyed. In the end Jugurtha was betrayed into the hands of the Romans through the treachery of his own father-in-law, Bocchus, King of Mauretania. The Romans turned the eastern frontier of Numidia into a Roman *cordon sanitaire*, held down by a chain of military settlements filled with war veterans. The westernmost provinces were taken by King Bocchus as his reward for treachery, while the central heartland of Numidia was ruled by Jugurtha's half brother Gauda (105–81 BC).

For a generation this heartland retained its freedom, but its fate was sealed when Juba I (62–46 BC) gave his wholesale support to Pompey (106–48 BC) who was about to lose the civil war against Julius Caesar (c. 101–44 BC). Caesar landed in North Africa near the Tunisian town of Mahdia in 46 BC and marched quickly north to defeat the much larger Numidian-Pompeian army that awaited him passively at Thapsus. In the aftermath of the battle Juba I staged a suicide duel with a Roman legionary, watched by a slave who had strict orders to kill the survivor.

Caesar's African Policy

Julius Caesar's actions, however beneficial in Rome, were entirely rapacious in North Africa. First, he levied extortionate fines on the rich cities, although many were theoretically allies of Rome. Leptis Magna alone had to furnish him with three million pounds of olive oil a year. Later his surveyors stole the territories of such ostensibly free cities as Hadrumentum (Sousse) and Thysdrus (El Jem), as well as a vast rectangle of fertile coastland, and settled them with landless Italians, the urban poor of Rome and discharged army veterans.

Juba's kingdom of Numidia suffered an even worse fate. It was annexed as a new province of the empire, renamed Africa Nova, and placed under the stewardship of Sallust, a Roman money lender who had lent vast sums to Caesar during his rise to power. The extent of the extortions he inflicted on his province shocked even his Roman contemporaries, and on his retirement to Rome Sallust was able to build a palatial villa, where he settled down to write his history of the Jugurthine War.

A new round of civil war started after the murder of Julius Caesar in 44 BC. The Roman legions based in Africa Nova (Algeria) and Africa Vetus (Tunisia) fought each other in support of different candidates. By 36 BC Augustus (30 BC–AD 14), the heir of Julius Caesar, had achieved mastery in North Africa, five years before victory at the battle of Actium in 31 BC gave him control of the whole Roman Empire.

The Augustan Legacy

Augustus was neither a great general nor a charismatic demagogue. His genius was political, his greatest virtue patience and his lucky destiny was 50 years of power, which enabled him to transform Rome from a predatory military machine into a stable empire. First, he deprived the Roman nobility of any military authority and reduced the Roman army to a functional level. Secondly, he created a streamlined bureaucracy recruited from talented provincial Italian families like his own. Thirdly, he began the process of co-opting the native ruling classes into the imperial ruling class by appointing them as provincial magistrates. This policy, the *Pax Romana*, allowed for an unprecedented period of prosperity and creativity which would, over the next century, enrich and transform North Africa.

COLONIAL SETTLEMENTS IN NORTH AFRICA

Augustus' immediate concern after his victory at Actium in 31 BC was to halve the size of the Roman army without causing mutiny and a new round of civil war. The veterans could only be amicably discharged with a pension, but this was beyond the fiscal resources of the state, so they were partly paid in land. Faced with the need to settle about 200,000 veterans, Augustus established colonies throughout the empire, but was particularly attentive to North Africa. Drafts of veterans were sent to all the colonies established ten years before by Julius Caesar, as well as those established fifty years earlier by Marius. In addition, 17 new colonies were established along the fertile lands of the Mejerda valley (northern Tunisia) and along the western littoral of the supposedly independent kingdom of Mauretania. Only a small fraction of these had any defensive role. The major determining factor in their foundation was Augustus' desire to be rid of his excess soldiers. These veterans were not the smallholding heroes from the pages of Livy, they were petty squires dependent on dispossessed local peasants and share-croppers to work their land. The veterans' lives centred on their concubines and old comrades in the local town, not on their fields. Many failed to make a living as North African farmers, sold up their portion and moved to a more urban life in one of the coastal cities.

Others prospered, slowly expanded their holdings, served their turn as magistrates and watched their grandchildren marrying into the local, landed élite: a medley of proud Berber lords from the hills, successful Italian merchants, scheming bailiffs and old Punic dynasts. A methodical analysis of inscriptions suggests that even at the height of the colonial period, some 51 per cent of the magistrates of North Africa were from the native, Punic-speaking aristocracy. Clearly there were marked limits to the extent of colonial settlement.

AFRICA PROCONSULARIS

In 27 BC Augustus merged the two existing provinces (Africa Vetus and Africa Nova) to create the single province of Africa Proconsularis, which stretched from eastern Libya to central Algeria. The proconsul of Africa commanded the legions that protected the southern frontier of this extensive province. It was one of the few important military commands that Augustus left open to the Roman nobility and it thus formed one of the crowning honours of a traditional senatorial career. Beneath the proconsul, Augustus made certain that his officials controlled everything of strategic importance: the ports, roads, frontiers and corn supply, as well as maintaining a careful watch over the loyalty of the legions. These salaried officials usually held the same post for five years, while the proconsul was appointed annually.

The details of the various wars fought out on the southern frontier of the empire are lost to us, save for one illuminating passage from the Roman author, Pliny. In 20 BC, L. Cornelius Balbus arrived as the new proconsul of Africa and was immediately faced with widespread rebellion, although it was only a year since his predecessor had been awarded a triumphal honour for his decisive defeat of these same tribes. Leaving the western districts under the command of his junior officers, Balbus gathered his forces for an attack on the Garamantians in the south. The expedition successfully penetrated the fringes of the Sahara, occupying Cydames (Ghadames) on the way to seizing Garama (Germa), the capital of the Garamantians, in the deep south of the Fezzan oasis. It was a spectacular coup, against the citadel of one of the most militant and confident of the Berber tribes. However, the long-term consequences of Balbus' coup were strictly limited. Even the trading oasis of Cydames was too far south to be permanently garrisoned, and the Berber tribes continued to put up tenacious resistance to Roman conquest. It is intriguing to speculate on the importance of Balbus' origins, from a Punic family in Spain. Perhaps he had access to detailed information about this ancient Carthaginian trading route, which would not have been available to a purely Roman governor.

THE REFOUNDATION OF CARTHAGE, 39–29 BC

The refoundation of Carthage had always been a central policy of the Roman populist party. There was a widespread belief that the obliteration of Carthage in 146 BC had turned the mother goddess against the Romans, who had been punished with the madness of civil war. As early as 122 BC the Roman statesman Gaius Gracchus had led 6,000 colonists to the ruins of Carthage, which he had renamed Junonia as an act of appeasement to the goddess, but the project foundered against aristocratic opposition. Julius Caesar had decreed Carthage's revival exactly a century after its destruction, in 46 BC, and had even completed a detailed street layout, but he was assassinated before he could achieve it.

So Augustus began the restoration in 39 BC by piously dedicating a new shrine to the mother goddess Ceres. Henceforth, the city's coins would bear the corn sheaf of the goddess, and her spring festival became the principal event of the North African year. By 29 BC a rectangular grid-plan of streets, aligned to the shore, covered the old Punic ruins with hundreds of *insula* – islands of housing. At the elevated centre of this grid, on the site of the old Byrsa citadel, stood a gleaming new Capitolium. Here temples and libraries stood beside the basilica, the great public hall of justice, where the governor presided over a court of final appeal. At the heart of the Capitolium, a grateful entrepreneur who had made a fortune manufacturing tiles for the new urban development, paid for an altar dedicated to the clan of Augustus. It was loosely modelled on the altar of peace in Rome and the careful symbolism of its carvings can still be admired in the Bardo museum in Tunis.

JUBA II OF MAURETANIA

During the reign of Augustus the kingdom of Mauretania (western Algeria and Morocco) gradually fell under Roman dominion. The major instrument of this expansion was a native Berber prince, Juba II (25 BC–AD 23), who provides a perfect example of Augustus' co-option of the native ruling class. Born a Numidian, the son of Juba I, Juba was Punic by culture, Greek by education and became a Roman by experience. He had been taken to Rome as a child, to grace the African triumph of Julius Caesar. He was brought up in the household of Augustus and the gratitude he felt to his patron was further confirmed when he was married to another royal orphan-in-exile, the beautiful Cleopatra Silene, 15-year-old daughter of Mark Anthony and Cleopatra.

In 25 BC Augustus judged Juba the perfect candidate for the throne of Mauretania, ruled from Iol (Cherchel in Algeria). Juba II and Cleopatra responded in kind by renaming the capital Caesarea in his honour. They ruled over a glittering, cultured city, which they turned from a sprawling Berber citadel into a classically organized city adorned with a theatre, library and imported Greek and Egyptian statuary. Juba, like the ideal of a philosopher-king, found time to write critiques on art and the theatre, as well as compiling a voluminous series of histories, a geography of Africa and a treatise on the medicinal uses of euphorbia. The western limits of Juba's kingdom are not known precisely. Excavations at the capital of Volubulis in Morocco, which Juba II ruled via a deputy, have revealed a sizeable town as far back as the third century BC. The coast of Morocco, however, consisted mainly of independent Punic city-states, like Sala, Lixus and Tingis (Tangier).

THE REVOLT OF TACFARINAS, 17–24 AD

Tacfarinas was the last great leader of resistance to Roman rule in North Africa, and the heroic story of his rebellion has been preserved for us in the histories of the first century Roman historian, Tacitus.

Tacfarinas was of the Musulamii, the Berber tribe who occupied the Aures mountain range in south-east Algeria. Ironically Tacfarinas had learned the craft of war serving in an auxiliary Roman regiment, which suppressed other Berber uprisings against Rome in another region. He deserted and returned home to the still independent Aurès Mountains where he forged a disciplined guerilla army from a motley band of bandits and free-booters. Tacfarinas proved himself a master of guerilla warfare. For seven long years he frustrated innumerable search and destroy missions launched against him. He infuriated the Emperor Tiberius (42 BC–AD 37) by proposing peace in exchange for territory. His name, whispered ever more approvingly in the markets of North Africa, gradually assumed heroic status. The death of Juba II in AD 23 presented Tacfarinas with the perfect opportunity for a general uprising. His agents had secured the support of other free Berber tribes, such as the Garamantes, as well as fermenting rebellion amongst landless peasants within Africa Proconsularis. That year the whole of North Africa, from Libya to Morocco, was swept up in the heady excitement of Tacfarinas' revolt.

The Senate appealed to Tiberius to take direct control and reinforcements were rushed in from other provinces. Tiberius' appointee settled down to the unglamorous task of constructing a network of small field fortresses, but it was his successor, Cornelius Dolabella, who reaped the victory in AD 24. Tacfarinas, no longer the captain of swift-moving bands of horsemen, but a general in command of a vast unruly army, marched north from his tribal stronghold to take control of Juba II's capital of Caesarea. Dolabella seized the opportunity presented by a visible enemy and led a surprise attack on Tacfarinas' army-of-rebellion which had camped at Auzia, just 50 miles south-east of Caesarea. It was a slaughter, not a battle, and when Tacfarinas heard of the death of his son he galloped heroically into a thicket of javelins. The revolt was over, and just 14 years later the permanent Roman garrison in the province was reduced to only two legions.

KING PTOLEMY AND AEDEMON'S REVOLT

Juba's young son Ptolemy (23–42), who assisted in the suppression of Tacfarinas' revolt, was only able to secure his inheritance with the assistance of Roman troops. Ptolemy was declared an official friend and ally by the grateful Senate while his youth, wealth and distinguished ancestry guaranteed him an enthusiastic reception in Rome. However his popularity masked an unpalatable fact of *realpolitik*, which was that with the successful pacification of North Africa, Rome no longer needed a client king ruling over Mauretania.

One morning the crowds in the Coliseum roared such a voluble greeting to King Ptolemy that it seemed to Emperor Caligula that it eclipsed his own. Caligula plotted the murder of his cousin (they shared Mark Anthony as a grandfather) and the simultaneous annexation of Mauretania which took place in AD 42 . Yet again the fig was not quite ripe for the picking.

Aedemon, a Berber councillor of Ptolemy's, raised the tribes of western Mauretania in rebellion against Roman rule. Volubulis took the side of Rome, and defended by M. Valerius Severus, a native Mauretanian, the city held firm. But it took four Roman legions over three years to subdue the surrounding country. It was good schooling for the Roman commander, C. Suetonius Paullinus, who twenty years later subdued Boadiccea's rebellion in Britain. However, Aedemon's resistance is indicative of the fate of the conquest of the far west of North Africa, where the Romans never succeeded in subduing the tribes of the Middle Atlas nor those of the Rif Mountains and so were unable to connect their coastal province by road to the rest of their North African domains. The capital of Volubilis, far from governing the province of Mauretania Tingitana from a geographical centre, formed its most south-westerly salient, protected by a ring of five forts and an alliance with the neighbouring Baquates tribe. In times of trouble, the province naturally looked to Roman Spain for aid, rather than to the rest of North Africa.

The Pentapolis

Cyrenaica (eastern Libya), once a province of Ptolemaic Egypt, had been in administrative limbo ever since its last ruler, Ptolemy Apion (116–96 BC), had bequeathed his royal power to Rome in 96 BC. In the immediate aftermath of victory Augustus settled a draft of Roman veterans on the five Greek cities of Cyrenaica. Despite the land confiscation and brutality inherent in every colonial settlement, Augustus won the undying regard of the Cyrenaican Pentapolis by joining them administratively with the Greek island of Crete, confirming their customary laws and allowing Greek magistrates to judge civil cases.

CHAPTER FIVE

Daily Life in Roman North Africa

With resistance crushed throughout the region, North Africa settled into a period of peace and prosperity. The physical remains of this era, the ghostly ruined buildings and towns which dot the landscape, are an extraordinary heritage, impressive in detail and diversity, but above all in scale. Six hundred urban settlements have been located in North Africa from the Roman period, testimony to the transformation of the empire achieved by Augustus. Before his reign there was nothing positive about the Roman presence in North Africa, while in the 200 years that followed, the region grew progressively more prosperous, populous and powerful. This golden era was capped by the reign of the Severan emperors, a North African dynasty that ruled from Rome over the halcyon decades of the Roman Empire (193–235).

Local Autonomy

It is often incorrectly presumed that the Roman Empire was responsible for the construction of the magnificent Roman remains. In fact most of the Roman architecture in North Africa was commissioned by local dignitaries who were proudly embellishing their own home towns. At Leptis Magna for instance, both the magnificent colonnaded market-place and the theatre were built by just one citizen, Annobal Rufus. Dougga's elegant town centre was created by the Gabinii, a local family of landlords. Even triumphal arches and temples, so emphatically dedicated to the emperors, were constructed and paid for by the local municipalities. Detailed examination has revealed that the indigenous Punic unit of measurement, the 20-inch cubit, was used in preference to the Roman foot of 12 inches. This is even true of such prestigious imperial projects as the aqueduct that bought water from Zaghouan to Carthage. Another form of underlying cultural continuity is the use of vertical stone beams in all construction work, a distinctive Punic feature known as *opus Africanum*.

Each town was the centre of a canton, a petty republic which ran its own affairs. A property-owning democracy formed the Popular Assembly, which approved proposals, passed honorific decrees and elected magistrates. It was presided over by two town consuls, who were known either by the old Punic title *suffetes* or the Latin *duoviri* . Day-to-day administration was in the hands of the *muhazim* or *aediles*, while the influential council of elders, the *ordo decurionem*, was composed of all the ex-officials. It was the towns, determined to prove more civic-minded than their neighbours, that built the various public facilities: dams, markets, aqueducts, bridges, cisterns, amphitheatres and circus tracks. Baths, temples, theatres and charity schools tended to be philanthropic gifts from prominent citizens. The local magisterial class were even trusted to supervise the collection of the tithe-tax, which was sent to feed the city of Rome each year.

The local Punic-speaking ruling class, even at the height of Roman colonial settlement, remained numerically dominant. An educated North African read literature and philosophy in Greek, used Latin in the lawcourts, but spoke Punic at home. Punic names, Punic deities, Punic titles and Punic speech remained in widespread use. The Emperor Septimius Severus' sister (a scion of one of Leptis Magna's leading families) was still such a Punic-speaker that she was hardly able to communicate when she visited Rome in the early third century, while even as late as the fifth century, St Augustine refers to the survival of Punic up-country.

In order to give true credit to the North African mason and his North African patron it is tempting to turn pedant and talk in terms of buildings from the Roman period, rather than Roman buildings. It seems that Rome's combination of local democracy with distant overlordship was a form of government particularly suited to exploit the latent energies of the Berbers. It tapped their genius for conciliar government at local level, yet prevented the fierce canton rivalries from turning into war, thereby allowing the peaceful flowering of native talent.

PROCONSULS AND LEGATES

The reforms of Augustus had ended the era of carpet-bagging governors such as the historian Sallust. The new breed of salaried governors sat lightly on the shoulders of the region. In the words of Emperor Tiberius, a governor should be a good shepherd and 'shear, not flay his flock'. The North African provinces comprised Mauretania Caesarensis (governed from Caesarea), Mauretania Tingitana (Volubulis), Cyrene-Crete and Africa Proconsularis, whose proconsul lived in Carthage with subordinate legates at Leptis Magna and Hippo Diarrhytus.

The governors, equipped with nothing more than a detachment of Rome's urban cohort as a police force, presided over the great festivals, soothed local rivalries, inspected the cities' annual accounts, licensed all clubs and societies and acted as a court of final appeal. Abuse of their power was checked by the fact that military command and the supervision of financial matters were the responsibility of independent officials reporting directly to the emperor. Another check on administrative abuse was the imperial cult, which Emperor Vespasian (AD 69–79) had established as a vehicle for expressing political loyalty in the provinces. The *flamens Augusti*, the priests of the cult, were recruited from amongst the rich provincials who would gather at the provincial capital to elect priests and supervise the temples. This gathering created an officially sanctioned council for discussing the common concerns of the province, while the high priest had the useful privilege of corresponding directly with Caesar, over the head of the governor.

Tribute from North Africa

Whatever his propaganda, each emperor had two paramount political concerns: how to feed the city of Rome and how to pay the legions which patrolled the endless frontiers. Each year the provinces were, therefore, committed to sending a tribute to Rome in the form of a tithe or *tributum soli*. North Africa paid this levy in corn and olive oil which were collected in state granaries, usually located at a port. The shipping of the cargo was organized by private merchants, but imperial officials maintained the essential infrastructure of harbours and roads. The grainfields of North Africa were so vital to the empire that they were known as its breadbasket. They provided Rome with two-thirds of its annual grain needs (while Egypt provided the rest). The second major form of tribute was the poll tax, the *tributum capitis*, which was paid in coin into the *fiscus*, the provincial branch of the state treasury. The *fiscus* paid local staff and administration expenses, and sent detailed accounts back to the central treasury, the *aerarium* at Rome.

IMPERIAL REVENUE

Money to pay the legions was principally raised by indirect taxation from both Roman citizens and provincials alike. The *vilicus maritimius* collected duty on all goods crossing a maritime frontier as well as the death tax, levied at 8 per cent. The *vilicus terrestris* collected a 4 per cent tax levied on the sale of slaves, a 5 per cent tax levied on the manusmission of slaves and all custom duties at land frontiers. To maximize custom collection Tiberius divided the empire into ten custom zones.

Despite all these charges, state revenue was never sufficient and had to be supplemented by the emperor's privy purse. This was filled by legacies (it was impolitic, perhaps even dangerous, for the rich to make a will without favourable mention of the emperor) and revenue from the vast *saltus*, the imperial estates. As well as the whole of Egypt, the *saltus* in North Africa included all land previously held by the Cyrenaican, Numidian and Mauretanian kings. It also commanded the heights of the ancient economy by instituting a monopoly of all mines and quarries. The workforce was supplied by the courts, who punished serious crimes with a life sentence at the quarry face, *damnatio ad metella*. The *saltus* was comparatively modest in Africa Proconsularis until Nero, in order to confiscate their estates, executed six Roman senators (who between them owned half of agrarian North Africa) on charges of treason.

The III Augusta Legion

At the end of Augustus' reign the population of the empire was 100 million, of which one million were Roman citizens. The security of the empire was based on a standing army of volunteer Roman citizens

Charioteers – detail from mosaic

divided among 28 legions. This force of 150,000 men, originally enough to secure the vast frontiers of the empire, was gradually augmented by provincial legions. Provincial officers were recruited from the *collegia iuvenum*, a club which served as a cadet corps and was established in provincial towns for the young men of the equestrian order, the local upper class. The *collegia iuvenum* was a central institution of provincial life, with its own baths, library, council chamber and cult temple. There is a well-preserved example at Makhtar (Tunisia) which occupies a prime site on one side of the old forum.

In Africa, by the end of the first century AD, the southern border was policed by the III Augusta Legion, assisted by a shifting galaxy of auxiliary cohorts, which could bring the numbers up to some 25,000 men. Military responsibility for the frontier of Mauretania Tingitana (Morocco) was normally assumed by the legions serving in Spain, whilst the military requirements of the province of Cyrenaica-Crete were linked with the great Roman naval base of Alexandria and the Egyptian-Syrian garrisons.

The III Augusta watched over the central Saharan frontier of North

Africa (Algeria, Tunisia and western Libya) as well as keeping an eye on the tribes of the southern mountain regions. The border was never absolute, since it ran across nomadic lands and the tribes continued to migrate across it seasonally, bringing vital trade and labour, which was needed at times of harvest. The III Augusta Legion made good use of the natural frontiers of the region, the mountain chains, salt lakes and sand deserts, and established their frontier lines across the plateaux. The *limes*, the actual frontier line, was an unglamorous ditch and wall, made of dry stone and pounded wet clay. Positioned regularly along its length were 14-metre square masonry watch-towers, while larger isolated forts, such as Ksar Ghilane in the Tunisian Sahara, were designed as bases for mobile patrols. Another valuable form of intelligence was derived from policing the tribal markets, which were a barometer of the political mood of the borderlands. None of these precautions proved to be failsafe, and even at the height of empire, in the second century, the desert tribes brushed through the *limes* twice and occupied substantial portions of Mauretania.

In AD 128 the Roman emperor Hadrian (117–38) travelled south across the breadth of the province to the fringes of the Sahara to review the III Augusta at Laembaesis (Algeria). In this, the best preserved military camp of the Roman world, it is possible to hear the echo of Hadrian's all-too-modern address to the troops, which survives inscribed on a column base. He congratulates them for performing so well under adverse conditions:

> In my recollection you have not only changed camp twice but actually built new ones . . . But you were not at all remiss . . . the centurions were quick and brave as usual . . . despite the heat, you avoided being tedious by doing promptly what had to be done . . . that the care taken by my legate Catullinus has been outstanding is apparent from the fact that such men as you are under his command.

Life on the Land

The vivid collection of North African mosaics, which portray life in an agrarian villa, testify to the importance of agriculture and the countryside in Roman North Africa. Interestingly, they have all been found in town houses, which fits in with what we understand of agriculture at the time. A typical landowner lived in the town and visited the country, where he might control thousands of acres and hundreds of lives. Much of this land he would farm as a *conductor*, a tenant, who, at occasional auctions bid for leases on fields belonging to the town, some great absentee senatorial landlord, or even the emperor.

No two villas in these mosaics look the same, and none would look out of place in modern North Africa, for they share a taste for stern exteriors and secluded internal courtyards. The ground floor, where all the storerooms and workshops were located, was of solid, stone construction, well guarded by a single secure door beside which the steward had his room. The lighter upper floor, often framed by corner towers and boasting a balcony, was reserved for the owner's family. Just outside the house stand ovens and bathhouses, while the simple round huts, the *mapalia*, of the workforce are a little further off. This workforce was largely made up of resident communities of *coloni*, tied peasants who paid the landlord a third of the harvest on the threshing floor (or as we might say gross), whether the crop was barley, wheat, grapes or olives. For vegetables and beans, a fifth was due. In addition each *colonus* worked six days on the landlord's home farm: two days of ploughing, two of cultivating and two of harvesting. There was never sufficient residential labour for the harvest, so local landless peasants, itinerant gangs of labourers and nomads were hired as required.

The rewards of methodical farming could be great. Some indication of North Africa's rapidly expanding agrarian economy is revealed by the growth in tribute, which was based on a fixed percentage of the harvest. In Julius Caesar's day the tribute from North Africa brought in 50,000 tons of wheat a year. By AD 46 this had increased to 500,000 tons, a tenfold increase in just 100 years. Side by side with this tenfold growth in ploughland during the first century was the simultaneous expansion of orchards and vineyards. It was a society that fed on wine (that was seldom allowed to age more than a year) from the top to the very bottom. Even the mean-minded Roman statesman Cato budgeted an amphora of wine a month for each slave. In a good year 120 amphorae of wine could be expected from just two acres of vines.

OLIVES AND THE INTERIOR

The Romans had never bothered to survey land over 500 metres in height or with less than 400 millimetres of rainfall a year, as it was rightly deemed useless for wheat. However, this fallow land provided a hard-working peasant with an opportunity for self-advancement, for the olive, providing the trees are planted 30 metres apart, can successfully be grown in the dry steppe and on hillside terraces. Protected by the legions from predatory raiders, with an efficient road system that stretched as straight as an arrow to the closest port and with a growing population assuring a continous market for olive oil, the ground was clear for a second agrarian boom.

Olive oil was no fashionable accessory, but a vital requirement of the ancient economy: as soap, a favourite sauce, cooking oil, as medicine and as a source of light in lamps. Gleaming new steppe cities, laid out with grid-like precision like Sbeitla, emerged in the second century on the back of the prosperity brought by olive oil. New inland centres of pottery manufacture were established, initially to churn out storage amphorae for the oil, which later developed a healthy export trade in lamps, figurines and red-slip tableware.

Town Life

While Roman North Africa was dotted with small towns, the most populous towns were all on the coast. As well as vast quantities of wheat and olive oil, their ports traded in textiles, dyed cloth, carpets, cloaks, finished leather, pottery, Numidian marble, sponges, cured fish, rare woods, herbs, wild beasts for the games and rare items from the trans-Saharan trade. The greatest of these towns was teeming Carthage, whose population (perhaps as high as 400,000) ranked it as the third city of empire, after Rome and Alexandria. Here the North Africans indulged in all the urban pursuits that we associate with Roman town life in Italy.

The most distinctive feature of all towns was the open square at their centre, known either by the Latin word *forum* or the Greek *agora*. This stone-paved piazza was enclosed by a colonnade and was reached by a couple of steps, which safeguarded it from wheeled traffic. It was the political, legal, social and commercial centre of the town. Here, in a short morning stroll, a citizen could hear the rhetoric of the lawcourts, the exchanges of the merchants, the gossip of the town, the ritual of the temples and the bargaining of the shopkeepers. For around the forum clustered the *curia* (senate house), the open-sided *basilica* (law court), half a dozen temples, a dozen smaller shrines and the entrances to smaller market squares lined with shops and offices. Scattered across the forum, casting lengthening shadows in the evening light, stood a plethora of votive statues and inscribed plinths commemorating the generosity of one citizen, the distinguished public career of another, the visit of a proconsul or one of the endless victories or gestures of generosity of the emperors. Amongst these ossified relics of the great and the good, the citizen body would assemble to elect magistrates, to vote on proposals and to hear speakers whose practised rhetoric spilled out from the terrace of the capitolium temple to fill the packed forum with mellifluous sound.

AQUEDUCTS AND BATHS

North Africa's most famous aqueduct, which brought water from a temple on Mount Zaghouan to the cisterns of Carthage, was 56 kilometres as the crow flies but 132 kilometres as the arched aqueduct wanders. The engineers had to devise a route which would keep the gradient steady – steep enough to ensure a steady flow, but not so strong as to burst open the sealed pipes. When the water arrived it was divided equably by the town's water commissioner, between the cavernous reserve cisterns on the hilltops, a few wealthy private customers and municipal structures such as baths and public fountains. When the aqueducts ran, water would be freely available in every quarter of the city. The women of the house could fill their jars from the cool collecting basins that stood beneath opulent colonnaded fountain heads, while drinking troughs stood brimful at the city gates. Such a state of affairs was not always possible in drought-prone North Africa and no villa was without its own private roof-fed cisterns. Beneath the paved streets drains took away foul water, although very few houses had latrines, since everyone used those by the bathhouses.

The baths were open to all who could pay a small fee and on great

Monumental bas-relief: Victory with trophy

public holidays even this was waived. They were palatial edifices the like of which the world has never seen before or since: paved in mosaic, riveted with marble, heated, decorated with statues and filled with the sound of splashing water. The routine of bathing began with a visit to the *forica*, the opulent latrines where neighbours defecated in companionable proximity, chattering over the events of last night from their shaded stone seat, looking across to where the sun played on a gurgling fountain. Moving round to the principal entrance of the baths you arrived at the *apodyterion*, the changing rooms, undressing in the *vestibularium* and anointing yourself with oil in the *unctarium*. Then, some exercise in the sundrenched courtyard of the *palaestra*, followed by scraping away of oily dead skin with a strigil in the *destrictarium*. A succession of progressively heated marble chambers – the *sudarium*, *caldarium* and *laconica* – helped to sweat out ill-humour, and for an additional charge you could abandon yourself in the *laconica* to the ministrations of a skilled masseur. Immersion in the *tepidarium* bath prepared you for the cold pool of the vaulted *frigidarium*, which was decorated with the best statues and mosaics. From here you could start the process again, or in some cases make use of the *natatio*, a large outside swimming pool, or wander freely through the shops, library and gardens attached to the bath complex. Baths were usually laid out with a symmetrical floor plan, which provided for two sets of hot chambers. This was to do with maintenance, for different admission hours, rather than walls, kept the sexes apart. In North Africa the dried residue from the olive oil presses made for an abundant fuel with which to stoke the hypercaust heating system. The natural hot springs of North Africa were also enthusiastically exploited for their curative effects. A concerned valetudinarian could sample a dozen such establishments within a day's journey of Carthage.

URBAN ENTERTAINMENTS

A striking feature of the ruined towns of North Africa are the many buildings associated with public entertainment: the theatres, amphitheatres and circuses. At the great public festivals, such as the pre-eminent North African festival of Ceres, which took place from 12–19 April, countryfolk would flock in to town to join in the dawn-to-dusk entertainments.

The theatre season ran from the festival of Cybele on 4 April to the people's games in September, and consisted of Greek tragedies, interspersed with debates, lectures, farces, pantomimes, circus acts and comedy in Latin. The front three rows of the *cavea* were reserved for the thrones of the town's leading citizens – its senators, magistrates and priests. Next came rows for the equestrian class followed by seats for the ordinary citizens. A colonnaded promenade ran round the summit of the theatre with a shrine to Ceres, or some other attribute of the mother goddess, placed at its centre. Awnings could be attached to this colonnade to provide shade. When the Emperor Caracalla (188–217) sent his favourite actor to play at Leptis Magna's theatre his visit was commemorated by a votive statue inscribed familiarly 'he was the best turn of his day . . . acclaimed in Verona, Vicenza, Milan and Rome'.

GLADIATORIAL GAMES

The most important entertainments held in the amphitheatres were the gladiatorial games. The magistrate presenting the show arranged matters with the *lanistae*, professional managers who ran stables of gladiators, provided wild beasts and arena attendants, as well as acting as referees on the day.

The night before a show, a symbolic gladiatorial duel with muffled weapons was followed by a lavish public banquet. In the morning, as a warm up, those sentenced by the magistrates to *damnatio ad bestias* were killed in the arena. First, they would all be exhibited in chains before being led out to their individual deaths; normally there was some form of torture, before they were mauled by wild beasts and finished off by a gladiator. Then it was time for the *venatio*, the wild beast hunt. A circus or dancing troupe would entertain the crowd while the amphitheatre was transformed into a more suitable setting. An alternative interlude was for miniature catapults to fling tokens, which could be exchanged for prizes, up into the poorest seats. The gladiators specializing in wild beast hunts, the *bestiarii*, were a professional group, fighting and working with animals in a way not far removed from a professional English huntsman today. They might slaughter antelope, wild ass and ostriches with arrows, spear wild boar, fight wild cats or face enraged bulls. In addition, they managed fights between animals, arranging for predatory cats to kill in the arena or for pairs of chained animals, such as bears and bulls, to fight one another.

In the lunch hour it was the turn of robbers, arsonists and murderers to kill each other. The first pair were brought forth, one armed, one just dressed in a tunic. The business of the first was to kill the latter, which he seldom failed to do. After this feat he was disarmed and led out to confront a newcomer armed to the teeth and so the butchery continued until all lay dead.

In the afternoon a fanfare of lutes, trumpets and horns announced the major event of the day, the gladiatorial duels. First, the gladiators paraded in fine embroidered cloaks, their weapons carried by valets, before giving the famous collective greeting to the presiding magistrate, *Ave, morituri te salutant* ('Hail, we who are about to die salute you.'). The duels were accompanied by music, the orchestra celebrating each successful parry and blow with a fanfare, by fervent betting and by roars of applause from the crowd. Gladiators, when disabled, could usually appeal to the crowd, who would wave handkerchiefs or gesticulate with their thumbs upright crying *mitte* ('let him go') or reversing their thumbs in a jabbing motion and screaming *iugula* ('slay him'). The passions aroused were intense, hawkers sold food and drink to quench thirsts and appetites along the benches while prostitutes did a thriving trade in the dark vaults.

Events in the circus, the 500-metre long chariot-racing track, were less bloodthirsty but equally exciting. Twelve four-horse chariots, three in each team (the reds, the whites, the blues and the greens) raced seven times anti-clockwise round the central *spina*. The progress of the race was recorded on the *spina* by a row of seven stone eggs being removed from their posts or dolphins spouting water into a line of basins. North Africa was renowned as the home of the best horses, and the Berber hinterland was famous as the breeding ground of charioteers. One such African charioteer of genius had seven statues raised in his honour along the racing track at Constantinople, with a detailed inscription of his stream of victories won until death stole him from the circus, aged 67.

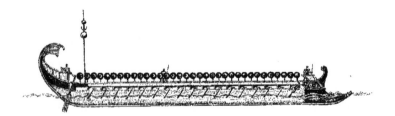

CHAPTER SIX

The Golden Age of Roman North Africa, 69–235

It was only a matter of time before the citizens of North Africa began to play a decisive role in the affairs of the empire at its heart, in Rome. The route had been opened by Claudius (41–54), who was the first emperor to fill empty seats in the Senate with upper-class provincials. In his defence he spoke of 'transferring to this city all outstanding persons, where ever found' to assist in the direction of the Roman Empire. This enlightened policy was largely responsible for the longevity of the empire and its success.

Vespasian accelerated the process after he fought his way to the throne in AD 69 and was the first to award a North African with the broad stripe and gold ring of a senator. This process of assimilation reached its natural fulfillment when Spanish-born Trajan became emperor in AD 96 and climbed the last barrier of prejudice. By the end of the second century, a third of the Roman senate originated from North Africa.

This strong representation of North Africans was not just due to the efficient exploitation of their agricultural estates. From the first century the region had produced a stream of men of rare ability, whose influence was felt throughout the empire. To follow the careers of four such talented North Africans (Lucius Quietus, Lucius Apuleius, Marcus Fronto and Septimius Severus) allows a vivid insight into the empire at its most glorious, multicultural and tolerant apogee.

Lucius Quietus, the Darling of the Legions

It was in Trajan's reign that a North African first came within a heart beat of wearing the purple of the Caesars. Lucius Quietus (?–117), far

Trajan's triumphal arch, Timgad, Algeria

from being brought up as a model Roman in a provincial forum, was the son of a tribal lord from unconquered central Morocco. Lucius' father and his warriors had supported the Roman legions in their attempt to subdue Mauretania Tingitana (northern Morocco) during Aedemon's revolt in AD 46. This useful ally, on a notoriously difficult frontier, was honoured with the gift of Roman citizenship. Lucius served as an auxiliary officer in the Roman cavalry, recruiting from the free tribes of Morocco. Emperor Domitian (81–96) rewarded him with equestrian rank but later dismissed him for insubordination. Since practically every officer of calibre had been mistreated by this paranoid ruler this commended rather than harmed Lucius in the eyes of his brother officers. In due course it was one of these, a Spanish legionary commander called Trajan (98–117), who occupied the throne. Lucius served as Trajan's cavalry commander during the tough conquest of Romania – you can see his bareheaded Berber cavalry on Trajan's column in Rome. He was made a senator, provincial governor and even appointed consul. The high profile of cavalry in the war against Parthia further strengthened his standing, while a brilliant rearguard action, which saved the whole army from destruction, made Lucius the darling of the legions. Only the quick action of Hadrian, supported by Trajan's widow, prevented Lucius being acclaimed emperor on the death of Trajan. Hadrian had the infantry under Lucius' command quietly disarmed, but the North African cavalry proudly refused to surrender their arms and abandon their heroic commander. They had to be slaughtered to a man before Hadrian was in a position to order the execution of his rival. Lucius was clearly an exceptional general, and although it seems unlikely that he would have made a better ruler than Hadrian, the wisdom of the Roman meritocracy is abundantly clear. In previous centuries Lucius would have been a rebellious scourge, like Tacfarinas or Jugurtha.

Lucius Apuleius and the Golden Ass

The only complete Roman novel that is still read for pleasure is *The Golden Ass*. It defies categorization, for it is both a romance, a bodice-ripper, a comic satire, a patrician put-down and a deeply religious work. It was written by a North African, Lucius Apuleius (born 123 AD), whose character has been described as 'superficial, colorful, excessive, disordered, intemperate, and redundant'. Apuleius was, in short, as entertaining in life as in his writing, while his fellow citizens saw another side to him, raising an inscription that praised him as a 'platonic philosopher' and an 'ornament to the community'.

Apuleius came from Madauros (M'daourouch in Algeria), an agricultural centre inland from the port of Hippo (Bone). The town was a modest place – even in its heyday there were only 1,200 seats in its theatre. Yet despite the bad Latin revealed in the epitaphs found in the old forum it had a good academic reputation, and St Augustine was later educated there. Lucius Apuleius was born at the summit of local society, his father had been a *diumvir*, a town consul, and left a fortune of two million sesterces when he died. Lucius' inheritance allowed him a life of agreeable scholarship, but his devotion to Greek and Latin literature never conflicted with his pride in his Numidian ancestry. By his thirtieth birthday he had studied, and debauched himself, at the university cities of Carthage, Athens and Rome and was down to his last three slaves. Rather than devote himself to practising law in the capital, for which he was abundantly well trained, he took ship back to his North African homeland. At Oea (Tripoli) he lodged with one of his numerous student friends and ended up marrying the widowed mother of the house, who was wise, very rich and only ten years his senior. His friend was delighted by the match but unfortunately died, and a gaggle of disapproving cousins formally accused Lucius of witchcraft. It was the *cause célèbre* of 158, with public interest so intense that the trial had to be staged in the theatre at Sabratha before the proconsul. Lucius, who conducted his own defence, was at last put to work, and his brilliant destruction of the charges against him is preserved for us in his *Apologia*. The acquittal seems to have settled something restless within him, for Lucius then settled down to write and teach.

Marcus Fronto, 100–166

Marcus Cornelius Fronto was born in 100 at Cirta, the old Numidian capital, but his family originated from the small town of Calama (Guelma) some 74 kilometres inland from Hippo. Fronto, just like his near neighbour Apuleius, first studied at Carthage before moving to Rome in his early twenties. There he applied himself to law, but more specifically to an analytical study of Latin, its history, origins, true form and purpose. Fronto became an acknowledged master whose services, either as legal consultant or practising lawyer, were in continuous demand. His style was highly mannered, almost archaically correct, but he was a vigorous champion of spoken Latin. Fronto, like some archetypal Oxbridge don, carefully acquired status. He married into a collateral branch of the imperial family, served as tutor to the heir to the throne, acquired the villa of Maecenas (Augustus' highly cultured friend) and in due course was honoured with the office of consul. His influence was not limited to Rome, for he exercised a diligent correspondence with all the rising talents of the next generation. His correspondence with his old pupil, the emperor Marcus Aurelius (161–80), is distinguished by an affectionate but underlying disagreement which does them both credit. He was the central figure in the

highly urbane intellectual circle preserved for us in the Latin grammarian Aulus Gellius' *Attic Nights*, but he always remained proud of his
nomadic Berber ancestors and indulged himself in poetic yearnings for
the sharp clear skies of his youth.

Septimius Severus, 145–211

The apex of North African influence in Rome occurred under
Septimius Severus, the first North African to ascend the throne of the
Caesars, and his reign marks the high tide of the Roman Empire as an
enlightened state.

Septimius was born at Leptis Magna in 145, into a wealthy and
distinguished family of Punic lineage. His father was a retiring man who
had avoided a public career, although a large number of his relatives
had risen to high rank. One member of the family had been trusted
with updating Leptis Magna's constitution, another had been a senator,
another had risen to become consul, while a more distant branch had
left North Africa altogether and established themselves as landed gentry
in Tuscany. Septimius' political career, assisted by this network of
well-connected cousins, had a certain inevitability to it, providing he
proved diligent. By the time he was 45 he had worked his way up the
approved career ladder of legal, military and administrative posts to
become one of the 24 consuls appointed for the year 189.

His career could well have ended here, had not a chance posting to
Syria, some seven years before, opened up alternative avenues. In Syria
Septimius met both his political patron, the governor Pertinax, and his
second wife, Julia Domna, the resourceful scion of a dynasty of high
priests to the Syrian sun god. It was also in Syria that Septimius first
received warning of his bright destiny when he was addressed as 'king'
by the oracle of Baal at Apamea.

In 189 three key military commands (Syria, Britain and the Danube)
came up for appointment. Pertinax, then prefect of Rome, secured the
Danube command for his friend Septimius, whose competent but
uninspiring career seemed to threaten no one. In 193, after the death
of the mad Commodus, Pertinax assumed the throne. His rule was cut
short after 87 days, when he was murdered by the Praetorian Guards

The Severan dynasty: Septimius Severus and his wife Julia Domna

who then auctioned the throne to the highest bidder. This shameful transaction revealed a number of North Africans in high positions, for Aemilius Laetus, commander of the Guard, came from Thina (Sfax), while Didius Julianus, the winner of this infamous auction, came from a well-known Hadrumentum (Sousse) family.

On hearing of the murder, Septimius at once marched on Rome with his Danube legions to disband the perfidious Praetorian Guard. The cowed Senate acclaimed him emperor, but it took four years to destroy the rival generals in Syria and Britain. In 197 Septimius celebrated his supremacy with a drastic purge of the Senate. Roman street gossip credited him with exacting a long-awaited revenge for Hannibal and Carthage. It was a romantic notion, for Septimius' proscription was just as remorseless to the senators from North Africa as to those descended from the old families of Rome.

The reign of Septimius Severus was an astonishing *tour de force* on practically every level: intellectual, legal, spiritual and military. The emperor and his formidably intelligent wife sponsored and popularized the last great revival of pagan philosophy, the neo-platonic school, as expounded by Plotinus (205–70) and his biographer Porphyry in Alexandria and Rome. The Severans were the last truly pious dynasty of Rome, meticulously attending to their religious duties, as well as restoring shrines and creating new temple complexes. The great legacy of the empire, Roman law, was virtually created during the reign of Septimius reign by his handpicked (mostly Syrian) jurists, whose innovative and incisive judgements formed the foundation of the famous codification of the law achieved centuries later by the emperors Theodosius (379–95) and Justinian (527–65).

Septimius freed Egypt from the slavery imposed upon it by Augustus, creating self-governing councils, reforming the law and improving the lot of the peasantry. Elsewhere in the empire he struck hard against the senatorial plutocracy, abolishing the corrupt practice of tax farming and opening up the imperial administration to the provincial middle class. He abolished the privileged status of Rome and Italy, making way for his son's celebrated grant of citizenship (the Constitutio Antoniana of 212) to all the free inhabitants of the provinces.

The emperor also abolished the restriction on marriage within the army and began to create local militias to protect the frontier and free up the legions as a mobile battle force. Septimius and his redoubtable wife Julia Domna (known as the 'Mother of the Camp') led from the front, personally reviewing the entire frontier defences of the empire, and leading aggressive campaigns on the Danube, and on the Persian, Syrian and Scottish frontiers. Nor did Septimius neglect the security of his homeland. From 202 to 203 he directed a concerted advance into the Saharan steppe, pushing Roman rule to its southernmost limits. Behind this forward line Septimius settled a militia of veterans in a special *limitanei* (tax-free frontier) zone, equipping them with land, livestock and slaves.

SEVERAN ARCHITECTURE

It was also a golden period of architecture. The baths of Caracalla and the Severan arches in the forum are some of the most astonishing structures in Rome. In his home town of Leptis Magna, Septimius combined the construction of a monumental new quarter with radical innovation. The Severan arch, aside from boasting some of the finest examples of Roman carving, also experimented with baroque forms. Bold vertical pediments were thrown up into the air like pinnacles from the corner columns. The grand harbour avenue formed the Roman world's first monumental arcade, while the massive basilica beside the new forum stands like a preface to the Christian architecture of the fourth century.

The Gordian Rebellion of 235

The Severan dynasty continued for 24 years after Septimius' death, hampered by near-mad males but sustained by two more remarkable generations of women from the Syrian family of Julia Domna: Julia Maesa and Julia Mammaea. In 235 Julia Mammaea and her son Alexander Severus were assassinated and their deaths marked both the end of the golden age and the end of North African political influence.

After the murder a cabal of rich North African landlords conspired to nominate an alternative candidate to the throne. Their motives were partly affection for the Severans, partly disgust at the usurpation of the throne by Maximinus (235–8), a simple Thracian soldier, but mostly a reaction to the extortionate taxation ordered by the new emperor. They championed Gordian, a venerable Roman senator of proved administrative ability, who was then serving as proconsul of Africa. Gordian's candidacy was accepted by the Senate and by most of the provinces. He and his co-emperor son (Gordian I and Gordian II) briefly ruled the empire (238) from the governor's palace at Carthage, while plans were perfected for the journey to Rome. However, the North Africans had failed to secure the support of Capellianus, legate of the III Augusta Legion, who marched on Carthage, defeating the small army led against him by Gordian II. On hearing of the defeat and death of his son, Gordian I took his own life. It was a wise decision for Capellianus was not content to merely restore order. He directed a bloody social purge, punishing the landed class for daring to prefer a man of senatorial background to Maximinus, the choice of the army. In Herodian's words

> when Capellianus entered Carthage he killed all the leading men who were still alive after the battle, and he plundered the temples and seized the money of private persons and the public funds. And he attacked all the other cities that had taken down the dedications to Maximinus, killing the gentry and exiling the common citizens. He also gave orders to the soldiers to put fields and villages to the torch and loot.

In particular Capellianus targeted the city of Thysdrus (El Jem, Tunisia), which had first sparked the revolt by attacking Maximinus' tax officials.

In a further twist, Maximinus was supplanted in 238 by Gordian III (238–44), a grandson of Gordian I. Gordian avenged his kinsmen by destroying the III Augusta Legion, whose very name was obliterated. Throughout North Africa you will find that their name has been hacked off official inscriptions.

Military Anarchy, 235–84

Capellianus' terror campaign in North Africa marked the birth of a new military order in the empire. The landed class were no longer the power brokers, and in North Africa this fall from high political grace is particularly marked. The exuberant flowering of architecture, the superb mosaic floors and the boom in assertive, confident public buildings during the Severan period is followed by a complete architectural void. Not a single inscription, let alone a new building, has been identified between 244 and 270.

In the half century following the murder of Alexander Severus, 28 soldiers were proclaimed emperor, only one of whom died before he could be deposed. Imperial statues were made with a replaceable head so that official portraiture could keep pace with the bloody succession of soldier-emperors. Each new accession entailed a donation to the legions who had assisted the emperor, which was in turn raised by a fresh round of confiscatory taxes and coinage devaluation. It was a period of bewildering politics where the only hope of survival lay in a studiously maintained apolitical profile and where a demonstration of wealth brought down extortionate tax demands on the whole community.

Architecturally this was a miserable period, but there is no evidence of depopulation or a downturn in agricultural production in North Africa. There were clearly still large amounts of disposable wealth around, evidenced by the many hoards of coins discovered from this period. Political uncertainty, devaluation and the constant need for hard cash to pay soldiers, meant wealth needed to be highly mobile to keep it out of the rapacious hands of Rome.

The social and moral vacuum left by the disintegrating empire made way for what was to become a vital force in North African history for 400 years, the Christian Church.

From Pagan to Christian,
284–393

Although the adoption of Christianity as the official religion of the Roman Empire was of paramount importance to European history, in North Africa Christianity lasted only some 400 years before being eclipsed by another great religion from the Middle East. Nevertheless, in this short period the religion took on some distinctively North African characteristics and provoked a schism of violent bitterness, which lasted for most of the period.

The Early Church

For over two centuries, the Christian faith had survived partly underground. The first communities had been Jewish, but most of these were destroyed during the Roman suppression of Jewish revolts in AD 71 and 110. The communities that survived were those following the example of St Paul, which had gradually shed their Jewish identity and its unpopular rites of circumcision and dietary laws. They proved to be exceptionally adaptable. The Syrian homeland of the faith was a land of many languages – Aramaic, Greek and Hebrew – and the Church from its earliest days was never restricted to one linguistic identity. Indeed the feast of Pentecost, when the apostles are recorded as speaking in many tongues, was no doubt partly a metaphor for this adaptability. From the beginning, the Church was conceived as a missionary organization, following the example of Christ. Missionary activity was also, as St Paul first suggested, the only sure manifestation of the Grace of God.

Mosaic: The Lady of Carthage

A TREASONABLE OFFENCE

What made these early Christians objectionable to the Roman state was not so much their beliefs, nor even their ceaseless proselytizing, but their refusal to sacrifice to any of the old deities or to offer so much as a prayer to the official cult of the deified emperors. To the majority of the population, such a refusal seemed a direct attack on the harmony of society as well as the fertility of the land. It was also treasonable and could be punished by death.

In practice, official persecution of Christians only occured when the emperor needed a scapegoat, after natural disaster had fanned popular rage. The first persecution, which resulted in the execution of the two charismatic leaders of the early Church, St Peter and St Paul, in AD 64 occurred when the Roman emperor Nero needed someone to blame for the great fire of Rome in 61. The normal governmental attitude was one of tolerant disdain, as defined by a letter from Emperor Trajan to governor Pliny:

> this wretched cult . . . must not be hunted out . . . pamphlets circulated anonymously must play no part in any accusation [but] if they are brought before you and the charge against them proved, they must be punished, but in the case of anyone who denies that he is a Christian, and makes it clear that he is not by offering prayers to our gods, he is to be pardoned.

Few Christians, when faced with the choice between a horrifying death in the amphitheatre or an easy (and arguably temporary) apostacy, could resist making the latter choice. The noble army of martyrs was a small and select group.

THE FIRST NORTH AFRICAN CHRISTIANS

Christianity entered North Africa through the polyglot coastal cities, with the first communities established at Carthage, Tipasa, Cyrene and Tingis. The first North African Christians to be recorded are six martyrs who came from the small inland town of Scillium, who were tried before pronconsul Vigellius Saturninus on July 17, 180 in Carthage. The trial transcript survives, carefully copied by the Church as a record of its early heroes:

> The pronconsul asked 'What are the things in your box?' to which Speratus, the leading Christian of the group, replied, 'The Books, and the letters of Paul, a just man'. The pronconsul declared his own faith, 'We, also, are religious, and our religion is simple: and we swear by the genius of our lord the emperor, and pray for his welfare, as you ought to do.' To which Speratus replied, 'The Empire of this world I do not recognize; but rather I serve God whom no man has seen nor can see with human eyes.'

The proconsul, in a spirit of humanity, offered them 'a postponement of thirty days [to] reconsider' but the six refused and were sentenced to death.

Another well-chronicled trial of six Christians took place in Carthage in 203. It was also supervised by a lenient judge, the procurator Hilarion who appealed to Perpetua, a well-educated young mother, 'spare your father's white hairs; spare the tender years of your child. Offer a sacrifice for the safety of the Emperors.' However, this little group of Christians had already fixed their desires on the heavenly rewards of martyrdom and not even their public torture in the amphitheatre would shake their faith.

It is almost certain that their deaths were watched by at least one sympathetic witness for Tertullian, born in Carthage in 155 AD, was then in full flow, pouring forth a stream of Christian pamphlets after a late conversion. Tertullian's theological beliefs were later considered too heretical for him to be included amongst the canonical 'Fathers of the Church' but his literary influence can hardly be overrated. He virtually created ecclesiastical Latin (the language of the Christian West for the next thousand years) with his lively, bold and witty style. He invented new words and phraseology as well as perfecting a ruthlessly destructive invective and a high authoritarian moral tone that would later become a characteristic of medieval writing. Tertullian has an exhaustingly exact opinion on everything: from female deportment, dress, marriage, medals and military service to such theological matters as the bodily resurrection. It is as if the passion of the early martyrs has been transformed into a clearly written legal code. Tertullian, who wrote enthusiastically and lyrically about actively seeking martyrdom, somehow managed to survive in Carthage, for his first biographer, St Jerome, says 'he is said to have lived to an advanced age'.

The Spread of Christianity in the Third Century

Despite the example of the heroic martyrs it is impossible to imagine that the impressive classical humanism of the high empire, in the first and second centuries, could be replaced by an introverted, restrictive, demanding moral faith such as Christianity. With the arrival of military anarchy in 235 however, it is all too easy to appreciate the attractions of Christianity. The Church made a virtue of the necessity of political quietism and self-sufficiency. It offered the absorbing occupation of moral self-inspection in exchange for the vanished urban display of the past. On a practical level it also offered a system of mutual support to its members in contrast to the arbitrary exactions of the tax officials. The continuous political disorder also appealed to rather than dismayed the Church, for it offered reassuring proof of the end of the world whose imminence was strongly believed in.

The Christian communities were also highly adaptable. Their treasures (gospels, epistles and acts) were, like the silver of the generals, all highly portable. They placed no faith in, nor had any responsibility for, the upkeep of buildings. The site of the humble tomb of a martyr meant much more to them than all the perfumed courtyards, marble temples and smoking altars of antiquity. They had no fear of defilement or accidental pollution; a 'church' could be formed wherever a few believers could come together, their rites demanding nothing more than verbal prayers, bread, wine and the kiss of peace.

THE DECIAN PERSECUTION

Both the spread of Christianity and the increasing bankruptcy of imperial Rome, with its monetary inflation, heavy taxation and military defeats, made increasing persecution inevitable. Decius (249–51) was the first soldier-emperor to organize a concerted empire-wide campaign against the Church. He set up local committees to supervise a loyalty oath to the state cult of Rome and the deified emperors. Certificates (*libelli*) were awarded stating that 'we have sacrificed to the gods all along, and now in your presence according to orders I poured a libation and sacrificed and tasted of the sacred offerings' before the approved witnesses. As an attempt to winkle out Christians the oath failed, although it provided opportunities for local graft. Certificates were traded, some sacrificed with 'crossed fingers', others hid during the period of oath-taking, but many Christians simply betrayed their faith.

Within the Church there was controversy about how to re-admit these temporizing *libellatici* (certificate holders) into the Christian fold. Matters were further complicated because many of these lapsed Christians had obtained a certificate of forgiveness (*libelli paci*) by confessing to those Christian martyrs who were in prison because of their faith. The Gospel of St Mark (xiii, 11) credited Christians in prison with unique access to the Holy Spirit and so they were much in demand as confessors. But for the admirable leadership of the bishop of Carthage, St Cyprian, the Church in North Africa seemed likely to split on this contentious issue.

ST CYPRIAN OF CARTHAGE AND THE VALERIAN PERSECUTION

Cyprian is the very model of a good bishop. His life is also a characteristic example of the cultural shift that took place in the middle of the third century. Cyprian was born in Carthage in 200 to prosperous pagan parents. Throughout the heyday of Severan North Africa he was at the forefront of North African society, a successful barrister at the lawcourts who was also a professor of rhetoric at the university of Carthage. His conversion to Christianity only occured in 246, but as there were very few men of respect, position and learning in the early Church he was made bishop of Carthage just two years later. He was devoted to the unity of the Church, to letter writing (some 60 of which have survived) and to pastoral care. His humane conduct during the plague of 252 is said to have won him more converts than any preacher. The next year his moral authority was further demonstrated when he collected 100,000 sesterces in order to ransom a group of citizens from their kidnappers. Cyprian well understood that the Church, if it was to function as a compassionate institution, had temporal needs, but he was also passionate enough to take inspiration from the heroic evangelism of the martyrs. He proved to be a natural diplomat, remaining in constant touch with his one superior, the bishop of Rome, while acting as the avuncular primate to all the lesser bishops of North Africa. Eighty-seven bishops responded to his call to attend a regional council held covertly in Carthage in 256.

A new round of official persecution, launched by the Emperor Valerian in 258, specifically targeted the Church leadership and its economic resources. The proconsul handled the trial of the celebrated Bishop Cyprian, with all the courtesy to be expected between members of the *honestiores* (educated men of property) class. St Cyprian also exhibited the most graceful manners and left instructions that his executioner should be generously tipped. He was beheaded on 14 September just outside Carthage.

Even as St Cyprian was being executed it was clear that some critical threshold had been crossed, for the authorities were powerless to prevent him being escorted to his execution by a crowd of well-wishers. Two years later, in 260, the Emperor Gallienus issued an edict of toleration, which ushered in a 40-year period of coexistence.

The Reforms of Diocletian, 284–303

It was Diocletian who finally restored the authority of the state during his 20-year reign as emperor (284–305). He curbed internal dissidence, secured the frontiers, reorganized provincial administration, established a system of imperial succession, attempted to curb inflation with price control edicts and divided the empire between an eastern and a western ruler. In his authoritarian reformation of empire, civil life was to be as disciplined as the military vocation. The peasant was to be tied to the land, the craftsman to the town, the merchant to a fixed price, just as the soldier was tied to the defence of the frontier.

North Africa was part of the western empire which was administered by Maximian (284–305), Diocletian's loyal co-emperor. Maximian was the first ruler since Septimius Severus to repair the network of roads, forts, walls and ditches that formed the Saharan frontier zone, in a prolonged military campaign from 297–8. He oversaw directly the creation of a new military structure that placed the provincial militia or *limitanei* under the command of the *dux* (duke) while the professional mobile army, which was doubled in size, was commanded by the *comes* (count). The cavalry was for the first time conceived as an equal and permanent part of the Roman army rather than being formed from native auxiliaries. Whatever the change in training and status of the cavalrymen, North Africa retained its accustomed place as the nursery of horsemen. The permanent cavalry garrison of 16 squadrons was the largest on any imperial frontier, for these squadrons, aside from their local duties, continued to recruit and train Berber youths for service overseas.

The administrative boundaries were altered in 303 to create seven smaller and more manageable provinces. Algeria was divided between the four provinces of Mauretania Caesarensis and Mauretania Sitifensis in the west, Numidia Cirtensis in the north-east and Militana in the south. Tunisia was divided between the northern province of Zeugitana and the southern province of Byzacena with Tripolitania to its east. For

Ghirza: Libyan mausoleum

the first time since the Punic Wars, the region also enjoyed a precarious unity as 'Africa', one of the eight *dioceses* of the western empire.

There were two areas in the far east and the far west of the region that were excluded from Diocletian's diocese of Africa. Cyrenaica was severed from its old connection with Crete and renamed Upper Libya (or the Pentapolis) with a civil governor posted at the coastal city of Ptolemais. Lower or 'Dry Libya', which included such oasis communities as the oracular shrine of Siwa, was governed from Derna, also on the coast. Initially the disciplining of the militant Marmaric tribes of the desert was in the hands of the 'Duke of Egypt, Thebaid and the Two Libyas', but as this splendid officer resided on the Nile at distant Luxor, a Duke of the Pentapolis was later appointed.

In the far west the Berber tribes had destroyed Roman rule over Mauretania Tingitana. From the available archaeological record it looks as if the walled town of Banassa on the River Sebou fell first, sometime after 259, followed by Thamusida after 270. The provincial capital of Volubulis, its circuit wall guarded by 40 towers, its approaches watched by five outlying forts, must have fallen after 280. This is the last date on which the governor and the neighbouring Baquates tribal chief met to erect a stone altar to a '*foederata et diuturna pax*' – a federated and lasting peace. Co-Emperor Maximian who campaigned in Mauretania Tingitana in 298, understood that it would be too expensive in men and resources to reconquer the interior. Roman authority was henceforth restricted to the neighbouring ports of Tingis and Sebta (Tangier and Ceuta), which were placed under the administration of Spain. From Tingis merchants kept up links with the string of trading towns along the Atlantic coast such as Lixus and Sala, which survived as urban communities despite the 'Diocletian withdrawal'. There were also continuing links with the proud tribes of the interior, for a reduced form of urban life returned to Volubilis after the excitement of the initial sack.

DIOCLETIAN'S PERSECUTION OF 303

Apart from a few isolated instances, it was only at the end of this long reign that indifference to Christianity was replaced by organized hostility. In particular it was Diocletian, irritated by a succession of palace fires that he blamed on Christians, who was instrumental in organizing the last great persecution in 303.

After 40 years of tolerance, the Church had become a highly visible institution, and was an easy target for the imperial officials. They destroyed Christian places of worship, forbade meetings, confiscated sacred vessels and hunted down the scriptures, which were publicly burnt. Obdurate Christians who refused to assist the authorities were imprisoned, some were tortured, but it seems that only a few were executed. The intensity of persecution depended on the mood of the officials, who with the exception of the fiercely pagan governor of Numidia, proved to be comparatively mild in North Africa. Most Christians were content to hide their beliefs for a while, but a distressingly large number turned *traditores* and assisted the authorities in tracking down gospels and sacred vessels. The bishop of Carthage, Mensurius, meekly handed over a number of gospels, but later acquitted himself on the slightly specious grounds that they were heretical and deserved to be burnt. At the same time Caecilian, the archdeacon of Carthage, made public the breach between the temporizing church officials and the martyrs. He picketed the jail and halted the flow of pilgrims who had been giving alms and confessing to the imprisoned Christians. Caecilian deplored the noisy publicity of these martyrs and considered their fate to be self-inflicted. Those within the Christian community of Carthage may have had some sympathy with his actions, but to the Christian populace at large Caecilian appeared to be trying to starve the martyrs into apostasy.

The Birth of Donatism, 305–16

In 305 Diocletian retired to his palace at Split on his native Yugoslavian coast and the persecution, at least in the western half of the empire, gently subsided.

He left the North African Church riven between the martyrs and the established church. There were bitter personal recriminations over who had betrayed the Church, whether they had automatically forfeited their sacerdotal office, whether they could be forgiven or ever accepted back into the Church. It also reopened the questions first posed by Cyprian: to what extent could the moral failings of a priest diminish the power of the sacraments? Was the Church to be a society of saints or a school for sinners? The dispute echoed around the empire but was most acutely felt in North Africa, where the traditional Berber respect for a man of honour seems to have reinforced the party of martyrs. The Numidian interior had suffered greatly and was littered with the tombs of martyrs, whose friends could not but judge harshly the discredited Church establishment based in the coastal cities.

The dispute came to a head in 312, when Caecilian, the archdeacon, was hurriedly elected bishop of Carthage. His enemies used the pretext of technical reasons to invalidate his election and to elect a rival bishop. Donatus was a man of such moral authority, impassioned oratory and intellectual fortitude that the party of martyrs was thereafter known as the Donatists.

CONSTANTINE THE GREAT, FIRST CHRISTIAN EMPEROR

A period of dynastic struggle followed the retirement of Diocletian and Maximian in 305. One of the leading contenders for power was Maximian's son, Maxentius (306–12), who inherited much of his father's old power base in the western empire. But in 308 the African leadership revolted against Maxentius, who invaded and fought a fierce campaign against the African legions, which included the sack of both Carthage and Cirta. The defeat of Maxentius in 312 at the battle of Milvian Bridge by Constantine's army (the first Roman force to have fought under the sign of the cross) was celebrated throughout North Africa as the destruction of a hated oppressor. Constantine (306–37), who despatched Maxentius's pickled head to Carthage, could have sent no more welcome gift to the city fathers.

The next year, Emperor Constantine sent another healing gift to North Africa, the publication of the Edict of Milan, which granted Christians complete legal equality and religious freedom, as well as ordering the return of all Church property confiscated during the persecutions.

This latter clause was impossible to enforce without first defining which was the true Church in North Africa. The rival bishops of Carthage, Caecilian and Donatus, were both summoned to explain their claims before the bishop of Rome, Pope Miltiades. He had a personal interest in the issue for he was also a North African churchman who had been accused of being a *traditor*. Miltiades' judgement came down in favour of Caecilian, but the Emperor Constantine, clearly impressed by the moral character of Donatus and his supporters, intervened. He ordered a re-trial at Arles and later dispatched a judicial investigation to Carthage. At length Caecilian and the established Church secured the grudging support of the emperor. They celebrated their delayed legal victory with the assistance of the army and launched a misdirected persecution of the Donatists in 316, which once again surrendered the moral high ground to the martyrs. In Donatus' telling phrase, 'the true Church is persecuted not persecuting'.

Donatism, while strong amongst intellectuals, the poor and people of principle in the cities, also enjoyed strong, at times almost universal, support from the rural interior. Donatus, who came from a Numidian oasis community, was uniquely able to articulate the spiritual yearnings of the forgotten hinterland. The emperor called a halt to the persecution the next year, and granted the Donatist Church toleration, but continued his official backing of the established Church. For the next 40 years the Donatist Church was subjected to a kind of guerilla persecution, although the longer this continued the greater the mystical devotion of Donatus' followers. Although none of his writing was allowed to survive by his Catholic opponents, and he can only be known through the tracts of his enemies, even they never attempted to impugn his integrity. Despite the violent sectarianism, it would be unwise to exaggerate the cultural differences between Catholic and Donatist. No architectural differences can be detected between their churches, nor was there ever any major doctrinal division between them. The Donatists are, however, thought to have white-washed their churches and shrines in a manner still commonplace throughout the Maghreb.

Christ and the Sun God

Even Constantine, who had the devout St Helena for a mother, first approached Christianity through his devotion to the pagan sun god. He was not alone. Solar monotheism was the most popular form of paganism in his day and provided an easy spiritual path to Christianity. Tertullian, some two centuries before Constantine, wrote about the popular confusion between Christ and the sun god, for the Christians also worshipped on Sunday and prayed towards the east. Another influential North African Christian writer of the second century, Clement of Alexandria, made the connection even more emphatically when he wrote of 'Christ driving his chariot across the sky like the sun god' and quoted the old testament prophecy that Christ was 'the sun of righteousness'.

Constantine deliberately encouraged this fusion of belief by continuing to display the old pagan divine sunburst on his coinage (which in time would become transformed into the Christian halo). It was also in the early fourth century that 25 December, the day of the winter solstice, the birthday of the sun god, became accepted as the nativity of Jesus. In his new eastern capital of Constantinople, the emperor, at the same time as he was building the great church of the apostles and that of St Sophia, was also raising in the forum a large statue of himself in the style of the sun god. The mosaic floors of North Africa bear vivid witness to the almost seamless continuity of sacred images between the pagan and Christian periods. The peacock of Venus with its incorruptible flesh becomes a Christian symbol for the Resurrection, the vine leaves, grape harvest scenes and wine bowls of Dionysius become associated with the chalice of the Christian communion, while the shepherd bearing a sacrificial lamb on his shoulders up to the hilltop shrines of Saturn is transformed into the Christian 'Good Shepherd'.

Constantine actively supported Christianity during his long reign, but neither he nor his immediate heirs made any attempt to force it upon their pagan subjects. The transformation from a pagan to a Christian society was a very gradual process and one that was long resisted by patricians and peasants deeply attached to the old ways. As late as 380, St Augustine could write about the city of Carthage as brimming with parades in honour of Caelestis-Tanit, the wild Bacchanalian dances and orgies held in honour of the goddess Cybele. He was exaggerating of course and we know from the archaeological record that the city at this time also boasted a dozen churches. Only a moralist could overlook these unmissable structures, such as the six-aisled basilica of St Cyprian (now within the grounds of the Tunisian presidential palace), which was built over a Christian cemetery. Another six-aisled basilica, also built over an old Christian cemetery, was dedicated to the early martyrs, St Perpetua and St Felicity. In size, both gave precedence to Damous el-karita basilica which, with its wide nave and ten aisles, was the largest church in North Africa.

CHRISTIAN INVERSION OF SACRED GEOGRAPHY

Carthage was typical in that all its major churches were constructed on the outer fringe of the classical city. It was long thought that this was due to the opposition of conservative landowners refusing them city-centre sites near the old pagan sanctuaries, but it was also due to a radically new attitude to the sacred. The classical world had kept the gods, the living and the dead, religiously apart. Temple sanctuaries were for the gods, temple courtyards used by ritually clean worshippers, while the dead were always taken beyond the clearly defined gates of the inhabited city to the necropolis, the city of the dead. To the pagan world it was an unthinkable pollution to confuse the two cities, let alone introduce anything dead into a temple. Yet this is exactly what the Christians did, constructing their great churches above tombs, burying their dead beneath the floors of churches and even instituting the kissing of the bones of martyrs. Christianity, to anyone educated in the classical world, deliberately inverted all the rules of sacred geography.

THE ARCHITECTURE OF CHRISTIANITY

The persecution of Diocletian had razed all existing churches, enabling a harmonious Christian architecture to be created across the empire during Constantine's reign. Excavations, assisted by the vivid depictions that survive from fifth-century North African floor mosaics (such as those from Tabarca and Qsar Libya), allow for comprehensive reconstructions.

The basilica, the Roman lawcourt, was taken as the model for Christian churches, in deliberate preference to the thousands of existing religious temples. The basilica was composed of a wide central nave (lit by upper windows), which was flanked by lower side aisles, with apses at either end. Roman magistrates, surrounded by their legal assistants, were customarily seated on a throne in the apse to judge court cases, retiring behind a curtain to decide on a sentence, which would be written out and read by a junior official. The Church simply followed Roman legal practice, replacing judge with bishop. The major internal innovation was the addition of the altar, whose sanctity was stressed by a protective canopy. Initially the altar was placed near the centre of the nave but by the late fifth century it had been moved to the eastern apse and stood behind a low stone screen. The eastern apse, approached by a stairway, was raised above the nave and equipped with benches, known as *synthronon*, for the lesser clergy. The western apse, particularly in North Africa, was often occupied by the sarcophagus of an honoured martyr, although this practice gradually faded away as the west end became the entrance. The more elaborate churches would have three doors, preceded by an enclosed outer courtyard where a central fountain allowed worshippers to wash. Those who were preparing themselves

A fifth-century Christian tomb mosaic at Tabarka

for the Christian life, the *catchumens*, were usually restricted to the
courtyard while the outer aisles and the centre of the church with its
altar were reserved for baptized Christians. The rite of baptism, which
offered complete forgiveness of sins, had enormous importance in
the early Church, but nowhere greater than in North Africa where
excavations have revealed a large number of elaborate baptisteries.
The fonts were either marble-clad cruciform troughs or lip-shaped
bowls whose curved walls were clad in mosaic, the entire structure
shaded by a domed balcony. The candidate was dipped in the water
thrice after each affirmation of belief in the Trinity, was then
anointed with oil and hands laid on him for the gift of the Holy Spirit.
Milk and honey were then presented as tokens of the Promised Land.
A labyrinth of rooms surrounded the font, through which the neophyte
would have processed, an architectural reflection of the importance of
this spiritual journey.

The Church as a Pillar of State

Constantine, who saved the Church from persecution, also helped destroy its virtue for he transformed it into a pillar of the state. He gave bishops the power of magistrates and with it the appropriate dignities of a court title, staff, mitre, pallium and the right to have their hands kissed. He also increased their local prestige enormously by directing that over a third of provincial revenue should be dispensed through Church charities. The spiritual responsibilities of the bishops were increasingly swamped by these secular demands. The palace of the bishop was thronged by a stream of local clients patiently, but obstinately, waiting for their patron's assistance: help in the preferment of a nephew, the release of a prisoner, the deferral of a tax, a recommendation to a school or just a letter of introduction.

As a corollary of these new powers the Church organized itself to be a mirror to the secular administration of the empire. The Council of Nicaea clearly defined the rules for the election and behaviour of bishops and placed them under the supervision of a senior metropolitan bishop. This was nothing new to the North African Church which had always accepted the primacy of Carthage, but they now began to stress his importance within the whole Church by respectfully addressing him as 'Papa' and demoting the pope at Rome to a mere bishop. The Church enthusiastically inherited the old civic rivalries over precedence and the extent of provincial boundaries. Indeed the only dissenting votes cast against the Council of Nicaea (despite all its high theology) were from two North African bishops, from Cyrenaica, who refused to accept the supremacy of the metropolitan of Alexandria.

Constantine also attempted to put some of the new morality into practice and devised laws for the protection of children, slaves and peasants. He forbade branding on the human face and put an end to gladiatorial combat. He encouraged the special role of Sunday as a day apart: for rest, prayer or as the most suitable day for weekly rural markets. The seven-day week was an alien concept to classical society, which organized the year into months, each with their own festivals. However, the triumph of the seven-day week had as much to do with popular astrology as Judeo-Christian practice. To this day the days of the week bear the planetary names devised by ancient Babylonian astrologers.

Circumcelliones, *Ascetic Heirs of the Martyrs*

At the same time that Christianity became a prop to the state, there was an ascetic reaction to maintain the old purity of the martyrs. The earliest and most famous ascetic was St Anthony, who in 300 gave away his inheritance and forsook the cosmopolitan joys of urban Egypt to pursue a life of solitude in the desert. His heroic struggle to know God, beset by the dangers of possession by evil spirits but befriended by the wild beasts, was vividly chronicled in his biography, written by Athanasius, the Greek father of the Church. The *Life of Anthony* proved a continual inspiration to a rich assortment of heroic ascetics: those anchorites, eremites, hermits and stylites who still bewitch our imagination. The Catholic bishops were suspicious of these wilful, independent-minded holy men, but the creation of settled communities of ascetics, governed by rules and a spiritual director, gradually calmed their fears.

All the worst fears of the bishops were encapsulated by the *circumcelliones,* the indigenous popular ascetic movement of North Africa, which found a natural ally in the Donatist Church. As early as 340 there are reports of bands of itinerant ascetics who congregated round the tombs of martyrs. They were given their name because they walked *circum cellas,* circled around the rural shrines in prayer. They had their own organization, their own dress (the rough Numidian woollen cloak that likens them in more than one way to the Franciscans), held vows of poverty, avoided marriage and had a sister organization for women known as *sanctimoniales.* Their spiritual practice was based on an almost continuous series of long pilgrimages, which allowed them to attend the festivals at distant shrines across the breadth of the country, fed by gifts of food from the villages they passed. They earned fierce loyalty from the peasantry by mocking the pretensions of the landlords, chastising debt collectors and burning down palatial villas, although they were seldom armed with anything more offensive than a stave. They had no fear of punishment for they courted martyrdom with a fervour that at times led to suicidal acts. In times of hardship, their numbers were swelled by landless labourers and impoverished peasants, while during an official persecution they could melt away into the land. Their militancy made them notorious, at times an embarassment, even to the Donatist bishops. The movement survived until it was swept away by Islam.

To an extent the strict monastic rules, like the one established by St Benedict in 529, were a reaction to the dangers that wandering ascetics presented to the Church. There were Catholic monasteries in North Africa, but these are only known through literary sources, such as the communities founded by St Augustine (354–430) at Thagaste and Hippo. Fulgentius (who was later to become a Vandal bishop) started his spiritual journey in a monastery established on the island of Kneis. Excavations on the nearby Tunisian mainland have uncovered a number of sixth-century churches, which may have been associated with this foundation.

The Catholic Donatist Feud

A decade after Constantine's death in 337, there were over 200 Donatist bishops in North Africa. Donatus, aware that the emperors were having difficulties with the Catholic majority, decided it was time for a renewed appeal. It backfired horribly. The imperial officials sent to investigate sided so strongly with the Catholic Church that a whole cycle of riots, massacre and counter terror was unleashed across the region. In 347 the Emperor Constans (337–50) sent Macarius, bishop of Aelia Capitolina, to lead a military campaign against the schismatic Donatists and to hunt out the *circumcelliones*. This brutal repression, the *tempora Macariana*, served only to rekindle Donatist fervour which survived the death of their revered leader in 355. Julian, the last pagan emperor (361–3), had no particular love for the Donatists, but was interested in encouraging discord between Christians. In 361 he gave permission for all exiled bishops to return home, restored Donatist property that had been confiscated in 347 and ended official support for the Catholics. The Donatists seized their chance and unleashed a terror campaign that forced many humiliated Catholics into a second baptism. Valentinian (364–75) was the last ruler to promote a policy of religious tolerance.

In North Africa this happily coincided with the gentle leadership of the Donatist Church by the theologian Parmenian, from 363–93. Valentinian's reign was otherwise a decade of barely controlled disasters. In the year 365 a series of earthquakes literally toppled all the coastal cities of the eastern Mediterranean while a decade later the first barbarian tribes began to pour across the Rhine. It was not the only frontier where the Romans suffered, for rebellion was also rife amongst the tribes within and outside the Saharan frontier.

CHAPTER EIGHT

Bishops, Barbarians and Byzantium,
400–647

Our knowledge of fifth-century North Africa is seen through the writing, if not the eyes, of two towering intellectual figures, St Augustine, bishop of Hippo and Synesius of Cyrene, bishop of Ptolemais. Their lives testify to the final triumph of the Christian Church just as the Roman Empire was being overwhelmed by the invasions of German tribes. It was such a tribe, the Vandals, led by their redoubtable warlord Genseric (429–77), who seized control of North Africa. They established themselves in the villas of the Roman landlords and ruled as an alien military aristocracy for 100 years. They left nothing but an infamous name behind, but this was created from their piratical raids on the European coast rather than from their largely pacific rule of North Africa. In 533 their rule, which had become largely restricted to Tunisia, was ended by the invasion of Belisarius, which turned North Africa into a province of the Byzantine Empire. It is customary to dismiss the Byzantine rule from 533–647 as a destructive period. It is indeed overshadowed by the greater glories of the Classical and Islamic civilizations, but viewed in its own light it was a time of *kosmesis*, *ktisis* and *ananeosis* (adornment, foundation and renewal).

Synesius of Cyrene, a Pagan Bishop

The life of Synesius of Cyrene gives a graphic example of the central place Christianity had come to occupy in late fourth-century North Africa. He straddles the divisions between the ancient and medieval worlds, like some delicately poised fulcrum that links two apparently opposed forces with effortless ease.

Synesius was born into a family of landed aristocrats who could proudly trace their ancestry back to the first Greek colonists who came to Cyrene with King Battus in the seventh century BC. In common with most young men of his class he studied not at the Latin-speaking university of Carthage, but at Greek-speaking Alexandria where he became devoted to the neo-platonic school of philosophy. It was here that he began his lifelong correspondence with the female philosopher and mathematican Hypatia, whose classes often included a number of lovesick students. Hypatia sought to cure one youth of his obsession by asking him 'is this what you desire?' as she tossed him one of her blood-soaked sanitary towels. Her outspoken vigour made her a natural opponent of Christian fundamentalists and in 415 some half-educated monks, encouraged by the bishop of Alexandria, assassinated her.

After Alexandria, Synesius moved to Athens, the mother of philosophy, but the fourth-century city proved a bitter disappointment so he returned to manage his inheritance, an estate that lay to the south of Cyrene. In 400 he was selected to be Cyrenaica's ambassador to the court at Constantinople. His loyal address (the *de regno*, delivered as a philosophical oration) to the new Emperor Arcadius poured elegant scorn on the succession of corrupt and cowardly officials who had impoverished his province by failing to protect it from barbarian raiders. After three years residence at Constantinople he came back to a heroic welcome, having won a number of tax concessions from the court. He loved the simple joys of rural life on his estate and wrote:

> as to the emperor, as to the favourites of the emperor, no one, or hardly any one, speaks of them here. Our ears have rest from such stories. No doubt men know well that there is always an emperor living, for we are reminded of this every year by those who collect the taxes: but who he is, is not very clear.

Seven years later the city of Ptolemais petitioned Synesius to become its bishop. Synesius, who had not even been baptized, proved a most reluctant candidate, having no desire to give up either his wife, ostrich hunting or philosophy. He was permitted to keep his wife and his grave doubts on the Resurrection, and proved to be a dutiful bishop. The last years of his life were spent quarrelling with imperial officials and helping develop a local militia, based on fortified farmsteads, which formed a credible defence system against the incursions of the *Macae* and *Austuriani* tribes. One of these raids destroyed Synesius' beloved estate, after which he wrote 'all is lost, all is destroyed'. It was a genuine cry of despair from a landed proprietor who had accepted Christianity, not out of faith but from civic duty.

St Augustine of Hippo

Quite the reverse is true of North Africa's greatest contribution to Christianity, St Augustine. Whether he is thought of as a philosopher, theologian, politician, churchman or writer, St Augustine has had a towering influence over western Christendom, even though he is largely forgotten in his native North Africa. His seminal works, *City of God*, *Of the Trinity* and *Confessions* are intellectual milestones in human thought. The former two are more quoted from than read, although the latter with its vivid psychological insights has a renewed appeal to twentieth-century taste. His theological teaching, which was largely concerned with the correct balance between free will and predestination, original sin and divine grace, proved a direct inspiration to the Reformation 1,000 years later, although his position as one of the 'four doctors of the Latin church' remains unassailable. His life also provides a fascinating insight into fifth-century North Africa.

Augustine was Numidian through and through, born in the overwhelmingly Donatist town of Thagaste (Souk Ahras in Algeria), one of the children of Patricius, a pagan minor landowner, and St Monica, a devoted Catholic. He was sent to Madauros, Apuleius' home town, to get a better schooling and although he loathed it and never learned Greek (reading the classics only through Latin translations) he was a promising enough student for it to be worth sending him on to higher education. His father struggled for a year to raise the money for university and once there Augustine enjoyed himself enormously, making friends, finding lovers, discovering theatre, the circus and the baths, but also winning academic prizes. He returned home to teach rhetoric at Thagaste and, having cut his teeth, moved back to Carthage where he took a concubine and taught for seven years. During this period he was a Manichean, a member of a heretical sect whose belief in a dark god of earthly power opposed to the god of light drew on elements of Buddhism, Gnostic Christianity and Persian Zoroastranism.

Feeling stuck in a rut he took the bold step of moving to Italy, but had a difficult first year in Rome looking after his concubine and their son. The next year, at the age of 30, his luck changed. Augustine was appointed professor of rhetoric at Milan and was converted to Christianity by the city's princely bishop, St Ambrose. Before he returned to North Africa there was a hideous domestic scene when his mother dismissed his concubine, who was the mother of his son and his companion for 15 years, so that she could find a more suitable heiress.

In 388 they returned to North Africa, but St Monica died at the port of Ostia just as they were embarking. Augustine returned to Thagaste to establish a monastic community composed of like-minded male Catholic intellectuals. In 391, despite his express wishes, he was made auxiliary bishop for the city of Hippo Regius and proved himself almost immediately to be an exemplary choice. Four years later he was made bishop and became the principal Catholic activist in North Africa, pursuing the vendetta against the Donatists with annual councils, missions and a stream of closely argued pamphlets. He founded a new monastery at Hippo and launched the political campaign that in 405 finally convinced Emperor Honorius (395–423) to declare that the Donatists were heretical. Quoting the gospels, 'compel them to come in', St Augustine justified the use of force including torture, but drew the line at execution. In 411 he achieved his patiently orchestrated Catholic-Donatist summit and despite some comic touches (all 284 Donatist bishops refused to sit down with sinners – the Catholic bishops) and a lot of bickering over Caecilian's election a century ago, it produced a second condemnation.

Thereafter, Augustine increasingly dedicated himself to his writing, which was specifically designed to answer two contemporay challenges. One was the widespread belief that Rome had fallen (it had been sacked by Goths in 410) because Christianity had weakened the empire. The second came from a humane British monk, Pelagius, who could not believe that we inherited sin from Adam and the act of our conception or that unbaptized babies went to Hell. Pelagius, who had once tried to visit Augustine, stopping off at Hippo on a journey between Rome and Jerusalem, was also spurned by another great doctor of the Latin church. St Jerome called him a corpulent dog weighed down with Scots porridge. *The City of God*, which was composed in 19 episodic, if not repetitive, chapters was written between 413 and 427. Two years later, during the Vandal siege of Hippo, the great bishop died, more concerned with the recent conversion of a physician than the crumbling state of his nation.

Vandal Conquest

The Vandal conquest was a short-lived but dramatic interlude in North Africa's history. The military prowess of a single German tribe allowed it to carve out a great kingdom for itself, despite being completely cut off from contact with its old homeland so that its numbers could not be replenished by new migration. Nor did the Vandals make any attempt to assimilate themselves into North African society, which they kept at a distance through their alien language, hybrid Arian church and caste-like pride in their military abilities.

As late as 400 the Romans were not familiar with the Vandals, who were still dwelling amongst the swamps, forests and sandy plains that lay between the Oder and Vistula rivers. In 406 they stormed across the frozen Rhine, in order to escape the Huns to their east and to pillage Gaul. By 409 they had crossed the Pyrenees and settled in southern Spain. In 426 Genseric, their vigorous new leader, took the city of Cartagena and created the Vandal fleet which soon proved itself with the capture of the Balearic islands. Three years later a rift between the Dowager-Empress Placidia and Boniface, the last military commander of Africa, provided a pretext for the invasion of North Africa. In 429 Genseric led 80,000 of his Vandal people across the straits of Gibraltar from where they marched rapidly east along the coast of Algeria, closely supported by their fleet. Boniface tried to block their advance, but his small field army was forced back behind the walls of Hippo Regius, which resisted siege for 14 months only to be stormed in 430. St Augustine had already died, but he had discussed with his clergy what should be done in the event of defeat. They had decided to draw lots:

half were to share the fate of their parishioners, half to leave in order to keep the faith alive. Genseric established his capital at Hippo and in 433 made an opportunistic treaty with the empire, which legally established the Vandals as *foederatii*, allies in charge of the defence of Numidia. By 439 he had recovered his strength and returned to the offensive. He marched quickly on Carthage, which had only recently been enclosed with defensive walls. The citizens of Carthage proved remarkably uninterested in the fate of the empire and flatly refused to leave their seats at the race track just because the Vandals had attacked. There could not have been greater contrast between the siege of Punic and Roman Carthage. In 444 the emperor officially surrendered his sovereignty to the Vandals.

VANDAL RULE

Elsewhere in the fallen provinces of the empire, the barbarian conquerors had awarded themselves a percentage of land (a half, a third, two-thirds) from the great estates of the landed proprietors. Genseric was more brutal. All the Roman landlords were expelled from North Africa and their estates given to Vandal warriors, who became an exclusive ruling class. There was no dispossession of the peasantry, who were required to continue working the land for their new masters, nor of the *conductores,* the middle-class leaseholders, who continued to manage rural affairs. The Vandals took quickly to the aristocratic lifestyle of conspicuous consumption and hunting, but sometimes went to surprising lengths to ape their predecessors. Inscriptions at Cuicul (near Theveste) and Ammaedara reveal the continuation of the imperial cult, conducted by Vandal *flamines* (priests of the cult).

Having rewarded his people, Genseric's second policy was to cut out completely the expense and inconvenience of guarding the frontier, controlling the mountain tribes and ruling the steppe. Most of the vast region of Roman North Africa that lay west of the Hippo-Theveste road was effectively abandoned as Genseric invested the various Romanized-Berber chiefs as local kings. Genseric had unwittingly returned to the frontiers of the old Carthaginian Empire, the fertile and defensible region that is roughly defined by the modern state of Tunisia. It was a drastic but effective policy, suitable to the Vandals who had no experience of imperial administration, regular taxation nor tedious garrison life.

Genseric's third policy, state piracy, held the political balance of his new kingdom together. Every spring the Vandal fleet sailed from the harbour of Carthage to pillage the islands and coastline of the Mediterranean. The coasts of Sicily, Sardinia, Greece, Italy, Spain and Yugoslavia were methodically plundered and in the gloriously successful year of 455, Rome itself was occupied for a profitable fortnight. Material wealth and slaves poured into the kingdom, keeping the Vandal warriors happy and willing to accept royal commands. The recently elevated Berber kings were also invited to participate, along with their cavalry, in these exciting and rewarding annual expeditions. When the eastern emperor struck back at this scourge of civilization, dispatching two fleets from Constantinople against Vandal Carthage during the 460s, Genseric destroyed them both.

Genseric's progeny: Huneric, Thrasamund and Hilderic

During his long and successful career Genseric transformed himself from an elected war leader to a hereditary king. In a move appropriate to this new standing his son Huneric married Eudoxia, the daughter of Emperor Valentinian. His first wife, a Visigothic princess, was divorced and sent home having been mutilated on a trumped up treason charge.

When Genseric died, he was succeeded by Huneric (477–84) who knew well that a proper east German king should have been elected at Thing (the general assembly of the army) from the most talented men of royal blood. To make sure of his hereditary succession, therefore, he began a methodical purge of his kin. This blood-letting was succeeded by the persecution of the Catholic Church after a Vandal church council held at Carthage in 484 had upheld Arian theology. Five thousand Catholic clergy are reported to have fled Huneric's persecution and escaped west to take refuge with the Berber kings.

Huneric died later that year and was succeeded by two nephews, who amicably divided the royal authority between them. Gunthamund concerned himself with military matters while Thrasamund presided over the Vandal court at Carthage, a place of not inconsiderable learning. Amongst the surviving works from this period are Dracontius' tragedy on the theme of *Oresteia*, a collection of classical myths reworked into verse, three books of hexameters entitled *De Laudibus Dei* (which were much admired by Milton) and an *Apologia*.

In 523 the throne passed to Hilderic, an elderly cultivated homosexual, who was possibly more proud of being a grandson of Emperor Valentian III (425–55) than of Genseric. Hilderic halted the persecution of the Catholic Church, welcomed back the exiled bishops, opened friendly relations with the eastern empire and started a row with the hitherto friendly Ostrogoths in Italy. The defeat of a Vandal army by Antalas (who had created a Berber kingdom in the centre of Tunisia) finally broke Hilderic's dwindling authority. In 530 he was deposed by Gelimer, his more militant cousin, although if we are to believe the Byzantine historian Procopius, the fine German manhood of the Vandals had already gone to seed in the sun. Procopius' description, not unlike the moral warnings of a headmaster, should be enjoyed for its own sake rather than for any particular insight:

> Of all the nations I know the most effeminate is that of the Vandals. They spent all their days in the baths and enjoyed a table abounding in all things, the sweetest and best that the earth and sea produce. And they wore gold very generally, and clothed themselves in garments of silk, and passed their time, thus dressed in theatres and hippodromes and in other pleasurable pursuits, and above all else in hunting. And they had dancers and mimes and all other things to hear and see which are of a musical nature or otherwise merit attention among men. And most of them dwelt in parks, which were well supplied with water and trees, and they had great number of banquets. Finally, being lovers of the earth, they delivered themselves without reservation to all manner of sexual pleasures.

The Berber Hinterland

While the Vandals were pleasuring themselves on alien soil, the rest of North Africa had been returned to its indigenous rulers, whose authority had remained dormant under the Roman policy of co-opting the native ruling class into that of Rome. The quick emergence of these

Romano–Berber successor states testifies to the enduring resilience of traditional structures within the fabric of imperial administration, and they continued to dominate the interior for 250 years.

As well as Antalas, who defeated the Vandals in central Tunisia, in the far west (northern Morocco) the Baquates tribe remained the dominant power. Their memory is kept alive by the massive 'royal tomb' at El Gour, a drum some 40 metres wide built from finely dressed stone using Roman units of measurement. It was constructed sometime between the mid-sixth and the mid-seventh century.

Another forgotten Berber dynasty is recorded by the Djedar tombs dating from the sixth and seventh centuries, which crown the hilltops of the Jebel Lakhdar necropolis. These stepped pyramids (the largest of which would have originally stood 40 metres high) are made from finely dressed stone and conceal underground corridors and funerary chambers. Even the desert itself gave birth to a powerful Berber confederation, the Lawata, who had first come to the attention of the Romans in the late third century. They dominated the desert fringe from southern Tunisia to Egypt, absorbing into their confederation all the ancient Berber tribes of the area. Their strength was based on the vast wealth of the sophisticated trading oases of Siwa, Augila and Garama. These oases were famous for the ancient worship of Ammon, an ancient Libyan monotheistic religion, which worshipped the supreme deity as a divine couple, male Ammon and female Murzuk. Ammon was personified by the sun and by a sacred bull, Murzuk by the moon and by a sacred cow.

The fourth-century tomb of Tin Hinan, in the Hoggar Mountains of the central Sahara, gives proof of the wealth that flowed along the ancient trade routes of the Sahara and helps explain the strength of the Lawata. The circular outer wall of Tin Hinan's mausoleum, which overlooks the Oued Abalessa from a small hill, stands 12 metres high and is 6 metres thick at its base. This perimeter wall enclosed an earlier fort or shrine, and Tin Hinan's tomb was found in the last of its 11 rooms, preserved by the climate and the respect of the Tuareg for their legendary ancestress. The desert queen, wrapped in a protective cover of red leather worked with gold leaf, lay on a wooden couch secured with twisted tassels of coloured cloth and leather. Her face had been

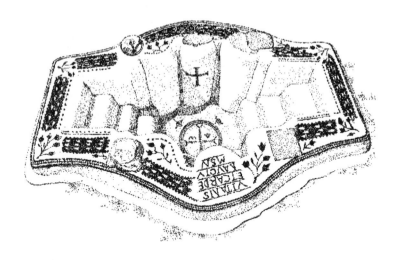

Baptismal font

screened with a white veil and three ostrich feathers, two emeralds had hung from her ears, nine golden bracelets lay heavy on her right arm, eight silver bracelets on her left while her neck had been garlanded with necklaces. Over 300 beads and precious stones were counted, including amethysts, cornelians, 'Punic' core glass, emeralds and gold. Around her couch a crystal vase, a stone idol of the mother goddess, Roman coins in a wooden bowl, a bronze mirror and a golden classical pendant gave further witness to her eclectic taste and her wide-ranging trading connections. Her 'tall, slim and aristocratic' skeleton has been exhibited in the museum of Algiers since her discovery in 1927. Her androgynous physique and the 12 warriors found buried in an outer ring of tumuli around the mausoleum continue to attract a bubble of speculation from those who quest after the 'mysterious Sahara'.

ROMANO-BERBER SOCIETY

In 1928 the discovery of a sealed jar, hidden in a remote stone wall about 60 miles south of Tebessa, has allowed an intimate view of Romano-Berber society. The jar contained 56 wooden tablets that related to a dismantled estate, the *fundus Tuletianos*, in the 490s. From this sub-Saharan village on the border between the Aurès and the Vandal kingdom one might have expected a cry of woe such as that recorded by Gildas, a contemporary British writer. Instead the documents are distinguished by their complete parochial ordinariness: the sale of a slave, a leasehold, a dowry list and various legal and financial statements. The emotional heart of the tablets centres on the marriage of Juliana to Geminia, a modest heiress worth several hundred olive trees. Geminia, in addition to her orchards, was a descendant of Falvius Geminius Catullinus who had once owned the whole *fundus* as well as other properties. The Geminius family had come down in the world, but they were by no means beaten. Most of the tablets concern their patient acquisition of odd parcels of land, although their largest single purchase is only a matter of 37 olive trees. A careful analysis of the tablets by Eugene Albertini (after whom they are named, in preference to their authors) has revealed a high degree of Latin literacy, knowledge of Roman law and respect for female property rights in this small village. The *fundus* is otherwise an entirely Berber zone in matters of dress, jewellery, consumption and the patient intricacies of dry farming the desert fringe.

The Byzantine Conquest of 533

Meanwhile on the coast the cycle of foreign invasion continued. In 533 Emperor Justinian (527–65) dispatched General Belisarius with a fleet of 500 ships and an army of 16,000 from Constantinople to the shores of modern-day Tunisia to dispose of the troublesome Vandals once and for all. The Byzantine army included a large and advanced cavalry composed of mercenary Huns, mounted bowmen and some of the first knights in chainmail, securely mounted on a new breed of warhorse with the aid of stirrups. Spurred on by the prophetic dream of an Egyptian bishop and enjoying either good intelligence or a great deal of luck, the expedition landed south of Carthage while the Vandal fleet was in Sardinia and the army embroiled on its north-western frontier. Belisarius marched unopposed up the coast and, having defeated a Vandal force ten miles outside the city walls, entered Carthage propitiously on the feast day of St Cyprian. Trapped in Carthage by the arrival of the main Vandal army, he sent his heavy cavalry in an unexpected and successful sally, to storm out of the city gates. The Vandal siege, the Vandal army and Vandal rule over North Africa was broken in one cavalry charge. The whole campaign had taken just three months.

With victory came new provinces for the emperor, all the fabulous loot acquired in a century of Vandal piracy and the last king of the Vandals, now a contrite pensioner. The king, Gelimer, fled west to a mountain-top citadel before being tempted by Byzantine offers and agreeing to surrender. Justinian proved as good as his word. He settled a large Anatolian estate on Gelimer and recruited the defeated Vandals into his guard regiments.

The Romano-Berber kings, who had remained aloof from the conflict, sent loyal delegations asking for imperial recognition of their titles. After a century without Roman military overlords or tax officials during which, according to one Berber inscription, they had 'never forsworn, nor broken faith, either with the Romans or the Moors' their request was hardly out of order. Belisarius officially recognized their position, although most of his successors proved entirely faithless in their dealings with the Berber kings.

SOLOMON AND THE IMPOSITION OF BYZANTINE RULE

Belisarius left behind an Armenian general, the eunuch Solomon, as governor of North Africa. He offered back the land to descendants of the landowners dispossessed by the Vandals, disbanded the Arian Church, re-established the imperial tribute of corn, to Constantinople rather than Rome, reintroduced the tax man and restored the Catholic Church to its accustomed position beside the hierarchy of secular administration.

After a mutiny of several years, in which the Byzantine soldiers refused to fight in Solomon's expansive wars against the Berber kings, Solomon was forced out of North Africa. Only abundant promises and a team of hand-picked envoys from Justinian managed to win over the rebellious troops. In 539 Solomon was reappointed governor and given complete control over both the military and the civil administration.

He applied a rigid discipline and proceeded to advance into the Aurès and push the frontier west. Over the next five years Solomon devoted the energies of the state to an enormous building programme that fortified the Byzantine province of Africa. The open cities and villa-dotted countryside of the past was transformed into a medieval landscape of small walled towns surrounded by fortified manor houses. His engineers energetically and ruthlessly quarried their way through the glorious old civic edifices of the High Empire (many of which had already been subdivided and partly quarried by later occupants) in order to use the ready-dressed stones and columns in the construction of curtain walls. Precious marble veneers and pagan statuary were smashed and burned in kilns to produce copious quantities of lime mortar. Other structures from the past (temples, forums, triumphal arches, theatres, amphitheatres and baths) were immaculately preserved if they were by chance found useful, and incorporated within a fort. Whole cities, such as Leptis Magna and Sabratha, were reordered and confined within a much diminished circuit of walls. At the same time sewer systems were overhauled, aqueducts reconnected, harbours cleared and grandiose churches erected to dominate the new urban centres. It was a truly massive programme of public works, which was only achieved with the Emperor Justinian's continual support. There was also a renewed energy for a single definition of religious faith, which led to the persecution of all who deviated from Catholic Orthodoxy: Donatists, Jews, Arians or pagans.

It is a customary mistake to dismiss the Byzantine period as a fragile interregnum between the Roman and Islamic periods. But there is nothing ephemeral about the forest of Byzantine marble columns that rise from the ruined churches of Apollonia or the insistent imagery on the mosaic floor of the church at Ksar Libya (Gsar-Elbia) which repeats the watchwords *kosmesis*, *ktisis* and *ananeosis*, (adornment, foundation and renewal). The three great rectangular military fortresses, which were constructed on the south-western frontier zone at Tebessa, Thelepte and Ammaedara, would alone have required over a million labouring days in their construction.

The defences were soon to be tested, largely due to the appointment of Solomon's nephew Sergius (a brutal, arrogant officer loathed by his own soldiers as well as by his enemies) as governor of Tripolitania. The Lawata, complaining that Byzantine soldiers had been raiding their settlements despite a truce, had been invited to make a new peace at Leptis Magna. The Lawata sent 80 delegates to negotiate with Sergius on behalf of the whole confederation. This Byzantine governor, in violation of all civilized behaviour and every notion of honour, murdered 79 of these envoys in the infamous massacre of Leptis Magna of 543. The whole of the southern frontier promptly errupted in revolt and although Solomon won an engagement outside Tebessa, his army once again deserted him. He made a brave but hopeless stand at Cillium (Kasserine) where he was overwhelmed by the Berber tribes. The death of Solomon was considered sufficient vengeance by the Lawata who were then prepared to make peace with the empire. The deliberately insulting reply from Constantinople, the appointment of Sergius to succeed his uncle, fanned the revolt to even greater heights. The Byzantine army was destroyed outside El Kef, Carthage was threatened and for two years the tribal armies seemed poised to dismember the province. Only their jealousies, lack of unity and Solomon's castles preserved a semblance of Byzantine authority.

Order was reimposed after the appointment of John Troglita as the next Byzantine governor. The eponymous hero of Corippus' epic poem, the *Johannides*, John had long experience of the kind of warfare and diplomacy required in North Africa. With persistence, particularly in taking the war into the desert confines, he reaped a decisive victory in the south in 548. His struggle against the Berber kings was resolved as much by the honourable treaties he concluded eventually, as by the actual fighting. Sadly, John was an exception in the succession of governors and for the rest of the century North Africa lurched from one border war to another, with a Berber army again reaching the gates of Carthage in 596.

THE HEROIC HERACLIADS

The Emperor Maurikios (582–602) tried to halt these recurring and disastrous abuses of power by appointing a powerful viceroy to guarantee continuity in policy. He created the office of exarch of North Africa and in 595 appointed Heraclius, one of the Byzantine Empire's most admired generals, to this near-autonomous post. Heraclius was an inspired administrator who completely won the trust of the Berber kings and initiated a 50-year period of peace and prosperity.

In 602 the usurper Phocas (602–10) murdered the Emperor Maurikios in Constantinople and brought the empire to its knees in just a few years of paranoid government. By 608 Heraclius could tolerate the madness no more and withheld the corn tribute due to Constantinople, at the same time sending his son Heraclius and cousin, General Nicetas, to raise a volunteer army of 3,000 from the province of Cyrenaica. With an equal number of Lawata tribesmen, they marched overland to seize control of Alexandria and Egypt, thereby seizing Constantinople's other source of corn. Phocas was promptly deposed in a popular uprising, and Heraclius acclaimed as the new emperor (610–41).

Heraclius' inheritance was racked with problems. Swamped by barbarian and Persian armies in the east, he even considered moving the capital to Carthage in 620. He triumphed eventually against the Persian invaders and his reign became a decisive milestone for the eastern Roman Empire. For it was under Heraclius that Greek became the official language of the empire, which was henceforth ruled not by a Caesar, an Imperator or an Augustus, but by the *Basileus*. This recognition of a long-acknowledged language division encouraged the ever-deepening ties between the Latin-speaking African Church and the Roman papacy.

The position of exarch was filled first by Nicetas and later by other close relations of the Heracliad dynasty, George and then Gregory, who presided over the last decades of Christian North Africa. The peaceful conditions on the frontiers allowed for a surge in Christian missionary activity as Catholic and Donatist preachers competed with each other to penetrate the most reclusive mountain and oasis communities to make conversions. The exarchs assisted in the foundation of monasteries and nunneries in lonely places as well as in the heart of fashionable Carthage. Christians of diverse belief poured into the city, refugees from the Arab conquest of Syria and Egypt in 641. In 642 the danger surged ever closer to Carthage. Cyrenaica fell to the Arabs and the following year they brushed aside the elaborate Byzantine defences of Tripolitania.

In the midst of the alarmed babble of citizens and refugees, Abbot Maximus, the charismatic preacher, distracted the worried populace with his passionate denouncements of heretical beliefs and the errors of the imperial court. Maximus' biographer records that, 'not only clerics and bishops but also magistrates and people alike hung on his words, and clung to the saint like iron filings to a magnet'. These sophisticated urban dwellers looked to Maximus in vain, for Islam, the new burning force from the east, would in a few years sweep them all away. In 647 the first Arab army would penetrate Tunisia. The culture, religion, language, literature and even the physical survival of Carthage, the millenial capital of North Africa, was doomed. The invaders brought with them a new language, new religion, new literature, a new way of life, new cities and a new pride for the land of North Africa.

CHAPTER NINE

The Arab Conquest,
647–710

The coming of Islam in the seventh century provided North Africa with a completely new model of government, a new passion and a new faith, around which life and politics have pulsed ever since. For Islam is not just a religion, it also offers a political example and a code of law. In international terms it offers unity with Muslims the world over and, in literary Arabic, a world-wide language. Based on the five pillars of Islam – faith, prayer, alms-giving, fasting and pilgrimage – the Muslim world presents a remarkable face of unity. The annual pilgrimage to Mecca has had enormous influence, for it has gathered together and inspired the intellectual and religious leaders of North Africa in their attempt to create the 'pure land' of the Islamic ideal. Without some understanding of Islam, it is impossible to understand North Africa.

Pre-Islamic Arabia

Although it is straying way beyond the geographical frontiers of North Africa to look at the birth of Islam in Arabia, it is in many ways truly central. The life story of the Prophet Mohammed (570–632), known from infancy by every Muslim of every class in every age, lies at the heart of the religion, as an inspiration to all believers. By contrast North Africans may summarily dismiss the historical narrative of those who have held power in North Africa with a wave of the hand.

The Arabian peninsula before Islam was a cultural backwater, a land of tented camps and scattered oases. Largely pagan and politically fragmented, it was encroached upon periodically by its powerful neighbours, Byzantium, Persia and Abyssinia. The only focus of order was the city of Mecca, which sat astride the spice route. The ancient Kaaba sanctuary at the centre of Mecca, which contained images of all the deities honoured in Arabia, was the focus of an annual festival. The pilgrims, protected from tribal feuds by a month-long truce, flocked to Mecca to worship, trade, settle debts, negotiate marriages, arbitrate peace and celebrate. It was the undoubted centre of Arabic life and the only place that could support a non-tribal population – a fascinating medley of missionaries, refugees and merchants – Persian Zoroastrians, Coptic Christians from Egypt, Jews, Jacobite Christians from Syria, pagan Africans, Nestorians from Iraq as well as local soothsayers, healers, religious thinkers and poets. This tolerant city of many faiths was controlled by the Quraysh, a confederation of local clans who governed through a council of elders.

The Prophet Mohammed

In 570 Mohammed was born into the Bani Hashim, a distinguished, but impoverished clan within the Quraysh confederation. Wet-nursed in the desert by a bedouin tribeswoman, the young Mohammed, thrice orphaned by the successive deaths of father, mother and grandfather, passed into the care of his uncle's household at the age of eight. He earned his keep as a shepherd before graduating to work on the great camel caravans that were dispatched twice a year from Mecca. The well-travelled, good-looking Mohammed soon earned the respectful epithet *al-ameen*, the trusty, due to his scrupulous honesty, and in 595 he accepted the proposal of marriage from his wealthy, twice-widowed employer, Khadija. Ill-matched only in age, they had a number of children during their 26-year marriage although none of their sons survived childhood.

Mohammed, who may have been an intimate of the Hanif, a free-thinking group of philosophical monotheists, became increasingly dissatisfied with the pagan religious life of the city. He used to escape the bustle of the pilgrimage month by meditating in a cave on nearby Mount Hira. There, aged 40, he received his first religious revelation, which terrified him. These revelations, delivered as a recitation by the Archangel Gabriel, continued throughout his life and would collectively form the Koran. For three years he kept the divine messages within his private circle of family and friends, but in 613 he was bidden to go out and preach publicly, by a revelation that began 'Rise up and warn'. Mohammed's warnings were concerned with the nature of the one God, the moral and religious conduct required of mankind, and the Day of Judgement at the end of the world. The leaders of the Quraysh rejected his preaching with a mocking scorn that was gradually replaced by hostility and the persecution of his followers. The Prophet Mohammed was protected by the Bani Hashim clan, but many of his followers were forced to flee Mecca. In 620 the death of his uncle and of his wife Khadija made his position even worse.

Two years later the Prophet Mohammed migrated to an oasis 12 days north of Mecca, whose community openly acknowledged him as Prophet. The oasis was hence known as Medina-al-nabi, the city of the Prophet. This migration, the *hegira*, marks the start of the Muslim calendar, in which year one corresponds to AD 622. In the following years the Prophet clearly defined the religious, ritual and ethical practices of this first Muslim community. There were prohibitions against alcohol, gambling and usury, and definitions of accepted moral behaviour in a diverse range of matters from war, dress, divorce and legal evidence, to the giving of alms. The role of the individual and the status of women were strengthened against the ubiquitous power of the clan, but without upsetting the central unit of community life, the patriarchal family. At Mecca the Prophet had hoped that his revelations would be welcomed by Jews and Christians as well as pagans, but at Medina he realized the need for a completely independent religious community.

Although at first Medina faced a number of attacks by the Jewish tribes and by the Meccans, the Prophet's growing influence over the bedouin desert tribes eventually was decisive. For without their agreement, Mecca's highly vulnerable caravan trade would never reach its destination. During a truce in 628 the Muslims of Medina performed their first pilgrimage to Mecca. This incorporation of the Kaaba into Muslim worship calmed many of the Meccans' worst fears. Two years later, the city surrendered unconditionally to the Prophet who showed great magnaminity in victory. He cleansed the Kaaba of idols, granted amnesty to his enemies and presented gifts to his adversaries. In the following two years a combination of armed raids, official embassies and Muslim missionaries brought all the disparate communities of Arabia into the fold of the Prophet.

The Caliphate, 632–44

Arabia would have turned its back speedily on these achievements but for the firm leadership of the Muslim community at Medina. After the death of the Prophet in 632, the leading Muslims assembled and chose Abu Bekr, one of the first Muslims and a father-in-law of the Prophet, as his caliph or successor (633–6). There was no question of the caliph inheriting any prophetic gifts, for Mohammed was declared to be the last in the long line of prophets who had communicated God's will to mankind. Abu Bekr acted as a traditional tribal sheikh, a chief, leading the community and arbitrating its disputes. As Abu Bekr declared before he was acclaimed at the mosque, 'he would obey the *sunna*, the well trodden path of the Prophet, and that people should obey him as long as he obeyed it'.

Abu Bekr's compact between ruler and ruled elevated the *sunna* as the highest authority. The Koran, the complete collection of the divinely dictated recitations of the Prophet Mohammed (divided into 114 unequal *sura*, chapters) stood at the pinnacle of this authority. The secondary source was the Hadith, a diverse collection of the sayings and actions of the Prophet Mohammed. From these two sources a third compilation would later emerge, the Sharia (the holy law or traditional path), which was a collection of all the approved interpretations, judgements and decisions based on the Koran, the Hadith and historical precedent.

Abu Bekr's first requirement as caliph was military leadership, a role he fulfilled with gusto. As well as bringing the last of the Arabian tribes into the fold, he sent armies north to Syria, east to Persia and west to Egypt. Within a decade of the death of the Prophet, the Muslim Empire rivalled that of Alexander the Great. The speed and extent of the Arab conquest is astonishing, since the Muslim armies had no technical advantage with which to explain their success. One of the most convincing explanations was the exhausted state of both the Byzantine and Persian Sassanid Empires, which had devastated the Middle East in a generation of warfare. The violent swings of fortune of that war had taught the indigenous population to shun political involvement and to welcome impartially any 'victorious' power. However, primary importance must be given to the military capability of the Arab tribes whose martial virtues were continously honed by clan feuds and the testing enviroment of the desert. Islam enforced a disciplined unity over them which turned a bedouin raid into a conquest and a tribal confederation into an empire. Without the leadership of the Muslims of Medina and Mecca the tribes always would have consumed their strength in internecine warfare. Fighting under the banners of Islam they could not fail. If they fell in battle they became heroic martyrs with the promise of paradise, if they survived they were transformed into a conquering aristocracy.

The Conquest of North Africa

While it had taken only a decade to conquer western Asia, it took the Muslim-Arab armies 50 years to subdue North Africa. They were opposed by two quite separate powers, Byzantium and the Berber kingdoms. Byzantine power was based on the fortified coastal cities protected by the imperial navy, while the Berber tribes, long prized as mercenaries in European armies, were the full military equals of the Arabs. The conquest succeeded due to persistent determination and a central leadership that could draw on the resources of a vast empire. The Berbers were by comparison disunited and their military opposition was weakened, time and time again, by their innate attraction to Islam.

After the conquest of Alexandria (643), which had been ordered by Abu Bekr, the Arab general Amr ibn el-Aasi, acting entirely on his own initiative, advanced west across the desert into Cyrenaica. He brushed aside the local militia, while the Byzantine field army avoided battle by withdrawing behind the walls of Teuchira. The other cities of the Pentapolis surrendered, only the walled town of Barca, with its primarily Berber population, offering any resistance. When the Barcans eventually submitted, the Arab invaders felt an immediate affinity with the town and its people. Amr ibn el-Aasi wrote 'If my own possessions were not in the Hijaz, I would live in Barca and never leave it, because I know no land more peaceful.' A later chronicler wrote that the Barcans 'are the most generous people in the Maghreb, and the passion of civil war never affects them'. Barca was chosen as the seat of the governor of Cyrenaica, who constructed a great mosque for the use of Arab armies on their way west.

The governor's chief role was to collect the provincial tribute, raised from a percentage of the harvest and a poll tax levied on all non-Muslims. The poll tax was assessed in advance and raised by the existing community leaders. Amr ibn el-Aasi assessed Cyrenaica at 13,000 dinars, but added a sub-clause that this could be paid in young Berber slaves. It was illegal to enslave 'people of the book' (as Christians and Jews were known) and as Cyrenaica was almost entirely Christian, this clause probably referred to the still pagan Lawata who had also made their submission to Amr ibn el-Aasi. It initiated an ugly precedent, for the Arab-Muslim ruling class developed a passion for young Berber slaves in preference to any other race.

The next year Amr ibn el-Aasi led his army across the Sirte desert and stormed the Tripolitanian walled cities of Leptis Magna, Oea and Sabratha, while one of his junior commanders, Oqba ben Nafi, rode south into the Libyan Sahara to raid the Lawata oasis of Zawila. In 645 the unsanctioned two-year expedition returned to Egypt laden with slaves, booty and tribute. Uthman, an aristocrat from Mecca's old Quaraysh confederation, had just been elected third caliph (644–56) and was determined to impose greater central authority. Amr ibn el-Aasi was removed from the governorship of Egypt and replaced by Abdullah ibn Saad. In 647 Abdullah received orders to lead an army of 20,000 Arab cavalrymen into the west.

BATTLE OF SBEITLA, 647

The Exarch Gregory had been preparing the defences of Byzantine North Africa ever since the walled cities of Tripolitania had been so suddenly, completely and ominously subsumed by the Arabs in 644. In 646 with the cautious backing of the pope in Rome and the passionate support of Abbot Maximus in Carthage, he had declared his independence from Constantinople. Gregory moved his administrative headquarters down to Sufetula (Sbeitla, the capital of the southern steppe), the better to face the Arab attack with the support of the allied Berber kings. But the Byzantine-Berber army was annihilated at the battle of Sbeitla, Exarch-Emperor Gregory perished and Abdullah ibn Saad was induced by a vast sum to return east. Although it looked as if the whole of southern Tunisia, the olive-rich province of Byzacena, had fallen into the hands of the Arabs, it was in fact too early for permanent occupation. The Byzantine navy still controlled the sea and the caliphate was paralysed by civil war.

OQBA BEN NAFI, COMMANDER OF THE WEST, 670–84

In 660 Muawiya, the victor of civil war, became the fifth caliph, moved the capital of the Islamic empire from Medina to Damascus and established the dynastic rule of his Ommayed family.

Muawiya was the very embodiment of a tribal sheikh, a master of the art of *hilm* – ruling without offending the touchy dignity of the Arabs. He organized his fellow Arabs into a nation-in-arms, segregated in garrison cities known as *misr* and rewarded with a privileged existence from the *Ddwan*, the military payroll. Islam was still conceived as the religion of the Arabs, and non-Arab converts continued to be taxed as if they were subjects.

In 670 the caliphate was ready to renew the conquest of North Africa, and appointed the veteran campaigner, Oqba ben Nafi, as commander of the army of the west. The previous incursions had removed any obstacle to Arab advance deep into central Tunisia, and Oqba ben Nafi was able to select Kairouan (literally the 'caravan') as his headquarters without any opposition. Here he constructed a great mosque where his army could pray right beside his residence, the *dar al-imara*, government house. Kairouan was a good military base, supplied with clear water from deep wells while the surrounding steppe provided plentiful grazing for the horses of the cavalry. It was also close enough for Oqba to launch an almost continuous series of profitable raids on the Berber kingdoms to the west and the Byzantine coastal cities to the east.

For some reason, perhaps court intrigue, perhaps dissatisfaction at his

Tuareg of the Sahara

progress, Oqba ben Nafi was replaced in 675 by a new commander, Abdul-Muhajir Dinar, who initiated a more dynamic policy of negotiating with the Romano-Berber kingdoms. Abdul-Muhajir Dinar was particularly successful with Kusalya, the king of Mauretania, who converted to Islam and became a client-monarch with a residence near Kairouan. This promising policy was shattered by the return of Oqba ben Nafi in 682. The old warrior, disgusted by any pact with the Berbers, deposed Kusalya and Abdul-Muhajir Dinar and had them bound in chains to humiliate them. He was also determined that no one should ever doubt his leadership again, and led his army on an epic march to discover the boundaries of the furthest west. A mesh of romantic legends has descended over this extraordinary campaign, and transformed Oqba ben Nafi from bloody Arab conquistador to apostle of the Berbers, with magical powers to match his missionary zeal. There is no reason to doubt, however, that Oqba ben Nafi reached the Sous valley of south-western Morocco and spurred his horse across the sands of Sidi R'bat out into the Atlantic surf and swore, 'O God I take you to witness that there is no ford here. If there was I would cross it.'

During the march King Kusalya made his escape and awaited his opportunity for vengeance. Later that year Oqba ben Nafi returned across the pre-Saharan steppe and camped at the Roman fortress of Tahuda just outside the oasis of Biskra. He may have been on a hunting expedition, for he was protected only by a small escort when Kusalya ambushed him. The tomb mosque that was later raised over the tomb of Oqba ben Nafi is considered one of the holiest and certainly one of the oldest Muslim shrines in North Africa. After Oqba's death, Kusalya reoccupied his old palace outside Kairouan and, staying true to Islam, presided over his Berber subjects while treating the remaining Arabs of the Kairouan garrison with respect. However one of Oqba ben Nafi's subordinates, Zuhahayr ibn Qay, had fled east to Egypt and eventually returned to Kairouan with reinforcements. Kusalya was forced to withdraw and died in a battle. Zuhahayr ibn Qay next turned his attention to the Byzantines who had made good use of Arab difficulties by reoccupying a number of coastal fortresses, including one in Cyrenaica. This threat to the long line of communication between Egypt and Kairouan could not be suffered. However Zuhahayr ibn Qay died during the seige.

HASSAN IBN NUMAN AND AL-KAHINA, 693–704

These various setbacks encouraged the Ommayad caliph Abdul Malik to assemble a sufficient force for the conquest of the Maghreb. In 693 an Arab army of 40,000 under the command of Hassan ibn Numan left Egypt and, side-stepping any of the lesser outposts on the way, marched straight on the Byzantine capital of Carthage, which was successfully stormed. Hassan then moved along the northern coast and defeated a combined Byzantine and Berber army that was barring his way to the second great port of Tunisia, Bizerte. The Arab army may then have continued along the north coast, for at a battle fought at Nini river it was worsted by the priestess Al-Kahina, the leader of the Jawara tribe whose citadel was near the Algerian town of Bijaya (Bougie). Her victory seems to have inspired other Berber tribes to fall on the Arabs, for Hassan was forced out of central Tunisia and defeated for a second time near the coastal oasis of Gabes. The remnant of the Arab army retired to the safety of Cyrenaica and in 697 a Byzantine fleet recaptured Carthage.

Despite her great victories, Al-Kahina was enough of a priestess to be filled with foreboding for the future. She ordered a scorched earth policy to frustrate the expected Arab counter-invasion and instructed her sons to become Muslim and take service under the Arabs. They were not alone. At least two Berber regiments, numbering 6,000 horsemen each, served as part of Hassan's second army of conquest.

In 697 Hassan ibn Numan led this new army west and at the second battle of Gabes managed to defeat the Berber confederation. Al-Kahina retreated west, pursued by the Arab cavalry, and made a last, long-remembered stand at Tubna, although dozens of locations in North Africa, including the great Roman amphitheatre at El Jem, also claim to have been the site.

Hassan ibn Numan recaptured Carthage in 698. Believing its coastal situation too vulnerable to attack, he founded Tunis, slightly inland, as the new Islamic face to age-old Carthage. Tunis, which sits on a hill between two inland lagoons, was turned into a naval port by the construction of a canal, La Goulette (the throat), which linked the lagoon to the sea. Hassan imported shipbuilders from Egypt to construct an Arab fleet with which to oppose the traditional Byzantine naval supremacy. With this fleet at his disposal he methodically sacked the various Byzantine coastal forts that were dotted along the North African shore. The last act of the Byzantine navy was to evacuate a large proportion of the urban Christian population to crowded Constantinople or to such nearby Byzantine territory as the islands of Sicily, Sardinia and the Balearics.

The Conquest of Spain

By 704 Musa ben Nasser had taken over from Hassan ibn Numan. Between 705 and 710 the Arab army criss-crossed the Maghreb accepting the submission of Berber tribal leaders, who professed Islam and proved their loyalty by surrendering hostages and assisting in the raising of Berber regiments. To guard this vast new territory Musa established three military bases, at Tlemcen in western Algeria, at Tangier in northern Morocco and in the Tafilalet oasis in south-eastern Morocco, which controlled an important Saharan trade route. The Arab army was still based at Kairouan, while these new bases were largely manned by Berber troops. Even the first governor of the Tangier garrison, Tariq ibn Ziyad, was a Berber.

In 711 Tariq ibn Ziyad led a foray of 7,000 Berber cavalrymen across the straits of Gibraltar to test the defences of Visigothic Spain. He landed at the craggy peninsula that has ever been associated with him (Jebel al-Tariq, Tariq's mountain, is the origin of the word Gibraltar) and advanced north to engage King Roderic (710–11). At the battle of Barbate river, fought outside Jerez la Frontera, Tariq destroyed the Visigothic army and established Muslim rule over Spain. In the great cities of Cordoba and Toledo the Jews and Catholics greeted Tariq as a liberator from the hated rule of the Arian Visigoths. The fruits of this great, and surprising, Berber victory were hurriedly snatched by the Arab ruling class, who poured in to occupy the sweet lands of Spain. In the next decade the Berber legions would push their way across the Pyrenees and, after their victory at Toulouse in 721, penetrate deep into the heart of France.

Emir of Ifriqiya

Musa ben Nasser was made the first independent governor of North Africa, which had hitherto been ruled from Egypt. His province, Ifriqiya, stretched from the Atlantic coast of Morocco to western Libya. Cyrenaica remained a province of Egypt. The governor, who was addressed as 'Emir', presided over 24 *kuras* (districts) each ruled by an *amil*. The density of districts gives some indication of the taxable wealth and pattern of control, for Tunisia was divided into 11 *kuras*, Morocco only two. There was no separation of powers. The emir was an omnipotent military and religious viceroy around whose person ranged the four departments of state: *jund* (army), *rasil* (post and intelligence service), *kharaj* (taxation) and *bit el-mal* (treasury).

As a conquered territory Ifriqiya had to pay both land and poll tax, and although there was now no legal justification for the enslavement of the Berbers, it had become too profitable a trade to curtail. Emir Musa ben Nasser is estimated to have enslaved 100,000 Berber youths, of whom he dispatched the customary fifth to his master, the caliph, in Damsacus. The Arab-Muslim élite justified the continued slave raids by accusing the Berber tribes of frequent apostasy (one Arab source claimed the Berbers rejected Islam 11 times), while a convenient, but totally, fictitious Hadith stated that the Berbers could never become Muslims because they had eaten the prophet God had sent them. This racism conflicted with the growing awareness that Muslim converts should be treated as equals to the Arabs. Two factions developed within the Arab ruling class. Qays wished to maintain a militant, ever-expanding, but highly centralized Arab Empire. Yemenis wished to transform the caliphate into a peaceful, decentralized Muslim state. The Ommayads were ultra-Qays, and only one enlightened member of the dynasty, Umar II (717–20), attempted to transform the caliphate from an Arab to a Muslim Empire.

In 718 Umar II dispatched a learned Muslim as the new emir of Ifriqiya, reformed the system of taxation, forbade the enslavement of Berbers and dispatched ten scholars to teach true Islam to the Berbers. On his death in 720 however, this policy was reversed and the following emirs all returned enthusiastically to the profitable business of enslaving their subjects. Some good was done however, for the scholars of Umar II settled down in Kairouan, the congenially Arab-speaking capital, and were the seed from which Kairouan emerged as the religious and intellectual centre of the Maghreb.

Signs of future discord between ruler and ruled were not hard to detect. When Emir Yazid (720–4) ordered that all Berber soldiers were to be tattooed with their names on the right arm and 'guard of Yazid' on their left, they murdered him. Worse was to follow with the appointment of Ubayd Allah al-Habbab in 734, who took slave raiding to new heights. He first appointed his sons as the two district governors of Morocco and then joined them at the head of an Arab army, which swept through the south of the country netting thousands upon thousands of slaves. Nor was this just an example of entrepeneurial abuse of authority, for the emir was acting on written instructions from Caliph Hisham (724–43), who carefully listed the physical types of slaves he was after. A delegation from Kairouan took a petition of complaint to the caliph's court at Damascus, but they were never even granted an audience.

CHAPTER TEN

Revolt and Reaction: Kharijites and Aghlabids, 739–903

Underlying dissatisfaction with the arrogant rule of the caliphate erupted in the eighth century in a series of revolts that reversed the Arab conquest and saw much of North Africa in the hands of a patchwork of secessionist states. Tunisia remained an uneasy part of the caliphate for another 50 years until an Arab general established the dynastic rule of his Aghlabid family. Despite the intriguing diversity of these states, the ninth century was a largely peaceful, prosperous and constructive period in North Africa's history.

Zenith of the Caliphate

The Ommayad caliphs had never been loved by the Arabs, but they had been acknowledged reluctantly for their efficiency. During the 720s and 730s their authority began to loosen as their conquests slowly ground to a halt. The second Arab siege of Constantinople had failed in 719, the Christian kingdoms of Armenia and Georgia halted any further advance in the Caucasus, the fortress of Multan on the Punjab marked the furthest Arab advance into India, while in 732 the twin battles of Poitiers and Tours expelled the Berber-Arab army from France and pushed Islamic rule back south of the Pyrenees. The military rigour of the Arab armies had begun to dwindle as desert warriors became landlords, interbred with their subjects and adjusted to comfortable city life. Records from one Arab garrison-city provide graphic proof of this trend, for while in 670 it could produce 50,000 warriors, in 730 it could field only 15,000. A tax revolt from 725–6 shook Arab rule in Egypt, and in the Arab homeland historic rivals of the Ommayads began to re-emerge. However, it was in the furthest reaches of North Africa, at Tangier in 739, that the Ommayad Caliphate was first overthrown.

THE TANGIER MUTINY AND BERBER REVOLT, 739–43

By 739 Tangier had been a Muslim-Berber stronghold for a generation and one that took justifiable pride in its single-handed conquest of Spain. That year the Arab governor of Tangier, Umar ibn Abdallah Muradi, levied a poll tax on his subjects which was assessed at enslavement for one in five members of the population.

This insulting assessment inferred that the entire population, proud Muslim-Berber soldiers, converts to Islam, and Jewish and Christian Berbers were no better than pagans. The garrison, led by Maysara (a one-time water-carrier from the Arab citadel of Kairouan), mutinied against Arab rule and were soon masters of Morocco. In 741 the Berber rebels, now under the command of a more experienced Berber chieftain, decisively defeated the Arab army of the west at the battle of

the Nobles, which had an unexpected effect on Arab settlement patterns. In the aftermath of the battle some 12,000 Arabs of Syrian lineage fled the shores of North Africa and found permanent refuge in Spain. Caliph Hisham sacked his emir and a new governor was sent out at the head of a fresh Arab army. This force advanced deep into northern Morocco, but on the banks of the slow-moving Sebou river it was utterly destroyed. Two rebel Berber armies now advanced on the Arab capital of Kairouan, but the governor of Egypt responded to the emergency by rushing in reinforcements, which by 742 had secured the city from attack.

In three years the Berber rebellion had destroyed two Arab armies and ended the rule of the caliphate over Morocco and Algeria. It revealed a discipline and unity of purpose that had been all too rare in the long annals of Berber resistance. This new unity was provided by Islam. It is a neat paradox of history that the Berbers were only capable of resisting the Arab conquest after they had first been converted by the Arabs to Islam. Indeed due to the wide-ranging influence of Muslim missionaries of the Kharijite sect, the Berbers came to believe that they were championing the purest form of Islam against the corrupted beliefs of the Arabs.

Kharijite Origins

The Kharijites (those who 'went out' – secessionists) first emerged as a distinct sect in Arabia in 657, during a succession dispute to the caliphate. They were passionately concerned to preserve the original purity of the Prophet Mohammed's first community and were strongly opposed to dynastic succession to the caliphate. They believed rather in the conditions of leadership set by Abu Bekr, who had declared that he should be obeyed as leader only for as long as he obeyed the example of the Prophet Mohammed. In line with this contractual leadership the Kharijites preferred the more modest title of 'Imam' (leader) to that of 'Caliph' (successor). They believed that the leader of the Muslim community should be elected purely on the basis of his religious learning and personal piety, with no restriction due to race or class. They also believed that a Muslim should be judged by his actions, not the rituals or declaration of faith. A true Muslim adhered strictly to the ethical and moral code taught by the Prophet Mohammed. Sin was a form of apostacy that could eradicate any of the benefits of belief or the scrupulous performance of public prayers.

If there is much in their doctrine to commend them, the political actions of the Kharijites were in violent and often disastrous contrast. In the world of Islamic scholarship they are notorious as the first to destroy the the unity of the Muslim community and the first to descend to terrorism. It was a Khariji who assassinated Ali, the last of the rightly-guided caliphs, although doctrinally he was a close ally. The death of Ali led directly to Ommayad rule, the very antithesis of their beliefs, against which they plotted violent insurrection. The subsequent Ommayad repression split the sect into the Ibadi, who were politically moderate, and the extremists, such as the Kharijites, who became the terrorist underground.

In order to propagate their faith the various Kharijite sects dispatched missionaries to the furthest corners of the caliphate. The missionaries, often hailing from the sophisticated cities of the Muslim heartland, carried with them an inherent intellectual prestige. However, unlike the arrogant Arab ruling class, they preached a powerful message of racial equality within the true community of believers. The contrast between this and the naked greed of the Arab governors made the Kharijite doctrine intensely attractive.

The dissemination of Ibadi beliefs is comparatively well chronicled. The Iraqi city of Basra was the centre of the Ibadi community, and in 719 its leader, Abu Ubayda Muslim, sent one of his accredited *hamalat al-ilm* (transmitters of learning), by the name of Salma ben Sa'd, to set up an Ibadi presence in Kairouan. Salma was followed by other teachers who had particular success in the Tripolitanian hinterland, converting the Berber tribes of the old Lawata confederacy.

The Kharijite missionaries were particularly successful amongst the vital Muslim-Berber soldiers of the Moroccan garrisons. It is likely for example that Maysara, who led the Tangier revolt, was a key Kharijite agent. It has also been suggested that the tradition of the Donatist Church (with a similar history of persecuted puritanism), made the Berbers particularly receptive to the Kharijite missionaries.

THE BENI MIDRAR OF SIGILMASSA, 744–909

The Berber garrison of southern Morocco assumed the authority that had hitherto been exercised by the Arab district governor. The Kharijite convictions of the soldiers were convincingly expressed by the election of a black Muslim as their first imam. Midrar (757–83), a Berber warrior of the Miknassa tribe from central Morocco, who had played a prominent part in the Tangier revolt, became the second imam. In 757 he established the dynastic Beni Midrar state with the foundation of the city of Sigilmassa in the centre of the Tafilalet oasis which was well sited for the trans-Saharan trade on the southern reaches of the Tafilalet oasis. He was succeeded by his son Al Yasa ibn Midrar (790–823) who extended the boundaries of the imamate, which grew prosperous from trade and from silver, mined in the vicinity of the Draa valley. Sigilmassa soon became the acknowledged centre of the western Saharan trade routes (a position it would keep for over a thousand years) frequented by Andalucians, Jews, sub-Saharan blacks and the veiled Berbers of the desert. It was defended by a wall pierced by 12 fortified gates, and its busy markets sprawled around the central mosque.

BERGHOUATA: THE HERETICAL STATE OF ATLANTIC MOROCCO

Another of the leaders of the Berber revolt, Tarif, returned to his tribal homeland on the Atlantic coast and established a Kharijite state from a confederacy of tribes that became known as the Berghouata. The Berghouata occupied the fertile grainlands south of the port of Sala Colonia (modern Rabat), which had been colonized by the Carthaginians from the fifth century BC but never incorporated into the Roman Empire. Yunis ibn Ilyas, a descendant of Tarif who led the confederacy from 842–84, also felt himself touched by the gift of prophecy. He created his own holy book, which was written in the indigenous Berber language. Berber is not a written language, but this particular region of North Africa already may have possessed its own Punic-derived script. Yunis' Berber monotheism was closely modelled on Kharijite Islam, although it incorporated a number of adaptations to diet, prayer and marriage that were more in keeping with Berber traditions. The Berghouata heresy was anathema to all the orthodox Islamic states, and although it never spread, it obstinately survived all assaults for several hundred years. When it was finally subdued all traces of the religion were expunged. Our knowledge of this obscure sect comes from the historian El Bekri who had access to the report of a Berghouata embassy sent to Spain in the tenth century.

Even more intriguing is the account of a more orthodox Berber Koran in the Jebel Hadid hills, just south of Berghouata territory. Seven Berber holy men from the Regrada tribe, well versed in the Jewish and Christian scriptures, are said to have journeyed to Mecca in the seventh century to find the comforter whom Jesus, in the Gospel of St John, promises to send after He had gone. They identified the Prophet Mohammed as that comforter, some years before the *hegira*, and took back an early version of Islam, which they preached, in Berber, in their homeland. The tombs of the seven saints are known and still venerated.

The Idrissid Monarchy of Central Morocco, 789–828

After the overthrow of the Arab governors by the Berber revolt, central Morocco returned to its habitual patchwork of tribal identities. The centre of the region was the town of Walila, which partly occupied the proud architectural remnants of the old Roman provincial capital Volubulis. Walila was presided over by a council of chiefs professing Jewish, Christian, Kharijite and orthodox Muslim beliefs.

It was in this obscure town, on the furthest reaches of the Muslim world, that an Arab prince, Idris ibn Abdullah, took grateful refuge in 788. His proudest possession was the friendship of his ex-slave Rashid, who had shared the dangers of his epic journey across Arabia, Syria and the breadth of North Africa. The journey had begun in 786 at the battle of Fakh outside Mecca, where Idris had fought for his kinsman Husayn, the great-great-grandson of the Prophet Mohammed, against an Abbasid army. After their victory, the Abbasids had hunted down the survivors, but by making his way to Morocco Idris felt that he had at last escaped the furthest reaches of the vengeful caliph. The depth of his Koranic scholarship soon attracted attention and when it became known that he was a *sharif* (a descendant of the Prophet Mohammed through his daughter Fatima's marriage to Ali) he became the acknowledged holy arbitrator for all the surrounding tribes. This position was clarified in February 789 when the most powerful Berber tribe in the vicinity, the Awraba, acclaimed him imam.

Idris' sanctity is still celebrated in Morocco, but his period of leadership was short, for in May 791 he was killed by an agent of Caliph Harun al-Rashid. Idris had neither wives nor children, but fortunately Rashid, his faithful ex-slave, was aware that Idris' young Berber lover was heavy with child. She was watched anxiously that summer and in August she gave birth to a boy, Idris II, for whom Rashid acted as regent. In 802 an Aghlabid agent (working on behalf of the Abbasids) assassinated Rashid, but was killed before he could endanger the young *sharif*. The next year, at the tender age of 11, Idris II (803–28) was acclaimed imam in the mosque of Walila. Idris was the only orthodox Islamic ruler in Morocco and his court soon attracted a stream of Arab refugees escaping persecution after some failed revolt. Within a few years Idris II had created an orthodox Arab enclave in Morocco complete with an officially appointed *qadi*, a chief *vizier* (minister) and a 500-strong regiment of Arab cavalry. Idris II increasingly found his authority constrained by the conciliar traditions of the Berber tribal chiefs. In 809, with the Berber chief of the Awraba tribe dead at his feet, he felt free to move from Walila to the newly established, and entirely Islamic, city of Fez. In 818 a failed rebellion in Cordoba sent a flood of Arab refugees to Fez, and a decade later a similar failed rebellion in Tunisia against the Aghlabids brought further Arab stock.

In just a few decades, Fez grew from a sparse, administrative headquarters to a densely populated Arab city composed of two separate walled quarters looking at each other across the Oued Fes. The right bank was occupied by the quarter of the Andalucians, who were considered to have the prettiest women and whose men were strong, brave fighters and good farmers. The left bank, where Idris II's el-Aliya palace and army barracks also stood, became known as the Kairouan quarter after the refugees from Tunisia. They were more elegant and better-educated than the Andalucians, but given to luxurious living. The latter qualities in due course became the typical characteristics of a Fassi, a citizen of Fez.

IDRISSID PRINCIPALITIES

Idris II was accepted as imam by most of the tribes of central Morocco by the time of his death in 828. His eldest son Mohammed (828–36) divided this inheritance amongst nine of his twelve brothers. This sub-division broke the tentative unity that Idris II had enforced personally upon central Morocco, but in many ways it was a beneficial process. The younger Idrissid princes were forced out of Fez and founded new towns in the hinterland, where they functioned as respected tribal arbitrators and orthodox missionaries. The Idrissid princes might look militarily powerless beside the example of their father, but they came to form an important part of the culture of Morocco. The Idrissid conversion of various Berber tribes is remembered in dozens of affectionate and legendary tales. Sidi Kacem, the fourth son of Idris II, refused to accept any of his inheritance and took to a life of pious poverty on the Atlantic shore where his tomb, outside Tangier, is still a centre of wide veneration. Another brother, Sidi Aissa ibn Idris, is buried in a reclusive High Atlas valley where he was killed by the pagan Ait Attab tribe. The tribe was subsequently converted to Islam by a miraculous whirlwind that emerged from Sidi Aissa's grave every spring and devastated their crops. Once they had honoured the martyr with a tomb and built their first mosque, the whirlwind ceased its destruction.

Mohammed, the eldest son, continued to rule from Fez, which grew as a commercial centre despite the political fragmentation. The city's increased standing was confirmed during the reign of Yahya ben Umar (849–63) by the construction of two great mosques, one for the Andalucians, one for the Kairouan quarter. The old market town of Sefrou, just a day's ride north of Fez, remained a jealous rival. It was the capital of a coalition of Kharijite Berber tribes who had resisted Idris II's authority and fought his successors. In 866 and 917 they managed to capture Fez and had the satisfaction of assisting in the deposition of its last Idrissid ruler, Yahya IV (905–23), in 923.

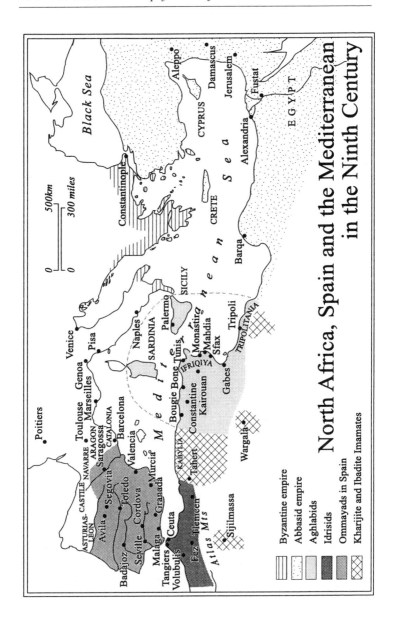

North Africa, Spain and the Mediterranean in the Ninth Century

The Rustamid Ibadi Imamate of Tahart

In Algeria the 739–43 revolt cleared the way for a Berber tribal confederacy, the Beni Ifran, to assume a dominant position. Their base was in the western plains, where in 765 they founded Tlemcen (ever after the capital of western Algeria) over the ruins of a Roman marching camp. At the core of the Beni Ifran confederacy was a proud remant of the Lawata, who had been driven out of Tripolitania by Arab slave raids and had fought under Al Kahina before being forced ever further west. Faced with a renewed Arab threat from Kairouan in the 770s they naturally joined forces with the Berber tribes of central Algeria who were being led by a charismatic Ibadi imam, Abdul-Rahman ibn Rustam (777–84).

Rustam was an attractive character whose life story reveals the wide-ranging contacts and fluid mobility that was possible within the Islamic world. Neither Berber nor Arab, he was Persian, a trader based in Kairouan who was converted to the Ibadi faith by one of the *hamalat al-ilm* (transmitters of learning). He was such a promising convert that he was sent to receive final instruction from the Ibadi leadership in Basra, Iraq, and in due course returned to North Africa. Rustam founded the town of Tahart in central Algeria as an Ibadi centre for the Berber tribes. By 771 he was exercising sufficient authority to lead 15,000 Berber warriors against Tubna, the Arab forward post in eastern Algeria. The next year the defeat of the Ibadi community in Tripolitania by an Arab army immeasurably increased the importance of Tahart, which was henceforth defended by stone walls and a central keep, the fortress of Ma'suma (the safeguarded one). Tahart had other, natural advantages, for it sat astride an important trade route and possessed an assured supply of sweet water. The patterns of trade and the seasonal migration of the pastoral tribes naturally brought many of the Berber tribes of Algeria through the meadows that stretched below its walls. Such government business as was necessary would be transacted in a series of reciprocal feasts exchanged between tented encampment and town. Rustam acted as the ideal arbitrator, for his Persian origins removed any suspicion of bias in favour of one Berber tribe, whilst his scholarship assured access to the true path of the Prophet Mohammed. Unlike the elected leader

Ali ben Hamed, caliph of Constantine

of a Berber tribal confederation, he did not need to act with the consent of a council of clan chiefs. He imposed no unwanted authority on the tribes and received the alms-tax in kind, a tithe of crops and herds which was scrupulously used for the benefit of the poor, widows, orphans and for the Koranic education of children. On Rustam's death, the Ibadi leadership (mindful of their doctrinal opposition to dynastic succession) could yet find no more suitable imam than Abdul-Wahhab, his son. Abdul-Wahhab (784–823) presided over the increasingly prosperous and peaceful Rustamid imamate.

Tahart was marked by its tolerance, not only for other forms of Muslim belief, but for the Jewish and Christian traders who sheltered within its walls. Abdul-Wahhab pursued a pacific foreign policy, establishing good relations with both the Beni Midrar of Sigilmassa and the Aghlabids of Kairouan. In 812 he did lead an assault on Tripoli, held by an Aghlabid garrison, but the peaceful resolution of this military adventure so angered his fellow Ibadis in Tripolitania that they elected their own leader. However under al-Aflah (823–72), the third Rustamid imam, the Tripolitanian's loyalty was won back by his saintly demeanour and distinguished scholarship.

Arab Emirs at Kairouan, 742–99

The continued presence of the caliphate in North Africa had been safeguarded by the prompt action of the governor of Egypt when he had reinforced the citadel-city of Kairouan in 742. Three years later a combination of Muslim civil war and local intrigue ousted him. Command of the Arab army passed to Abdul Rahman ibn Habib, leader of Kairouan's influential Fihrid clan which was composed of Oqba ben Nafi's descendants, who had settled permanently in the Maghreb since the conquest. The Fihrids had led the Arab army at the battle of the Nobles, and had been instrumental in organizing Arab migration to Spain where they had briefly set up an independent emirate (750–6). They were courageous and resourceful, the very embodiment of the *jund*, the landed class of Arab knights, who were dedicated to the continuous expansion of Islam through military conquest. Far from sinking into a siege mentality against the Berber majority, Abdul Rahman ibn Habib led the *jund* in raids on Algeria, Byzantine Sicily and Sardinia. In 754 he paid lip-service to the new Abbasid dynasty which had supplanted the Ommayads, but resolutely refused to dispatch the Berber slaves who had in the past been sent as a present beside the written *baia* (loyalty oath). Two years later however a *jund* raid on southern Tunisia, against the Berber Nafzawa tribe, resulted in a catastrophic defeat. The Nafzawa, joined by the other Ibadi tribes of Tripolitania, rode north to occupy Kairouan where an Ibadi state was proclaimed. Arab chroniclers claim that orthodox Muslims were hunted down, women and children enslaved and the great mosque used as a stable for horses. This may just be propaganda, for it accords ill with the known tolerance of the Ibadi state that was soon to be set up by Rustam, who was deputy-governor of Kairouan during this Ibadi occupation of 756–61.

In 761 an army dispatched by the Abbassid caliph reoccupied

Kairouan and established an advance base at Tubna in eastern Algeria. After four unsuccessful campaigning seasons the Abbasids returned home leaving an Arab nobleman, Al-Aghlab ibn Salim, as the emir of Ifriqiya. Al-Aghlab was to enjoy posthumous fame as the father of the founder of the Aghlabid dynasty, but his own authority was constantly opposed by the *jund*. He died in 768 trying to quell a mutiny, and the Abbasid caliph was forced to send a new governor with a new army. The new governor, recruited from a noble Arab family long settled in Iraq, the Muhallabs, had greater success in holding the balance of power. It has been argued that the strong links between his family and the Ibadi leadership at Basra may have helped them negotiate a peace with his Ibadi neighbours in North Africa. Over the next few decades three generations of Muhallab governors presided successfully over the unruly politics of Kairouan. In 793 a fourth potential Muhallab governor was deposed by yet another *jund* mutiny, and over the next six years a succession of Abbasid governors tried to restore order in vain.

The Foundation of the Aghlabid Dynasty

By 799 the ground was well prepared for Ibrahim ibn al-Aghlab (800–12), a career-officer in command of the Abbasid garrison at Tubna, to launch a *coup d'état*. He marched his disciplined troops on Kairouan where he declared the restoration of order. He granted amnesty to the *jund* and at the same time opened secret negotiations with Harun al-Rashid, the celebrated Abbasid caliph (786–809), in Baghdad. By February 800 the negotiations were concluded. The caliph, bored by the continual expense and inconvenience of this distant and rebellious province, granted Ifriqiya as a hereditary fief to Ibrahim ibn al-Aghlab. Instead of receiving 100,000 dinars a year (the annual cost of governing Ifriqiya) Ibrahim agreed to provide the caliph with an annual tribute of 40,000 dinars. Outward forms of loyalty were carefully observed, such as calling out the Friday prayers in the name of the reigning caliph. The red and black ensigns of the Abbasids continued to be flown and each new Aghlabid emir respectfully petitioned Baghdad to approve his succession. In all practical matters however, the Aghlabids were independent sovereigns, as their coinage proclaimed.

THE NATURE OF AGHLABID AUTHORITY

Ibrahim ibn al-Aghlab became ruler through his skill as a soldier, coupled with a fine sense of political timing. He held power, but neither he nor his successors could claim to be respected arbitrators chosen by the Muslim community to keep them on the path of the Prophet. As a result, neither the scholarly religious establishment known as the *ulema*, nor the *jund*, felt anything but guarded hostility towards the Aghlabids.

Like all military rulers who have imposed themselves on Muslim societies, the Aghlabids had to construct their own sources of power. Ibrahim ibn al-Aghlab's first action was to move his court from Kairouan, whose resident population looked to the *jund* and especially the *ulema* for leadership. The *dar al-imara*, first founded by Oqba ben Nafi beside the great mosque of Kairouan, was abandoned in favour of the glittering new palace complex of al-Abbasiya, which was defended by walls and stood 2 kilometres from the city gates. Ibrahim's security was based on the personal loyalty of the Abbasid Tubna garrison, but this was gradually replaced by guard regiments of foreign slaves whose only loyalty was to their Aghlabid masters. The emir's agents acquired the pick of the black male slaves brought up from the Sudan on the trans-Saharan caravans, and purchased European slaves from Italian merchants. This contrasting colour scheme was both elegant and politically expedient, for the *abids*, the black guards, and the *saqaliba*, the white guards, were goaded into furious competition with each other.

Although assured of physical security in their palace the Aghlabid emirs were continuously faced with rebellion in their dominions. The *jund* had spread out from the garrison-cities like Kairouan and transformed themselves into landed aristocrats, watching over their fertile estates from fortified manor-houses. To balance the military power of the far-flung *jund*, the Aghlabids slowly developed alliances with the Berber Ibadite tribes beyond their domains. This understanding began in 812 when Emir Ibrahim I (800–12) and the Rustamid imam Abdul-Wahhab negotiated zones of influence during the Ibadite siege of Tripoli. The Ibadi Berbers were left in control of the

Tripolitanian hinterland and the Tunisian desert while the Aghlabids held the coast and the cities of Gabes and Tripoli. This agreement proved an enormous encouragement to trade, opening up Aghlabid Tunisia to the trans-Saharan trade, which was securely in the hands of the Ibadi. The peace also denied the *jund* any further opportunities to make war, and the Arab outposts on the Algerian border, at Setif, Mila, Tubna and Balazma were reduced to humdrum garrison duty. *Jund* disaffection at this state of affairs exploded in the revolt of 824, where for a period the rebels held both Tunis and Kairouan. The revolt was only finally subdued in 827 by an 'Aghlabid army', almost entirely recruited from Ibadi Berbers. In the aftermath the walls of Kairouan were levelled to make it an open city.

To find a permissible outlet for the bellicose activities of the *jund* the Aghlabids renewed the war against Christian Sicily. A great expedition was launched in 828, backed up by almost annual campaigns. A series of *ribats* (monastery-like castles garrisoned by warriors dedicated to the holy war) served as recruiting centres for the Sicilian war, for sea-borne raids as well as for defending the Tunisian coast against Christian counter-attack. The *ribats* which still stand at Sousse, Monastir and Mahres are some of the most beguiling examples of early Islamic architecture. In European parlance these sea-borne ventures are known as the Saracen raids, and have entered deep into the folklore of the Christian Mediterranean. Some of the raids were remarkably successful including, following the Vandal precedent, a sack of Rome in 846. From the perspective of the Aghlabids the policy was a brilliant success, for it calmed the *jund* and they reaped the bonus of the rich island of Sicily, which finally fell to the Muslims in 909.

The *ulema* meanwhile, horrified by the Aghlabid delight in wine-making, professional dancers and usury, were further incensed when Emir Abdullah I (812–17) levied a fixed tax, payable in coin, on the peasantry. The Aghlabid state, with its standing army, salaried administration and impressive building projects, could never have been financed on the Koranically approved alms-tax in kind. Indeed, ironically, the firm financial foundations of the Aghlabids allowed them to win over individual members of the *ulema* by appointing them as *qadi* (judges), a position of great respect with a salary attached.

During the Aghlabid period an important legal revolution was slowly transforming the whole Muslim world. A succession of influential *qadi* were dissolving the last barriers between Arab and non-Arab Muslims to create a single Muslim legal tradition. Kairouan made its own contribution in the persons of two great ninth-century legal scholars: Ibn al Furat and Sahnun. Sahnun (the most revered and influential of the two) had once been Furat's pupil. His preference for the uncompromisingly Koranic-based judgements of the Medinan *qadi* Maliki was immensely influential for the future legal system of the Maghreb, which is based on the Malikite school to this day.

THE CULMINATION OF AGHLABID RULE

For the bulk of the population Aghlabid rule was a golden period of peace, prosperity and construction. The wounds of a century of warfare were slowly healed as abandoned fields and orchards were brought back under cultivation, agricultural populations grew and the surplus streamed into fast-emerging markets, coastal ports, the glittering capital of Kairouan and the emir's treasury. Tunisia received its definitive urban shape in this period, when the Aghlabid emirs laid out the curtain walls and internal streets that would define the great coastal cities of Sfax, Sousse and Tunis, which still dominate the nation. The emirs demonstrated their piety with an impressive religious building programme, including the great mosque of Sousse, the Zitouna Mosque in Tunis and the definitive reconstruction of the Great Mosque of Oqba ben Nafi at Kairouan. Few dynasties can hope to match this extraordinary architectural creativity, which has continued to delight worshippers and pilgrims for well over a thousand years. The reign of Abou Ibrahim Ahmed (856–63) saw the triumphant completion of all three of these magnificent structures. It also witnessed the joyous spectacle of the nightly Ramadan procession when the emir walked from his palace to Kairouan's Great Mosque along a festooned pathway, distributing alms in a festival mood. At such times the historic rivalry between *ulema* and the dynasty must have been almost forgotten.

Abou Ibrahim Ahmed was succeeded to the emirate by his 13-year-old son, Mohammed II (864–75), whose carefree reign was divided between the joys of hunting and the sensual delights of palace life. The emir died young, worn out by less than a dozen years of ardent pleasure, but not before he had won the affectionate nickname of *Abu Gharaniq* (father of the cranes), because of his endless enthusiasm for sending hawks in pursuit of these stately birds. Mohammed II had left the cares of state in the hands of his kinsmen, who succeeded him to the throne.

Ibrahim II (875–902) had been an exemplary governor, but proved a tyrannical monarch. He increased the number of slave-guards based at Reqqada, his new palace complex 10 kilometres south-west of Kairouan, until he had a totally obedient army of 10,000 at his command. He delighted in demonstrating his absolute power. A leading *qadi* who opposed the emir's land confiscations was tortured to death and a prominent nobleman was publicly crucified in Kairouan. In 893 he assembled the *jund* at the outpost of Balazma as if for a campaign, but then had them all massacred. Even the Abbasid caliph was shocked, and encouraged the increasingly mad Ibrahim II to abdicate in favour of his son, Abdullah II in 902. The bloodshed continued. A year later Abdullah was murdered on the instructions of his own son, Ziyadat Allah III (903–9), who then proceeded from patricide to fratricide, ordering the death of his brother, the popular commander of the army. The dynasty was in a state of terminal decay, and within six years it would be banished from North Africa by a new and potent political force, the Fatimids.

CHAPTER ELEVEN

The Fatimid and Ommayad Adventures,
909–1090

Tenth-century North Africa was dominated by two rival powers, the Ommayads based in Spain and the Shiite Fatimids in Tunisia. The rise to power of both dynasties reads like the most improbable fiction, shot through with secret societies, exiled princes, impregnable fortresses, reclusive mountain kingdoms and tribal viceroys. Despite their picaresque origins, however, the states they established were sophisticated and highly centralized. Like a long drawn-out chess game, the Fatimids and Ommayads, both of whom claimed to be caliph, manoeuvred for dominance over the neutral territory of Morocco and western Algeria. By the middle of the eleventh century this pattern of authority had been broken. The Ommayad state had imploded while the ambitions of the Fatimids had led them out of North Africa into the fatlands of Egypt. They left behind a dynasty of Berber viceroys, but the whole extraordinary chronicle of events was swept away, as if it had been a dream, by a widespread return to nomadism ushered in by the westward migration of the vast Beni Hilal bedouin from Arabia. The effect was profound, for as Ibn Khaldoun lamented: 'the Arabs (by which he meant bedouin Arabs) are incapable of good government and bring the desert with them'.

Ommayad Emirate of Cordoba, 750–912

The affairs of Al Andalus (Muslim Spain) are inextricably linked with North Africa from the year of its conquest in 711 to its fall in 1485. This is especially true of the tenth century when Ommayad Spain frustrated the extension of the Shiite Fatimid Empire over all the Maghreb.

The story begins with the battle of the River Zab, in Iraq in 750, when the last Ommayad caliph, Marwan II (744–50), was defeated by the Abbasids who secured their new tenure on the throne by the wholesale slaughter of the old dynasty. The most obscure descendants of the ruling clan were hounded out of the alleys of Damascus and dragged to their death, but one of the caliph's own sons, Abdul Rahman ibn Marwan, somehow escaped the slaughter. He headed for the safety of Morocco where he was entertained hospitably by the Miknassa tribe for a number of years. In 756 political unrest in Spain gave Abdul Rahman the opportunity to depose the Fihrid emir and establish his own independent state, the Ommayad emirate of Cordoba. After the conquest of 711 Spain had been settled by a small Arab élite (the Berber army of Tariq was denied any of the fruits of its victory) who presided over communities of Christians and Jews. These useful, tribute-paying non-Muslims would later become known as Mozarabs due to their assimilation of Arabic language and culture. Hisham I (788–96) kept the emirate in tune with the prevailing orthodoxy by adopting the Malikite school of Islam, which was championed by the scholars of Kairouan. However, in foreign affairs the Ommayads followed an expedient policy of alliance with the unorthodox Berber states, were they Kharijite, Ibadi or even the heretical Berghouata. This not only allowed them privileged access to the trans-Saharan trade, but also kept the territories of the Abbasid caliph at a safe remove. Abdul Rahman II (822–52) developed a close connection with the Rustamids of Tahart, helping them resist Aghlabid pressure on the Algerian frontier. The prosperity of the late ninth century seems to have disarmed the antagonism between the Ommayad and Aghlabid emirs. They both declined promising opportunities to meddle in each others' misfortunes, such as the Spanish revolt of 880 and the re-emergence of Byzantine power in Sicily in 840.

This *laissez-faire* attitude was dramatically reversed in the tenth century. Abdul Rahman III, who came to the throne just two years after the Fatimids siezed Tunisia, proved himself a worthy adversary to their vast ambitions.

Abu Abdullah, Architect of the Fatimid Empire, 892–911

The Fatimids imposed their rule over North Africa for 150 years, although they were not from the Maghreb nor particularly interested in the region. North Africa was no more than a convenient stepping stone to their real ambition, which was to rule over the Middle East. For all the glamour of their empire and the brief unity they brought to the region, overall they were an alien and destructive force.

The Fatimids had complicated origins as a sect within a sect of Islam. They represented the extreme monarchical wing of Shiite Islam, which holds that Ali (the cousin, son-in-law and closest disciple of the Prophet Mohammed) was his rightful successor. The Shiites believed that the future leadership of Islam should have followed the bloodline of Ali and Fatima (the only daughter of the Prophet to produce grandchildren). This dynasty was also believed to be divinely inspired and an infallible interpreter of Islam, whose theocratic powers turned political disobedience into a form of apostasy. Yet these presumed powers were in painful contrast to the neglected position the Fatamid dynasty held within Muslim society.

By the ninth century the sect was concentrated on the small Syrian town of Salamiyya, from whence it dispatched a steady trickle of devoted missionaries into the wider world. One such missionary, Abu Abdullah al-Shii from the Yemen, was instructed to take the Fatimid message to the Berber tribes of the Kabylie mountains. To do this he waited patiently in Mecca where he befriended a party of Berber tribal chiefs from the Kabylie who were performing the pilgrimage. They were impressed by his gentle hospitality, his learning, piety and intelligent interest in North Africa. They pressed him to bring such learning to their homeland, and although Abu Abdullah initially pretended no interest, a year later, in 892, he was established in the Kabylie mountains as a respected teacher and preacher. His personal asceticsm and scrupulous respect for the law contrasted powerfully with the exploitation of the Aghlabid tax officials and frontier garrison. This was further highlighted by the Aghlabid emir, Ibrahim II's notorious massacre of the *jund* in the fortress of Balazma in 893.

Many of the tribal chiefs proved reluctant to surrender their authority to Abu Abdullah's Fatimid theocracy, however well he explained it. It was not until 902 that he established secure leadership of the Kabylie Berbers from his central base of Tazrut. In 904 Sitif, an old centre of power in Algeria, fell to the Berber-Fatimid legions who slowly tightened their grip over the Zab and Aurès Mountains. By 908 Fatimid armies had begun to advance into Tunisia and within a year were in possession of Reqqada, the barrack-palace of the Aghlabids. The last emir, Ziyadat Allah III (903–9), fled unmourned by his subjects, taking his treasure and his crimes with him to the security of the Abbasid court. Later that year Abu Abdullah marched west to seize control of Tahart, the Rustamid capital, before proceeding hundreds of miles south-west to seize Sigilmassa, heartland of the Beni Midrar. The latter had become especially important to Abu Abdullah for his master, Ubaydalla Said (who had secretly left Syria to take command in North Africa) had been held captive there for a decade. The winter of 909 saw a triumphal progress for Abu Abdullah as he escorted his revered master across the huge territory of Fatimid authority that stretched from southern Morocco to Libya. In January 910 Ubaydalla Said was installed in the palace of Reqqada where he announced that he was not only imam of the Fatimids, but the Mahdi (the righteous leader of Islam whose arrival indicates that the end of the world is at hand). His loyal lieutenant Abu Abdullah, who had worked all his life to hear the former announcement, was unenthusiastic about the latter claim. Within a year he and his family had been murdered on the instructions of Ubaydalla Said.

The Fatimid Empire of Ubaydalla Said, 910–34

The Kabylie Berbers rose up in revolt to protest at the callous reward meted out to Abu Abdullah. The revolt was soon repressed and the Berbers of the Kabylie Mountains continued to form one of the core elements of Fatimid military strength. The other great strength of the Fatimid state was its efficiency, which allowed it to impose and enforce a whole catalogue of new taxes with which to support its military ventures. New direct and indirect taxes were levied, customs and tolls collected on roads and bridges, at ports and markets, and not even the nomads and the Meccan-bound pilgrims escaped an assessment. The ruthless nature of Ubaydalla Said's rule was also revealed by his forcible imposition of Shiite forms of prayer and religious law on the reluctant population. The two Malikite scholars who were brave enough to protest were flogged to death publicly and their naked corpses dragged by mules through Kairouan, smearing the streets with their blood. The savage martyrdom of two such eminent scholars silenced public criticsm.

In 914 Ubaydalla Said felt strong enough to proceed with his principal ambition. A Fatimid army marched east, supported by the Sicilian fleet, and although it occupied Alexandria briefly, ultimately the expedition was chased out of Egypt. This military defeat checked his immediate ambitions, which were henceforth concentrated on building up Fatimid strength. In 915 the Fatimid capital moved from Kairouan to the new city of Mahdia on the Tunisian coast. The twin urban quarters of the new capital extended inland while the fortified residence of the Mahdi, entered either through the sea gate or the fortress-like land gateway, extended out along a rocky peninsula. Mahdia, part palace, part barracks, part religious sanctuary, all fortress, was the creation of a paranoid mind, only reluctantly attached to North Africa.

OMMAYAD-FATIMID RIVALRY

By 917 Ubaydalla Said was ready to direct his attention to the conquest of Morocco. A Fatimid army seized control of the emirate of Nukur, which controlled most of Morocco's Mediterranean coast, and assisted their local allies (the Miknassa) in establishing authority over Yahya IV (905–23), the last Idrissid ruler of Fez.

These actions were opposed vigorously by Abdul Rahman III (912–61), the Ommayad ruler of Spain. Before the year was out Abdul Rahman's fleet had restored the emir of Nukur to his strategically located realm, henceforth under the protection of the Ommayad state. Abdul Rahman also sought to counter the religious propaganda of the Fatimids by digging up his own family's neglected titles, such as *al-nasir li din allah* (defender of the religion of God). In Sigilmassa Ommayad agents supported the exiled Beni Midrar dynasty and fomented two rebellions against the Fatimid governors. Each time a Fatimid army restored order, but in the third rebellion of 977 an Ommayad client successfully re-established the emirate.

Ommayad agents were also successful in sponsoring a widespread revolt against Fatimid authority in Morocco in 931. The Miknassa, who dominated central Morocco from their newly established city of Meknes, and the Beni Ifran confederation, who dominated western Algeria from Tlemcen, became clients of the Ommayads. The loyalty of these new tribal allies was assured by the establishment of two Ommayad garrisons at the key Moroccan harbours of Melilla and Ceuta. These bridgeheads were the limits of Ommayad territorial ambition, for they were content to control other key cities, such as Tangier and Fez, through sympathetic tribal lords.

The Rif mountain tribes, recently united into the Beni Gannun Emirate by al-Qasim, an Idrissid prince, struggled hard to maintain their independence from either of the two powers. In 950 with Ommayad influence at its height, the Beni Gannun were forced to acknowledge the suzerainity of Cordoba. The Fatimid general Jawhar reversed the situation in the well-orchestrated campaign of 958–60, but once the Fatimids had moved to Egypt the Ommayads felt secure to strike back. General Ghalib's expedition of 973 once again re-established the Ommayad protectorate over northern Morocco. Buluggin, the first Zirid emir (972–84), knew the area well for he had led a Fatimid assault on Tlemcen just before he assumed power. In 979 he personally led an army that pushed the Ommayads back to Ceuta, although he failed to take that city by siege. This was to be the last round, for none of Buluggin's successors managed to penetrate west of the antagonistic confederacy of Berber tribes based at Tlemcen, in Algeria. Nor could the Ommayads afford an aggressive foreign policy, for the accession of the ten-year-old Hisham II (976–1009) marked the beginning of their gradual decay. Power was exercised by his vizier whose unpopular rule was only enforced by recruiting Berbers into the army. It was in this period that Spain received its major influx of Muslim Berber settlers, who were given the highland areas as all the fertile land had long since been appropriated by the Arabs. By 1002 the Arab ruling class had reasserted its power and established dozens of petty states, the so-called *Muluk Al Tawa'if* (the party kings) and in 1031 the last shadow of unity was removed when the Ommayad caliphate of Cordoba was abolished.

Despite the long rivalry between the Fatimid and Ommayad Empires, there had been recognizable limits to the conflict. It was a war by proxy fought out amongst allies, that never escalated into a set piece battle between rival armies. Neither side attempted to extend the antagonism beyond the strategic chess-board of Morocco and western Algeria. Even during Abu Yazid's insurrection Abdul Rahman III made no effective move against the Fatimids, although he did send the rebel leader a caftan of honour.

ABU YAZID, THE OLD MAN ON THE DONKEY

In the same period the Tunisian heartland of the Fatimid state was consumed by a much more intense struggle. Al Qaim (934–46) had allowed no let up in the fiscal exploitation and doctrinal tyranny established by Ubaydalla Said. He vigorously and successfully suppressed any opposition amongst his North African subjects, but like a suppressed volcano it exploded under the leadership of Abu Yazid.

Abu Yazid, or the old man on the donkey as he was known, was a historical figure who has also become a powerful symbol of popular resistance to the exploitation of governments. The image of the simple old Berber countryman armed with a cloak and a donkey opposing the exquisite perfumed figure of the caliph secure in his castle, surrounded by his elegant court and his formidable regiments, has become an enduring feature of folk tales. Abu Yazid was born south of the Sahara, around 880, within the compound of a family of Berber merchants. He was brought up on the trans-Saharan caravan routes but was educated by an Ibadi master in southern Tunisia, followed by a stint in the Ibadi schools at Sigilmassa. By this time he was ready to teach himself, in the Ibadi schools of the Rustamid capital of Tahart. After the Fatimid conquest of Tahart he settled in the Jerid, the region of fertile oases in Tunisia, where his standing amongst the population grew to such an extent that in 937 he was imprisoned by the Fatimid police. A group of supporters rescued him from prison in Kairouan, after which he took to the security of the Aurès Mountains of Algeria. Much to everyone's surprise, a Fatimid force sent to hunt him down in 943 was itself defeated by Abu Yazid's supporters. In 944 support for the saintly Ibadi preacher

Old man on the donkey

snowballed amongst the tax-oppressed Berbers. Within six months the whole edifice of Fatimid rule was in flames with Al Qaim hemmed in behind the walls of Mahdia. Even the Arab establishment offered its support to Abu Yazid, not their usual practice with Berber Ibadi preachers, so violent was their antagonism to the Shiite doctrines of the Fatimids.

However, the Fatimid fleet was left in undisputed control of the sea, which rendered Mahdia near impregnable. It was equipped with great storage cellars and its deep wells (although so near to the sea) drew sweet water by directly tapping aquifers. Supplied with fresh produce from Sicily, conditions in the besieged city were always much better than in the massive, but disordered camp of the besiegers that stretched as far as the eye could see beyond the walls. In folk tales the caliph is portrayed feeding his pet fish in mirrored halls while his astrologers carefully calculate the end of this malign period of misfortune. The failure to capture Mahdia broke the fragile unity of Abu Yazid's coalition of supporters. The important coastal cities of Tunis and Sousse were the first to rebel and Abu Yazid was soon forced to abandon the siege of Mahdia. In 946 the accession of a young Fatimid imam, Ismail al-Mansur, completed the rotation of the wheel of fortune. Abu Yazid's depleted army was defeated outside Kairouan and he was forced back into the mountains. In the summer of the next year the 70-year-old was finally captured by the Fatimids. He died in prison soon afterwards.

The Zirid Dynasty, 972–1051

By the reign of al-Muizz (953–75) the Fatimids had recovered their resources sufficiently to contemplate renewed adventures. In 958 General Jawhar led the long-delayed Fatimid counter-attack on the Ommayad protectorate that had been established over much of Morocco and western Algeria. In 968 political chaos in Egypt presented the Fatimids with a long-awaited opportunity to return to the Middle East. General Jawhar was sent east and by July 969 had seized control of Egypt for his master, who ordered the foundation of Cairo. In four years the new capital was ready for occupation and the triumphant Fatimid court sailed east, never to return to Mahdia.

For the appointment of a governor to rule North Africa in his stead, al-Muizz continued the long-established Fatimid policy of favouring the Berber tribes of the Kabylie Mountains, who had always provided the core of their military support. They alone had remained loyal to the Fatimids during the testing years of Abu Yazid's rebellion. Ziri ibn Manad who had ruled central Algeria for the Fatimids from the Kabylie town of Ashir, would have been al-Muizz's first choice, but he had died in 971. The mantle fell to his son Buluggin ibn Ziri who had already proved himself a capable general in the Fatimid invasion of western Algeria in 970.

Buluggin's capable administration soon established the Berber Zirid family as the ruling dynasty of North Africa. His position was inherited by al-Mansur (984–96) who ruled a cohesive state that stretched across Tunisia, central Algeria and the Tripolitanian coast. His authority in western Algeria and central Morocco was only respected when enforced by a Zirid army. The capital returned to Kairouan, or more properly

A detail from the Fatimid-built Great Mosque minaret at Sfax

to the walled palace of Sabra Al-Mansuriya, which stood beyond the city walls.

The accession of Badis (996–1016) was marked by a splintering of authority, for shortly after his accession he was persuaded to appoint his uncle Hammad governor of the old Zirid family fief. By the end of Badis' reign Hammad was openly ruling eastern Algeria as a separate state from his new capital of Qalat Beni Hammad, near Msila. There was never an out-and-out war, but the Beni Hammad constantly put the resolve of their Zirid cousins to test in a series of border clashes.

It was during the reign of al-Muizz, the fourth Zirid emir (1016–62), that the last ties with the Fatimid caliphs in Cairo were broken. The reign began with bloodshed as anti-Shiite riots swept through the cities and towns of Tunisia, resulting in 20,000 deaths. Finally the North Africans achieved their long-delayed revenge for the Fatimid persecution of the Malikite *ulema*. The riots struck the death knell to the spiritual authority of Shiifism in North Africa, and also to the very survival of the Shiite minority formed during a century of Fatimid authority. The popular standing of the great Malikite scholars of the day was immense. Ibn Zayd who had created the *Risala*, a handy synopsis of Malikite law for the use of the *qadi*, was the hero of Kairouan. His brother in flesh, as well as religion, Muhriz ibn Khalaf, heroically defended orthodox Islam in Tunis and was later revered as the city's patron saint. Short of appealing for the assistance of a new Fatimid army, accompanied no doubt by a new governor, there was no way that al-Muizz could reverse this tide of popular opinion. Indeed by the end of his reign he had decided to swim with the flow, and between 1041 and 1055 he gently broke the last religious and political connections with the Fatimids. The Fatimid caliphs were not concerned enough to send an army, but they did take the opportunity of ridding themselves of a hydra-like nuisance.

The Hilalian Invasion

Fatimid authority in Egypt was being threatened by the growth of an anarchic community of Arab nomads that was effectively beyond the control of government judges, tax officials and the police. This community had grown from Arab bedouin clans who had casually migrated into the Egyptian desert after the first Muslim conquest. Their numbers had grown, swollen both by migration from other desert tribes and by peasants escaping their burden of debt and continual servitude, until they numbered a quarter of a million. They were so proudly Arab that they took Islam as their birthright, but often revealed a very tentative grasp of its principles. Clan loyalty rather than the community of believers remained the unshaken basis of their existence. Living on the fringe of the settled community, they had recently become aware of their numbers and their power and had grown ever more assertive. Not even the caliph dared test the loyalty of his army against the 50,000 young warriors that the clan chiefs could lead into battle. Instead of risking conflict Caliph al-Mustansir (1036–94), working on the advice of his worried Egyptian ministers, decided to flatter this pest. In a series of graceful audiences he inflated the pride of the clan chiefs by requesting their assistance in quelling the rebellion of the Zirid emirs and fed their ambition by officially allocating them the administration of various different provinces.

The ruse worked. In 1051 the great nomad presence migrated west. This vast confederation was known as the Beni Hilal (the children of the Moon). Although Cyrenaica was officially part of Fatimid Egypt and in no state of revolt it was the first area to be settled, by a faction of the Beni Hilal thereafter known as the Beni Sulyam. The Beni Hilal continued westwards, brushing their way through the Zirid army at the battle of Haydaran (near Gabes) in 1052. They proved themselves to be most unusual conquerors, for they were not interested in possessing towns or cities, but instead took possession of the grazing grounds of the southern steppe.

The Zirid emir, safe behind the walls of Kairouan, searched in vain for some paramount chief with whom he could negotiate. Between 1053 and 1057 he tried to recruit some of the Arab clans into his army, and to co-opt clan chiefs into his dynasty by marrying them to his daughters, but all in vain. There was literally no one in command of the migration of the Beni Hilal in a way that the emir could understand. The clans all wished to be free of any subservient relationship with a government or with each other. They had land, held with the dignity of an official grant from the caliph, and they wished for nothing more than to be left to enjoy their own particular form of clan-feuding freedom.

By 1057, with his authority visibly disintegrating around him, the emir left Kairouan for the coast and the well-defended citadel of Mahdia. Two decades later the process of westward migration brought the Beni Hilal to the gates of his cousin al-Nasir, the Hammad emir of eastern Algeria. In 1090 the Beni Hammad emir abandoned his inland capital and founded the new town of Bijaya on the site of an old Romano-Punic port.

LIFE IN THE INTERIOR

This move to the coast was a graphic statement of a new order. Tunisian and Algerian government would hereafter be restricted to the fertile farmland of the coasts, their capitals not in the steppe land but on the coast. The interior of the country (with one or two exceptions) passed out of their effective control. Government in the interior could only be enforced by the presence of the army. The Arab clan chiefs might be persuaded to accept the suzerainity and the judgements of a ruler, but they were impossible to tax. At a stroke the taxable basis of government was reduced by a half. The chroniclers bemoaned the almost complete destruction of urban life in the interior, the ruin of the great olive orchards and the end of the revenues that had enriched the landowning class, the royal courts and indirectly the literate urban scholars. However, the speed with which the traditional structures collapsed suggests that there was also a social revolution acting beside the Arab migration. A century of high taxation, ruthlessly enforced by an alien Shiite minority, combined with the repression that followed the high hopes of Abu Yazid's rebellion, developed into a yawning gap between ruler and ruled.

For the bulk of the peasant population, the destruction of town-based government by the Arab migration must have been a welcome relief. The tax-oppressed, army-assaulted, revolution-churned villages could be abandoned for a nomadic pastoral life assisted by sporadic grain cultivation. Those settled, Berber-speaking villages and olive groves that did remain were gradually marginalized as the steppe and high plateaux became primarily dedicated to pastoralism. Familial clusters of black woven tents accompanied the annual movement of the flocks from the summer to the winter grazing grounds. Over the centuries a system of clientage, intermarriage, Koranic education and genealogical adoption of Berber communities into the lineages of the Beni Hilal clans slowly converted the steppe to Arabic speech. It was a long, uneven and largely unchronicled process, which left the Berber language untouched in the mountainous regions. In the nineteenth century much energy was devoted to examining tribal genealogies and labelling the Arabic-speaking nomad tribes of the steppe as either pure Arab, pure Berber or mixed Berber-Arab. No reliable conclusions can be drawn as to the ethnic contribution that the Hilalian invasion made to the bloodline of the contemporary Maghreb, although on a cultural and lingusitic level it was of enormous importance.

The Fatimids, undisturbed by the chaos they had unleashed in the Maghreb, continued to rule Egypt from the beautiful, elegant city of Cairo until the twelfth century, when their inability to deal with the Crusader state of Palestine finally led to their deposition by Saladin, a Kurdish prince. The lineage survived the fall from power although there have been further schisms, reformations and hidden periods. The Aga Khan (the leader of the worldwide Ismaili community) is a lineal descendant.

CHAPTER TWELVE

The Almoravids,
1042–1147

By the middle of the eleventh century the authority of the Zirid and Hammid emirs had been reduced to the cities of Mahdia and Bijaya. The Ommayads of Cordoba, who had exercised a long protectorate over Morocco, were no more. Muslim Spain was divided into thirty-two feuding principalities. North Africa had also reverted to a patchwork of local lordships, interspersed with the militant presence of nomadic Arab clan chiefs.

Under the circumstances, it was inevitable that another unifying force would impose itself from above, but this time it came from a new and unexpected direction. The Almoravids emerged from the Saharan desert to impose an Islamic-inspired unity upon the political anarchy. From their heartland in the western Sahara they carved out an empire that stretched over the modern states of Mauretania, Morocco, northern Mali, western Algeria and Spain. No one before or since has managed to secure such divergent latitudinal boundaries, from the foothills of the Pyrenees to the River Niger. Their astonishing achievement was partly due to the military capabilities of the desert tribes when united under a forceful Islamic leadership. More interestingly, however, it was also a reflection of the vital importance of the trans-Saharan trade.

The Integration of the Sahara into Islamic North Africa

The arid steppe land that precedes the actual Sahara desert had marked the outer limits of the territorial ambitions of Carthage, Rome and Byzantium, which were all agriculture-based empires. The desert

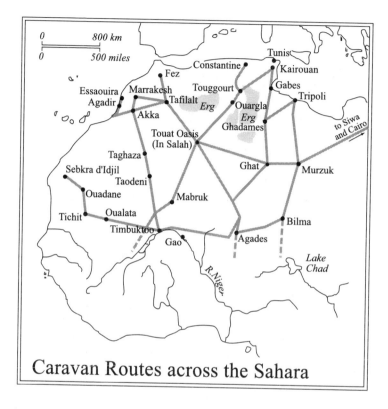

0   800 km
0   500 miles

Tunis
Constantine   Kairouan
Fez
Essaouira Marrakesh Touggourt   Gabes
Agadir   Tafilalt   Tripoli
Akka   *Erg*   Ouargla
                    Erg   to Siwa
Touat Oasis   Ghadames   and Cairo
(In Salah)
Taghaza
Sebkra d'Idjil   Ghat   Murzuk
Taodeni
Ouadane
Tichit   Oualata   Mabruk
Timbuktoo   Bilma
         Gao   Agades
                              *Lake
                              Chad*
R. Niger

Caravan Routes across the Sahara

defences established by these various states acted as a permeable frontier that controlled, but did not seek to prohibit, the movement of the nomads who provided labour for the harvest, whose flocks dunged the fields and who traded their excess livestock. Armed expeditions were occasionally dispatched south of this frontier zone to overawe the desert tribes, but there was never an attempt to annexe the desert region or seize control of the Saharan carrying trade from the indigenous communities. Indeed, many of the Roman frontier forts (such as Ghadames and Bu Njem) were sited beside the time-honoured market places of the Berbers, where the trans-Saharan caravans were broken up and the goods auctioned off to coastal traders. Although the exotic nature of the goods allowed for handsome individual profits, in the great scale of things it was of minor importance compared to the export of North African wheat and olive oil.

It was only during the Islamic period that the Sahara was linked comprehensively with the rest of the region. The speed of the Arab conquest of North Africa had been made possible because of the way the Arabs treated the desert as a highway rather than an obstacle. From the very first Arab incursion into the North African province of Cyrenaica in 643, they were also interested in controlling the Sahara. An Arab force under Oqba ben Nafi subdued the Fezzan and Zawila oases while his superior conquered the coast. It gave the Arab conquerors immediate control of the inland caravan routes, which had previously been controlled by independent tribal powers such as the Garamantes and Luwata. Similarly, the Arab advance west into Morocco avoided the traditional path of conquering armies (along the fortress-strewn Mediterranean coast) and cut across the semi-desert west of the oasis of Biskra. These inland routes were put to immediate use by merchants, messengers, military reinforcements and Mecca-bound pilgrims, for they were less dangerous than maritime travel.

In Cyrenaica the string of famous classical coastal cities was soon abandoned as they were vulnerable to attack from the Byzantine navy. So while Ptolemais and Apollonia slowly declined into picturesque ruin new Islamic urban centres, such as Ajdabiya, Msus and Mekilli, emerged along the caravan trails that were established south of the agricultural zone. The Arab conquest caused a progressive geographical shift to the south throughout the region, as camel replaced boat, oasis caravanserai supplanted coastal ports, and steppe land acquired a new importance as the breeding ground for camels and horses. All the new Islamic cities founded in North Africa (Kairouan, Tahart, Tlemcen, Fez, Meknes and Sigilmassa) reflect this dramatic shift from the coast to the interior.

The exploitation of the desert fringe paid an unexpected and immediate dividend when a number of silver mines were found, particularly in southern Morocco. The silver, eventually traded with the Aghlabid emirs at Kairouan and from there to the Middle East, was of significant quantity. Recent metallic analysis has hinted that perhaps a third of all early Islamic silver coinage originated here.

The Gold Trade of the Western Sahara

Camels had been an essential part of the North African landscape for
centuries, but it was not until around the fourth century that effectively
they had become acclimatized to the western Sahara. The local breeding
of camels, backed up by the importation of better varieties of date palm,
made the commercial crossing of the western Sahara a possible, if still
hazardous, enterprise. The caravan crossing was as meticulously
organized as a military campaign. Thousands of camels would be
assembled in adjoining communities (so as not to exhaust the
grazing) and fattened up, while great quantities of dates and barley
were packed and goatskins filled with sweet water. A consortium of
the chief merchants would appoint a caravan commander, whose most
important task was to plan the route and negotiate with the veiled
desert tribes for the caravan to be guided, guarded and replenished
throughout their territory. These negotiations required intimate

Mausoleum Dehmani, Kairouan

knowledge of the varying influence of the desert tribes, their component clans and families. Crossing the desert took about two months, ideally divided between three marching sessions of ten days interspersed with two fifteen-day rest periods when the camels could be watered and grazed.

There were two major routes to the famous trading towns of Timbuktoo and Gao on the Niger river bend. The central route stopped at the Touat oasis, while the westerly, more arduous and exclusively Moroccan route passed through Taghaza and Taodeni. In addition there was the old 'Garamantian crossing' (favoured by Tunisan and Libyan merchants), which led south from Ghadames and Ghat towards Lake Chad. Berber traders carried metal weapons, silver beads, copper and woollen cloth to West Africa where they traded it for black slaves, ivory, rare woods, scents, ostrich feathers, kola nuts and hides.

The most lucrative trade, however, was the exchange of salt for gold. Fortunately for the Berber traders, there was no West African source of salt, while the rest of the world craved gold. Salt could be aquired *en route* across the desert at two isolated hell-holes in the centre of the Sahara, the salt mines of Taodeni and Bilma, worked by a population of marooned slaves. The source of gold remained a closely guarded secret for centuries, although it is now thought to have been the equatorial marshland of Bambuk at the confluence of the Senegal and Faleme rivers. The Berber merchants of the Saharan caravans only knew that their West African counterparts acquired the gold dust from up-country traders who toured scattered communities of subterranean miners. These reclusive miners used feathers to pan the worked earth for the particles of gold, which were then packed into quills. The supply of West African gold sustained the rulers of North Africa for almost 1,000 years. Fortified mints were established on the northern extremities of the great caravan routes where the gold dust was assessed, smelted and struck into coin.

Berber Merchants and the Kingdom of Ghana

These trans-Saharan trade routes were the conduits through which Islam arrived in West Africa. In direct contrast to North Africa, this was a peaceful and slow process which worked through the existing political structure.

Sometime before the fourth century the kingdom of Ghana was established at the steppe capital of Kumbi (the burial ground) Saleh. By the eighth century the negro Soninke dynasty ruled Ghana with similar rival kingdoms in the west (Takrur) and east (Kawkaw). They were extensive states, governed by sacred kings who ruled through an elaborate layer of courtiers and governors. The Arabs at the time of the conquest of North Africa already knew that Ghana was the source of the gold that they seized during their conquest of the Berbers, but we have no evidence that they crossed the Sahara in force. After the Berber revolt of 739, control of the three major trans-Saharan trade routes was secured by the Berber Ibadite states centred on Sigilmassa, Tahart and the Tripolitanian hinterland. The Ibadi merchants were the acknowledged masters of the trans-Saharan trade throughout the eighth and ninth centuries. Their strategic control of the gold market and the caravans of black slaves did much to establish their legitimacy in the eyes of their orthodox Islamic neighbours. This pattern was disturbed when the Fatamids seized control of Tahart and Sigilmassa in 909. Many Ibadi merchants migrated south to escape the rule of the hated Shiite governors and to keep control of their lucrative trade. For instance Imam Yaqub, the last Rustamid ruler of Tahart, found safe refuge in the Saharan oasis of Ouargla (central southern Algeria). He proved a rallying point for his community, and a century later in 1053, a successor established a purely Ibadi community in the neighbouring Mzab valley at the newly-built town of Ghardaia. The strong religious ethos of the Mzab community is still felt by travellers passing through this oasis in the Algerian Sahara.

The diaspora of the tenth century proved to be the great period of Ibadi merchant missionaries, who extended the faith deep into the furthest reaches of the Sahara. In Saharan market towns such as Tadmakkat and Awdaghust, which lay well north of the negro kingdoms of West Africa, there was a suprisingly cosmopolitan society, filled as they were with commercial agents, including representatives of the great Jewish trading families from Cairo, Kairouan, Cordoba and Fez.

Tribespeople in desert tents

In the same period the migration of Muslim adventurers had established distinct quarters in the capital cities of the West African kingdoms, such as Gao. The Muslims, due to their numerical and literate skills, were employed by the royal courts as secretaries and administrators. These faithful servants were soon invited by their religiously tolerant masters to construct mosques. Not a few managed to rise to ministerial positions. Over the tenth century a significant portion of the native West African ruling class adopted Islam, which was usually practised as an elegant addition, rather than an alternative, to the seasonal round of pagan festivals whose joyous rituals centred around beer-drinking, feasting, sacrifice, processions, music and dance.

RIVALS FOR THE TRADE
By the middle of the eleventh century a four-cornered struggle had developed between the Saharan trading towns, the West African kingdoms, the Berber tribes of the western Sahara and such North African oasis–cities as Sigilmassa. The first round was won by the kingdom of Ghana, which in 990 extended its authority north over both Awdaghust, the Saharan trading town, and Taodeni, the lucrative salt mine.

For a long time it was thought that the rise of the Almoravids was a

Berber backlash against this negro expansion. However, the situation was much more complex and intriguing. The Almoravids, after their initial conquest of the central Sahara in 1054, proceeded to ally themselves to the king of Ghana. Together they 'squeezed out' the various Berber middlemen, such as the Ibadi trading network, the Saharan trading towns and the Muslim merchants resident in Ghana. By 1070 the Almoravids had become, as it were, sole agents of the Ghanaian kingdom in both religion and trade. They imposed the Malikite law code of orthodox Islam on all Muslims, hounded out dissidents and established absolute control of the caravan traffic. The ruling Almoravid and Ghanaian élite intermarried. They may also have co-operated in waging holy war on the enemies of Ghana such as the Susu people, who as pagans could be legitimately, and profitably, enslaved.

Tribal Chief and Missionary: Yahya and Ibn Yasin, 1035–59

The oasis-city of Sigilmassa had been one of the keys to the trans-Saharan trade ever since its foundation in the eighth century. The turbulent politics of the tenth century, when Ommayad agents had backed a number of native Ibadi revolts against the Fatamid governors, had kept the city in continuous spiritual and religious turmoil. In 970 the two-power rivalry had been resolved with the establishment of an independent emirate, which controlled southern Morocco and allowed nothing to disrupt the caravan trade. The Berber tribesmen of the western Sahara (the ancestors of the bluemen so beloved by modern tourists) were a familiar and vital component in the expanding fortunes of the city of Sigilmassa. They were known collectively as *al-mulath-thamun* because of the distinctive male custom of wearing the litham, the mouth veil. They were composed of three important tribes: the Massufa, centred on the oasis of Taghaza, the Guddala of the Atlantic coast and the Lamtuna of the far south.

In 1035 Yahya, a wealthy and pious Guddala chief, performed the pilgrimage to Mecca. On the long journey he kept a look out for a promising young scholar, but failed to persuade any suitably qualified intellectual to give up his urban existence to teach in the desert. On his return journey he stopped off at Kairouan, the great centre of Maghrebi orthodoxy, where all intellectual attainments were taught in the shaded arcades of the great mosque. One of the great professors of the city advised Yahya to make contact with Wajaj, one of his most promising ex-pupils, who had returned to his Moroccan homeland. Yahya was very impressed by the religious centre in the Sous valley that Wajaj had established, staffed by students from Kairouan whose Arabic scholarship had not destroyed their attachment to their Berber homeland. This was just what Yahya had dreamed of creating in his own desert homeland, to set his people on the true path of the Prophet.

Ibn Yasin, one of Wajaj's keenest disciples, was dispatched south under the patronage of this desert lord. There was much work to be done, for the desert tribes still retained a number of their ancient customs, such as the habit of keeping nine wives. Ibn Yasin, loyally supported by his patron, established a public treasury to be filled by the tithe tax and imposed the full weight of the Malikite law code. This inevitably brought Ibn Yasin into conflict with the traditional clan chiefs, who sought to drive the meddling scholar away. But instead of meekly returning home to the Sous valley, Yasin looked to the example of the Prophet. Just as the Prophet had left Mecca for Medina, so Yasin migrated with his few supporters and established a *ribat* (a fortress of the faith) somewhere on the Atlantic shore of the western Sahara. His followers became known as *al-murabitun* (the men of the ribat), which was later corrupted into the familiar 'Almoravids' by the Spanish.

By 1042 this community, reinforced by zealous young men from all the desert clans, had become a force to be reckoned with in the politics of the western Sahara. Their scrupulous respect for the letter of Islamic law was combined with impressive military discipline. Against the straggling armies of their tribal opponents the Almoravids could field an army of closed ranks of infantry, backed up by a cavalry force held in reserve. In time-honoured desert tradition the camels were seated in a circle at the rear, to create a living wall behind which bagagge and non-combatants could shelter. In case of a reverse the army could fall back on this position, which no horse could be persuaded to charge, so great is their dislike of the camel.

The Almoravid Emergence, 1053–61

The great breakthrough in the fortunes of the Almoravids came with the conversion of the chief of the Lamtuna tribe. Ibn Yasin increasingly could concentrate his energies on the religious reformation of the desert tribes while the Lamtuna tribal leaders used their well-honed military and political skills in the prosecution of war. In 1053 the Almoravids struck north, seizing control of Sigilmassa and the next year took Awdaghust, so securing both ends of the trans-Saharan trade. Three years later their authority was tested by the revolt of Sigilmassa, which succeeded in massacring its Almoravid garrison. The Almoravids stormed the city a second time and then proceeded with the conquest of the oasis valleys of southern Morocco. By 1059 Abu Bekr, the military commander of the Almoravids, was sufficiently in control of southern Morocco to cross the High Atlas and assault the Berghouata confederacy of the Atlantic coast. Ibn Yasin died during the bitter fighting against this long-established Berber heresy, but within the year Abu Bekr had secured their outward submission. To secure these important new territorial gains Abu Bekr established a forward military base just north of two of the most important passes across the High Atlas mountain chain. A thorn-laced earth embankment marked out the tented encampment of the Almoravids centred around Ksar al-Hajar, the tower of stone. Thus was the city of Marrakech born.

In 1060 Abu Bekr moved south quickly to deal with a desert revolt led by the Guddala that threatened the core of their dominion, the control of the trans-Saharan trade. He appointed a trusted Lamtuna cousin, Youssef ibn Tachfine (1061–1106), as deputy and presented him with a wife, Zaynab, the daughter of a notable from Kairouan. Ibn Tachfine, the lean desert warrior, and the cultured Zaynab made a resourceful pair, as was demonstrated the next year when Abu Bekr returned north. He was welcomed with great honour and presented, so the popular tale goes, with a cascade of the most sumptuous gifts so that, in the words of Zaynab, 'he should not be short of anything in the desert'. Abu Bekr was being given more status, but less power. He was sage enough to accept this division of authority, which also made sound tactical sense. Abu Bekr could concentrate on the expansion of Almoravid influence in the south while Tachfine led the army in the north. Tachfine was courteous enough to continue making a great public show of recognizing his cousin as his senior until Abu Bekr's death.

THE CONQUESTS OF YOUSSEF IBN TACHFINE, 1061–1106

In 1061 the Almoravid army, under the command of Tachfine, marched north to conquer Morocco. Tachfine's policy was to befriend the towns and settled agricultural communities, but to be ruthless to all those who held power or contested his. His fiercest opponents were not walled cities or mountain peoples, but the tribal confederations of central Morocco and western Algeria. In 1069, when Tachfine finally seized control of Fez, he ordered the massacre of the garrison at the same time as pushing forward an ambitious scheme of civic improvements. The walls that had kept the Kairouan and Andalucian quarters apart were torn down, the principal mosques were rebuilt and the water system subjected to a complete overhaul. Hill springs were tapped to supply street fountains and public baths, while engineers diverted the riverbed to power watermills. The Almoravids, coming from the desert, cared passionately about the correct use of water. To control the city, Tachfine erected a citadel, which also served as the headquarters of a great army camp. This has long since disappeared, but the Almoravid defences that have survived in Morocco (atop Jebel Amergou in the Rifs and Jebel Zagora in the Draa valley) are impressive in both scale and detail.

From 1070 to 1082 Tachfine concentrated his efforts on a remorseless frontier war, which gradually extended Almoravid rule over the western half of Algeria. After 1082 he turned his attention to subduing northern Morocco, including the famously bellicose Rif tribes. Tachfine destroyed the last enclave of Kharijism on the Mediterranean coast and established a new city, confusingly named Fes-el-Bali, to civilize this wild mountain region.

Since 1082 the Muslim princes of Spain had been appealing to Tachfine for aid against the Christian king of Castile. There had been a long history of the Arab ruling class of Spain employing the Berbers to fight their wars. When Tachfine finally responded to their appeals, he came not as their mercenary servant nor as their ally, but as their master. In 1086 he landed on the Spanish shore and personally led the Almoravid army to victory against the Castilians at the battle of Zallaqa. Within a few months the Muslim princes were appealing to Castile for aid against the Almoravids. One by one they were removed, so that by the year 1110 all of Muslim Spain was administered by Almoravid governors. El-Mutamid, the poet prince of Seville, was exiled to southern Morocco where the view of the High Atlas mountains taunted him with cherished memories of Al-Andalus.

ALMORAVID GOVERNMENT

Tachfine's climactic victory at Zallaqa was followed the next year, in 1087, by the death of his cousin Abu Bekr. Tachfine had become one of the most powerful Muslim monarchs in the world, but was nothing if not devoutly orthodox. Respectfully he petitioned the symbolic head of the Islamic community, the Abbasid caliph at Baghdad, for titular recognition of his authority and was granted the title of *amir al-muslimin* (Prince of Muslims).

He was the very model of a Muslim ruler, whose vast power and disposable wealth never tempted him from his simple, almost ascetic tastes. He continued to wear the woollen garments of a desert herdsmen, woven for him by the women of his household, and kept to the habitual Saharan diet of fresh milk and barley cakes enlivened by feasts of camel meat. The success of the Almoravid movement was dependent to a large degree on his extraordinary physical health. Tachfine led the Almoravid army personally for 45 years, driven by a consistent and genuine passion to create a unitary Muslim community. On one level he was extraordinarily successful, for after Tachfine we hear no more about Shiite communities, the Berghouata heresy or Kharijite enclaves. North Africa (with the exception of a few Ibadi pockets) became remarkable within the world of Islam for its orthodox homogenity.

Although the Almoravid army was recruited exclusively from the desert tribes of the western Sahara and specifically from Tachfine's own Lamtuna tribe, Tachfine's military conquests were often greeted with popular support, as they swept away petty emirates, tribal chiefs and corrupt princely dynasties. The Almoravid governors who replaced them were bound to follow the precepts of orthodox Islam to the very letter. Taverns were closed, musical instruments destroyed, illegal taxes abolished and the booty of war fairly distributed. Salaried scholars, steeped in the Malikite school, were incorporated officially into every level of government. Even a *qadi*, a provincial judge, was forbidden to pass judgement unless he was assisted by four consultants trained in Islamic law. The most revered of these legal scholars (known individually as *faqih* or collectively as *fuqaha*) were appointed to a permanent council, the ultimate religious authority, which accompanied Tachfine wherever he went. It was consulted before any important decision of state although its authoritative advice was delivered to the ruler in the respectful terms of a *fatawa*, a legal opinion. It was a convincing attempt to create a purely Islamic state, and although it had flaws it was the model adhered to by most subsequent rulers of North Africa for the next 1,000 years.

The chief, but almost unavoidable, flaw of the Almoravid system was raising the letter above the spirit of law. It was the triumph of the lawyer over the thinker. This was particularly acute in the Malikite tradition, which did not encourage the use of analogies, or rational argument in reaching a judgment. The legal manuals of the Malikite scholars were held in such regard at school, court and government that at times they seemed to supersede the original sources of Koran and Hadith. The Islamic ideal became increasingly suffocated by a narrow, single-minded, conservative legalism completely inimical to new thought or the motivating spirit of religion. The universities' single ambition was to produce *fuqaha* for the next generation. There was no room for theology, philosophy or mysticsm, which were treated with outright hostility. The public burning of the works of al-Ghazzali, the intellectual hero of medieval Islam, in the centre of Marrakech provides shocking proof of the narrow-minded culture of the Almoravids. Two of the leading mystical Islamic thinkers of Andalucia, ibn al-Arif and ibn Barrajan, were arrested by the Almoravid authorities and died in custody before their opinions could even be heard.

TACHFINE'S HEIRS, 1106–45

In 1106 the great desert warrior was succeeded by his son Ali ben Youssef. The first decade of Ali's reign took the empire to its territorial apogee as the new emir of the Almoravids conquered Madrid and then Lisbon before capturing the Balearic islands in 1115. In 1125 the tide turned, and an Almoravid army was defeated by the Aragonese at the battle of Arnisol near Lucena. It was the first major defeat in a half century marked otherwise only by victory. Granada was selected as the new capital of Almoravid rule in Spain and the burden of war was reflected in the ever more exploitative taxation of its Jewish and Christian subjects. Suspicion as to the ultimate loyalties of these non-Islamic citizens led to a destructive cycle of repression and deportation.

The declining military situation in Spain, although it had no practical effect on North Africa, sounded the slow collapse of Almoravid authority. Ali took the precaution of defending his capital of Marrakech with a circuit of walls, establishing fortresses in the foothills of the High Atlas and recruiting a mercenary force of Christian cavalry. These were wise precaution, for the city was besieged in 1129, although its successful defence somewhat restored Ali's position. His successor Tachfine (1143–5) died at Oran, having tried to suppress a revolt in western Algeria.

The end of the Almoravid Empire came suddenly in 1147, with a simultaneous revolt in Spain and the second siege of Marrakech. Ishaq, the last emir, died defending the walls of his capital. The victors deliberately levelled all evidence of the old dynasty in Marrakech. One small domed washing room, the ablutions annexe to an Almoravid mosque, was buried in a protective layer of rubble. It was excavated in 1948 to great acclaim, one historian even declaring that 'the art of Islam has never exceeded the splendour of this extraordinary dome'. The calligraphic frieze round this sole survivor of Almoravid rule identifies its creator as Ali ben Youssef.

CHAPTER THIRTEEN

The Almohad Empire,
1147–1276

It is all too easy to confuse Almoravid with Almohad, for these two successive empires have much in common beside their first four letters. Both united the Maghreb for a century, starting off as a movement of Muslim reform. Both were founded by charismatic Berber scholars and were based on the military prowess of a core group of Berber tribes, and both used the southern Moroccan city of Marrakech as their capital.

With so much in common it is little wonder that they were such bitter enemies. The Almoravids were only supplanted by the Almohads after 20 years of warfare. They were also close neighbours. The Almohad headquarters in the High Atlas mountains was no more than a two-day ride from the Almoravid capital of Marrakech. On a clear day the two citadels were almost within view of one another.

However, there were differences between the two. The Almohad Empire extended right across the breadth of North Africa from southern Spain to Tripolitania. These frontiers, although they never incorporated the old Saharan domains of the Almoravids, are the closest historical expression of the dream of a united, Islamic North Africa. The Almohads also took the independence of the Maghreb to its zenith. Ibn Tumert (1125–30), the Almohad founder, refused to acknowledge any of the traditional Islamic authorities except the Prophet. His successors ackowledged no higher political authority and took the caliph's title for themselves. All later rulers of North Africa would be content, if not proud, to acknowledge their role within the wider Arabic community.

Mohammed Ibn Tumert

The founder of the Almohad movement was a Berber through and through, although his education took him to the forefront of the Islamic intellectual world. He was born in 1080 in Igilliz, an obscure mountain village in the Anti Atlas Mountains of southern Morocco. Educated locally, possibly in the very same Sous valley *ribat* where Ibn Yasin had first taught, he left his homeland at the age of 26 dissatisfied with the dry legal learning taught by the Malikite scholars and questing after a purer source of Islam. He travelled north to Cordoba, still one of the greatest Muslim cities, and from there travelled east to perform the pilgrimage at Mecca. He spent a further ten years as a disciple, sitting at the feet of revered teachers in Cairo and Baghdad, before he felt confident enough to return to the west in 1117.

He travelled slowly across the Maghreb as a recognized and revered man of religion. He lived in many of the major Maghrebi cities, preaching at Tunis, Bijaya and Constantine before arriving at the Almoravid capital of Marrakech in 1121. The ruling Almoravid emir, Ali ben Youssef (1106–42), was then at the height of his powers. None of his subjects doubted his personal piety or his role as the upholder of Islam, particularly while his armies remained victorious against the Christians in Spain.

Ibn Tumert seems to have deliberately set himself the task of undermining the religious foundations of Almoravid authority. He was astute enough to pick issues, such as the use of the litham (the male mouth veil) and the personal freedoms allowed to Saharan women, that struck at the proud traditions of the desert tribes. These could only be outlawed by the Almoravid emir at the risk of alienating his army. A conference assembled to decide if such practices were un-Islamic broke down into an angry dispute between ibn Tumert and the *fuqaha*, the Malikite scholars of the Almoravid establishment. Ibn Tumert claimed a moral victory, and continued his inflammatory preaching until the emir ordered his arrest. This decisive, public break with the Almoravid government may have been what ibn Tumert was seeking all along. Certainly he moved rapidly to avoid capture, travelling south to the safety of his

Woman from the Anti Atlas Mountains, Morocco

mountain homeland, where he was acclaimed by an influential tribal chief, Abu Hafs Umar.

POWER POLITICIAN OR PASSIONATE REFORMER?

Ibn Tumert's motivations have never be satisfactorily determined. His four-year journey across the Maghreb seems accidental, but his actions once in Marrakech seem to be part of a premeditated plan. The majority of historians, who have consistently stressed the rivalry between the three main Berber language groups of Morocco (the Sanhaja, Zenata and Masmuda), have stressed his role as a leader of the Masmuda. In their view, the clash between the Almoravids and Almohads is a reflection of the traditional rivalry between the nomadic Sanhaja of the desert and the sedentary Masmuda of the Atlas Mountains.

An alternative view sees ibn Tumert as a passionate man determined to destroy the pedantic authoritarian legalism of the Almoravid *fuqaha* which stood in the way of true religion. The persecution of celebrated Sufi thinkers and the public burning of the revered works of the Persian professor of religious law, al-Ghazzali would certainly have damned the Almoravids in the eyes of such a man. It was also true that there was no possibility of debate with the *fuqaha*.

The actual substance of his religious disagreement with the *fuqaha* is eminently reasonable. Ibn Tumert condemned their habit of treating the Malikite law code as some parallel revelation, and recommended that they keep to the original sources, the Koran and the Hadith. He was particularly incensed by the *fuqaha's* literal misreading of the Koran, which had led them to give human attributes to the one God. Ibn Tumert rightly stressed that the indivisibility and unrepresentable form of God were completely central to Islam. This passionately held belief led to his supporters being known as *al-muwahhidun* (the unitarians), which was later corrupted by the Spanish into the familiar 'Almohads'.

THE MAHDI IN THE MOUNTAINS, 1121–30

Whatever road ibn Tumert had taken to reach a state of armed rebellion, he proved himself totally committed once he had arrived there. Abu Hafs Umar, the Berber lord of the Anti Atlas Mountains, assured him devoted support in his homeland. His religious stature grew rapidly until he was recognized as the Mahdi, a Messianic figure who will establish an Islamic Empire just before the end of the world.

In 1125, the year when the Almoravid regime was shaken by military defeat in Spain, he felt it propitious to establish a new centre of operations at Tinmal. The new base occupied a well-watered, but secluded mountain valley, which also controlled access to one of the most important passes across the High Atlas Mountains. Here he established the core of his new Islamic state, ruling through the existing structure of the indigenous mountain chiefs. In the time-honoured example of the Prophet Mohammed, ibn Tumert's authority was based on his position as chief arbitrator, moral guide and religious instructor of the community. The traditional law codes were rejected in favour of direct reliance on the injunctions contained in the Koran and Hadith. He was assisted by an inner council of ten disciples who, with a further

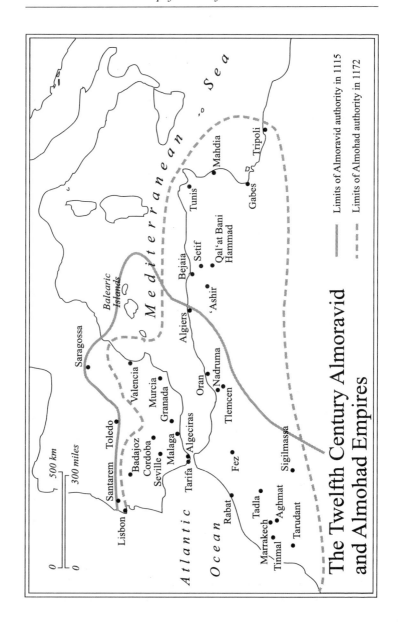

The Twelfth Century Almoravid and Almohad Empires

Limits of Almoravid authority in 1115

Limits of Almohad authority in 1172

40 representatives, made up the great assembly of the Almohads. Right from the start this community was designed to function as an army, constantly increasing its authority and defending itself from attack.

The better to destroy this guerilla base, the Almoravids established a forward base at the fortress of El Halal, a 150-acre natural plateau, which they embellished with a curtain wall and fortified gates. Its silhouette still dominates the High Atlas foothills. In 1129 the Almoravids mounted their big push. Three separate military columns advanced into the High Atlas Mountains in order to trap and destroy the Almohads at Tinmal. They were all repulsed and the Almohads, exultant at this triple victory, swept down from the hills to besiege Marrakech. For 40 days they attacked the city, before being caught off guard by the Almoravid cavalry.

Abdel Moumen's War against the Almoravids, 1130–47

Later that year, in August 1130, ibn Tumert died. It could not have occurred at a worse moment, so his ten disciples kept his death a secret for three years in order to safeguard their endangered community. Abdel Moumen (1130–63), his oldest and most loyal disciple, was chosen to be ibn Tumert's 'spokesman' and was in due course confirmed as his successor. No one doubted Abdel Moumen's commitment, for he had been a devoted follower of ibn Tumert since they had first met on a dusty track outside the village of Millal in eastern Algeria in 1118.

Abdel Moumen was determined never to risk another battle in the plains against a superior force of Almoravid cavalry. His strategy called for the piecemeal conquest of the mountain regions. By 1139 his control of the Anti, High and Middle Atlas Mountains was complete, and he felt confident of engaging the Almoravids directly. A series of grim battles was fought for control of the plains of western Algeria, which culminated in a decisive victory outside Tlemcen in 1144. The Almoravid emir, Tachfine ben Ali, was forced back into the port of Oran, but before he could be reinforced by his fleet, the Almohads stormed the city walls. Rather than face the ignominy of captivity, the emir rode his horse at a gallop over the cliff face.

The Almoravids did not know how to surrender. Their garrison at

Fez bravely resisted for nine months and the city only fell after Abdel Moumen constructed a dam upstream which, when released, swept a great hole through the walls. In 1147 Ishaq (the younger brother of Tachfine ben Ali) prepared to defend Marrakech against a second Almohad siege. The city resisted for 11 months and was only finally taken when the Christian mercenaries defending the Bab Rhemat gateway betrayed their charge and let in the Almohads. The slaughter was not confined to the mortal population, for the victorious Almohads also levelled the palaces and even the mosques of the Almoravids. Abdel Moumen ordered the construction of the Koutoubia Mosque over the ruins of the Almoravid palace. The first mosque was torn down soon after its completion, either because it had been built too hurriedly on insecure foundations, or because it was found to be incorrectly orientated towards Mecca. In Marrakech it is widely believed to be haunted.

THE ALMOHAD EMPIRE UNDER ABDEL MOUMEN, 1147–62

After the fall of Marrakech Abdel Moumen was in a position to dispatch an Almohad army across the straits of Gibraltar to Spain. Muslim Spain, which had been in revolt since 1144, had once again subdivided into a patchwork of principalities. Abdel Moumen preferred to leave this hornet's nest well alone, and was content for his army to occupy only the corner that controlled the crossing to North Africa.

Most of the Almohad expeditionary force was soon recalled so that Abdel Moumen could consolidate his authority methodically over all the regions of Morocco. In 1151 he led the Almohad army east, seizing Algiers and Bijaya and so destroying the last enclaves of the Beni Hammad emirs. The Arab nomads of the Hilalian migration, who had now been settled on the North African steppe for a century, felt threatened by the Almohads. Over the next year messengers journeyed quietly between the encampments of the various Arab clans plotting insurrection. In the spring of 1153 the Arab warriors secretly assembled in southern Algeria to advance north on the Almohad position. The two armies met in battle that April, and Abdel Moumen's disciplined formations decisively routed the Arab cavalry. Abdel Moumen dealt with the Arabs as if they were a permanent part of Maghrebi political life. He recruited some into his army, confirmed others in possession of their land while ordering other tribes to move further west and south. This latter migration was directed specifically at his two remaining enemies, the Berber tribes of the western Sahara (the unconquered core of the Almoravid Empire) and the tribes on the Atlantic coast of Morocco who had persisted in resisting Almohad authority.

At about this time Abdel Moumen began to concentrate his thoughts on his succession. Against the spirit of the movement, he was looking for a way to establish his son Mohammed (an unworthy centre for his affections) as the future ruler of the Almohads. Gradually Abdel Moumen appointed his other sons and loyal supporters to the principal commands, so that when he made the actual announcement, in 1154, he was ready for the inevitable reaction. Two of ibn Tumert's surviving brothers led the revolt against Abdel Moumen's betrayal of the theocratic intentions of the Almohads. But the loyalty of the Almohad army, after 25 years of victories, was no longer in question. They stood firmly behind their commander and crushed the revolt, which centred on Fez and Marrakech. Abdel Moumen used this opportunity for a purge of his enemies.

At the same time he sought to deflect criticsm by strengthening the personality cult that surrounded ibn Tumert, and ordered the construction of a great sanctuary mosque at Tinmal. The privileged position of the six original Almohad tribes (all from the Anti Atlas and High Atlas Mountains) who formed the core of the Almohad army was confirmed. Abdel Moumen also made certain that the 50-man grand assembly was continuously consulted and honoured. The only addition to the power structure was the co-option of Abdel Moumen's Kumya tribe, from the Tlemcen region, into the Almohad ruling élite.

The most promising offspring of the Almohad leadership were prepared for their future high status in the empire at a college attached to the household of Abdel Moumen. They were trained in the arts of war as well as administration, and were also expected to memorize the works of ibn Tumert alongside the Koran. Abdel Moumen made certain that the other disciples of ibn Tumert, who arguably had an equal claim to authority, should share in the rewards of the empire. Early supporters such as Abu Hafs Umar continued to enjoy positions of responsibility and great honour.

The religious members of the original Almohad community also held a privileged position within the new regime. They were given the title 'Almohad scholar', awarded a salary and appointed as legal advisers to the various imperial governors. As there were not enough Almohad scholars to go around, lesser officials known as 'town scholars' were also employed. In theory the new Islamic state had banished the despised lawcodes that stood between the believer and the Prophet's relevation, but this did not always work in practice. Many of the traditions and practical details derived from the Malikite lawcode remained in force, although officially unacknowledged.

By 1159, Abdel Moumen felt secure enough to continue with the conquest of the Maghreb. He marched east at the head of a 200,000-strong army supported by a strong navy. It proved to be more a triumphal procession than a military conquest and within a year Tunisia and Tripolitania had been incorporated fully into the empire. He set up the local capital in the bustling city of Tunis, where it has remained ever since.

Only then did this most methodical of strategists switch his attention to the various independent principalities of Muslim Spain. Another vast army was patiently assembled within the walls of Rabat, supplies were gathered and the Almohad fleet was summoned to its harbour. Abdel Moumen's next move was presumed to be southern Spain. Anxious Christian kings dispatched ambassador after ambassador in order to find out the destination of this great invasion force. Luckily for them, it was fated never to sail, for in 1163 Abdel Moumen died.

Between Nomads and Normans: Zirid Tunisia, 1057–1159

The Almoravids and Almohads deservedly monopolize attention during the eleventh and twelfth centuries. Until Abdel Moumen's triumphal procession through Tunisia and Tripolitania in 1159, however, a very different fate had befallen the eastern Maghreb.

The migration of the Arab nomads had destroyed the Kairouan-centred authority of the Zirid emirs by 1057. They moved to the coast, and although their authority was often effectively restricted to the walls of Mahdia, they managed to survive and prosper in a reduced way. They concentrated all foreign trade through the city and managed to maintain a small but useful navy. Now and then they were invited to arbitrate some intractable tribal dispute, but otherwise their control over the countryside was negligible. To the outside world the Zirid emirs presented a more convincing face of authority, and they continued to be approached by ambassadors and foreign merchants. This concentration of all political and economic activity within the bounds of one city was reflected in Mahdia's alternative name during this period, which was Ifriqiya.

The market towns, oasis settlements and coastal farmland that had survived the spread of nomadism soon settled down to a modest mode of existence. These communities usually survived as clients of a powerful nomad clan, and although this relationship was often based on a reasonable exchange of skills and products it could also degenerate into a predatory form of feudalism. For instance the city of Tunis, which had become a client of the Riyah tribe in the late eleventh century, realized that it would be destroyed if it continued to meet the extortionate demands of its 'protectors'. The leading citizens sent a desperate appeal to the Beni Hammad emir at Bijaya, but he was in no better position to offer practical help than his Zirid cousin in Mahdia. However, he did send one of his sons, Abdelhaq ibn Khorassan, to investigate the situation.

Abdelhaq plunged into the problem, organized a militia and repaired the walls so that Tunis, under his leadership, was soon able to defy the Riyah on her own. Abdelhaq next turned his enquiring mind to the development of new manufactories and the creation of an export trade. Under the stewardship of his two heirs the prosperity of this city state continued. The Khorassan emirs of Tunis, as they were known, were an example to their age, living openly amongst their fellow citizens in a palace, not a walled fortress. The Khorassan Mosque and mausoleum, close to their palace, Dar Hussein (now a branch of the National Library), also bear testament to their confident, but disciplined taste in architecture.

The Norman-Sicilian Invasion of Tunisia, 1120–60

In 1035 a civil war between rival emirs of Palermo first allowed a Christian army, made up of Italians and Norman knights, the opportunity to invade Muslim Sicily. Prince Abdullah, son of the ruling Zirid emir of Kairouan, led 6,000 Berber warriors to repel this unwanted intervention but he was defeated in 1040 at the battle of Troina. In another symbolic encounter the same year, the emir of Syracuse was unhorsed in single combat by William Hauteville, who was henceforth known as 'Iron Arm'.

It was William's half-brother, Roger (1072–1101), who was destined to become the first Norman count of Sicily. But for the crippling effect of the Beni Hilal migration on North Africa from 1051, it is very doubtful if Roger, or any other intrepid Norman adventurer, could have achieved this, and it is revealing that Sicily was only effectively conquered between 1061 and 1092. The comparative ease of Roger's conquest was largely due to his regard for his Saracen subjects, who continued to hold their property and their faith, share in the government of the island and even serve in his army. His rule was a rare and gloriously successful example of tolerance and cultural diversity. Roger I had no interest in quixotic crusades. He made a firm and lasting peace with Temim, the Zirid emir, and refused to join the swashbuckling Italian expedition launched against Mahdia in 1087.

Roger II (1102–54) continued his father's wise policy of tolerance. He was celebrated for his encouragement of Muslim scholarship and for the translations he commissioned for his trilingual court where Arabic, Latin and Greek were all spoken. One of his greatest examples of patronage is the so-called 'Book of Roger', the *Nuzhat al-Mushtaq*, or 'Description of Africa' by al-Idrisi, which remains a prime source for twelfth-century North Africa. Roger II harboured a strategic rather than an academic motive in this scholarly commission, for by 1120 he had begun to plan the conquest of the North African coast. His first venture, a raid on Gabes, was an abysmal failure, but he was a patient man who looked to the long term. In 1121 the accession of Hassan, a 12-year-old, to the Zirid throne, seemed to present the perfect opportunity. In 1123 a Sicilian invasion fleet left Palermo for Mahdia, but Hassan, proclaiming a *jihad* against the Christians, was able to rally the inland tribes to his defence. The Sicilian army was driven back into its ships and the fortress they had garrisoned, isolated by the Zirid fleet, soon fell.

Roger II was disheartened but not discouraged. Over the next decade a series of hit-and-run raids depleted the coastal population of Tunisia and wore down the resistance of the towns. In 1135 he finally secured his first permanent foothold, the Tunisian island of Jerba and thereafter in quick succession he established garrisons in Tunis, Tripoli, Gabes, Sfax and Bone before seizing control of Mahdia in 1154. The fall of Mahdia effectively established the Normans of Sicily as rulers of the North African coast from Tripoli to Cap Bon.

It is tempting to speculate on the possible growth of a twelfth-century kingdom that bestrode the straits of Sicily as deftly as it did the barriers of religion. A multi-cultural state united by trade and prosperity, glorying in diversity and yet developing a fusion of Norman, Byzantine and Islamic culture might have had a profound influence on the history of the Mediterranean. Yet the whole elaborate edifice of the Sicilian-Norman conquest of the North African coast had been achieved in a political vacuum. It toppled like a pack of cards when the Almohad army and navy advanced upon Tunisia in 1159. In January 1160 the last Norman garrison in North Africa evacuated the fortified peninsula of Mahdia peacefully in exchange for safe conduct to Sicily, probably taking with them the last remnants of the Christian population of North Africa.

Abu Yaqub Yusuf

Mohammed, the chosen heir of Abdel Moumen, presided over his father's vast army for just 40 days. The 50-strong assembly of the Almohads judged him unfit to be caliph and elected his younger brother, Abu Yaqub Yusuf (1163–84), in his place. His reign was, in the words of the chroniclers, 'that of a true King'. Abu Yaqub Yusuf was the Saladin of the West, famed for the sureness of his word, his generosity, his singleness of purpose, intelligence and statesmanship.

The Great Mosque at Tlemcen

Although his personal energy was largely to be consumed by frontier wars and the suppression of rebellions, he presided over a rare period of peace. He organized a fair system of taxation, which produced abundant revenues to be spent on public works, the defence of the Almohad Empire, the patronage of scholars and the encouragement of religion. It was his personal interest and protection that encouraged the work of two of Islam's greatest scholars, Abu Bakr (1107–85) and ibn Rushd (1126–98), who are better known in Europe as Abubacer and Averroës. Ibn Rushd's work in translating and producing a detailed commentary on the philosophy of Aristotle is acknowledged to be one of the starting blocks of the Renaissance. It was dangerous intellectual territory, for the orthodox Muslim establishment distrusted philosophy as unwarranted speculation. Muslim intellectuals countered this hostility by arguing that it was just another way of arriving at the same truth that had been revealed by the Koran.

After his succession, Abu Yaqub Yusuf discharged the vast tribal levies assembled by his father and reduced the army to its Almohad core. He then moved to suppress the Rif tribes of northern Morocco, who had as usual used the uncertainty to revolt. It was a long campaign, but by 1166 Abu Yaqub Yusuf had finally crushed the Ghomara tribe who were at the heart of the rebellion. Although Marrakech was the capital of the Almohad Empire, the reality of government required an almost continuous cycle of administrative processions and military campaigns. The ruler was as likely to be found at Seville, Granada, Tlemcen, Tunis, Fez, Rabat or Taza, all of which were embellished with grand mosques and walled enclosures suitable for a tented army. In 1171 Abu Yaqub Yusuf at last found himself free to lead an army across the straits into Spain. Even the cynical Andalucian warlords were impressed by his conduct of the war, which was directed at relieving the beleaguered Muslims on the poor northern and western frontiers rather than annexing the rich provinces of the south-east. Gradually they rallied to his service and by 1172 most of Muslim Spain was incorporated within the boundaries of the Almohad Empire. In 1183 Abu Yaqub Yusuf was called back to the troubled Spanish frontier by a joint Castilian-Portugese offensive. He died the following year from wounds received while leading an assault on the castle of Santarem.

Yaqub al-Mansour, Prince of Architects

He was succeeded by his son, Yaqub al-Mansour (1184–99), who also spent much of his reign defending the boundaries of the empire. His victory against the Christians at Alarcos in 1195 won him the proud title *al-mansour* (the victorious) and stabilized the Spanish frontier, but the political situation in Tunisia kept him busy enough. A year after his succession the Arab tribes of the steppe rose in revolt, led by an Almoravid prince from the Beni Ghaniya dynasty, which continued to rule the Balearic islands. Although he was able to reimpose authority in the centre of Tunisia, Yaqub al-Mansour never managed to destroy the rebel army, which used the Tunisian desert as a safe refuge.

Yaqub al-Mansour's chief renown rests not so much on these military campaigns as on the glorious flowering of Almohad architecture that occurred during his reign. The Oudaia gate and El-Hassan mosque in Rabat, the Koutoubia, the Kasbah Mosque and the Ageunaou gate in Marrakech and the Giralda minaret in Seville argue eloquently for his inclusion in a list of the world's most exalted builders. Anyone who has stared up at the unfinished summit of the El Hassan minaret (work on which stopped on the day of Yaqub al-Mansour's death) instinctively realizes the intimate connection between the caliph and his buildings. The genius of Almohad architecture lies in its bold, massive forms, enlivened by restrained, yet intricate and delicate, decorative detail.

It is easy to imagine that Yaqub al-Mansour, who had achieved so much in ordered stone, also attempted to impose the same order on human society. Yet here he was not so successful. The first books to be burnt publicly in his struggle to resolve the contradictions of the Almohad faith were those of his father's philosopher friends. So died, after a gloriously brief period, official support for rational Islamic philosophy. Next he burned the lawbooks of the Malikite legal tradition without legitimizing any of the other three traditions, the Hanafi, Hanbali or the Shafii schools. Instead he commissioned a new synthesis, which although an admirable idea in itself, effectively handed back religious interpretation to the legal scholars. Perhaps most damaging of all to his own authority, but a fine testament to his personal piety, was his desire to strip away the mystique attached to ibn Tumert. He denied that ibn Tumert was the infallible Mahdi and discouraged the use of his writing as a primary form of sacred literature. He was also very suspicious of the great influx of Sufism that was sweeping the Maghreb. Rather than alienate these brotherhoods, a wiser but less honest ruler could easily have embraced them by attaching them to the cult of ibn Tumert.

The Decay of the Almohad Empire, 1213–76

Caliph Mohammed en Nasir (1199–1213) brought the Almohad Empire to its territorial apogee with his conquest of the Balearic islands in 1203. Having successfully subdued the base of the Almoravid Beni Ghaniya dynasty at last, he was able to subdue their rebellion in Tunisia. Before he marched back home to Marrakech in 1207, he appointed

Abdul Wahid, son of Abu Hafs Umar, viceroy of Tunisia. Abdul Wahid only accepted on condition that he would be relieved in three years time, although in fact he loyally remained in his post until his death in 1221. Few could have realized that this administrative appointment was to be the foundation of a dynasty that would rule Tunisia for 300 years.

In 1213 the authority of the Almohad Empire, just like that of the Almoravids before it, received its first shock from a military defeat in Spain. The actual engagement, fought just south of a notorious bandit-infested mountain pass, has subsequently become a Spanish legend, although its importance lies in the subsequent political consequences. Mohammed en Nasir retired to Marrakech only to die the following year, and was succeeded by a child. Almohad unity imploded, as the ruling tribes struggled for precedence during the long minority of Caliph Youssef al-Mustansir (1214–24). The credibility of the dynasty was rocked again in 1227 when an Almohad prince, al-Mamun (1229–32), led a revolt in Spain against Caliph al-Adid. Al-Mamun, backed by a Castilian army, marched south to seize control of Marrakech in 1228. In 1229 he officially renounced the doctrines of ibn Tumert and returned to Malikite orthodoxy.

With the authority of the empire in tatters, provincial governors and tribal warlords began to carve out their own petty states. In Spain, the power vacuum allowed the Christian kings to carry all before them. Ferdinand III of Castile (1217–52) captured Cordoba in 1235 and Seville in 1248. Only the mountainous south-east, reinforced by a flood of Muslim refugees, remained safe. In 1231 Mohammed I (1230–72) had established himself as the independent ruler of Granada. His heirs, the Nasrid emirs, preserved the independence of their beautiful and wealthy mountain kingdom by the prompt payment of annual tribute and by exciting the natural rivalries that existed between the Christian kingdoms of Castile, Aragon and Portugal. The Alhambra Palace, which they built overlooking Granada, remains the most dazzling expression of secular Hispano-Mauresque architecture.

The Almohads were not quite dead yet. A determined attempt to revive the empire was launched by Caliph Abu Said (1242–8) in 1244. After a four-year campaign he seemed on the point of subduing northern Morocco and western Algeria when he was killed in a small engagement outside Tlemcen. The disaster of his death in 1248 was compounded by the total destruction of the leaderless Almohad army as it crossed the Moulouya river on its way back to Marrakech. This massacre by the Beni Merin tribe destroyed the last Almohad hope. Southern Morocco was ruled for two more decades by Almohad princes residing behind the walls of Marrakech. The last caliph, Ishaq, reigned only over Tinmal, but even this mountain sanctuary was stormed in 1276. A long file of captives, the last of the Almohads, was then led down the mountain pass and executed publicly outside Marrakech.

CHAPTER FOURTEEN

Medieval Dynasties: Merenids, Zayyanids and Hafsids, 1250–1400

By 1250 the Almohad Empire had been replaced by the rule of the Merenids in Morocco, the Zayyanids in Algeria and the Hafsids in Tunisia. It was a period of extraordinary contrasts. The capitals of these dynastic states grew into sophisticated, well-ordered cities that had few equals anywhere in the world. Intellectual life soared to unequalled heights. Architecture reached its dazzling apogee. Yet in the same period the political structure degenerated into a morass. Armies of the three rival dynasties criss-crossed the Maghreb in ferocious pursuit of an illusive imperium. The bewildering chronicle of external wars was only equalled by internal intrigues, in which son deposed father, brother struggled against brother, uncles fought nephews and viziers deposed their masters. The armies were made up of tribal levies led by their own ambitious warlord chiefs stiffened by companies of Christian mercenaries, unlike the highly-motivated religious armies of their predecessors. None of the three ruling dynasties came to power as champions of Islam, yet despite their mercurial family politics, they survived. Where the upright, bold and pure leadership of the Almoravids and Almohads lasted just three generations, the Merenid, Hafsid and Zayyanid sultans ruled for over 300 years.

To understand these apparent contradictions one has to look not only at political events, but also at the changing nature of North African society. No longer was the region divided exclusively by tribe. Local towns and cities of growing sophistication were attracting a mix of people whose loyalties included their trading partners and religious fellow-travellers. The spread of mystical Islam had made religion a personal affair of the heart and set up local centres of charity, so leaders no longer needed to espouse Islam as part of their political agenda. Meanwhile the great cities had become self-sustaining entities, with their own charitable social work foundations, from which the governing dynasties could remain aloof in their self-contained, well-defended quarters.

Mystical Islam

There have always been two sides to Islam, formal worship and the intimate, enthusiastic search of the mystic. The latter is known as 'Sufism', a word derived from the Arabic for wool (*suf*) which refers to the cheap woollen cloaks worn by its early, self-denying adherents. Sufism is neither a schism, a heresy nor a formal movement, but a simple attempt to focus on the animating spirit of religion rather than its outward observance. The first mystical practices are said to have been taught by the Prophet Mohammed to his daughter and son-in-law, but were considered too demanding and spiritually dangerous for the mass of mankind, and so were never written down. They were reserved for pious initiates who received verbal instruction from an approved master. A continous succession of master-disciple relationships down the generations preserved the venerable link back to the Prophet.

SUFI MASTERS

The Muslim principalities of Spain produced a disproportionate number of Sufi masters, including Ibn al-Arabi (1165–1240) 'the seal of the saints', who is acknowledged to be the greatest Muslim metaphysician of them all. In his works *Meccan Revelations* and *Wisdom of the Prophets* he leads his disciples towards an all-encompassing deism which, although well suited to the twentieth century, has been treated with great suspicion by orthodox Muslims. It was, however, the Persian al-Ghazzali (1059–1111), more than any other man, who prepared the way for the great spread of Sufism. He occupied an unimpeachably orthodox position, as the professor of Islamic law in the caliph's own city of Baghdad. Al-Ghazzali was honest enough to realize that he was as enamoured of his high salary, honoured position and wide public recognition as of any true service, or even ultimate faith in his religion.

He battled with his conscience for years before a nervous breakdown helped him to take to the open road. He lived the life of a wandering ascetic for ten years before concluding that simple piety is more important than any amount of learning. His long search had brought him back, full circle, to the traditional practices of Muslim religious life. In his two most important works *Deliverer from Error* and *Revivification of the Religious Sciences,* al-Ghazzali united the parallel paths of the Sufi mystical search with the legalistic practices of Islam. It was these works that the orthodox Almoravids had burnt so misguidedly in the public square of Marrakech. For they were not designed to sweep away the old, dry, legalistic interpretations of Islam, but to bolster them with additional mystical devotions. Islam, freed from acting only as a political and legal agenda, was encouraged to act as a deeply rewarding and personal religion.

Abu Madyan al-Andalusi (?–1197), based in the Algerian capital of Tlemcen, was an especially influential and respected North African master. Following in the footsteps of al-Ghazzali he managed to blend the bright poetry of Andalucian mysticism with detailed study of Islamic law. Other revered North African figures include Sidi Harazem of Fez (familiar to any traveller in Morocco as a mineral water brand-name) and Abdessalam ibn Mchich (?–1228), who taught in the forbidding Rif Mountains of northern Morocco. His spiritual heir was Abou al Hassan ech Chadhili (?–1258), a fellow Rifian, whose spiritual celebrity is commemorated by dozens of shrines scattered throughout the Maghreb. Also known as Sidi Belhassen, this well-travelled ascetic (who introduced coffee-drinking from the Yemen) is revered as a founding master by no less than 15 separate brotherhoods.

Groups of disciples would organize themselves into brotherhoods around a charismatic master, who was usually referred to as the 'sheikh'. The *zaouia*, or collection of buildings that gradually arose around such a sheikh, often included a mosque, a teaching hall, a charitable kitchen, some accommodation for travellers, the sheikh's private retreat and in due course his revered tomb. Subsidiary branches might be formed during his lifetime by disciples or by his designated heirs, who were often his lineal descendants. Regular attendance at a *zaouia* was seldom a formal, or even an exclusive, undertaking, in the manner of Christian monasteries. The lodges prided themselves on their hospitality and a city-dweller might frequent half a dozen *zaouia* without any major conflict of interest.

As Sufism spread across North Africa in the twelfth and thirteenth centuries it became ever more diverse. There were brotherhoods that stressed ethical behaviour, piety and Koranic learning. Others immersed themselves in gnostic thought, speculative cosmology, theosophy and religious syncreticsm. Still others sought to lead disciples towards an ecstatic revelation of God through techniques of dance, music, prolonged contemplation or the repetition of prayer. Popular religion was reflected in the belief in the powers of the sheikhs who were credited with miracles of healing, the power to bless, to intercede at the Day of Judgement and to interpret dreams, as well as to protect the fertility of crops and flocks.

The mystical achievements of these brotherhoods have never been adequately chronicled, although some of their spiritual activity is preserved in the biographies of sheikhs, their collected sayings, anecdotes, letters and favourite folk tales. The best of these, like the parables of Jesus, operate on a number of different levels.

THE POLITICAL ROLE OF THE SUFI SHEIKHS

Humility, charity, silence, inner tranquility and an indifference to the things of the world were the social attributes of the Sufi. Passionate political involvement was the very antithesis of their nature. The coming and goings of sultans, viziers and their armies was as nothing to the affairs of the next world. Yet at the same time the sheikhs played a valuable social role, particularly in the areas of mountain and steppe traditionally dominated by tribes rather than government. A respected sheikh had an appeal that transcended tribal loyalties. His word, or letter of recommendation, could provide security for travellers and merchants that mere money would never have secured. His whitewashed *zaouia*, often visible from afar with its accompanying cluster of trees, was acknowledged as a safe refuge from tribal feuds and clan vendettas. He alone could be trusted to arbitrate a settlement or judge a case without tribal bias. The *zaouia* often organized a school for the conventional Koranic education of children as well as providing charity for the sick

Arabic calligraphy

and the poor. A well-run *zaouia* could offer all the services of efficient government with none of the exploitation and arbitrary powers that went with it. The sheikhs asked the surrounding communities only for what they needed, and from all accounts it was given gladly.

The Cities

At the start of the fourteenth century the three cities of Fez, Tlemcen and Tunis dominated the North African political landscape. Their dazzling, sophisticated urbanity was expressed physically in the clear definition provided by their encircling walls. One side of the walls looked out over sunbaked cemeteries beyond which the countryside stretched towards the horizon, while on the other squatted the teeming, seething city whose bustling, narrow alleys were shaded by tall houses. Within the walls were concentrated all the high art, craft, trade and literate life that defined the Arabic identity of the nation. Outside these oases of civilization lay the land of the Berber tribes, whose self-sufficient lifestyle was linked to that of the cities by thin threads of trade that did little to diminish the mutual hostility. At their height in the fourteenth century, Tlemcen and Tunis had populations of 100,000, while Fez seldom numbered less than 125,000 within its walls. All these cities retain memories of this golden age, but Fez is exceptional in its retention of a strong medieval identity.

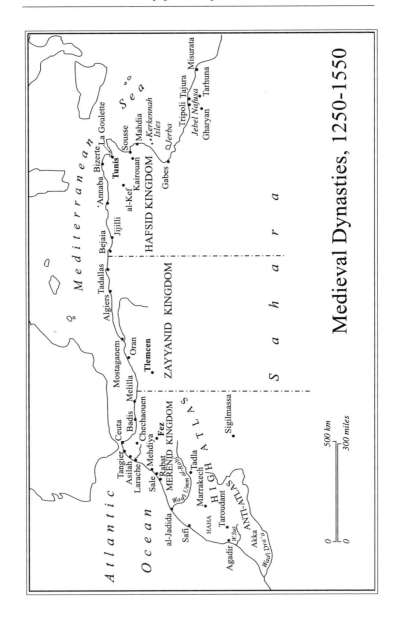

Medieval Dynasties, 1250-1550

CITY GOVERNMENT

Entrance into the city was controlled by eight gates, watched over by detachments of the garrison. Each night the city withdrew into itself as the great, riveted, wooden gates were bolted shut at dusk and not opened again until dawn. These gates often grew into small fortresses as their defence was elaborated by the addition of towers, inner courtyards, Z-shaped passages and internal gates. In Fez the Gate of the Lion evolved into the state prison while the western gate, embellished by an Almohad castle, became the residence of the governor. Governors were appointed by the sultan to command the garrison, judge criminal cases and order public executions, which usually took place just outside a prominent city gate.

Within its outer walls a city such as Fez was subdivided into 18 quarters, each of which was closed off by internal gates at night. Each quarter acted as a self-sufficient town, with its own mosques, schools, water fountains, communal ovens and bath-houses. The most distinctive quarters were those set aside for specific populations, such as the Jewish *mellah* in Fez or the *rabat en nassara* of Tunis, which housed Christian mercenaries. A council of the most important residents selected a headman to represent their quarter and assist the *qadi*, the city-judge, in the civic administration. The *qadi*, chosen from among the chief scholars of Islamic law, occupied the summit of prestige amongst the native citizenry. He acted as rector of the university and censor of intellectual life as well as judging personally all civil cases, although he appointed a deputy to look after marriage and divorce procedures. Through a permanent staff of some 40 secretaries and accountants the *qadi* supervised the various pious foundations that had been established over the centuries by wealthy citizens. These foundations financed the hospitals, schools, bath-houses and charitable kitchens, which so impressed European visitors. Collectively the foundations provided an admirable system of healthcare and poor relief, but their charitable concerns stopped abruptly at the city walls. Second only to the *qadi* in urban prestige was the *muhtasib* (the magistrate of manners) who kept watch over the honesty of the market places, checked weights and measures, looked to the proper conduct of the public baths and organized a weekly medical for the prostitutes of the city.

TRADE GUILDS

Working beside the *muhtasib* were the various trade corporations of the city who, like the guilds of medieval Christendom, enforced standards, protected their monopolies and established apprenticeship systems under the leadership of a council of masters. In Fez there were over 150 guilds, each under the protection of a patron saint and often linked with a Sufi brotherhood. They ranged in prestige from that of the 300 nameless hereditary porters to the guild of water engineers, who required a lifetime of study to understand the labyrinth of underground aqueducts, pipes, springs, drains, culverts and streams that flowed through the city.

The cloth industry was the largest industry in Fez. At its height it employed 20,000 workers under the direction of 500 master-weavers. Second in size, but much greater in complexity, was the leather trade, where collectively three rival corporations ran the city's four tanneries. In addition there were different guilds for each stage of the process from de-hairing, tanning and dyeing the hides to processing them into saddlebags, slippers and harnesses.

Bakers and grocery shops were scattered through the quarters of the city. Tunis had 700 licensed grocers, 1,200 animal-powered flour mills and 4,000 people permanently employed in the daily baking and distribution of bread. The various trades were concentrated together in streets named after them or within a *fondouk*. A *fondouk* could take many forms, but at its most basic it was a secure courtyard for travelling merchants who could stable their animals on the ground floor and live amongst their merchandise, in self-contained apartments on the balconied upper storeys. They worked as miniature city quarters, dedicated to a particular trade, or to traders from a certain city or distant land. Tenancies varied from a few days for an intinerant trader, to near-hereditary leaseholds for well-established artisans like silk-weavers or metalsmiths. Such skilled artisans tended to deal, not directly with the public, but through trade-dominated auctions. The retailers occupied the hundreds upon hundreds of small booths that lined the alleys and courtyards of the city centre, just as they do today. The booths were no haphazard arrangement. Sultans took it upon themselves to construct magnificent covered bazaars, whose domes, vaults and arcades remain one of the ubiquitous delights of North Africa. Rents in many of the most prestigious covered bazaars went directly to support a mosque or a Koranic school. Dealers in perfume and books, the most precious and desirable merchandise, occupied the streets closest to the mosque. The *souk el attarine*, the market of scent, is still located beside the great mosques in both Fez and Tunis. The great Koutoubia Mosque in Marrakech was named after the *souk el kutubiyyin*, which once surrounded the mosque with the bustle of scribes, copyists, binders and booksellers.

SEATS OF LEARNING: THE QARAOUYINE AND THE ZITOUNA

There were two great universities in North Africa, synonymous with the great mosques at the centre of Fez and Tunis, the Qaraouyine and the Zitouna. Lectures were given in the courtyard and the prayer hall of the mosques between morning and noon prayers. Stress was laid on verbal communication, recitation and memorizing. At the heart of the curriculum was Koranic interpretation, study of the Hadith, Arabic language and Islamic law. Smaller classes might assemble in the houses of individual professors or in the various *medersa* (residential colleges) that were established during the thirteenth and fourteenth centuries. The Hafsid sultan, Abu Zakariya, established the first *medersa* in North Africa in Tunis in 1249, for the study of Almohad doctrine. His initiative was followed a generation later in Fez whose oldest college, the Seffarine, was built in 1280. The foundation of a *medersa* was an act of generosity beyond the means of all but the sultans. Aside from the initial cost of construction (which in itself was often enormous) the colleges needed a permanent endowment to pay professors and administrative staff and to feed students who were invited to reside free for seven years. Perhaps the greatest of all is the jewel-like Attarine Medersa of Fez, built by the Merenid sultan, Abou Said. The geometrical abstractions of its cut-tile mosaic allied to successive layers of arabesque carving in tile, plaster, marble and cedar wood all conspire to create a symphony of harmonious design entirely suited to reflective meditation and recitation.

NORTH AFRICA'S FINEST: IBN BATTUTA AND IBN KHALDOUN

These seats of learning produced a handful of men whose erudition has made them famous to this day. Ibn Battuta was, despite his extraordinary exploits, a typical product of the university education system of North Africa. He was of Berber ancestry, born in Tangier in 1304 to a prosperous family of lawyers. After completing his studies he qualified as a scholar of Islamic law but decided to complete his education with a pilgrimage to Mecca. He continued travelling for the next 25 years, taking intermittent employment as a judge, ambassador or consultant on law as he explored the widest reaches of the Islamic world all the way to Indonesia and China. His scholarship made him an honoured guest in any Muslim state, but having settled down for a year and married a local girl he was generally ready for new adventures. He returned to Morocco in 1354 where he dictated his travels to a scribe in Fez, breaking off his narrative to explore Spain and West Africa. The latter journey, made at the instigation of the Merenid sultan, may have had a strategic motivation, although Battuta's scornful description of local customs and the horrors of desert travel must have proved some discouragement. Many of his contemporaries treated his traveller's tales with suspicion, but where they can be checked they have proved accurate. He died in Morocco in 1377.

His contemporary, ibn Khaldoun, is a towering figure in the intellectual history of North Africa, the only true equal to St Augustine, although his writing, far from inspiring a whole culture, was to remain forgotten for 500 years. Aside from his work as a historian and encyclopaedist, he was the first man to explore the philosophy of history, invented sociology, pursued a political career and acted as a revered scholar of Islamic law.

He was born in Tunis in 1332 although his parents both came from aristocratic Arab families that had been settled in Muslim Spain for centuries. He had a good education, which prepared him for government service, although his agile mind was too free and fond of intrigue to make of him a dutiful servant. At one time or another he lived in all the great cities of the Maghreb as he moved from the service of one dynasty to another. In 1362 some new scandal encouraged him to leave

North Africa altogether and serve the Nasrids of Granada, but after two years as their ambassador to Castile he was disgraced and imprisoned. He later recovered his freedom, but had to move east, and finally settled in Cairo where he became chief judge of the Malikite community. In Alexandria he watched helplessly as the ship that was bringing his entire family and library to join him sank without trace. His prestige was such that he was chosen to be the Egyptian ambassador to the all-conquering Mongol emperor Tamerlane, before his death in 1406. His principal work is *The Book of Examples,* a general history of the Muslims and especially those in North Africa, although it is the extensive volumes of the modestly-titled *Muqaddimah* (Introduction) upon which his intellectual celebrity rests. His concepts, especially the cyclical nature of history, have had an enormous and wide-ranging impact.

THE KASBAH

No sovereign of this period, however well loved, wished to be entirely surrounded by his citizenry. Sultans lived with their family and their treasure behind strong fortress walls, guarded by their most loyal servants. For popular insurrection was by no means unknown in the cities, and invariably swept all before it.

The Zayyanids resided in the Mechouar, a rectangular fortress that abutted the southern perimeter wall of Tlemcen. The Hafsids of Tunis also dwelt within Almohad walls. They resided in the fortified walls of the kasbah, which Abdel Moumen had constructed on the summit of the city. The kasbah's principal gateway, Bab Integemi, led directly into the city and housed a permanent garrison. A second gate led into the Bab Menara quarter, where the military establishment dwelt. A third gate, Bab El-Ghdar, opened directly onto the countryside. Daily prayers were the only time when the Hafsids mixed with the people, but even this was curtailed when in 1233 Sultan Abou Zakariya constructed the Kasbah Mosque within the fortress walls.

In 1276 the Merenids took their security one step further by establishing a completely separate government city a clear 750 metres west of the outer walls of Fez. Officially inaugurated as El Medinat el-Baida (the white city) it has always been known as Fez el-Jedid (new

Fez). Fez el-Jedid was protected by a moat and a double circuit of walls reinforced with square towers. Within the safety of these walls the sultans located all the machinery of government: an extensive palace, barracks for their mercenary guards, the mint and the treasury. Baths, bakehouses, a market, a choice of three mosques and a new aqueduct allowed the government city to function completely independently of the teeming thousands in old Fez.

The Dynasties

As we have seen, the medieval rulers of North Africa barely needed the active support of the population, but they did require the two vital ingredients of power: soldiers and money. Every sultan wished to be able to tax the population efficiently, but outside the fertile coastal plains and well-watered valleys tribal resistance seldom made it worth the military effort involved. The chief source of government revenue came, therefore, from customs collected from merchants at the ports of the Mediterranean and in the Sahara. The flow of gold across the Sahara was the most vital and easiest component in government finances of the period. The sultan's percentage of the gold trade contributed as much as 60 per cent to his revenue, effectively paying for wars of conquest, beautiful university colleges, palaces, courtiers and Christian mercenary guards.

Despite the flow of refugees pouring out of Muslim Spain, there were not sufficient resources to support a professional standing army. The sultan's rule was based ultimately on the military strength of his tribe, reinforced by co-opting other warlike tribes, or at least their leadership, into the ruling élite. One of the principal arts of government was the balance of this relationship between sultan and tribal warlord. The latter had to be suitably rewarded with a provincial governorship or ministerial post, checked by the role of junior members of the ruling dynasty in the surrounding administrative posts. The command of the army, for instance, was usually conferred upon the heir apparent. The three other most important posts were those of grand vizier (prime minister), public treasurer and *sahib al shurta* (chief of police).

THE RISE OF THE MERENIDS

The Beni Merin were the largest of the Berber tribes that occupied the steppe to the east of Morocco. They had personally witnessed the rewards of power, when their neighbouring Kumya tribe (from which Abdel Moumen was descended) had been co-opted into the Almohad élite. The Beni Merin had also served in the Almohad armies, but at a much lower level, as part of the great levies of tribal cavalry that were raised for specific campaigns. They had grown accustomed to Arabic speech and the political geography of the Maghreb. By 1216 the decay of the Almohad Empire had become apparent and the Beni Merin tribe began to flex its muscle.

In 1245 an astute tribal warlord, Abou Yahya (1245–58), assumed direction of the Beni Merin. He was immediately faced with the challenge of an Almohad army advancing under the command of Caliph Abu Said. Abou Yahya made a complete submission, surrendered all the possessions of his tribe, dispatched 500 Beni Merin warriors to serve in the cavalry of the Almohad army and retired to an isolated castle in the Rif Mountains. He bided his time, which arrived three years later. In 1248 the now leaderless Almohad army was returning to Marrakech, led across the eastern steppe by Beni Merin scouts, for whom it was home. The army was guided straight into an ambush organized by Abou Yahya at the crossing of the River Moulouya. In the ensuing massacre the entire Almohad army was destroyed. Those who could, like the Christian mercenary regiments, defected to Abou Yahya. Within two months Abou Yahya controlled all of central and northern Morocco.

A quick alliance between the Almohads in Marrakech and the Zayyanids in Tlemcen left Abou Yahya facing war on two fronts, a situation that continued until his successor, Abou Yusuf Yacqub (1259–86), had secured the eastern frontier with a series of three victories against the Zayyanids. There was no room for mercy in the ensuing struggle with the Almohads, and by 1276 the last of the dynasty had been hunted out. Abou Yusuf Yacqub went on to win popular renown by expelling a Castilian fleet from Sale and leading an army into Spain in support of Muslim Granada. It was also Abou Yusuf Yacqub who defined the future shape of Merenid rule by establishing Fez el Jedid and constructing the first *medersa* in Fez.

His successors would battle furiously to conquer Algeria and Tunisia, seeking but failing to re-establish the full glory of the Almohad Empire.

THE ZAYYANIDS

As in the case of the Merenids, the Zayyanids first rose to power as tribal warlords. However, if the Merenids were like wolves tearing at the great carcass of the Almohad Empire, the Zayyanids behaved like loyal Almohad mastiffs. They were the ruling clan of the Beni Abdul-Wad tribe, who were among the three most important tribes in western Algeria. Their power base was round Tlemcen and they had been early allies of the Almohads, loyally serving as cavalry in a number of campaigns.

In 1230 a Zayyanid chief was first appointed governor of Tlemcen by the Almohad caliph in Marrakech, but it was his successor Yaghmurasan ibn Zayan (1236–82), who took the title in 1236, who really set the dynasty on its way. He was a remarkable man, the very embodiment of a tribal leader, who ruled as much by personal example, tact and the sureness of his word as by his undoubted skill as a military commander. In 1242 and 1248 his territory was occupied by Hafsid and then Almohad armies, but each time he was reinvested with the governorship. After the death of Caliph Abu Said he put the dead sovereign's harem under his personal protection and made certain of their safe return to Marrakech.

The boundaries of the Zayyanid state fluctuated enormously, largely depending on their relationship with the powerful Maghrawa and Beni Tujin tribes who either accepted their situation as subordinate allies or rebelled in alliance with either the Merenids or the Hafsids. As long as the Zayyanids continued to control the north-south trade route between the port of Oran, via Tlemcen to Sigilmassa, however, these rebellions posed little threat. Tlemcen grew rich and prosperous from the trade and the Zayyanids established an able administration based on the skills of Andalucian refugees. After the extinction of the Almohads, the Zayyanids acknowledged the Hafsids as the representatives of legitimacy. It was not until the reign of Yaghmurasan's grandson, Abu Hammu I (1308–18) that they first introduced the rituals amd titles of address suitable to an independent dynasty. Abu Hammu I also followed the prevailing fashion by constructing the first *medersa* at Tlemcen, built specifically to house two renowned Malikite scholars, known collectively as the Awlad al-Imam. It was during this golden age of Tlemcen that Algiers became established as the second city of the state. In 1331 the Zayyanids almost succeeded in conquering Bijaya (which would have given them control of most of modern Algeria) but during the next 20 years their state was nearly subsumed by fighting between the Merenids and Hafsids. Abu Hammu II (1359–89) succeeded in reviving his ancestral domain, although even he was forced to abandon the capital of Tlemcen four times. His successors usually paid tribute to either the Hafsids or to the Merenids to secure their tenure on the throne. By manipulating the rivalries the dynasty managed to survive, so that as late as 1516 there was still a Zayyanid monarch, Abu Hammu III (1516–27), looking over the minaret-studded skyline of Tlemcen from the terrace of the Mechouar palace.

THE HAFSIDS

Hafsid rule over Tunisia evolved almost seamlessly from the Almohad inheritance. It started in 1207 with the appointment of Abdul Wahid as viceroy of Tunisia. Abdul Wahid, the son of Abu Hafs Umar (one of the great founders of the Almohad movement), governed Tunisia and eastern Algeria until his death in 1221. Although the Hafsids had great prestige amongst the Almohads, there was an interregnum of five years before another member of the family succeeded in getting himself appointed viceroy.

It was this viceroy's ambitious younger brother, Abu Zakariya (1228–49) who proved to be the true founder of the Hafsid dynasty. It took Abu Zakariya only two years to supplant his brother and in 1228 he received the official appointment. The next year al-Mamun, the Almohad caliph at Marrakech, officially renounced the doctrines of ibn Tumert and returned to the Malikite traditions. It proved the perfect opportunity for Abu Zakariya to renounce his obedience by posing as the champion of Almohad orthodoxy and to set up his own kingdom. Initially Abu Zakariya took only the title of emir, but by 1236 he began to style himself as the reigning Almohad caliph. His army almost kept pace with his ambitions, for by 1242 it occupied all of Tunisia and

The Chellah necropolis at Rabat, built by the Merenids
in the fourteenth century

Algeria, as well as holding such strategic Moroccan toeholds as
Sigilmassa and Ceuta. But this was the brief territorial zenith of the
Hafsid state, against which the Almohad caliph, Abu Said launched his
ill-fated campaign of 1244–8. The fighting brought home to Abu
Zakariya the precariousness of his position. The Hafsids, who originated
in the Anti Atlas Mountains of southwest Morocco, could call upon no
core of tribal support in their rule of Tunisia and Algeria. Their use of
tribal levies had to be carefully balanced if they were not to fall under
the power of an ambitious warlord. To counter this dangerous
dependence Abu Zakariya started the habitual Hafsid practice of using
Christian mercenaries and Andalucian refugees. They were, however,
a numerically small element within any army and loyal only for as long
as the sultan could afford to pay them.

His son and successor al-Mustansir (1249–77) turned his back on such
laborious and costly foreign adventures and presided over a glorious
period of pacific prosperity. European merchants flocked to the

extensive Hafsid domains. Due to the Mongol invasions which had devastated the Middle East, al-Mustansir briefly was recognized as the leading monarch of the Muslim world. In 1259 the sherifs of Mecca recognized him as caliph, while he had the satisfaction of receiving respectful embassies from Granada, the Merenids, Zayyanids and the West African kingdoms. At the same time, friendly trading treaties were signed with all the commercial powers of Christendom. The intellectual confidence of the period was reflected in the permission granted to the Dominicans to establish a Studium Arabicum (which housed the theologian Raymond Martin in Tunis from 1250 to 1260) and openly to preach to Muslims.

This dream-like state of tolerance and prosperity was shattered in 1270 when King Louis IX of France ordered the Eighth Crusade to disembark at Carthage. It was not a crusade and Louis had been badly led astray, yet again, by the ambitions of his brother, Charles of Anjou, who ruled Sicily in this period and wished to get his hands on Tunis. However, the resulting campaign exposed to the full the military weakness of the Hafsid state. Fortunately after two desultory battles had been fought in the midsummer sun the crusader army caught dysentery. The mailed knights disappeared into their tents and the life of the saintly King Louis literally drained away on 25 August. Al-Mustansir, who was on the point of abandoning Tunis, was instead able to make a favourable peace and regain some much needed face. Seven years later the old caliph died and Hafsid authority collapsed into political chaos as rival tribal chiefs supported different Hafsid claimants to the throne.

A decade later Abu Hafs (1284–95) was able to impose some order, but only at the risk of becoming dangerously dependent on Christian mercenaries who were all obedient subjects of the king of Aragon. Abu Bekr (1318–47) managed to expel these Spaniards before they became too firmly entrenched in the ports and islands of Tunisia, but his precarious achievement was wrecked by the Merenid invasions of 1347 and 1357. Abu Abbas (1370–94) had to start from the beginning, but this proved to be no bad thing. A succession of small engagements allowed him to build up a small, but personally loyal, army which he could expand at need by recruiting from rival tribes. In 1380 his efforts were vindicated when a series of popular revolts against oppressive local rulers allowed him to impose Hafsid governors in all the major towns. Aside from the state revenue now collected from customs there were great profits to be derived from the corsairs. *Al Jihad fil Bahr*, the holy struggle at sea, was just beginning to warm up.

CHAPTER FIFTEEN

Christian Crusaders and Corsair Captains, 1415–1578

It was in the fifteenth century that the battle for supremacy of the Mediterranean began in earnest. From 1415 to 1578 Muslim North Africa was locked in combat with Christian crusaders from the Spanish peninsula. The war served as a prelude to the great conflict between the two superpowers of the day, the Hapsburg and Ottoman Empires, which defined the religious frontiers of the Mediterranean as they are today. In North Africa the old medieval dynasties were swept away as military leadership passed to such victorious pirates, or corsairs, as Barbarossa and Dragut. Mastery of the Mediterranean had become the all-important prerequisite to the establishment of power on land as well as sea.

The Fate of Maghrebi Christianity

Had something remained of the Christian communities that once flourished in North Africa, the ensuing conflict might not have been as fierce. However, the fate of these communities is one of the unsolved mysteries of North African history. Their disappearance contrasts strongly with the Middle East, where communities of Christian Arabs, such as the Copts of Egypt and the Maronites of Lebanon, have survived as sizeable minorities into the twentieth century.

There were 200 North African bishops under the authority of the primate of Carthage before the Arab invasion in the seventh century. Yet by 1076 there were only three bishops left in Ifriquiya, and when the Sicilian occupation of the Tunisian coast came to an end in 1159, it seems that the last dwindling congregations of Christians left too. In the intervening period, emigration to Byzantium and conversion to Islam had taken care of the rest.

By the late twelfth century all the Christians in North Africa were known to have originated from the opposite shore of the Mediterranean. Substantial numbers of Spanish Christians served as mercenaries, others (who had been captured by corsairs) laboured as slaves, embellished the harems or, having converted to Islam, won their freedom. Their lack of tribal loyalties made the *mawali* (converts) useful royal servants and often they rose to the highest positions. The ports attracted flocks of Christian merchants buying up luxury goods and arranging for the export of more humdrum staples such as wheat, olive oil and dates. The Muslim principalities of Spain had always been the main conduit for North African trade, but as the re-conquest gathered momentum this pattern was broken. The new opportunities were eagerly grasped, especially by the merchants of Pisa, Genoa and Venice, who were all licensed to trade directly with North Africa in the Almohad period.

'Friendly' Aragon

In the thirteenth century the Spanish kingdom of Aragon pursued a notably pro-Muslim policy. It upheld the independence of Muslim Granada against threats from neighbouring Castile. In 1246 the ambassador of Aragon successfully discouraged Pope Innocent IV from directing a crusade to North Africa. Three years later Aragonese corsairs were officially prohibited from attacking Muslim ships. This astute policy soon won Aragon favourable treatment in both Zayyanid Algeria and Hafsid Tunisia, where it was treated as 'most friendly Christian neighbour'.

The ports of Oran, Bejaia and Tunis were opened to trade with the merchants of Aragon, although long-established Jewish trading dynasties still oversaw the dispatch of goods arriving via the camel caravans of Sigilmassa to the docks of Barcelona. As trade developed the Aragonese were permitted to construct their own permanent installations ashore, known as 'Catalan fondouks'.

These fondouks sheltered a self-contained world with shops, taverns, apartments, store rooms and a chapel, all under the control of a consul. In Oran the authority of the Catalan consul was extended to cover all resident European traders. Further privileges allowed the king of Aragon to collect half the customs levied from European traders as well as taking a healthy cut from the salaries of all Christian mercenaries employed by the sultan. Aragon's influence was further strengthened when its king won the right to appoint the commander of the Christian mercenaries. In 1288 the Zayyanids even sent their cavalry across the Mediterranean to fight for the king of Aragon against his neighbour of Castile.

'OVER-FRIENDLY' ARAGON

By 1350 however these good relations had deteriorated into a series of tit-for-tat seabourne raids and outright piracy. The relationship took its first lurch for the worse after Peter III of Aragon (1196–1213) seized control of Sicily in 1282. It was then an easy matter to provide military support to rival candidates for the Hafsid throne. Each act of assistance came with a price attached.

As early as 1284 Aragon occupied the Tunisian islands of Jerba and Kerkennah. In 1285 they were given the 'responsibility' of supervising the collection of customs. By the end of the century the Aragonese had so tightened their grip over the Hafsid state that they had virtually established a protectorate. Matters came to a head in 1311 when Sultan al-Lihyani thought it expedient to pretend interest in the Christian religion in order to be sure of Aragon's uncritical support. The celebrated Franciscan missionary scholar, Ramon Lull, was despatched to prepare him for conversion, composing a succession of theological pamphlets in Arabic in the process. But al-Lihyani had not the slightest intention of renouncing his faith. He was himself a Koranic scholar whose principal concern was to strip away the vestiges of Almohad theology and return to Malikite orthodoxy. This process, which he had begun in 1311 by removing ibn Tumert's name from the call to prayer, was not without some political risk, which was why he was so concerned to keep Aragon sweet. However, this delicate balancing act failed, and in 1313 a palace coup supported by a popular uprising forced the Aragonese to evacuate Tunisia, although it was not until 1335 that they were expelled from Jerba and Kerkennah.

This was the first round in a gradually increasing tempo of war. The Christian corsairs were based chiefly on the Aragonese island of Majorca while the Muslim corsairs liked to operate out of such Hafsid ports as Bejaia, Tunis, Mahdia and Jerba. In 1354 the Genoese fleet struck at the Muslim corsairs in Tripoli, in 1390 Aragon mounted an abortive six-month siege of Mahdia, and in 1401 they allied with the Venetians in an attack on Annaba.

Despite these attacks trade was kept alive by local arrangements. In fifteenth-century Oran there were Genoese and Aragonese merchant ships berthed in the same harbour as the Muslim corsairs. The corsair war brought new financial opportunities for the brave and well-connected, in the ransoming of wealthy captives, buying of captured cargoes and in negotiating protection deals with the corsair captains.

The Fall of Ceuta, 1415

The Christian kingdoms of Aragon, Castile and Portugal were too close to the Merenids, however, to be viewed with anything other than continual suspicion. Rather than cultivate close trading relations, the Merenids were concerned to bolster Muslim Granada as a strategic buffer against the aggressive Christian kingdoms.

In 1292 the Merenids voluntarily handed over their major Spanish bases, including Algeciras (with a splendid royal palace) and Ronda, to the Nasrid rulers of Granada. In 1372 the Nasrids enjoyed a last surge of power, which gave them control over Ceuta in North Africa and Gibraltar, the two pillars of Hercules. Thus in the fateful year of 1415 it was a garrison from Nasrid Granada that watched the sad fate of the ancient North African city of Ceuta.

King John of Portugal (1385–1433) singled out Ceuta as the object of a first crusade for his five young sons. It was a baptism of blood. Amongst the burnt-out ruins of the city, surrounded by files of thousands of captives and bloated corpses, the king of Portugal knighted his boys. The decision to establish a permanent Portuguese garrison at Ceuta was an almost accidental consequence of this royal foray, undertaken as much to snub Castile (with whom King John had already fought one war) as to stake out a claim to an African empire.

Yet Portugal's bright destiny was shaped directly by the sack of Ceuta, for Henry the Navigator was one of the young princes who had been knighted amidst the ruins. Henry devoted his life to the exploration of the Atlantic coast of Africa in an attempt to make contact with Prester John (a semi-mythical Christian king of Asia), seize control of the trade routes at their source and thereby utterly confound his Muslim enemies. His nautical expeditions led directly to the foundation of the worldwide Portuguese maritime empire.

Tangier and an End to the Merenids, 1419–72

The fall of Ceuta was a deeply felt humiliation. Conflict between rival members of the Merenid dynasty delayed and then weakened the long expected counter-attack. It was four years before the Merenid sultan Abu Said, assisted by the Nasrids of Granada, could mount an assault. The failure of this siege in 1419 discredited the sultan, who was deposed the next year in a popular insurrection. The governor of Sale, untainted by involvement in the failed siege, was eventually able to reimpose order. He ruled as vizier-regent for Abdul Haqq, a one-year-old Merenid princeling. In 1437 he repulsed a second Portuguese invasion, which had attempted to capture Tangier. Don Fernando (another of King John's sons knighted amidst the ruins of Ceuta) surrendered himself as a hostage in order that his troops be allowed to withdraw in safety. In captivity Don Fernando agreed to surrender Ceuta, but these negotiations were not recognized by his brother, King Duarte of Portugal. Don Fernando was fated to remain a prisoner of state, lodged for six years in the Bab Dekakane gatehouse of Fez el-Jedid. After his death, his mummified corpse stuffed with straw was hung by the heels from the gatehouse arch for another 29 years.

In 1457 Sultan Abdul Haqq at last managed to free himself from the lifelong tutelage of his vizier. But his brief exercise of personal rule was not happy, coinciding with the seizure by the Portuguese of Ksar es Seghir (the castle of the crossing), which stood halfway between Ceuta and Tangier. The old town, with its venerable mosque, was flattened and rapidly transformed into an imposing coastal fortress by an army of Portuguese masons. At the same time Abdul Haqq pushed through fiscal reforms which removed tax exemptions enjoyed by Sufi sheikhs and *shorfa*, those community leaders who could claim descent from the Prophet Mohammed. The prestige of the Idrissid *shorfa* was in the ascendant in this period. The tombs of both Idris I and Idris II, after centuries of neglect, had been rediscovered in 1437 and quickly attracted the popular veneration in which they are still held. That the population chose to look to the distant past to find their heroes was an obvious sign of their dissatisfaction with the Merenid dynasty. Abdul Haqq's tax reforms would have been difficult to implement at the best of times, but he compounded his political difficulties by appointing a talented Jewish financier as his vizier. In 1465 a popular rebellion led by the religious scholars of Fez tore down the Merenid state. The sultan was dragged through the alleys of Fez before his throat was cut like a sacrificial ram. A council formed from the religious leaders of Fez elected one of their number, Mohammed al-Juti, to be the imam of the new purified state. Al-Juti presided over the Islamic community of Fez for seven years. In 1472 Mohammed al-Shaykh, the governor of Asilah, reimposed military control over Fez and established the Wattasid dynasty. The Portuguese had not been slow to take advantage of the situation. In 1471 they finally seized Tangier before heading south down the Atlantic coast to capture the port of Asilah, followed by the ports of Larache in 1473 and Azzemour in 1486.

The Fall of Granada in 1492

These troublesome events in Morocco were to be overshadowed by a much greater tragedy, the fall of Granada. If the Greeks still raise a melancholic annual toast to Byzantine Constantinople (which fell to the Ottoman Turks in 1453), North Africa must be allowed to still sigh for Muslim Granada. For the city was the sole surviving testament to the glories of the Andalucian Arab civilization, with its fabulous architecture and elegant living, its literature, music, science and thought-provoking poetic mysticism. The loss of Granada, even to the poorest Saharan shepherd boy, remains a vivid scar dividing the modern world from the glorious past.

The independence of Muslim Granada had been maintained as much by the mutual antagonism between the three Christian Iberian kingdoms as by its own strength. In 1469 the feud between Castile and Aragon was healed by the marriage of Isabella, queen of Castile to Ferdinand, king of Aragon. Ten years later Castile and Portugal concluded peace with the treaty of Alcacovas. This treaty, which effectively sealed Granada's fate, also ambitiously divided North Africa into future spheres of interest. Morocco was to be the prey of Portugal while Spain inherited Aragon's old interests in Zayyanid Algeria and Hafsid Tunisia.

After 1479 a steady trickle of emigration drained the confidence of Granada, while its resources, at this critical moment, were riven by a dynastic feud. The first assault began in 1482, provoking desperate letters of appeal to various Muslim rulers (including one to the Ottoman sultan in 1487), but it was to no avail. One by one the great Muslim fortresses were reduced by King Ferdinand's massed artillery. The end came ten years later when Abu Abdullah, the last Nasrid emir to occupy the Alhambra Palace, was forced to surrender Granada in 1492.

The Iberian Crusade Against the Maghreb

Despite the tolerant provisions of the treaty between Ferdinand and Abu Abdullah, the 700-year-old culture of Muslim Spain was soon swept aside by the ardour of Christian fundamentalists such as Grand Inquisitor Torquemeda, Archbishop de Cisneros and Queen Isabella 'the Catholic'. They were as mad a collection as has ever disgraced the name of religion, inaugurating such a cult of terror and military pride that agricultural labour and craftsmanship came to be considered tasks unworthy of a Christian.

In 1499, the year that the first Spanish Muslims were forcibly converted to Christianity, Archbishop Cisneros preached a passionate sermon urging the creation of a Spanish Empire over North Africa. Two Castilian captains had meanwhile reported on the state of a number of North African coastal fortresses, including the Moroccan port-city of Melilla. They had found the forts ill-equipped and undermanned, with their garrisons near mutiny for lack of pay. Anxious not to damage their valuable new understanding with Portugal, the Spanish waited until they had received official clearance from their neighbours to pounce. In 1497 Melilla was occupied by a Spanish garrison The response by the sultan at Fez was quick, but the powerful new cannons of the Spanish fleet kept his cavalry at a safe distance while masons hurriedly constructed new fortress walls. The death of Queen Isabella in 1504 reduced the chances of a full scale Spanish Crusade. In 1505 garrisons were planted at Marsa el-Kebir and Qassasa in western Algeria and three years later it was the turn of the Rif port of Badis to be seized by the Spanish, who turned the islet of Penon de Velez into a fortress. In 1509 the Zayyanid port of Oran was occupied, followed the next year by such key cities as Bejaia and Tripoli. Only in their attempt to occupy the Isle of Jerba the same year did the Spanish invaders meet with effective opposition, organized by the local sheikh assisted by two enterprising corsair captains, the brothers El-Uruj and Khayr al-Din Barbarossa.

El-Uruj the Corsair, 1516–19

These two brothers came from the island of Lesbos, the children of a Greek mother and a Turkish father. Fluent in Greek and Turkish, they speedily acquired knowledge of French, Italian, Spanish and Arabic from the polyglot crews who manned their corsair boats. Initially operating out of Alexandria, they later headed west where honour and great fortune could be made seizing prizes off the Spanish coast, running arms to the beleaguered Muslims of Spain and transporting refugees. By 1504 the two brothers had shifted their operations to the Sicilian straits and were working out of Hafsid ports such as La Goulette and Jerba.

El-Uruj's successful defence of Jerba in 1510 turned him into the heroic commander of the corsair captains. In 1513 the Hafsid sultan commissioned him to lead a naval assault on Spanish-held Bejaia while the Hafsid army pressed an attack by land. The joint operation was not a success and in the fighting El-Uruj lost an arm. But before the year was out he had launched a second assault on Bejaia, this time unhindered by assistance from the Hafsids. A pact with local Kabylie chieftains sealed Bejaia's land frontier more effectively than anything the Hafsid army had achieved. Three years later El-Uruj moved his corsair squadron west in response to an appeal from the people of Algiers, leaving his younger brother Khayr al-Din in command.

This extension of El-Uruj's authority turned him into a serious rival of the sultans, who now began openly to support the Spanish. In 1516 the Zayyanid sultan even sent an army to assist the Spanish attack on Algiers, but El-Uruj successfully defended the city. The following year El-Uruj turned his attention inland, deposing the Zayyanid sultan. In just two years El-Uruj had become the virtual master of Algeria, but he had made many enemies in the process. In 1518 a Spanish army trapped El-Uruj in Tlemcen. The city was besieged for six months, but before it was forced to surrender El-Uruj slipped over the walls with a few trusted men. His trail was picked up and he was hunted down before he could reach the safety of the coast.

Khayr al-Din, Known to the Christians as Barbarossa, 1520–44

The next summer the jubilant Spanish launched their second naval assault on Algiers, once again supported by a Zayyanid sultan. Khayr al-Din took over the defence of Algiers and was soon acclaimed a worthy successor to his brother. Khayr al-Din was fully aware that he did not have the resources to resist another attack by the Spanish or to face unaided the enmity of the Zayyanid and Hafsid sultans. In 1519 he dispatched gifts with a letter of submission to Istanbul and requested Ottoman assistance in the war against the Christians. The letter could not have come at a better time, for the Ottoman ruler, Selim I 'the Grim' (1481–1512), had just completed his conquest of Egypt. This gave the Ottomans, for the first time, a real interest in the naval balance of power in the Mediterranean and in the fate of North Africa. Selim I was also the first Ottoman sultan to assume the title of caliph and he wished to prove worthy of the title of ruler of all the Muslims. Khayr al-Din's submission was accepted, he was appointed regent of Algiers, and Ottoman troops equipped with up-to-date artillery were promptly sent to him. The arrival of these troops proved vital in shoring up Khayr al-Din's position.

By 1525 Ottoman assistance allowed him to turn Algiers into a securely fortified naval base, the home of a corsair fleet strong enough to take the war back into the Christian sea lanes. He was also the acknowledged master of central Algeria, although Khayr al-Din had learnt from his brother's fate to handle the politics of the interior with a lighter touch. He flattered the chiefs and ruled through the local lords even when he had the power to appoint his own deputies.

In the winter of 1533 Khayr al-Din sailed from Algiers to attend an audience in Istanbul. His meeting with the grave new Sultan, Suleyman the Magnificent, went well and in February he was promoted *kapudan pasha* (admiral of the Ottoman fleet) and given the task of conquering Tunisia. That summer Khayr al-Din advanced east from his old base to seize Tunis and defeat the Hafsid army outside the walls of Kairouan.

Emperor Charles V (1519–56) personally led the Spanish counter-attack. A fleet of 300 ships landed an army of 30,000 at La Goulette, which forced Khayr al-Din to evacuate Tunisia. A Hafsid prince was placed back on the throne, backed by a Spanish garrison which constructed a ring of star-shaped artillery bastions around the city of Tunis.

In 1538 the Ottoman fleet, commanded by Khayr al-Din, won a convincing victory at the battle of Prevese over the combined fleet of the Christian Holy League. Considering the state of affairs in the Maghreb at the start of Khayr al-Din's career it was a remarkable personal achievement. Such were the stakes that rumours circulated at the Ottoman court that Khayr al-Din was toying with the idea of an alliance with Charles V in order to set up his own kingdom.

In 1541, however, the Spanish launched a two-pronged offensive against both Jerba and Algiers. Under the Genoese admiral, Andrea Doria, they were successful in the south, but the third Spanish assault on the well-prepared defences of Algiers was a costly débâcle. Three years later Khayr al-Din felt the situation secure enough to retire to Istanbul, where he died peacefully a few years later. The great admiral, known to the Turks as Hayrettin Pasha, still presides over the naval landing station of Besiktas, where his mausoleum looks over the calm waters of the Bosphorus. No one man could be found to fill his place. His son inherited his position as the Ottoman regent of Algiers, an Ottoman courtier was appointed *kapudan pasha* while his place on the front line was assumed by his young protégé, Dragut.

Dragut, the Drawn Sword of Islam

Dragut had been one of Khayr al-Din's most promising young sea captains until he went missing. It was presumed that his ship had been sunk, but years later he was identified on the rowing bench of a Genoese galley. Khayr al-Din was forced to cede the island fortress of Tabarka in exchange for Dragut's release.

He was worth the price, for in 1551 he played a key role in the siege of Tripoli, which succeeded in expelling the crusading Knights of St John. Due to the jealousy of the Ottoman *kapudan pasha*, Dragut initially was passed over as regent of Tripoli, but two years later his talents were recognized. He turned Tripoli into a second Algiers, leading a series of audacious raids on the Christian coasts.

In 1558 his enslavement of the entire population of the Italian city of Reggio sent shockwaves throughout Christendom. A counter-attack was launched two years later, but Dragut surprised the Christian fleet in the shallow waters off the isle of Jerba. The Spanish garrison on the island was cut off from its support and after a two-month siege their last fortress was stormed. On the beach near the castle of Houmt Souk, Dragut constructed a grim pyramid of Spanish skulls as a warning to future invaders. Protected by an annual coat of whitewash, it stood for 300 years before being dismantled by the French colonial regime.

Dragut was equally industrious in the interior, where he used his Ottoman troops to discipline the tribes. For the first time since the Beni Hilal migration in the eleventh century, order was imposed on the powerful Arab tribes. Garrisons were established at key points on the caravan trails, but otherwise Dragut left the tribal leadership in place providing the annual tribute was forwarded to Tripoli and peace was maintained. Governors were appointed over the cities of Sfax, Gabes, Gafsa and even Kairouan. The wealth he aquired from the corsair war was lavished on the adornment of Tripoli, which he transformed from a grim Iberian fortress into an elegant Muslim city. The mosque that he built over a Spanish chapel remains one of the most exuberant and charming examples of the Ottoman-influenced Maghrebi renaissance. In 1565 he brought the full resources of his governorship to assist in the

Jabal Nafusa, the ksar at Kabao

great siege of Malta. His death, which occurred while directing an artillery bombardment, was a crucial blow to the prospect of an Ottoman victory.

Ali of the Sword, Uluç Kiliç Ali Pasha

Uluç Ali was born in Calabria of Italian parents, but was captured by Muslim corsairs while still a youth. He spent 14 years as a galley slave before winning his freedom and converting to Islam, when he took the name of Uluç Ali. He then commanded his own corsair craft and having distinguished himself on a number of Mediterranean cruises was promoted to admiral and later made Ottoman regent of Algiers (1567–80). In 1569 he led the second invasion of Tunisia and expelled practically all the Spanish garrisons that Charles V had planted. In 1570 all the energies of the Ottoman Empire were directed at the invasion of Cyprus, whose capture brought about a renewal of the Holy League (an alliance of Spain, the Hapsburg Empire, Venice and the Papacy). The next year Uluç Ali commanded the Algerian squadron during the epic battle of Lepanto, when the Ottoman fleet was virtually destroyed. It was hailed as a great victory for Christendom, but it was through no fault of Uluç Ali, for his squadron had fought with distinction and even captured a number of Spanish ships. In the immediate aftermath of the victory Don John, the Christian commander, undid Uluç Ali's work and once again placed a Spanish client, the Hafsid sultan Mohammed, back on the throne of Tunisia.

After the disaster of Lepanto, Sultan Selim II (1566–74) had sufficient dignity to greet Uluç Ali as a hero, renaming him Kiliç Ali (Ali of the sword) and appointing him *kapudan pasha*. All the available resources of the Ottoman state were placed at the admiral's command and within two years a new battle fleet of 200 ships had been launched. Under the strain of a shared victory, the Christian alliance had meanwhile broken apart. In March 1573 Uluç Ali was able to secure Tunisia once and for all. The brunt of the fighting was concentrated on the Spanish fortress of La Goulette, but once it had fallen in August the city of Tunis and the rest of the country were speedily occupied. Mohammed, the last Hafsid sultan (1573–4), was sent to an enforced retirement in Istanbul while the victorious Uluç Ali returned to his governorship of Algiers.

LITERATURE

One of the Spanish captives Uluç Ali had made at Lepanto was one Miguel Cervantes. After five years of slave labour in Algiers Cervantes escaped, but was recaptured and brought before the governor for sentencing. Cervantes' story made such a favourable impression on Uluç Ali that far from punishing the escaped slave, he ransomed him from his owner and returned him to Spain with a purse of money. All those who have delighted in *Don Quixote* are in Uluç Ali's debt while Cervantes pays his own tribute in Chapter 32 of the epic story.

The corsair war was also responsible for another literary composition. In 1518 some Italian-based corsairs captured an oil-laden galley off the island of Jerba, in which the scholar Al Hassan ibn Mohammed was travelling. The raiders passed their captive on to Pope Leo X who proved himself a most attentive and devoted patron. Mohammed flourished under his attentions and having converted to Christianity he took the name Leo Africanus and settled down in the papal library to write, *A History and Description of Africa*. Tradition relates that after the death of his patron he found Rome less congenial and quietly returned to Tunis, taking up the religion of his birth again before his death in 1554.

PEACE

In 1578 the Spanish and Ottoman Empires, which had been locked in a titanic war for the control of the Mediterranean for 100 years, at last signed a peace. The boundaries between Islam and Christendom agreed upon then have not been changed since. In North Africa the three Ottoman provinces based on the cities of Algiers, Tunis and Tripoli are the recognizable heirs of modern Algeria, Tunisia and Libya. Morocco, alone in the Maghreb, had managed to fend off the Christian threat without falling under the control of the Ottoman Empire.

CHAPTER SIXTEEN

The Ottoman Regencies of Algiers, Tunis and Tripoli, 1520–1818

Capitalizing on their defence of North Africa from invasion by Christian Europe, the Ottoman Empire established its own dominion in the three regencies of Algiers, Tunis and Tripoli. Ottoman rule, via an appointed pasha, was upheld by Turkish garrisons who remained determinedly aloof from the population. The success of the corsairs initially allowed this military caste to rest but lightly on the shoulders of the region. By the early eighteenth century local dynasties had assumed power over Tunisia and Libya whose growing prosperity was reflected in an intriguing fusion of Ottoman and Maghrebi culture. In Algeria, Ottoman rule evolved into a self-regulating military republic whose internal efficiency allowed it to survive unchanged for 300 years. By the early nineteenth century however, the European powers were beginning to reassert themselves in the Mediterranean, signalling an end to this period of Muslim rule. Behind the disguise of a British-enforced peace on the sea lanes, European imperial ambitions were once again emerging.

Ottoman North Africa

The Ottoman Empire acquired its first viceroy of North Africa when the corsair captain Khayr al-Din was recognized as regent of Algiers in 1520. Better known to the Christians as Barbarossa, Khayr al-Din was also addressed by the titles *beylerbey* (lord of lords) and *agha* (commander of the janissaries). Before his reign Algiers was an important port, but had never functioned as a political capital. Algeria had hitherto always been divided. The eastern half had been ruled by the Hafsid governor of Tunis while the west was ruled by its own dynasty of Zayyanid sultans based in Tlemcen. As the war progressed these dynasties vacillated between the Spanish and Ottoman camps, in an attempt to maintain their independence. By the middle of the sixteenth century there was no further room for manoeuvre. Their time had run out. The last Zayyanid left Tlemcen in 1551, the last Wattasid fled Fez in 1554 while the last Hafsid sailed out of Tunis in 1574.

The beylerbey of Algiers was left to rule the vast domains of central North Africa. These were divided in the customary manner. Constantine was capital of the eastern beylik, the smaller central beylik (due south of Algiers) was adminstered from Midea while the western beylik (the old Zayyanid kingdom) was eventually to be governed from the port of Oran rather than the old inland capital of Tlemcen.

Separate governors were appointed to Tunis, in 1574, and to Tripoli, in 1558, who reported directly to Istanbul. In the extent of their territory, and in the size of their corsair fleet and garrisons, these governors ranked far below the dignity of the beylerbey of Algiers.

BEYLERBEYS OF ALGIERS, 1520–1671

The 16th-century beylerbeys of Algiers: Khayr al-Din (1520–44), his son Agha Hasan Qusru (1544–67) and Uluç Kiliç Ali Pasha (1567–80) read like a rollcall of Ottoman heroes. All three rose to become *kapudan pasha* of the Ottoman fleet and to retire in great honour to Istanbul. After the peace signed with Spain the Ottoman court decided to contain the ambitions of this distant governorship. From 1587 the beylerbey was no longer chosen from the most dashing and charismatic of the corsair captains, but was an official appointed for a three-year term. These pashas had no chance to establish a local following. Their responsibilities in the booming port-city of Algiers, with its fleet of 75 corsair ships and Turkish garrison of 12,000, were all-consuming. Over the sixteenth century the population of Algiers had grown to 100,000 in addition to the 25,000 Christian captives held in the city.

Fortunes continued to be made by great corsair captains, such as Murad Rais, who cruised the Mediterranean in the 1580s. In Algiers these captains were serving officers in the navy, not the pirates or licensed Barbary privateeers of popular imagination. All ships and weapons captured during a corsair cruise remained the absolute property of the state. It was only the profits from the sale of captives and captured merchandise that were shared out amongst the crew. These profits were calculated in a fixed proportion based on rank, in much the same way that the British Royal Navy distributed prize money. Merchants also profited from the corsair war, acquiring captured merchandise at public auctions and speculating on captives who might later be ransomed. Poorer captives could only hope for release by one of the Catholic redemption socities, but were more likely to remain slave labourers all their lives. This surplus of skilled labour ensured that Algiers blossomed into one of the most beautiful cities of the world. Chroniclers remarked on the immaculate state of the streets, the beautifully kept gardens, the elegant houses and handsome pavilions enjoying views over dazzling sea and mountains.

The Military Republic of Algiers, 1671–1830

In 1671 a squadron of the Royal Navy under the command of Sir Edward Spragg swept into the bay of Algiers and sank seven of the best corsair ships. The *rais*, infuriated by the inadequate command of the shore batteries, assassinated the Ottoman governor, Agha Ali. They had no desire to seize control of the state, to sever their ties with the Ottoman Empire or in any way to reduce military discipline. They wished only for efficient leadership and met in council to select the most promising military officer as their commander. This elected leader was given the title of 'dey', an affectionate term used for a maternal uncle or a middle-ranking officer.

Thus was born the extraordinary military republic of Algiers, whose soldier élite was recruited from distant villages in Turkey. These youths were then shipped across the Mediterranean and trained to serve either as janissaries, disciplined foot soldiers skilled in the use of firearms and light artillery, as *sipahi*, the traditional Turkish light cavalry, or as marines. The Turkish soldiers lived in communal barracks that housed companies of a hundred men. They were paid a regular salary, which was increased to a gold coin a day during active service. They were forbidden to marry, but once their term of service was over they could

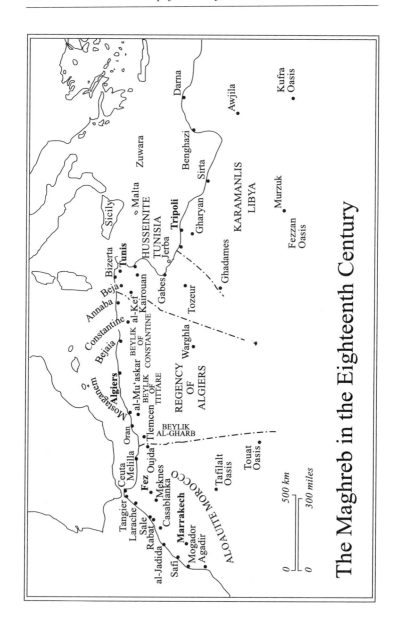

The Maghreb in the Eighteenth Century

settle down on their savings or take to a trade with a local wife or two. The Maghrebi-Turkish children produced from these unions were known as *kulughlis* and grew into a property-owning middle class. For all their wealth, the *kulughlis* were banned from military service, for no local interests were to be allowed to corrupt the zeal of the troops. The body of active Turkish troops were known as the *ujaq* and their interests were represented by their company commanders. These senior officers when assembled in *diwan al-asker*, the military council, exercised supreme power. Their paramount task was to elect the ruling dey, but this became a formality since he who served as *agha* and then *khazanadar* (state treasurer) always rose to the post. In addition to these high posts there was an inner council formed by the four secretaries of state, the cavalry commander and the commander of marines. Such a rigid career structure trained each successive dey in every aspect of government and kept political intrigue within narrow limits.

The Ottoman sultan continued to be honoured, although apart from the continual recruitment of Turkish troops from his domains, the regency of Algiers had become self-governing. A face-saving pasha was despatched from Istanbul, but he acted as ambassador rather than as governor. In 1711 the Ottoman court gave up on even this pretence and awarded the title of pasha to whoever was the ruling dey of Algiers.

THE DEY OF ALGIERS

The military republic of Algiers was an admirably meritocratic instution, particularly in the first 100 years when the Turkish military could be seen to be defending North Africa from the Christians and while the profits of the corsair war allowed the regime to finance itself.

About 95 per cent of the population of Algeria remained Berber or Arabic speaking and lived in agricultural villages, scattered mountain hamlets or tented encampments. Apart from the peace enforced by the three beys, who commanded detachments of janissaries at the provincial capitals, to these people the government of the dey of Algiers was a distant presence. He was better known to the tribal and religious leaders of the countryside whose friendship was secured by tax exemptions and stipends paid out of the state treasury of Algiers.

The combined population of Algiers and all the provincial towns probably numbered around 160,000, of which perhaps 10 per cent were partly of Turkish descent or enrolled in the *ujaq*. The dey of Algiers secured the support of the traditional religious establishment in the cities by awarding salaries to 120 leading scholars of Islamic law and by the judicious exercise of patronage. As representative of the Ottoman caliph in Istanbul, the dey of Algiers controlled all religious appointments, from the mufti of Algiers to the new imam of any one of the 130 neighbourhood mosques in Algiers. The Turkish military proudly kept to the Hanefite rite of their homeland, which they elevated to a position of precedence over the local Malikite tradition. This could have developed into a major source of friction, but in practice it worked remarkably smoothly as the intellectual quality of the Hanefite scholars sent out to the Maghreb was usually low and they often depended privately on the advice of their Malikite colleagues.

Oppression and Revolt, 1750–1830

By 1740 the strain was beginning to show. The corsair captains were no longer bringing in so many prizes, as the old Mediterranean trade routes lost importance compared to those of the Atlantic. Naval powers such as France and Britain had also acquired immunity for their merchantmen by a subtle blend of naval bombardment and quiet negotiations. The Algiers fleet was reduced to 20 ships, the army down to 7,000 men. The way out of this dilemma was obvious – to exploit the interior. The Turkish advantage in firearms and artillery was used to remorseless effect on the quasi-independent tribes. A few favoured tribes, usually those dwelling close to the provincial capital, were excused certain taxes in return for providing military service. Further to reduce the dangers of a general uprising, the politically sensitive Kabylie Mountains were placed under the direct responsibility of the dey. It was also during this period that the last Spanish possession in Algeria, Oran, was captured. It was taken by assault in 1708, lost again in 1732 and finally reoccupied in 1792.

TAXATION

Islamic taxation traditionally depended on the Koranically approved tithe of agricultural produce, but in fact this was only the beginning of the tax obligations. The Turkish army collected *lazma* (obligation) and *mauna* (support) as defenders of the faith, levied *ghamara* (indemnity) from the flocks of the pastoral tribes and also levied cash from the urban guilds, merchants and markets. In addition there was a twice-yearly demand for gifts to the provincial bey and his deputies to mark the major religious festivals. In their turn the three provincial beys sent a magnificent caravan of gifts to the dey of Algiers twice yearly. That from the bey of Oran transported great quantities of walnuts, butter and honey as well as bolts of fine woollen cloth from Tlemcen, silk from Fez, four horses, 50 black slaves, 20,000 gold coins and jewellery to half this weight.

The resistance of individual tribes to this crushing weight of taxation was never chronicled, but by the late eighteenth century it is known that resistance was being organized by certain Sufi brotherhoods. Their influence was pervasive yet could rarely be pinned down to any particular district by the army. Abdul-Kadir ibn al-Sharif, the sheikh of a district branch of the Darqawiyya brotherhood, led a classic guerilla campaign against the Turks from 1783 to 1805. The revolt was also supported by the newly established Tijaniyya brotherhood although its founder, Ahmad al-Tijani, was forced to flee Algeria to the safety of Fez in 1789. His son Mohammed al-Kebir led the resistance in the next generation until he was captured and killed by the Turks in 1827. He was a widely revered martyr, whose dying curse against the Turkish military republic was seemingly answered three years later when the French attacked the dey of Algiers.

Ottoman Tunisia: Pashas, Beys and Deys, 1574–1637

After the expulsion of the Spanish and their client Hafsid sultan in 1574, the Ottoman grand vizier Sinan Pasha personally organized the new government of Tunisia. The basis of Ottoman rule was a permanent garrison of 4,000 Turkish janissaries in Tunis who also guarded the coastal fortresses at Bizerte, La Goulette and Mahdia. The janissaries were divided into units of 100 men under the command of officers known as deys. The 40 deys could be assembled in the *diwan al-asker*, the military council, to decide policy in times of crisis. The routine of government was in the hands of the pasha, the governor, who was sent out from Istanbul for clearly defined terms of duty. He was assisted by the bey, the officer who kept the peace in the interior of the country and collected taxes. This arrangement lasted for 20 years before the deys elected one of their number to run the country. This quiet coup was achieved without disturbing any of the outward forms of loyalty to the Ottoman caliph. The dey of Tunis continued to rule with the assistance of the diwan, which was expanded by the addition of religious notables and the more respectable *rais*.

Under the enlightened leadership of Uthman Dey (1598–1610) and Youssef Dey (1610–37) Tunisia recovered from the devastation of the Hapsburg-Ottoman wars. Control of the south was recovered in a series of forceful campaigns, which by 1604 had established the present frontier with Libya. Tunis was rebuilt, ancient mosques were lovingly restored and new aqueducts, dams, fortresses and bridges constructed. The last wave of Muslim refugees from Andalucia, expelled by the intolerance of the Catholic kings, was welcomed by the deys with grants of land and a three-year tax holiday. The refugees brought new skills and helped develop a ceramic tradition from a blend of Ottoman, Persian, Maghrebi and Andalucian influences. These were used in the elegant new barracks, *medersas* and Hanafite mosques that the deys built in the centre of Tunis. The modest palace built by Uthman Dey and the elegant mosque built by Youssef Dey are vivid testaments to the taste of the period.

Barbary Corsairs

Corsair captains might fly the colours of Tunis (three silver crescents on a green ground) but they were placed under no effective discipline providing they paid over to the dey and his diwan their accustomed share from any prize. It helped that the lagoon foreshore of Tunis, although accessible to the sea, was not used by the corsairs who preferred the harbours of Bizerte, La Goulette and Porto Farina, which all faced directly on to the open sea. The corsair captains made use of galleys, which were capable of sudden decisive bursts of speed from their slave-manned rowing benches. Their low draught meant that they could be beached in any cove or take shelter behind sandbanks and in river estuaries not accessible to deep-bottomed, sailing craft. Their low silhouette also made them an elusive target for ship-based cannon fire and difficult to identify at a distance. The crews were divided between sailors who navigated the craft and the well-armed marines, whose sole job was to board the enemy craft.

The ports of Tunisia were also used by the frigates of the notorious Barbary renegades. These European *rais* had theoretically converted to Islam, but in fact neither knew nor cared for any religion. Such a captain was the Englishman John Ward, who boasted 'if I met my own father at sea I would rob him and sell him when I was done', or the Scotsman Mainwaring who flew the colours of Tunisia, Tuscany or Venice depending on the identity of his prey. The famous Dutch renegade Simon Danser betrayed masters once too often and on falling back into Tunisian waters was seized by the bey and hung for his crimes.

Tunis served as the financial centre for all this profitable activity, disposing of cargoes, arranging ransoms and exchanging contraband war materials. The Genoese, who had long specialized as financial middle-men between Islam and Christendom were gradually eased out of this position by the 'white Jews' of Livorno, who when settled in Tunis rigidly kept their distance from the native 'black Jews'. Even at the height of its activity, from about 1580 to 1680, the Tunisian 'fleet' seldom numbered above 17 ships. In 1654 an English squadron under Admiral Blake toured the Tunisian coast, bombarding the principal corsair ports. The Royal Navy achieved comparatively little destruction to either shipping or shore installations, but it was enough to get both sides down to some serious negotiation. Tunisia agreed not to attack English shipping in exchange for being provided with vital naval munitions with which to attack England's trading rivals. It was all very satisfactory and although France soon reached a similar, but not quite so nefarious deal, the corsairs continued to reap a handsome harvest from Spanish, Portugese, Scandinavian and Italian shipping.

Murad Osta and the Muradid Beys of Tunis, 1628–1705

The ruling class of Tunisia continued to recruit from the Turkish villages of Anatolia, but also relied on European converts to Islam. Some were volunteers but most had been captured young in corsair raids. Such was the fate of Murad Osta (1628–31) who was lifted from his Corsican village while a young boy. Once in Tunis he was circumcised, converted to Islam and trained in the arts of war, like any young Turkish recruit. While fighting in southern Tunisia the beautiful and brave young Murad caught the approving eye of his commander, Ramadan Bey, who promoted him and later trained him to be his successor. Murad proved an exceptionally talented commander and on becoming bey became such a dominant figure that Youssef Dey (1610–37) tactfully adopted Murad's own son as his heir. Such a chain of adoptions was the unlikely foundation of the dynasty of Muradid beys, which ruled Tunisia from 1628 to 1705.

The first three generations of Muradids proved themselves capable. For as well as prospering from the activity of the corsairs, they reopened direct trading links with Europe, welcomed the first consuls to Tunis, encouraged trade and new agricultural crops, established lucrative state monopolies and reaped the benefits of increased revenues produced from customs. Control over the distant southern and eastern frontier regions was increased, but by the late seventeenth century their grip began to fail. In 1675 the throne changed hands five times, in 1702 Murad III was assassinated and three years later the by now thoroughly discredited family was massacred.

Husseinite Beys of Tunis, 1705–1957

The collapse of the Muradid dynasty coincided with an invasion from Algiers. After a victory at El Kef, Tunis was besieged and it seemed probable that Tunisia might become the fourth province of Algeria. Resistance was left in the hands of Hussein ibn Ali Turki (1705–35), born of a Tunisian mother and a Turkish father who had been stationed at the castle of El Kef. As a half-caste *kulughli*, he was despised by the Turkish military caste, but Hussein proved a resourceful military leader who spoke Arabic as a native, and rallied the tribes to the defence of Tunis. He harried the Algerian army until it abandoned its siege and retreated to the safety of Constantine. The Turkish military caste took the first opportunity to rebel against Bey Hussein, but he mastered the coup and had the ringleader executed. Bey Hussein based his power on the *kulughli* caste, who were recruited into the military as were certain favoured nomad tribes of the eastern plain. He also maintained the janissary companies at full strength and tactfully continued to appoint a Turkish-speaking dey of Tunis.

The fruits of this promising political evolution were delayed by a 30-year civil war. It broke in 1728 when Bey Hussein's talented nephew, Pasha Ali (1735–56), who had been trained as heir-apparent, led a rebellion in the interior after he lost his position to Hussein's young son, Mohammed. This palace drama spread throughout the population, which divided itself between the Pashiyya (partisans of Pasha Ali) and Hussayniyya (supporters of Bey Hussein). The struggle between the factions, based on traditional political rivalries that had long been suppressed by military rule, exploded across Tunisian society. Although Pasha Ali had fought his way to the throne by 1735, his uncle continued to resist until the walls of Kairouan were stormed in 1740. The struggle continued in the next generation until Hussein's sons recovered the throne in 1756.

Eighteenth-Century Tunisia

Folk wisdom cautions an Islamic ruler to look to three things: the needs of the souk (the economy), the military and the men of the mosque. Bey Ali II (1756–82) and his heir Bey Hammuda (1782–1814) proved themselves exceptionally capable rulers who carefully balanced the different sections of society to create a harmonious and prosperous nation.

The bey was now the undisputed ruler of Tunisia, although he remained tied by bonds of tradition and respect to the Ottoman caliph in the same way that a Catholic monarch might acknowledge the Pope as his superior. The ruling bey would, with sumptuous gifts, petition Istanbul for the title of pasha, which honour was unfailing bestowed. Tribute was not paid (it was only once demanded, in 1835, but courteously refused on grounds of poverty), but the beylical court continued to send munificent personal gifts to the caliph–sultan. In times of great crisis (like the Greek revolt and the Crimean war) Tunisia freely offered military assistance to the Ottoman Empire. In return the beys continued to recruit Turkish soldiers for their army and received a quota of Mameluke slave boys from the Christian territories of the empire. In contrast to the Turkish deys, the beys moved their court out of the centre of Tunis to secluded palace enclosures such as the Bardo. Here were concentrated all the instruments of state: the principal army barracks, treasury, artillery depot, council chamber and the Mameluke courtiers who formed a permanent secretariat. A more exotic note was struck by the black slaves of the bey's personal bodyguard, the high walls of the harem quarters, lush ornamental gardens and opulent reception rooms.

THE ARMY

The army was maintained at 8,000 men, half of whom were *kulughlis*, although Turkish rather than Arabic continued as the language of the military. The cavalry was recruited from such favoured bedouin tribes as the Drid and Zuwawa. The latter, whose territory straddled the Tunisian-Algerian frontier (and who were employed by both nations) would later gain world-wide renown as the *zouaves* of the French colonial army. The army proved itself in war against the dey of Algiers,

Moulay Ishmael

from 1807–12, when the Husseinites asserted the complete equality of Tunisia against the claims of her powerful neighbour.

The army was also used in the twice-yearly administrative procession of the Bey du Camp, the heir to the throne. In June he marched up the Mejerda valley to the steppe capitals of Beja or El Kef. In November he marched south to the oasis city of Tozeur, returning to Tunis by March.

TAXES

The Bey du Camp collected taxes, bestowed gifts, convened audiences and confirmed the caids, the local governors, in office. The caids were a key link between the bey and his people. They were not government officials, but local notables who were charged with the collection of taxes and the administration of justice. A caid could appoint deputies, *khalifas*, over outlying villages and distant tribes, but might only have a few dozen armed retainers at his disposal. For his expenses he was permitted to keep all the profits of justice and added a percentage to the taxes he collected. Out of this largesse he was obliged to contribute twice yearly presents to the bey and the chief ministers of the court. This highly formalized 'corruption' was kept in check by the bey who consulted with rival local notables, received delegations of complaint and frequently made changes of office. On the isle of Jerba for instance the bey alternated the caidship among three ancient leading families.

The basis of government income remained the Koranically approved *ushr*, or tithe, assessed in livestock, wheat, dates or olives. Customs collected at ports produced another third of the revenue, while the rest was made up of a medley of specific taxes on rental income, profits derived from monopolies and the bey's personal control of the bulk of the export trade. The wealthy Jewish community alone paid the poll tax, which was judiciously directed to a separate account that paid the salaries of the leading Islamic scholars as well as providing stipends for their students.

The productive basis of the nation was the 400,000 share cropping cultivators who occupied the coastal plain, the northern valleys and the southern oases. Bey Ali II paid particular attention to their needs, abolishing a number of harmful state prerogatives, reducing the percentage of the tithe and reforming a number of abuses in the leasing of state lands. Hammuda continued this tradition, personally examining their complaints, managing his own model farms and exorting the virtues of work instead of casual charity. The 500,000 nomadic pastoralists paid a tithe assessed in wool, hides, wax and livestock.

CITY OF TUNIS

The city of Tunis, with a population of 80,000, matched all the other towns put together. Urban dwellers were immune from forced labour and military service, as well as the harsh justice and grosser tax abuses that might fall upon the country-dweller. Cloth-weavers, chechia hat-makers and perfumers occupied the summit of the manufacturing trade and their products were traded throughout the Maghreb, West

Africa and within the Ottoman Empire. Bey Hammuda was so proud of the Tunisian weavers, and so anxious to foster exports, that he refused to wear any other cloth. The work of jewellers, potters, rope, basket and leather workers was restricted to the domestic market. The scattered Jewish communities provided a disproportionate number of artisans, particularly jewellers, smiths and metal workers, for the arts of transformation were treated with suspicion by pious Muslims. The Jews stood outside the normal community, not only in their payment of the additional poll tax and levies for the upkeep of synagogues, kosher food and schools, but also because they had won the privilege of being administered by their own *caid al-Yahud*. The split between the indigenous community of 'black jews' and the immigrant 'white jews' was confirmed when the bey appointed two separate caids. Another isolated community was formed from the remnants of the Ibadi sect who had long been restricted to the isle of Jerba. In the seventeenth century they were permitted to settle and trade throughout Tunisia although their frugal habits, financial acumen and clannishness attracted jealousy usually reserved for Jews.

At the summit of the native, Arabic speaking society were the *ulema*, the scholars of Islamic law, judges, Sufi sheikhs, literate clerks and professors. The 30 most important received a handsome personal stipend from the bey in addition to their normal salaries paid by the *habous*, the pious foundations, which had been established over the centuries for the upkeep of mosques, *medersas* and *zaouia*. Tunis boasted some 300 mosques, 200 *zaouia* and 15 *medersas*, which housed the 800 students of the Zitouna university. In every principal town a *cadi* assisted the caid in the administration of correct Islamic law. In contentious cases the local *mufti*, or a council of regional scholars, could be called upon to give an authorative opinion. At the apex of national justice was the ten-man judicial council, *majlis al-Shari*, over which the bey presided every Sunday. Even in death the graduations of this complex society were maintained, a Turk or *kulughli* was garrotted by a silken rope lubricated in soapy water, bedouin were hanged, townsmen beheaded with a sword and Jews drowned. The passing of a death sentence would mark the end of a judicial session, whereupon the bey would withdraw in order to pray for divine mercy at the Day of Judgement.

Pashas of Tripoli, 1551–1711

After Dragut's death in 1565 no successor could hope to match his stature. A succession of dutiful officials sailed from Istanbul to Tripoli to hold the office of pasha for an average of three years. Just as in Algiers and Tunis, the pasha was assisted by a *diwan,* but unlike the other regencies this council included local notables right from the start. By the early seventeenth century southern Tunisia, which had been conquered from Tripoli by Dragut, was returned to the bey of Tunis. This loss of territory in the west was made good by an assertive policy to the south and east. The most important trans-Saharan trade route in this period ran due south from Tripoli to Ghadames then on to Ghat or Murzuk (in the Fezzan) before heading across the central Sahara to Bilma. The pashas made some attempt to control this route, but their military superiority was blunted by Turkish mercenaries in the employ of local rulers. The oasis of Fezzan agreed to forward an annual tribute, but it remained independent, more closely linked to the emirs of Bornu (modern Nigeria) than to Libya. In the east, a succession of campaigns by such long-ruling pashas as Mohammed (1631–49) and his kinsman, Uthman (1649–72) was responsible for first linking Cyrenaica's destiny with Tripolitania, rather than her ancient association with Egypt.

AHMED, FOUNDER OF THE KARAMANLIS DYNASTY

In 1711 whilst the pasha was away in Istanbul, the local *kulughli* commander of cavalry, Ahmed Karamanlis (1711–45), launched a coup. To celebrate his success Karamanlis invited all the Turkish officers to a great banquet that he organized in his villa in the palmery around Tripoli. The noise of musicians and dancers, and the warm glow of the fires could be seen and heard from a great distance as could the gorgeously attired guests riding out through the gates of the city in the evening light. None of the janissary officers was prepared for the oiled rope that was expertly tightened around their necks as they passed through the reception halls on their way to the central courtyard. In the morning light the 300-strong officer corps lay stretched out awaiting burial, and Ahmed moved quickly to establish the dynastic rule of the Karamanlis. His adult son, Mohammed, was named heir apparent and new beys were appointed for the provinces. A *diwan* was created from the *agha*, the admiral of the fleet, the *khazanadar* (state treasurer), the sheikh (mayor) of Tripoli and the pasha's deputy. The army was no longer an alien military caste, for the 1,500 Turkish-trained infantry and artillerymen were outnumbered by 12,000 local cavalrymen.

Ahmed repulsed two military expeditions sent out from Istanbul at the same time as dispatching presents and protestations of the fiercest loyalty to the Ottoman court. In 1722 Istanbul accepted the new status and appointed Ahmed pasha. He dealt ruthlessly with any opposition even when it came from respected religious figures or tribal lords. A series of military campaigns in the early eighteenth century confirmed the growth of the Karamanlis state. Murzuk, the capital of the Fezzan, was occupied and Derna established as the political centre of Cyrenaica. At the same time Ahmed invited foreign merchants and artisans to Tripoli and provided the encouragement necessary for the expansion of agriculture.

The corsair war was energetically relaunched from Tripoli, but under Pasha Ahmed's watchful eye. Successful corsair captains were welcomed back as heroes with celebratory salutes fired from the castle of Tripoli, but they were also kept under firm control. The ships of Spain, the Italian states, Denmark, Sweden and Holland could be plundered at will, but Ahmed permitted no attacks on French or British shipping. Indeed the pasha made certain that the resident consuls of the two major naval powers felt both secure and honoured in Tripoli. This sage management allowed the corsair fleet of Tripoli to grow just as that of Tunis and Algiers began to decline.

YUSUF KARAMANLIS AND THE AMERICAN WAR

The last years of Ali Karamanlis' long reign (1754–93) were disturbed by a bitter struggle between his sons, Yusuf and Hassan. Yusuf horrified contemporaries by arranging for his brother to be stabbed to death in front of his mother, after which he waged open war against his elderly father. The civil war that Yusuf unleashed allowed Ali Burghul, a disgraced Algerian corsair-admiral, to seize control of the city of Tripoli in 1793 with a mixed band of Greek, Spanish and Turkish desperadoes. Their extortionate 17-month reign of terror was followed by a raid on Jerba which goaded the Tunisian army into action. The pirates were destroyed and Bey Hammuda reinstated the Karamanlis family on the throne of Tripoli. By 1795 Yusuf, a worthy heir of Ahmed Karamanlis, was sole ruler. The corsair fleet, which had become unruly, was re-established under the capable direction of Murad Rais, the Scottish renegade Peter Leslie. Fortunes were earned from ransoming captives and from various protection deals set up with the smaller European nations.

The chance capture of an American ship carrying protection money to the dey of Algiers alerted Yusuf to the amount the young republic was prepared to pay. By the end of the year he too had been promised $52,000, but the US consul, warned that he was paying too much, tried to back out of the deal. This resulted in the celebrated war between Libya and the United States in 1801–5. During the blockade of Tripoli the US warship *Philadelphia* was captured after she ran aground on a reef. Her entire crew of 301 men was imprisoned in Tripoli where they were well cared for. Pasha Yusuf even had the prison warder, who had abused a young American cabin boy, executed. In the mean time one of the first US covert operations was started. Yusuf's only surviving brother reluctantly allowed himself to become embroiled in an American plot, which resulted in the march of an ill-assorted column of irregulars from Egypt across the Libyan desert to seize the port of Derna. There, supported by the US navy, this task force began to form a Cyrenaican tribal army with which to invade Tripolitania. It was a heroically unlikely achievement, but the quiet American who had masterminded the whole affair was ordered to drop these hastily acquired allies in 1805. The State Department had negotiated a peace with Yusuf, who released his hostages in return for $60,000.

Esteem for the Karamanlis was never higher. Yusuf's fleet of 24 warships was by now one of the largest in the Mediterranean and a firm alliance with the British (who had recently proved their strength by expelling the French from Egypt and seizing control of the island of Malta) seemed to make his position even more secure. A busy new trade developed at the docks of Tripoli, where the British navy was supplied with salted beef.

In 1816 a new order was ushered in when Lord Exmouth's fleet toured the harbours of North Africa. Under the implicit threat of the massed cannons of the Royal Navy the rulers of Tunis, Algiers and Tripoli released their last remaining Christian captives and officially ended the corsair war. Two years later the French fleet assisted the Royal Navy in enforcing the *Pax Brittanica* on the Mediterranean sea. Freedom of navigation is a fine principle. It is a pity that only 12 years after it was first enforced by Europe, the Europeans once again renewed their invasion of North Africa.

CHAPTER SEVENTEEN

The Saadian and Alaouite Empires of Morocco, 1510–1822

Unlike the rest of the Maghreb, Morocco managed to retain her independence and keep both the Ottoman and Hapsburg superpowers at bay. This was quite an achievement in itself, but under such rulers as the Saadian Ahmad al-Mansour (1578–1603) and the Alaouite Moulay Ishmael (1672–1727) Morocco went on to carve out a vast southern empire for herself. These glorious imperial achievements were both followed by civil wars, which fractured Morocco once again into a jigsaw of regional identities. Such times allowed the provincial leadership, usually based around a Sufi brotherhood or a warlord, to come to the political surface.

The Portuguese on the Atlantic Coast

In fact Moroccco faced a greater threat from the Portuguese than she did from Hapsburg Spain. This was partly because the Atlantic coast of Morocco was within easy sailing distance of Portugal and beyond the effective range of the Ottoman navy. The Portuguese could also concentrate their resources, unlike the Spanish who were militarily embroiled in Italy, France, England and the Netherlands throughout the sixteenth century. Possession of the Atlantic seaboard of Morocco also made sound strategic sense to the Portuguese as it secured the approaches to their lucrative trading stations in the Far East. As we have seen, by the end of the fifteenth century they had a firm grip on the Straits of Gibraltar through their possession of the five Moroccan ports of Ceuta, Ksar es-Seghir, Tangier, Asilah and Larache.

Between 1505 and 1521 they expanded south down the Atlantic

coast, taking Azzemour, El Jadida, Safi, Souria Kedima, Essaouria, Agadir and Sidi Rabat. There was nothing haphazard about the Portuguese occupation. Each town was garrisoned, new curtain walls were built round the captured towns, the harbours were improved and barracks, churches and artillery bastions were constructed diligently. To this day the coast of Morocco is ornamented with dozens of creeper-draped ruins constructed by the Portuguese.

RESISTANCE IN THE NORTH

As a result of this successful assault by the Christian Portuguese, the authority of the Wattasid sultans progressively crumbled. Leadership of the military struggle in the Mediterranean fell to a local northern dynasty based in the mountain citadel of Chechaouen, descendants of the Idrissids. Their strength was reinforced by the flood of skilled Andalucian refugees that poured into the region after the fall of Granada. The emirate directed a corsair war against the Christians in the Mediterranean through the towns of Tetouan and Targa, both heavily populated by refugees who had a real grievance against their former homeland.

By the early sixteenth century the emirate had been recognized by the Wattasid sultans in Fez. Their bellicose attacks on the Mediterranean constrasted strongly with the local understandings made along the Atlantic coast with the Portuguese. A treaty signed in 1530 between Emir Moulay Ibrahim and the Portuguese governor of Asilah established a chivalric code of conduct. Cavalry raids could carry off livestock, but were forbidden to despoil gardens, burn standing crops or orchards. Merchants who had been licensed by both sides were free to continue their business, markets were established and prisoners were exchanged routinely, and jousts were even organized with the Portuguese in times of peace. While it was undoubtedly an agreeable state of affairs, it essentially legitimized the permanent Portuguese occupation of the coast.

The authority of the Wattasid sultans was limited to the fertile central belt of Morocco, encompassing the great cities of Rabat-Salé, Meknes, Fez and their tribal heartland in the eastern plains. Unlike the Hafsid and Zayyanid sultans, the Wattasids followed a resolutely pro-Ottoman foreign policy beginning with their first alliance with the corsair captain El-Uruj in 1517. In truth they were protected from the full consequences of Ottoman expansionism by distance, and since they had long since lost control of both the Mediterranean and the Atlantic coasts they had nothing to fear from the ambitions of the corsair captains. In 1526 young Prince Ahmed (1526–45) succeeded to the Wattasid throne and his older cousin Ali Abu Hassun, ruling as regent, made a formal acknowledgement of Ottoman suzereignity in the hope of receiving military aid. In 1545 the establishment of a Turkish governor at Tlemcen brought the Ottoman Empire to the frontier of Morocco. It seemed just a question of time before the Wattasids became dependent on Ottoman aid and Morocco simply another province of the vast Turkish Empire. Instead a new dynasty, the Saadians, emerged from the south determined to maintain the independence of Morocco.

The Origins of the Saadians

Even before their final overthrowal in 1465, the Merenids had lost control of their Saharan provinces, although junior members of the dynasty governed southern Morocco from Marrakech. The Wattasids were in an even weaker position. Control of the lucrative trans-Saharan trade route fell into the squabbling hands of tribal lords. As Portugal acquired port after port without resistance, the need for an effective single leadership in the south became apparent. None of the tribes was prepared to submit to its neighbouring rivals, but in 1510 a council of leading sheikhs at last persuaded the tribes to acclaim Mohammed al-Qaim (1510–17) as their leader in the holy war against the Christian Portuguese. Mohammed al-Qaim was a revered *shorfa*, a descendant of the Prophet Mohammed, and head of the Saadian family, which had long been resident in the kasbah of Tagmadart in the Draa oasis valley.

Mohammed al-Qaim proceeded cautiously, carefully gathering support and resources. He moved to the coast, both to place himself at the head of the guerilla campaign against the Portuguese and also to watch over the overseas trade. From the isolated port of Tarkuku, tucked into the wild western foothills of the High Atlas, he developed a flourishing trade with English and Genoese merchants from whom he could acquire vital war materials. For no sixteenth-century army, were it ever so brave, could hope to proceed to war without assured supplies of gunpowder, shot and up-to-date artillery. Mohammed al-Qaim also assumed leadership of the Sufi brotherhood that followed the teachings of al-Jazuli, a great Moroccan mystic who had been persecuted by the Merenids before his death in 1465. The brotherhood, which had been pursuing a vendetta against the central government for decades, was particularly influential among the tribes of south-western Morocco and gave the Saadians the hardcore support they had hitherto lacked.

THE FORMATION OF SAADIAN MOROCCO, 1517–57

In 1517 Mohammed al-Qaim's two sons, al-Araj (1517–40) and Mohammed al-Shaykh (1540–57), jointly assumed leadership of the holy war against the Christians. From their base in the Sous valley they gradually expanded their control over Morocco through 40 years of near-continuous war. In the south the Saadian sultans were welcomed as liberators, in the north they were seen as conquerors, while on the Algerian frontier they were seen as invaders.

In 1525, al-Araj was in a position to occupy peacefully the city of Marrakech after the death of the last Wattasid governor. The occupation was welcomed, for only a few years before Portuguese cavalry from the coast had raided as far as the city walls. There was some desultory fighting between the rival Wattasid sultan of Fez and the Saadian sultan of Marrakech in the following years, but in 1536 al-Araj soundly defeated the Wattasid field army at the battle of Oued al-Abid in the Tadla plain. It marked a decisive shift in power, but in 1540 al-Araj was deposed by his brother, Mohammed al-Shaykh, who had been in command of the siege of Portuguese Agadir. The following year witnessed the great triumph of the Saadians, as they expelled the Portuguese from Agadir, Safi and Azzemour. In 1545 a triumphant Mohammed al-Shaykh advanced north and, in a series of running battles, defeated and finally captured the young Wattasid sultan Ahmed.

Four years later he captured Fez, from where the remaining Wattasid court fled to Algiers, where they petitioned for Ottoman support to regain their throne. Mohammed al-Shaykh, who now aimed at nothing less than the liberation of the whole Maghreb from both Christians and Ottoman Turks, dispatched an army of 30,000 men under the command of his son, al-Harran, into Algeria. Tlemcen was taken in 1551, but as

Procession of a Sufi brotherhood

the Saadian army pushed ever eastwards towards Algiers, the Ottomans were able to rally some of the local tribes against the Saadian invaders. The Saadian army was pushed back into Morocco after Prince al-Harran died in Tlemcen. In 1554 a successful Ottoman counter-attack allowed the beylerbey of Algiers to place a Wattasid sultan back on the throne in Fez, protected by a palace guard of Turkish janissaries. The rule of this last Wattasid sultan, Ali Abu Hassun, did not last the year. The Wattasids were not the only dynasty to perish that decade, for the last Zayyanid sultan of Tlemcen had fled to Oran in 1551 and died a few years later as an obscure refugee in a Spanish port.

Mohammed al-Shaykh's third conquest of Fez left him in no mood to temper his authority with any of the traditional concessions. The extensive gifts of land that had been made to the city's religious scholars, Sufi sheikhs and *shorfa* by past sultans were all revoked, the estates confiscated and their old tax exemption abolished. Nor were the military tribes or mountain districts to be excluded from the nation-wide tax system imposed by the Saadian state.

In 1556 the situation on Morocco's eastern frontier was as tense as ever. Mohammed al-Shaykh entered into a defensive alliance with Spain against the Ottoman Empire, while the Turks besieged the Spanish in their remaining Algerian bases of Oran and Bejaia. In 1557 the resourceful beylerbey of Algiers, Agha Hasan Qusru (son of Khayr al-Din) requested that Mohammed al-Shaykh nominally accept Ottoman suzerainty by striking his coins and making the call to Friday prayers in the name of the Ottoman sultan. Mohammed al-Shaykh, who still planned to expel the Ottomans from all North Africa, contemptuously rejected these demands. In October 1557, while leading a tax-enforcing expedition into the High Atlas Mountains, he was assassinated by a group of Turkish officers serving in the Saadian army. These Ottoman agents then rode like the wind with the sultan's salted head in a saddle bag. Once Agha Hasan Qusru had seen this grisly parcel for himself, he ordered the Ottoman army to advance into Morocco, but his ambitious schemes were frustrated at a battle fought east of Fez.

THE SAADIAN EMPIRE, 1557–1603

When the news of Mohammed al-Shaykh's assassination reached Marrakech, six young Saadian princes were executed to safeguard the succession by the governor. It was a brutal but effective act, which paved the way for the prosperous 18-year reign of Sultan Abdullah al-Ghalib (1557–74). After his attempt to seize Tlemcen from the Ottomans in 1560 had failed, Abdullah al-Ghalib turned his attention north. In 1562 he stormed the walls of Chechaouen and ended the Idrisid emirate's century-long rule. Despite the heroic Morisco revolt of 1568–70, Abdullah al-Ghalib gave no help to his Muslim brothers in Andalucia, for he felt unable to jeopardize his alliance with Spain while the Ottoman threat remained on the eastern frontier. His pious building projects, such as the construction of the Mouassine Mosque and the sumptuous rebuilding of the Ben Youssef Medersa in Marrakech, went some way towards counterbalancing the unpopularity of this foreign policy. Preserved from war, the state so prospered that the sultan was free to wreck his health in hedonistic indulgence of the pleasures found within his palace walls.

THE BATTLE OF THE THREE KINGS

He was succeeded by his son, Mohammed al-Mutawakkil, who assumed the throne in 1574, the same year that the Ottoman fleet conquered Tunisia. Two of Mohammed al-Mutawakkil's uncles (who had survived the royal purge at the start of Abdullah al-Ghalib's reign) now saw their chance. In return for recognizing Ottoman suzerainty they were promised military assistance. In 1576 the beylerbey of Algiers dispatched part of his Turkish army to depose Mohammed al-Mutawakkil and to instal Abdul Malik (1576–8), on the throne of Marrakech. The new sultan duly ordered that Friday prayers be called in the name of the Ottoman caliph, whose name also appeared on the Saadian coinage.

Mohammed al-Mutawakkil (who had fled to the fortress of Asilah and forged an alliance with the boy-king of Portugal, Don Sebastian (1557–78)) was not long in organizing a counter-coup. In 1578 a Portuguese field army of 25,000 landed at Larache and advanced inland led by their sovereign escorted by his entire court. Sebastian planned to seize Fez where Mohammed al-Mutawakkil would be crowned sultan and he himself would become emperor of Morocco. This quixotic dream was halted at a battle fought beside the slow-moving dirty waters of the River Loukkos. The Saadian army, formed from a combination of Turkish, Andalucian and Moroccan infantry, and crowds of tribal cavalry, destroyed the entire Portuguese army. It was a furious engagement, with 8,000 dead on each side. All three monarchs also died that day. The body of Mohammed al-Mutawakkil was found washed up on the river bank, Don Sebastian's corpse was found covered by the bodies of warriors that he and his desperate bodyguard had slain, while Abdul Malik died in his saddle, possibly poisoned by Turkish officers who feared that he was about to betray the Ottoman alliance.

Ahmad al-Mansour, 1578–1603

Abdul Malik's younger brother, Ahmad, assumed control of the Saadian state at the propitious hour of victory. He was not the only beneficiary that day, for on the death of the childless Don Sebastian, the entire Portuguese Empire fell to his cousin and neighbour, the already immensely powerful Philip II of Spain (1556–98). If this had happened earlier it would undoubtedly have embroiled Morocco in the destructive Ottoman-Hapsburg war. As it was both empires were clearly exhausted by a century of war and had only delayed signing a truce in 1578 due to Don Sebastian's unexpected invasion of Morocco. After the Portuguese defeat, peace was duly made. For the immediate future the Saadian sultan of Morocco was safe and also unexpectedly rich from the ransoms of Portuguese nobles captured at the battle of the Three Kings. The body of Don Sebastian was escorted respectfully to his cousin Philip, who replied with a gift of fabulous Indian gems. Sebastian's corpse was buried in Ceuta where it became the centre of a cult that believed he would rise again and lead Portugal to even greater glory.

In addition, the Saadian regime was nothing if not efficient in its collection of taxes from a population variously estimated to have stood between 3 and 7 million. As well as dues from the luxury goods of the trans-Saharan trade, customs revenues benefited from the boom in sugar exports and the mining of saltpetre, which was a vital component of gunpowder. With the money Ahmad al-Mansour (the Victorious) employed Turks to man his artillery and arsenal and to train the Saadian army in the latest weaponry. He also formed guard regiments of European converts and Muslim refugees fleeing the failed Morisco revolts in Andalucia. The Andalucians were formed into a regiment of lancers while the Europeans became a janissary-like corps complete with Turkish dress and discipline. The Ottomania of the period led to Moroccan army officers being addressed as 'bey', 'beylerbey' and 'pasha'. By 1585 Ahmad had developed a useful understanding with England, whose Barbary Company supplied cannons and warships to Morocco in exchange for being allowed to mine saltpetre. The two countries even dabbled with plans for a joint attack on Portugal whilst spying on each others munitions' manufactures.

The comparative security of the military situation allowed Ahmad al-Mansour to turn his attention to the Saharan trade routes. Not since his great uncle, al-Araj, had a Saadian sultan been able to concern himself with the family's former interest in the southern oases. In 1583 a Saadian army reoccupied the strategic oasis of Tuat, but the vital salt mines of Taghaza remained under the control of Askia Ishaq II, the Muslim ruler of Songhai. In 1591 Judar Pasha (a Spanish convert to Islam) led a Saadian army on a 135-day march across the Sahara. The superior firepower of the Saadian infantry destroyed the army of

Songhai and after a murderous campaign, trading cities such as Gao and Timbuktoo were all ruled by Moroccan governors. In 1594 Ahmad al-Mansour received at his palace in Marrakech his first tribute, 30 mules laden with gold. By the end of his reign ten tons had been delivered and the sultan gained another epithet; as well as *al-mansour* (victorious) he was also known as *al-dahhabi* (the golden).

At his glittering court in Marrakech Ahmad, who had long since disregarded his brother's token submission to Ottoman rule, imitated the protocol of Istanbul by giving audience behind a curtain and being shaded from the sun by a crimson parasol. He also abandoned the existing Saadian royal palace, a rather dark kasbah, and started on the construction of the al-Badi (splendid) palace. His youth, largely spent in exile, had given him familiarity with a number of cultures and command of an imposing array of languages. He was a capable scholar, had a good calligraphic hand and was an enthusiastic correspondent, fluent in Turkish, Spanish, Italian and Arabic. He filled the palace with a rich library and proved a munificent patron of poets, musicians, historians, religious scholars and Sufi teachers. His dealings with the common people were not touched with the same concern. He once answered a petition to lower the high level of taxation with the words 'the people of Morocco are lunatics and their asylum consists in oppression'. Like his contemporary Philip II of Spain he was a tireless administrator, presiding over a council every Wednesday, personally reading all the reports from his governors and insisting on the prompt dispatch of government business. His three most promising sons were appointed provincial governors of Fez, Meknes and Taroudant, each with his own arsenal, armoury, foundry and army.

THE END OF THE SAADIAN EMPIRE, 1603–26

Sadly Ahmad's Moroccan Empire dissolved after his death in 1603. His three sons fought so viciously over their inheritance that within a decade they had destroyed the country's fragile order and painfully acquired prosperity. One son, Mohammed al-Sheikh, traded the towns of Badis and Larache with the Spanish in return for their military support. Backed by Christian arms he ruled Fez from 1610 until his assassination three years later. He was succeeded by his son who was even weaker. In southern Morocco Prince Zaidan (1603–28) was expelled from Marrakech by one Sufi sheikh (who went on to marry his mother), but was able to return to the al-Badi Palace in 1613 as the client of another, from the High Atlas Mountains. By 1620 the authority of the two rival Saadian princes in Fez and Marrakech hardly extended beyond the walls of their own palaces. By 1618 the Moroccan garrison in Timbuktoo abandoned any pretence at obedience and proceeded to elect its own leader. The garrison went on to behave as brutally as any of the Spanish conquistadors and in the process of trying to locate the exact position of the goldmines terrorized the ancient trade out of existence. The supply of gold dust dwindled to a trickle and Saharan merchants increasingly moved away from this turbulent zone and made use of the route from Lake Chad to Tripoli, the ancient Garamantian way. Morocco had quite literally killed the goose that laid the golden egg.

Shadow Sultans and Powerful Sheikhs, 1614–64

Half a dozen emirates emerged in the power vacuum formed by the disintegration of the Saadian state. Based on the prestige of a town, a warlord or a Sufi brotherhood, these states provide a fascinating cross-section of the political possibilities in seventeenth-century Morocco.

One of the most colourful and richest was the Republic of Bou Regreg, which was largely the creation of Andalucian refugees. In 1610, in the midst of the Saadian sultan Mohammed al-Sheikh's shocking betrayal of Larache to Spain, King Philip III expelled all his subjects of Jewish or Muslim descent. Some 300,000 refugees poured into Morocco through the gates of such Spanish-held fortresses as Ceuta. Many of them settled in the twin cities of Rabat and Salé which stand on either side of the Bou Regreg river.

The community took to piracy as a profitable and expedient way to extract their revenge on Christendom. The ships of Salé ranged far out into the Atlantic sea routes as well as raiding coastal settlements as far away as Iceland and Cornwall. The Salee Rovers, as they became known, soon achieved a notoriety equal to the Barbary corsairs. Indeed many of the infamous renegade captains, such as Mainwaring, were as familiar with the harbour of Rabat-Salé as that of Bizerte or Porto

Farina. In a formula loosely based on the Ottoman regencies a governing council of elders which included sea captains, religious leaders and local notables, elected an annual president and appointed officials.

In the southern foothills of the Anti Atlas at Illigh, a Sufi brotherhood had long attracted the affection and respect of the turbulent clans and tribes of the mountains. During the collapse of Saadian authority, the grandson of the founding sheikh of this community, Abu Hassun, emerged as the master of the mountains. By 1631 his tribal army had subdued all the oasis valleys and seized control of Sigilmassa. Abu Hassun, who now controlled the trans–Saharan trade routes, the lucrative sugar fields, the saltpetre mines and who traded directly with Europeans through the port of Agadir, seemed to be in a position to repeat the Saadian ascent to power. But his steady expansion was halted by the superior army of the Djila sheikhs who had begun to push south across the High Atlas. Although their moment on the national stage had passed, the Anti Atlas sheikhs remained a powerful force at the centre of the politics of their region. Even today, the *zaouia* of Sidi Ahmed ou Moussa is still one of the spiritual centres of the region.

In 1560 Abu Bekr, a Sufi master from a well-established local family, established the *zaouia* of Dala (or Djila) in the foothills of the Middle Atlas Mountains, where he fed the poor and taught all who wished to listen. From this humble centre grew the influential Dalaiyya brotherhood, which under his son Mohammed ran schools, a highly regarded *medersa*, fed 7,000 pilgrims a day and became the accepted political centre for the Berber tribes of the Middle Atlas. It was the third sheikh, Mohammed al-Haj, who transformed Dalaiyya into an offensive power by creating a fortified camp where he formed a regular army from the fiercest of the Middle Atlas tribesmen. In 1636 this force was used to defeat an advancing Saadian army and to confine the sheikh of Illigh to his southern territories. Two years later Mohammed captured Meknes where he began to brush against the power of al-Ayyashi, the charismatic leader of the Arab Beni Malik tribe and a one-time Saadian general.

Al-Ayyashi had emerged as the dominant force in seventeenth-century central Morocco by co-operating with urban notables and leading the *jihad* against Christian garrisons at El Jadida, Mehdiya and Tangier. In 1631 he imposed an unwelcome overlordship over the republic

Berber musicians from the mountains

of Bou Regreg. Once assured of the support of the Dalaiyyan sheikh, Bou Regreg revolted. In April 1641 their combined army caught al-Ayyashi's force against the banks of the River Sebou and destroyed it. In the aftermath the Dalaiyyan sheikh forced all the great cities – Fez, Rabat-Salé and Tetouan – to accept his governors. For the next 20 years the sheikh of Dalaiyya ruled Morocco, but left the two titular Saadian sultans of Fez and Marrakech in possession of their royal palaces. This acceptance of the prevailing legitimacy was matched by a failure to lead the *jihad* against the Christian strongholds on the coast. Al-Ayyashi began to look like a martyr to the urban and religious notables, who felt nothing but disdain for the backwoodsmen, the uncouth Berber warriors of the Middle Atlas, upon whom Dalaiyyan power rested. In 1660 the old Dalaiyyan sultan was poisoned and the country rose in revolt. His sons struggled to master the situation, but by 1663 their Berber regiments had been forced to evacuate both Fez and Rabat-Salé.

As the Dalaiyya shrank back to its Middle Atlas core, a new round of fighting between various regional warlords began.

Moulay Rachid, the First Alaouite Sultan

Even the most sagacious of Morocco's seventeenth-century politicians could not have predicted the rapid ascent of the first Alaouites, whose dynasty rules Morocco to this day. Even now it is difficult to pinpoint exactly how they achieved control.

Moulay Rachid's Alaouite family were *shorfa* who had moved from Arabia to Morocco in the thirteenth century. Generation after generation they had provided local leadership, but never became especially rich or powerful, remaining gentleman-adventurers in their Tafilalet oasis homeland. Moulay Rachid's father, Moulay al-Sharif (?–1631), had at different times in his life been acclaimed sultan at Sigilmassa, Oujda and very briefly at Fez, but these were all in response to local emergencies in difficult times and never grew into any permanent authority.

In 1663, as the civil war escalated, some of the leading Arab tribes of the eastern plains accepted the leadership of the young Alaouite warrior, Moulay Rachid (1664–72). The next year Moulay Rachid established Taza as his forward base, killed his rival elder half-brother (the pious Mohammed) in battle and proceeded to launch a series of lightning campaigns. In 1666 he captured Fez and two years later he rendered the *zaouia* of Dala a smoking ruin and executed the last of the Saadians in Marrakech. Through his brilliant tactical command of a bedouin Arab army, which terrified Morocco's cities, Moulay Rachid had achieved sole control of the country.

THE ALAOUITE EMPIRE OF MOULAY ISHMAEL, 1672–1727

Just four years after his victory Moulay Rachid died, caught like Absalom in the branch of a tree during a wild midnight ride through the palace gardens of Marrakech. He was succeeded by his younger brother, Moulay Ishmael, under whose long reign Morocco rose to the heights achieved during the great days of Ahmed al-Mansour. At the start however, Moulay Ishmael's inheritance seemed far from secure, threatened by revolts in the cities, by Middle Atlas tribes, by his nephew

Moulay Ishmael

in the Sous valley, by a northern warlord and by the Turks of Algiers.

To face these considerable challenges the sultan (whose mother and favourite wife were black) formed a devotedly loyal negro army. Freeborne Muslim negros, existing black slaves or those fresh from the Saharan caravans were bought into these Abid regiments. The sultan provided his new troops with black wives and encouraged them to have children. At the age of ten the boys entered military colleges where they were trained to both build and fight. At 18 they were drafted into regiments and presented with a wife trained in domestic skills by palace service. By the end of his reign the sultan had a vast Abid army of 150,000. Half were garrisoned in the new capital Meknes, the other half were in barracks at the provincial cities of Salé, Taza, Sefrou and Azrou. The Arab cavalry inherited from his brother and infantry recruited from the Rif tribes were stationed in a chain of fortresses constructed on the frontiers.

The Algiers-backed northern revolt was crushed speedily in 1673, but it was not until 1678 that Moulay Ishmael defeated the Middle Atlas tribes (led by a Dalaiyyan sheikh) at the battle of Oued al-Abid. Finally, in 1686 he destroyed his nephew at Taroudant and reincorporated southern Morocco into his empire. Campaigns, which took the war into Algeria, resulted in a negotiated peace and an agreed frontier in 1696. Moulay Ishmael also began to recover control of the Sahara. From 1676 the distant oasis of Tuat had a resident Moroccan governor and 18 years later there was a Moroccan caid in control of the infamous Saharan salt mine at Taghaza. By the end of his reign Moroccan troops were in possession of all of the western Sahara as far as modern-day Mauretania and were even assisting a Senegalese emir to repel the French.

Moulay Ishmael also scored a number of prestigious victories over the remaining Christian outposts on the Atlantic seaboard. In 1681 he forced the Spanish out of Mehdiya fortress and by 1684 a prolonged siege had forced the English out of Tangier, which they had acquired in 1661 through the dowry brought to Charles II by his Portuguese wife. A direct assault regained Larache in 1689 and three years later Asilah was recaptured. On the Mediterranean coast the four Spanish positions were placed under siege-blockade by local governors. The sultan also encouraged the corsair captains from Tetouan and Rabat-Salé to wage war on Christian shipping. Moulay Ishmael, through his ownership of ships and his royal percentage, took around 60 per cent of the corsairs' profits. Those captives who were not ransomed were engaged in building activity at the new capital of Meknes, enveloped in miles of walls and protected by immense gateways and a vast new government quarter of palaces, barracks, store rooms, cisterns and paddocks. The sultan also directed the reconstruction of towns, bridges, ports, forts, mosques and shrines, and purged the land of the more unorthodox cults.

His authority, although it was directed to securing peace, expanding the frontiers and encouraging trade, was based on the power of his army married to the religious prestige of his holy lineage. He had no wish to mask his authority with elaborate consultations or to rule through existing notables. His trusted officials were all 'new men' who had risen entirely due to their favour with the sovereign. Throughout his long reign he deliberately humbled the *ulema* of Fez, ruined many leading merchants and delighted in arbitrary executions that revealed the full extent of his power. Legends of his cruelty increased with every year, but behind the fables was a consistent policy, albeit driven towards madness by 54 years of power filled by war and rebellion.

Decline, Fall and Partial Recovery of Morocco

Moulay Ishmael was a legendary lover, fathering hundreds of boys and unknown quantities of girls. When he died in 1727 he had done nothing to name, let alone train, an heir. Princes were elevated and deposed by different factions of the Abid army in bewildering sequence. It was only when the anarchy had reached critical levels in 1743 that Prince Moulay Abdullah was able to crush the remains of his father's black slave army at the head of a coalition of tribes. Even then the sultan found his authority restricted to the environs of the four government cities (Meknes, Fez, Marrakech and Rabat) and the coastal plain, and even this dominion was constantly tested by sedition.

In 1750 the exhausted sultan resigned in favour of his son, Sidi Mohammed, who had proved himself a prodigy of integrity. Sidi Mohammed, who had escorted his grandmother to Mecca aged nine, proved such an exemplary governor of Safi that the citizens of Marrakech had begged him to be their ruler. He won great renown by suppressing a revolt even though it was in his favour. Once raised to the throne he sought to unite his turbulent subjects by energetically renewing the *jihad* against the remaining Christian-held cities. Following the devastation of the Lisbon earthquake he succeeded in ejecting the Portuguese from their last toeholds in Morocco, the walled towns of El Jadida and Anfa (Casablanca).

A tribal rebellion in the south brought home to Sultan Sidi Mohammed the absolute need for the government to control the flow of exports and the import of arms. In 1760 he began work on completely rebuilding the harbour town and defences of Essaouiria through which all Morocco's external trade was then directed. Jewish merchants were moved in to handle direct contacts with the Christian merchants and customs were reduced to a flat, but enforceable 2 per cent. Business in this safe well-ordered enviroment boomed, and so to did the coffers of the state treasury. Sidi Mohammed also realized that the naval balance of power had shifted dramatically and that the corsair war was no longer worth the risk of naval bombardments and of disturbing the profits of trade. So whilst not incurring the domestic disgrace of officially abandoning the *jihad* against the Christians, he negotiated protection agreements with all the principal trading nations (even with the infant United States in 1786). These treaties not only bought revenue directly to the state, but did so at virtually no cost to the Moroccan fleet which, reduced to two frigates, in truth posed only a small threat.

The chosen successor amongst the sons of Sidi Mohammed was Yazid (1790–2) who was brave, pious and handsome, but cruel to the point of madness. His two-year reign excited widespread rebellion, but unfortunately his death from blood poisoning did not halt the fighting as his surviving brothers fought for the throne. A cholera epidemic in 1799 left Moulay Sliman (1792–1822) the sole survivor. Moulay Sliman, who had been inspired by the Wahhabi movement of central Arabia, was determined that Morocco should return to the original purity of Islam. Throughout his reign he attempted to suppress the influence of the Sufi sheikhs, dismantle the brotherhoods and isolate Morocco from dangerous contact with the Christian nations. This suspicion of Europe was turned to loathing by the atheism and political extremism of the French Revolution and the Napoleonic Empire. At one stage the sultan banned all exports from Morocco, imposed an intentionally crippling 50 per cent duty on imports and confined all Christian consuls and merchants to live in Tangier, where they dealt through the intermediary Jewish community. His dealings with the Sufi brotherhoods could not be so straightforward and although he managed to destroy many of these regional power centres, ultimately he was to be defeated. In 1818 he led an expedition into the Middle Atlas foothills to uproot a Derkawi *zaouia*, but the royal army was vanquished in a night attack. It is some measure of Moulay Sliman's personal integrity and the sanctity of the Alaouite dynasty that the victorious tribes insisted on treating their illustrious captive with every mark of honour. The sultan was feasted for the customary three days and then escorted respectfully, but firmly, back to the royal palace at Meknes.

The strength of character of this fundamentalist sultan is not in any doubt. He ignored the claims of any of his inadequate sons to the throne and instead nominated his nephew, Abdul-Rahman, to succeed him.

CHAPTER EIGHTEEN

Colonists and Consuls: the European Conquest, 1830–1930

The Industrial Revolution, first incubated in the manufacturing towns of France and Britain in the middle of the eighteenth century, propelled these two nations into a whole new dimension of power, militarily, financially and demographically. Britain would take over Egypt and the Sudan. France would impose her rule over virtually the whole of North Africa, the Sahara and West Africa, while lesser portions were set aside for her two Mediterranean neighbours, Spain and Italy.

For a politically-minded Muslim of the nineteenth century there were important questions to be resolved. How best do we resist the domination of Christian Europe? Do we import the Industrial Revolution into our society, which is to say we Europeanize ourselves, or do we recover our ancient strength by resisting all modernizing influences in order to return to the pure forms of an early Islamic society? It was seldom possible for an individual, let alone a political movement or a whole society, to determine which of these two paths to follow. Kemal Ataturk's Turkey and Wahhabist Saudia Arabia provide the two most extreme (and successful) examples of these political options. For the Maghreb there was no such possibility. There was no policy, no leader, who could have prevented the vulnerable North African littoral from falling into European hands in this period.

If the process of European domination can now be seen as historical inevitability, there were, however, enormous differences in the timing and depth of this 'colonial' experience. The different fates that befell Algeria and Morocco for example, are vital for understanding their very different political cultures. For all its doom-laden inevitability, the story of resistance to the European conquest from 1830 to 1930

257

remains a passionate narrative. It is impossible to think of the modern Maghreb without conjuring up images of resistance leaders such as Emir Abdel Kader of Algeria, Tunisia's Mameluke reformer Kherredine, Abdel Krim of the Moroccan Rif and Omar al-Mukhtar of Cyrenaica.

Algeria

THE FLY-WHISK AND THE 1830 INVASION

Pierre Deval, the French consul in Algiers, had been responsible for a serious breach of Algerian sovereignty by fortifying the French trading fondouks at Bone and La Calle. He had also arrogantly refused even to discuss the debts of France (stretching back to 1798) whose armies had been supplied with Algerian wheat. At an audience on 29 April 1827, Dey Hussein III (1818–30) flicked the face of this arrogant consul with his fly-whisk.

This breach of protocol was fanned into a national insult by a French government desperate to find a foreign scapegoat for troubles at home. The French prime minister, Polignac, having failed with a naval blockade, decided on invasion, ostensibly as part of Britain and France's joint anti-corsair campaign. On 14 June 1830 a French army of 37,000 landed and advanced on the city of Algiers. The dey had formally surrendered on 5 July and the city was looted profitably, more than covering the cost of the whole venture.

Polignac had planned to hand Algiers back in exchange for an enlarged French outpost at Bone, but at this critical moment a revolution toppled the government in France. Clauzel, the forceful local army commander, used this period of political indecision to force through a much more ambitious policy. Encouraging colonial settlement on the rich farmland around Algiers, he also attempted to set up the Husseinite dynasty of Tunisia as France's client rulers in Algeria. A flood of land-hungry French colonists and ambitious speculators streamed into the port of Algiers. In 1831 the appointment of Duke Rovigo as governor gave the policy renewed force. Rovigo was a stage-like representative of colonial villainy, an ex-chief of police who owed his position to his wife's affair with a government minister. He worked hand in glove with land speculators, luring tribal leaders to negotiations where he had already arranged for their judicial murder. Meanwhile the coastal cities of Oran, Bougie and Annaba were being occupied by the French army.

By 1834, when the new French government finally determined a coherent policy and appointed the first official governor-general, the political initiative had long since been assumed by a coterie of generals and colonists. For well over 100 years nothing altered this political configuration.

ABDEL KADER AND BEY HAJ AHMED, 1830–9

After the fall of Algiers the tribal hinterland seized the opportunity to revolt against the old regime. Leadership of the western tribes passed to Abdel Kader, the son of the sheikh of the influential Qadiriyya brotherhood. He was acclaimed sultan and soon proved himself an energetic and efficient guerilla leader, with 10,000 warriors under his command. As well as abolishing the onerous burden of the old Turkish taxes, his standing was further confirmed by the defeat of the French at the battle of Trezel in June 1835 and by his compassionate treatment of his captives, which even won him the respect of the local French general. In 1837 the French, secure in their control of the coast, recognized the authority of Abdel Kader in the Treaty of Tafna and supplied him with arms to enforce his rule over the interior.

By 1839 Abdel Kader was master of two-thirds of Algeria. In eastern Algeria, Haj Ahmed, the bey of Constantine since 1826, never lost his grip on the region. Despite his loss of the coastal districts to the French army he refused to recognize their authority and proudly upheld his position as legitimate representative of the Ottoman sultan. At one point he seemed on the brink of transforming his old province into an independent beylik. However, he placed too much trust in the power of the Ottoman Empire, whose navy had been soundly defeated by the combined British-French fleet at Navarino in 1827.

In 1836 the French government seemed happy with this restricted occupation, but their policy was effectively sabotaged again by General Clauzel. His attempt to storm Constantine in the winter of 1836 resulted

Ali ben Hamed, caliph of Constantine

in the humiliating retreat of a French army through the mountains with the loss of 1,000 men. This blow to French prestige forced the government publicly to pledge itself to a renewed assault the following year. In 1837 the walls of Constantine were breached summarily by sophisticated new artillery, but the resistance was fierce. The new governor-general died during the fighting and the French army was forced to fight for the possession of the city, house by house. After the fall of his old capital Haj Ahmad continued to direct resistance from the southern steppes. The extent of newly conquered territory made nonsense of the French government's policy of restricted authority and in 1839 the opening of a direct military route between Algiers and Constantine (across the territory of Abdel Kader) brought renewed warfare.

TOTAL WAR, 1839–48

France was now set on a course of conquest. An experienced general, Bugeaud, was appointed governor-general and placed in command of a superbly equipped army of 110,000 men. He orchestrated a brutal campaign of terror directed as much against the population as the elusive guerilla bands of Abdel Kader.

Villages, hamlets and orchards were destroyed and torture used to locate underground silos of grain, the few hoarded weapons, the hidden herds and the jewellery of the women. Prisoners were routinely massacred in a campaign that even General Bugeaud described as a manhunt. After three years Abdel Kader and the remnant of his army were forced to take refuge in Morocco. French naval bombardments of Moroccan ports, and incursions by the army across the border, forced the Moroccan sultan to outlaw Abdel Kader and agree upon a new eastern frontier with France.

In the fifth year of war the depredations of the French were answered by a massive but desperate insurrection. The redoubled brutality of the repression, now allied to widespread famine and recurring epidemics, wore down even the heroic resources of the Algerian tribes. By 1848, the ninth year of war, both Abdel Kader and Bey Haj Ahmed had formally surrendered. Only the Saharan provinces and the Kabylie Mountains continued to defy the French.

COLONIAL SETTLEMENT

At the conclusion of this brutal conquest vast new territories were confiscated for colonization. Far more successful than the military colonies, providing a livelihood for discharged French veterans, were the civil settlements, which attracted hard, resourceful men from France, southern Italy, Malta, Spain and even from Germany and Switzerland. By the end of the war there were 105,000 settlers in Algeria of whom less than a half were French. In 1845 these areas of European settlement were formally incorporated into France. The settlers became 'super-citizens', for unlike their colleagues in France, their local elected governments were paid for by taxes levied from a disenfranchised native under-class. The democratic fruits of France's Second Republic (established by the revolution of 1848) were entirely reserved for the European settlers. In the following years a series of droughts, intensified by locust swarms and plague, completed the sufferings of the Muslim population, which had declined by a fifth down to 2,300,000.

NAPOLEON III, 'KING OF THE ARABS', 1852–70

The Second Empire established by Napoleon III in 1852 coincided with a series of good harvests and a general upturn in the world economy. The colonists, reinforced by the rising generation of Algerian-born Europeans, acquired an increasing confidence and turned their backs on the troublesome exotic tropical crops favoured by the French government, such as cotton, tobacco and scents, to concentrate on the cultivation of vines and cereals that were more suited to the region. By the 1860s the profits from this agricultural boom began to fuel the expansion of the domestic economy as roads, dams, irrigation works and railway lines were constructed across the country.

Further expansion of colonial settlement was halted by the military administration of the interior, and a political rift began to develop between the army and the colonial leadership. The interior was governed by the *bureau arabe*, an élite corps of Arab-speaking army officers, assisted by a small technical and medical staff and reinforced by detachments of native troops. The colonists launched a campaign designed to discredit the *bureau arabe* and in 1858 they won the support of Prince Napoleon-Jerome who had just been made minister for Algeria. This naive young prince began to dismantle the administration of the *bureau arabe* and to replace it with locally elected communes. The communes were quick to use their wide-ranging judicial and administrative powers to acquire more land from the natives and encourage further European settlement. This new wave of land grabbing provoked a tribal uprising, which was suppressed by the military.

The unrest at last focused Napoleon III's attention on Algeria and in 1860 he inspected the situation for himself. He was the first French leader to do so and was appalled at the ugly reality. The colonial deputies who had so persuasively talked of 'assimilation' between the two races whilst in Paris, cynically were practising a vicious exploitation in Algeria. The emperor determined to reverse this and to achieve a 'perfect equality between natives and Europeans and a reconciliation between the races'. He looked forward to a time when the European settlers would return the land to its native cultivators and concentrate their energies in the towns. There they could use their superior technical skills to direct the renewal of Algerian commerce and industry. To that end Napoleon III hastily restored the military government of the *bureau arabe* and launched a massive programme of public works. These reforms were matched by a resurgence of Muslim confidence which resulted in the construction of new mosques, *medersas* and Koranic primary schools to replace those destroyed or expropriated by the conquerors. Napoleon III also decreed that from this time native Algerians were to be considered the legal equals of French citizens. It was an encouraging first step although its effect was severely limited by a provision that they could only exercise the full franchise if they abandoned their right to be judged in personal matters by Muslim religious law. This in effect restricted the native electorate to a tiny minority prepared publicly to renounce Islam.

Even this fair wind did not blow for long. In 1868 a two-year famine left half a million native dead while in 1870, to the great delight of the colonial settlers, Napoleon III, the man they derided as 'King of the Arabs', was toppled from power.

THE TRIUMPH OF THE SETTLERS, 1871–1930

In 1871 the Kabylie mountain region rose in a rebellion led by the egalitarian Rahmaniyya Sufi brotherhood. The insurrection, which rapidly spread south to the Hodna Mountains and the Saharan provinces, fielded 100,000 warriors, but crucially lacked an authoritative leadership. The successful French repression of the revolt was followed by an enormous fine of 35 million francs, which could only be met by enforced land sales at government fixed prices. Such was the extent of the new land made available that the government was able to offer a free farm to any European settler prepared to take up residence. While the military were encouraged to proceed with the conquest of the Sahara, the colonists dismantled the *bureau arabe*, replacing it with regional elective communes. The Muslim population elected up to a quarter of the councillors, but none of these Muslim deputies were permitted to elect, let alone act as mayor. And it was the salaried mayors who became the elected nobility, trusted with enormous 'emergency' powers over the natives, who could not so much as travel outside their village without a written permit. As well as their absolute authority over the Algerians, the mayors made administrative judgements independent of any court of law, drew up the local budget, imposed taxes and ordered collective fines, imprisonment and land confiscations. All legal cases involving property were taken out of the Muslim system of justice and handed over to colonial courts staffed with all-European juries. Using these powers to the full the colonists systematically impoverished the traditional leadership as they acquired ever more land. Between 1871 and 1898 colonial land holdings, already immense after 40 years of military conquest, more than doubled. Algerian wine filled the gap left after the destruction of French viniculture by the phylloxera virus, while dry wheat-farming techniques from North America were introduced successfully to the southern steppes.

Rivalries between tribes and brotherhoods were encouraged, while the unifying effect of literary Arabic and a classical Koranic education were discriminated against in favour of French or local dialects. Even the millenial nomenclature of the landscape was obliterated as new French names were given to ancient villages, towns and valleys. Inheritable surnames were imposed on the population instead of the traditional Muslim patronymics and much propaganda was made of the enlightened policy of refusing to allow the Church to evangelize. However, this prohibition was less out of respect for Islam than a fear that too great an involvement between Church and *indigénat* (native) might create clerical spokesmen willing to denounce the habitual injustices of colonialism. As it was, the Catholic Church remained silent and seemingly content to serve as the complacent institution of the settlers. Even such celebrated Christians as Father Foucauld, the desert-dwelling scholarly ascetic, was not averse to acting as a French intelligence outpost.

The remorseless corruption of the communes extended a net of complicity across the entire colonial community. In France the regime was protected by deputies elected only by Europeans. Only now and then would a conscientious Frenchman emerge to denounce the destruction of native Algerian society. The French historian de Tocqueville, back in 1848, had written:

> We have cut down the number of charities, let schools fall into ruin, closed the colleges. Around us the lights have gone out, the recruitment of men of religion and men of law has ceased. We have made Muslim society far more miserable, disorganised, ignorant and barbarous than ever it was before it knew us.

Two generations later, in 1891, deputy Burdeau would highlight the same failings, which the next year were intensified by Jonnart, an ex-interior minister, into a blistering report on Algerian corruption. An ex-prime minister presided over the subsequent enquiry, which put forward a package of reforms and assured the appointment of the admirable Jules Cambon (1891–97) as governor-general. The reforms were applauded loudly in parliament, but later betrayed systematically by a potent mixture of administrative obstruction and political deals brokered by Algerian deputies behind closed doors.

PIED-NOIR ALGERIA, 1900–30

At the end of the century the franchise was extended to the native Jewish community of Algeria who were not required, like their Muslim neighbours, to renounce the practices of their faith. The Jews, although co-opted into the political regime, were wary of their equivocal position and were regularly denounced by political extremists from both the left and right of the colonial political spectrum. By 1900 the colonial population of Algeria approached 600,000, the impoverished Muslim population 3,500,000. This ratio of one settler to six *indigénats* marked the apogee of European dominance. The policy of conferring French citizenship on the children of colonial settlers gradually created a homogenous French-Algerian or '*pied-noir*' citizenry from the diverse national origins of the settlers. At the same time an awareness grew of the cultural differences between a *pied-noir* of Algeria and a French citizen of the mainland. This sense of difference and isolation, and the passions it engendered, were brought to the world at large by the desert meditations of the maveric Isabelle Eberhardt (1877–1904) and the hard, sun-scorched imagery of the French existential writer Albert Camus (1913–60). Isabelle Eberhardt was the illegitimate daughter of an Armenian Russian Orthodox priest and the German-Jewish wife of a Tsarist general, who spent her short adult life in the Sahara. Her conversion to Islam as much as her personal habits, of kif-smoking, drinking, casual sexual affairs and desert travelling in male dress estranged her from prevailing colonial attitudes. Her marriage to a young soldier secured her French citizenship although she was tragically drowned in a desert flash flood in 1904 with a half-finished manuscript.

The first strivings towards autonomy were reflected in the creation of an elected colonial assembly in Algiers, which advised the Paris-appointed governor-general.

As the colonial regime entered its halcyon years in the first decade of the twentieth century, the accelerating dynamic of capitalism was already undermining the whole system. The mythical colonial ideal, an owner-farmer efficiently working his modest landholding with the assistance of modern machinery and local Muslim labourers, was losing out to larger commercial ventures. These great estates of 5,000 hectares made their profits by exporting wine and wheat to Europe. By 1930 half the value of Algeria's exports came from the export of wine. In the process colonial landholdings dropped to 26,000 individual properties, with three-quarters of the Europeans living in towns.

NATIVE ALGERIAN SOCIETY

The surviving Muslim farmers tended to operate only within the domestic economy. Farming marginal land, they were effectively denied access to agricultural credits, co-operative marketing and new irrigation schemes, and over-burdened with taxes. Given the choice they preferred to cultivate their own subsistence plots or work as share-croppers rather than fall into total dependence upon the European colonists as wage earners on the great estates.

As the field of opportunity for the Algerian peasant seemed to grow narrower and narrower, and a growing population put ever more pressure on the land, a new field of endeavour was opened up. In 1910 the first trickle of intrepid migrants made the journey across to the manufacturing towns of Europe. In a little over a decade there would be 100,000 Algerian workers labouring in Europe, usually in despised occupations and living in appalling conditions. Cash remittances from these emigrants assured the survival of entire families.

At the same period a small Muslim élite began to emerge in the towns and cities. Not from the old establishment, these were families that had risen to affluence during the French regime, as legal clerks, complacent councillors, interpreters or native officials. They were a tiny minority, treated with suspicion by the bulk of the population due to their secular habits, French schooling and divided cultural loyalties. Their future ambitions within Algeria were checked by both the 'old turbans' of native society and the *pieds-noirs*, but they found allies amongst the liberal French in Paris. Here they were free to champion a true policy of assimilation, which would extend modern education, grant fiscal and legal equality to the natives and gradually work towards an extension of the franchise. The maelstrom of the First World War (1914–18) suspended any political activity, but left the French government indebted to the 300,000 Algerian men who had helped it to victory. However due to the opposition of the *pieds-noirs* this debt was never honoured. Apart from a slight amelioration in their fiscal status native Algerians remained a disenfrachised underclass. Encouraged by French reformers a 'Young Algerian' movement, led by Emir Khaled (Abdel Kader's grandson) emerged from the widespread disillusion, although the brutal reaction of the colonial regime led to the arrest and enforced exile of many of its leaders. Even the French governor-general of Morocco at the time denounced this unthinking reaction as the 'simply criminal policy of Algiers'.

Tunisia

At the start of the nineteenth century Tunisia was a compact, industrious nation, which might well have participated on its own terms in the technological evolution that was transforming European society. This was not to be. The death of Hammuda Pasha in 1814 marked a critical watershed in good government, and thereafter the commerce and manufactures of Tunisia waned while those of Europe waxed ever larger. It is usual to blame the corruption of the bey's court for this erosion of national power and commercial confidence, although in truth the corruption was as much a symptom as a cause.

Hammuda Pasha's heirs, his brother Uthman (1814) and cousin Mahmud (1814–24), reversed many of his more liberal economic policies, reimposing monopolies and increasing taxation. The outspoken opposition of the old pasha's trusted *confidant* and chief minister, Yusuf Sahib al-Taba, was settled by his assassination in 1815. Yet this was the very period when Tunisia needed his wise counsel, for the fleets of France and Britain were touring the ports of the Maghreb in a graphic expression of the new balance of military power. In 1819 Lord Exmouth's fleet forced Bey Mahmud publicly to renounce the corsair war and to release the last few remaining Christian slaves.

INTRIGUES AND CAPITULATIONS

The realities of this new gunboat diplomacy were not lost on Bey Hussein II (1824–35), who early in his reign contributed a battleship to the Ottoman fleet that was destroyed at Navarino in 1827. During the French assault on Algiers he pursued an ingratiatingly pro-French policy, supplying cattle to the invading army and halting the passage of Ottoman officials and munitions. In exchange for this betrayal of his Muslim neighbour the French General Clauzel proposed to establish Bey Hussein's brother Mustafa as ruler of eastern Algeria and his nephew Ahmed as ruler of western Algeria. By 1832, this grand affair having failed, Bey Hussein started another intrigue – to establish a Husseinite prince on the tottering throne of Libya. If the Tunisian ambassador to Istanbul was hard put to defend his master's actions, Bey Hussein never witnessed their total failure. He died just a week before an Ottoman governor seized control of Libya. By 1842 Tunisia had little room for manoeuvre, caught between the French army to the west and an Ottoman army to the east; neither did it have moral grounds for complaint. Internally, Bey Hussein had also beqeathed a terrible legacy, for his 1830 agreement with France had established the so-called capitulation treaties, which gave European consuls the right to judge all cases involving their nationals. By sytematic abuse of this privilege the consuls, who granted their protection to native, Jewish and foreign merchants, gradually seized control of commercial affairs.

Bey Ahmed I (1837–55) had little knowledge or opportunity to interfere in economic affairs. He was passionately involved in the creation of an efficient modern army in the manner of his boyhood heroes, Sultan Mahmud II and Mohammed Ali of Egypt. He raised a conscript force of 26,000, but it remained half-trained and badly equipped. Sold short by foreign instructors and suppliers, his army failed to impress any professional observer. His other extravagances – a fledgling navy, a new administrative palace at Mohammedia and military assistance freely given to the Ottoman Empire during the

Crimean War – bankrupted the state. At the end of his reign the army deserted their barracks, the naval cruiser he built at La Goulette was found to be too big to sail up the canal into the open sea and his financial secretary absconded to Paris with the remains of the state treasury.

His successor Bey Mohammed II (1855–9) led a popular reaction against these failed modernizations and returned to traditional practices. During his short four-year reign he struggled against the growing influence of the two great powers, Britain and France. This could best be negated by playing on their antagonism, and on the personal rivalry between consuls Richard Wood and Leon Roches, but he was helpless if they sank their differences. In 1857 they forced him to grant a law that gave Europeans equal legal rights, which allowed them, for the first time, securely to purchase Tunisian land.

BEY MOHAMMED AS SADIQ, 1859–82

Bey Mohammed as Sadiq existed in the rarified environment of the Bardo Palace, where he presided over a colourful, corrupt but devoted court of ex-boyfriends. His beady eyes framed by a red fez and full beard provide us with a haunting image to put beside other charismatic figures of the period such as the playboy peace-maker Edward VII or Abdul Hamid, the paranoid autocrat at Istanbul. Another graphic image is of the growth of the Tunis New Town. At the start of Mohammed as Sadiq's reign it was emerging from the despised marsh at the foot of the old medieval walled city. By the end its high buildings stood above wide, well-ordered thoroughfares bustling with traffic and trams. The opulent cafés and bars, lit by gaslight, stood in brilliant contrast to the shaded, twisting alleys of the old city.

The bey inaugurated his reign with a new constitution, which proposed a limited monarchy with ministers answerable to a supreme council of 60. Supported by foreign consuls and Tunisian reformers, it was opposed by the religious establishment and France and ignored, as an irrelevance, by the bulk of the population. The latter was right, for the constitution was mere window dressing for a decadent autocracy grown dependent on foreign loans. In 1863 an especially fraudulent foreign loan was floated, benefiting in equal measure the Parisian D'Erlanger bank, the prime minister, Khaznadar, and a motley group of Arabic-speaking agents. Such was the extent of their 'commissions' that the Tunisian treasury received only a quarter of the sum raised. A year later the bey doubled the poll tax in order to meet the interest payments while removing the traditional tax immunities enjoyed by the religious establishment and the urban communities. The tax rebellion of 1864 engulfed the entire country. The three most interested nations, Britain, Italy and France, rushed in troops to protect their investments and their subjects. By cancelling the tax and manipulating local rivalries the bey slowly re-established his authority before extracting a piecemeal revenge at his leisure. He went on to raise more foreign loans in a fast tightening coil of debt, which by 1868 had exhausted all lines of credit. The European holders of near worthless Tunisian government bonds began to clamour for direct intervention. France was on the point of ordering her troops in, but due to heavy commitments elsewhere decided on a holding operation in concert with the other two interested nations.

KHERREDINE AND THE INTERNATIONAL FINANCIAL COMMISSION

The Bey was forced to surrender control of all financial matters to an International Financial Commission run by France, Britain and Italy, but with Tunisian representation. The officials on the commission proved to be men of integrity. Within two years they had consolidated the debt to 160 million francs and established a 7-million-franc ceiling for government expenditure, which allowed surplus revenue to service the debt. As a result of these reforms Tunisia acquired a financially responsible government. For his part the bey sought to guarantee Tunisia's fragile independence by petitioning to become a province of the Ottoman Empire. As the International Financial Commission continued its work the extent of corruption began to be exposed. The throne was excluded from criticism but prime minister Mustafa Khaznadar was dismissed in 1873 and later charged with embezzling 50 million francs.

The new prime minister, Kherredine Pasha, was one of the great Muslim reformers of the period. His life story expresses much of the innate contradiction of the times. Born in the Caucasus Mountains, he was one of the last generation of traditional Mamelukes, formed from

The consul Roustan presenting General Bréart to the bey on 12 May 1881

levies of slave boys (often Christian by birth), who were trained in
Istanbul to be future leaders of Ottoman society. Kherredine first came
to Tunis in 1839 as a young Mameluke official seconded to the beylical
court. Despite the role of France in North Africa he was a great admirer
of French civilization, having lived in Paris for four years. He was a
major force behind the 1860 constitution, and brought together his
ideas for the reform of Islamic society in a book called *Aqwam al-masalik*
(The Surest Path). As prime minister, Kherredine turned his back on
grandiose constitutional reform to concentrate on the efficient working
of the existing administration and the proper accounting of *habous*
(charitable trust) revenue. The confiscated estates of ex-prime minister
Khaznadar were turned into a multi-lingual school, the celebrated
Sadiqi College of Tunis, for the training of future civil servants. He also
set up a street-cleaning service and a new tribunal, which he hoped
eventually would replace the consular jurisdictions. The efficiency of
his government was even applauded by European residents. His
dismissal in 1877, at the joint urging of the French consul and the bey's
current boyfriend, sealed Tunisia's fate.

EUROPEAN RIVALRY AND THE COUP OF 1881

Kherredine's fall coincided with the end of the Franco-British rivalry over Tunisia. At the 1878 Congress of Berlin the European powers had agreed a division of the Mediterranean, which left North Africa in France's sphere of influence. Britain's various financial interests were acquired either by Italy or France, whose rivalry alone maintained Tunisian independence a little longer. The French imported twice as much into the country as did the Italians, but they had only 1,000 residents against some 3,000 Italians. The Italians also had the advantage of geographical proximity and better, if still spurious, historical claims. They could take comfort as well in the growing domestic opposition to another extension of the French North African Empire, which was seen in France as an expensive drain on resources. Viewed in the long term it seemed that Italy had a good chance of superseding France as the dominant foreign influence in Tunisia.

For these very reasons the French government decided to act quickly. On 30 March 1881, a pretext was concocted (some nonsense about the incursion of the Khroumir tribes into Algeria) to allow the French army to march into Tunisia, and the bey ordered his garrisons to surrender. Resistance came only from a few of the more independent nomadic tribes in the south and from the city of Sfax, where a populist Islamic leadership defied the governor and organized a spirited defence of the medieval city walls against the landing of French marines. On 12 May the bey signed the Treaty of Bardo, which gave the French control over foreign affairs and the military security of Tunisia.

THE FRENCH PROTECTORATE

The first French governor, Jules Cambon, found his powers too circumscribed and began delicate negotiations with the bey, the various European powers and the French parliament to increase them. At the Marsa Convention (1883) France took responsibility for the Tunisian debt, the International Financial Commission was disbanded, most of the foreign consuls surrendered their judical powers and French control of the administration was tightened. The existing administrative structure, from the court down to the provincial *khalifas*, was retained but all effective power was placed in the hands of the French resident-general, French directors who oversaw each ministry and the French *contrôleurs civils* who watched over the provincial caids. The latter were still paid a percentage of the tax they raised, although this percentage was halved and now had to be properly accounted for. The mass of the population found their new rulers models of honesty and diligence, following the example of Kherredine rather than that of Algeria's *pieds-noirs*. There was remarkably little attention paid to democratic forms apart from one or two consultative committees and the elective municipal council of Tunis.

In matters of justice the French proved scrupulously correct. Traditional Islamic courts settled matters of marriage, divorce, paternity and inheritance, while a new system of courts enforced a reformed penal and commercial code. French courts gave justice to European settlers and a mixed Franco-Tunisian tribunal settled mixed cases and all matters involving land. There was no confiscation of land or state-encouraged settlement. European settlers had to buy their farms at the going rate and were particularly encouraged to farm new land whose cultivation was made possible by mechanized farming and irrigation in the Tell, the hinterland of Sfax and the Mejerda valley. A slight twist in the law allowed Europeans to buy land belonging to the state and the *habous*.

As French control over the nomad tribes increased, a grid of new roads opened up the interior of the country. Those tribes who refused to submit took refuge in Ottoman Tripolitania. The Turkish government was in no hurry to give the French occupation of Tunisia (which was officially still an Ottoman province) any form of recognition, so the border remained undefined until 1910. The protectorate's encouragement of capitalist enterprise led to the discovery of mineral deposits in these western hills and in particular of vast phosphate deposits at Metlaoui. The mining companies took responsibility for the construction of an extensive railway network which transported the ores to new deep water ports on the Sahel coast. Perhaps the greatest gift the French brought was sanitary reforms and a minimum standard of healthcare which eradicated the recurring depredations of plague. Much of this work was pioneered by the Pasteur Institute, established in Tunis in the early years of the protectorate. Even today as you enter a Tunisian chemist you cross into something recognizably French. During the 70 years of the French

Protectorate the native population of Tunisia quadrupled from one to four million. The European population was concentrated in Tunis. In 1901 it numbered around 100,000, divided between a comparatively wealthy minority of French outnumbered by three times as many resentful Italians.

KHERREDINE'S HEIRS

Because French rule had only ever been defined as temporary, it was possible for Tunisian reformers to support their modernization of the country. Bashir Sfar, one of Kherredine's most ardent disciples, founded an Arabic newspaper, *al-Hadira,* which supported the protectorate but argued for a more radical policy. It championed female education, attacked the influence of the 'old turbans', especially the sheikhs of Sufi brotherhoods, and encouraged the French to use qualified Tunisians in their administration. By the turn of the century this group, overwhelmingly educated at the Sadiqi College in Tunis, had become known as 'Young Tunisians' in a clear reference to the 'Young Turks' who were busily revitalizing the Ottoman Empire.

The political awakening of the Tunisian masses was based on much more immediate and emotive concerns. The first mass demonstration occured in 1911, to protest at the perceived threat from a French quarry to the El Jellaz cemetery in Tunis, which was crowned by the thirteenth-century tomb of a revered Sufi master. The next year unrest was provoked by the accidental death of a Tunisian girl, run over by an Italian tramdriver. Apart from the outpouring of popular emotion, the second demonstration also called for equality of pay between European and Muslim tram staff. The French reaction was to impose martial law and imprison the Young Tunisians who had publicly supported these trade union demands. Political activity was obscured by the 1914–18 war, but the foundation of the Destour (Constitution) party in 1921 revived the Young Tunisian programme. It called for a democratic assembly, a free press and universal adult education.

Morocco

On his accession in 1822 Sultan Moulay Abdul-Rahman abandoned his uncle's unpopular fundamentalist policies, halting the persecution of the Sufi brotherhoods and opening the ports of the country once more to European traders. The sultan helped the Algerian tribes in their resistance to the French, but his own vulnerability was brought home by the bombardment of Tangier and Essaouira by the French navy in 1832. When, 12 years later, a French army marched into Morocco to destroy Abdel Kader's Algerian army, which included Moroccan volunteers, the extent of the defeat broke the sultan's authority. He withdrew his public assistance to Algeria and the tribes defied his authority right up to the walls of Fez and Marrakech.

As a counterbalance to the French, the sultan began to strengthen his relationship with Britain, who was always anxious to increase trade and frustrate its rival. As a corollary to British diplomatic support the sultan was forced to agree to the Treaty of Tangier in 1856. As well as freeing trade to the port the treaty introduced capitulations, the same judicial privileges for European consuls that had been so disastrous to Tunisian sovereignty. Nor was the friendship of Britain worth this high price. In 1859, as the sultan lay dying, the British did nothing to stop a Spanish army advancing from Ceuta and occupying Tetouan. This second public defeat by Christian armies brought a cascade of tribal revolt down on the tender authority of the new sultan, Sidi Mohammed ibn Adbul-Rahman (Mohammed IV). The Spanish left Tetouan only after they were paid 100 million pesetas, which was raised by handing over control of Moroccan customs to a British-Spanish consortium. Although the sultan gradually managed to impose his authority, in the later part of his reign this was counter-balanced by a remorseless growth in European influence on the coast. By 1900 there were over 10,000 Europeans settled in Morocco, mostly in Tangier and Casablanca, which were governed by foreign consuls who established postal services, built lighthouses, improved the docks and organized a sanitary service. A network of Moroccan agents under the judicial protection of the foreign consuls effectively denied the sultan any control of the domestic economy. The Moroccan dirham lost 90 per cent of its value and trade was conducted in European currencies.

MOULAY HASSAN, 1873–94

Sultan Moulay Hassan was an exceptional individual who attempted the almost impossible task of modernizing Morocco whilst maintaining his nation's unity and independence. On the one hand he had to continue the medieval tradition of annual military progressions through the tribal zones to collect taxes and administer justice, while on the other hand he had to perfect a programme of reform. At the international Conference of Madrid he attempted to reform the consistent abuse of the consular judicial privilege, but none of the European nations (except Britain) kept to the agreement of two agents per consul. He also tried to reform tax collection and end the exemptions enjoyed by the religious and political élite. The army was to be modernized by military instructors recruited from Muslim states such as Turkey and Egypt, but the European powers blocked this scheme. Instead Moulay Hassan had to send promising youths to be trained in Europe. He avoided becoming dependent on any one power by employing a French military mission, a British chief of staff and an Italian firm to build a new munitions factory at Fez. The sultan also kept a watchful eye on French incursions into Morocco's Saharan territory from their bases in Algeria. Having exhausted himself in the service of his country, personally dispensing justice in regions that had not seen a sultan for hundreds of years, he died on campaign in 1894.

THE IMPOSITION OF FRENCH RULE

Moulay Hassan's two sons each inherited one side of his character. The older, Abdul Aziz (1894–1908), was a European-minded reformer, while the younger son, Moulay Hafid (1908–12), was a patriarchal, scholarly traditionalist. Neither possessed their father's balance, magnanimity or vision. Abdul Aziz's increasing reliance on European advisers, many of them worthless commission agents, gradually discredited his authority. He was replaced by his brother in 1908, but by then it was too late to oppose the rapidly expanding power of France. At the 1906 Conference of Algeciras Britain was assured of the neutrality of the straits of Gibraltar and Spain was offered chunks of Moroccan territory in the north and south in return for French rule over the rest. German interests were bought off later, with the secession of a large portion of the Congo in 1911.

Legionnaire, Eastern Morocco *c.* 1908

French occupation of the country began at Casablanca in 1907, but it was not until 1912 that they were in a position to close the affair. Deserted by his foreign allies and hemmed in between the French army and escalating tribal dissidence, Sultan Moulay Hafid agreed to a French protectorate over Morocco in the Treaty of Fez. In the far south news of his surrender led the Saharan tribes to acclaim a local governor, El Hiba, as sultan in Tiznit. El Hiba, the so-called Blue Sultan, led his tribal army north to do battle with the French. Having liberated Marrakech he advanced along the road to Casablanca where his army was decimated by the machine guns and howitzers of Colonel Mangin at Sidi Bou Othman.

Two years later General Lyautey, the first French resident-general, had just achieved control over the central plains of Morocco when the First World War called a halt to further conquest. A skeleton French force, reinforced by the troops of their allies, the lords of the High Atlas, managed to hold on to the existing territory. It was not until 1921 that the French could continue their military advance, but that summer the whole future of European rule was called into doubt by a Rif rising led by local chieftain Abdel Krim. By the middle of July 1921 the tribes of the eastern Rifs had destroyed an entire Spanish army. By May 1924 Abdel Krim's 120,000-strong army of the newly formed Rif Republic had pushed the Spanish back to a few positions on the coast and the next year he struck south into French-held territory, fighting his way to within 25 kilometres of the old capital of Fez. It was an extraordinary achievement, but by the spring of 1926 the entire resources of the French and Spanish states had been marshalled against him. By the end of that year this joint operation, masterminded by Marshal Pétain, had crushed the rebellion. It is a tribute to the spirited nature of the Moroccans that it was only in 1936 that the last vestiges of tribal opposition to the French were finally crushed.

THE ADMINISTRATION OF MOROCCO

The port of Tangier and its immediate hinterland remained a demilitarized zone, an international city ruled, or rather misruled, by a council of consuls assisted by French and Spanish civil servants. On the opposite shore, linked by steamer, sat the smug British fortress of Gibraltar, the original cause of Tangier's limbo-like status. Tangier became a safe haven for remittance men, homosexuals, smugglers, bankers, spies, artists and writers. It took a leading role in the European-influenced world of Maghrebi literature and art. The city was the base for such great French masters as Delacroix and Matisse whose images still dominate foreign perceptions of North Africa, as well as being the chosen home of such British artists as James McBey and Sir John Lavery. Its streets have also left their enduring mark in the work of Camille Saint-Saëns, William Burroughs and the beat poets. It is, however, the long-term Tangier resident American Paul Bowles who first fully explored the Maghreb in the English language. Whether in his own novels, short stories, in recording traditional music or translating the works of such writers as Mohammed Mrabet he has had an enormous influence.

The Mediterranean coast of Morocco was the core of the Spanish Protectorate although they also ruled over a vast but sparse part of the

Moroccan Sahara. Spanish rule in both zones was military; colonial settlement was not encouraged and economic development was restricted to the cities of Tetouan, Melilla and Larache, united by 500 kilometres of twisting mountain roads. The effect Morocco had on Spain was at least as profound (or as destructive) as that of Spain on Morocco, for it was General Franco's command of northern Morocco and its native regiments of Rif tribesmen that proved crucial to the fascist victory in the Spanish Civil War.

The rich central regions of Morocco all fell to the French. General Lyautey, the first resident-general, was a man of peculiar vision who brought a lifetime of experience to his appointment. In the same way as in Tunisia the French maintained the existing social and political structures. The whole panoply of imperial Morocco, from the sultan with his many palaces, to the pashas of the cities, the caids of the provinces and the village council of notables was kept intact, but under close supervision by French officials. Apart from minimal improvements to water supply and sanitary arrangements the traditional cities were left untouched. The European settlers were housed in distinct 'new towns' whose wide, tree-lined boulevards overlooked by apartment blocks and cafés stood in graphic contrast to the native quarters.

The protectorate acted as a benign umbrella for the safe deployment of capitalism, having first constructed a bare infrastructure of roads and new administrative centres. It was the bankers and entrepreneurs who developed the mines and railways and who created efficient agricultural businesses, which could afford to invest in dams, mechanization and new irrigation schemes. These large estates, on land bought legitimately, amounted to approximately one million hectares, mostly on the fertile northern plain and on the irrigated lands around the cities of Marrakech, Beni Mellal, Meknes and Taroudant.

This pattern of development produced a very different political reality from that of Algeria or even Tunisia. For although there were over 300,000 Europeans living in Morocco, the bulk of colonial investment was controlled by a rich minority of 5,000. This group actively colluded with the traditional Moroccan élite, a closed world of urban merchants, provincial governors, religious notables and members of the ruling Alaouite dynasty.

One of the more distinctive, and notorious, features of French rule in Morocco was its political alliance with the Berber lords of the High Atlas Mountains. Formed of military necessity during the testing years 1914–21, the policy allowed the most forceful of these lords, Thami al-Glaoui, to construct a state within a state. His feudal domain, upheld by garrisons of the French Foreign Legion, stretched from the foothills of the High Atlas to the Algerian frontier. If it was a cheap form of government for the French, it also tied in with their policy to divide and rule. Tribal divisions were always respected and the particularism of the Sufi brotherhoods protected. On a grander scale the French hoped to expand the linguistic division between the Arab-speaking cities and plains, and the Berber-speaking mountain dwellers. Local customary law was given legal recognition, and the learning of French as opposed to Arabic was encouraged through a number of state-funded schools. The college of higher education established at Azrou aimed to create a body of Berber officers and administrators loyal to France.

Libya

In the early nineteenth century Karamanlis rule over Libya seemed firmly established. The dynasty had come well out of the war with America and was preparing to expand south down the Saharan trade routes. Three decades later, however, it was toppled in a coup orchestrated by its closest ally, the British consul. In the resulting confusion the Ottoman Empire acted quickly to save Libya from the rule of Christian Europe for another two generations. It was not until 1911 that an Italian army would land on the shores of Libya and find itself locked in a 20-year war of colonial conquest.

THE CONSUL'S COUP

Ever since he had established himself as pasha of Tripoli in 1795, Yusuf Karamanlis (1795–1832) had favoured a close understanding with Britain. After Britain had established its naval supremacy in 1805 an imbalance inevitably crept into the relationship. The proximity of the British fleet in Malta was used by the British consul, Richard

Mahmud Mosque minaret, Tripoli

Warrington to advance British influence over Yusuf Pasha. A large Maltese trading colony was established in Tripoli, Warrington befriended a number of powerful tribal leaders and established a network of British vice-consuls in all the chief towns of Libya. Even in the distant Saharan oasis of Murzuk there was an 'English House' to be found. The suppression of the corsair war undermined the finances of the Karamanlis state and as the pasha became dependent on loans he fell further under the influence of the foreign consuls. To reverse this dependence Yusuf Pasha planned to seize control of the trans-Saharan trade by the conquest of the Bornu emirate. This adventurous scheme was blocked by Warrington, who used his influence to direct the exploration of the Sahara by British officers. This was no mere scholarly inquiry, but an attempt to establish British influence over the central Sahara and the Sudan.

In 1825 the French appointed an energetic consul, Charles Rousseau, to keep a check on the growth of British power. An absurd duel developed as the two consuls competed to extract new privileges from the increasingly powerless pasha. Behind this escalating diplomacy stood the very real threat of a naval bombardment, or worse. In 1830, the year that the French seized Algiers, a French naval squadron forced Yusuf Pasha to limit his fleet and to sign a non-aggression pact. Alarmed by this sudden surge in French influence, Warrington launched a *coup d'état*. He bought up a large proportion of Yusuf Pasha's foreign debts at a healthy discount and then called on the pasha to honour them, backed by the threat of naval action. The pasha was in no position to pay and his attempt to raise sufficient revenue from his subjects sparked off a number of tribal revolts including that of the Ouled Sulayman, a close ally of Warrington. By 1831 the chief of the Ouled Sulayman controlled central Libya and had formally requested to be placed under British protection. In January 1832 the chief petitioned the British government to occupy the country and preserve law and order. Later that year the British fleet anchored off Tripoli with an ultimatum to settle the debts in 48 hours. Yusuf tried to raise an emergency levy, but faced with widespread disobedience he abdicated in favour of his son Ali (1832–5). Warrington refused to accept this and brought in his tribal allies to back the candidature of a rival Karamanlis, Yusuf's grandson Mohammed. Ali was left in control of Tripoli while Mohammed held the surrounding country.

Warrington had, however, overreached himself. The conservative British government had been replaced by liberal reformers who had no wish to get involved in the expensive rule of Libya. The French, sensing a change in the wind, energetically began to back the candidature of Ali. The situation, further complicated by Husseinite intrigue, had locked into a stalemate by the summer of 1834.

The Ottoman Empire, which had not directly governed Libya since 1711, was reluctant to abandon its support for the local Karamanlis dynasty, but now saw that there was no alternative if Libya was to be saved from the Christians. In May 1835 an Ottoman fleet steamed into Tripoli harbour, seemingly in response to a request for assistance from the embattled Ali Karamanlis. Ali was arrested and two days later

Mohammed Karamanlis, abandoned by both his foreign patron and his tribal allies, escaped east. Overwhelmed with despair he took his life outside the walls of Misurata. Suicide is rare in Muslim dynasties but not amongst the Karamanlis, for it was the chosen end of Ahmed, the founder of the dynasty, who had shot himself in the stomach at the end of his long reign.

DIRECT TURKISH RULE, 1835–1911

Although Karamanlis Tripoli had fallen overnight, it took the Turks six years before they subdued the Berber hillsmen of the Jebel Nafusa and the Ouled Sulayman of the Sirte desert. By 1842 the country was at long last at peace, divided into the four sub-provinces of Cyrenaica, Jebel Nafusa, Homs and Fezzan. It is fashionable to decry this late-Ottoman period and to see the Turkish garrisons as oppressive, but that is to ignore some enlightened attempts at reform. Harbours were dredged, artesian wells sunk and a modern system of education established in the chief towns, where Arabic was taught alongside Turkish and the major European languages.

Slavery, which was not officially prohibited in Libya until 1857, continued throughout most of the nineteenth century. Small illicit slave caravans continued to cross the Sahara, but even in a busy year this contraband consisted of up to 3,000 negro slaves, the majority of whom passed into domestic service in the more opulent and traditional households of the Middle East. Ever since the virtual extinction of the gold trade in the seventeenth century, slavery had been the last profitable item of the trans-Saharan trade. Libya's key role in this trade enabled it to enter the modern era with a substantial Saharan territory, which was only maintained by being assiduously guarded.

THE SENUSSI OF CYRENAICA

The Senussi brotherhood *(Sanusiyya)* was established as a direct reaction to European dominance over the traditional lands of Islam. The brotherhood was first founded in western Algeria in 1837 by Sayyid Mohammed ibn Ali al-Senussi (1837–1859), who was soon forced to escape from French rule and so moved east, establishing a new headquarters in the mountainous hinterland of Cyrenaica at Al Beida in

1843. Like the Wahhabbists of Saudia Arabia the brotherhood was not so much a mystical confraternity as a fundamentalist reform movement, which attempted to strengthen Islam against the Christian threat by returning to the true path of the Prophet. All European vices (such as smoking tobacco) were purged. The Senussi found the desert both a physical refuge from expanding European influence and a healthy return to the seventh-century lifestyle of the Prophet. Their main *zaouia* migrated ever further south, moving from Al Beida to the oasis of Jaghbub, from there to the oasis of Kufra in 1895 and on to Qiru in the central Sahara in 1899. Senussi brothers trained at the headquarters were sent out to each of the desert tribes. Their zeal and selfless scholarship made them valuable members of any nomadic community for they could teach, reveal the law and arbitrate in the interminable clan disputes. By 1900 there were over 143 branches of the Senussi brotherhood scattered across eastern Libya and the Sahara.

The Turkish governors in Benghazi developed a peaceful understanding with the Senussi brotherhood, whose absolute influence in the desert was useful in resisting European penetration. By 1856 this informal understanding was codified in a treaty with the Ottoman sultan, who formally exempted the brotherhood from tax and gave it the right to collect the Koranic tithe in its desert territories. Throughout the rest of the century the Senussi governed the interior while the Turks concentrated their administration on the coast.

THE ITALIAN INVASION, 1911–12

At the Congress of Berlin in 1878, France and Britain encouraged the Italians to look to the Ottoman province of Libya as their allotted zone of influence. Italy was not strong enough to proceed with direct colonization, but instead set about pouring resources into Libya, buying up land, establishing medical and educational missions and setting up Italian businesses and a postal system. In 1908 the success of this long-term policy of creeping infiltration was endangered by the Young Turk government, which called a halt to any further extension of Italian influence. After a sudden spate of German acquisitions in Libya in June 1911 however, the Italian government decided to strike. In late September, Italy declared war on the Ottoman Empire and sailed south to seize the five ports of Tripoli, Benghazi, Derna, Tobruq and Khoms. It was an act of unprovoked aggression, and the tribes of Libya flocked to support the small Turkish force. The 7,000-strong Turkish garrison led a spirited defence, which hemmed the invading army of 60,000 into the cities and inflicted heavy casualties. The Turks also dispatched 365 respectable young Libyans to be trained as modern officers in Istanbul and established three training camps in Libya itself. The calibre of the Turkish instructing officers, who included Enver Pasha and Kemal Ataturk (the two greatest Turkish commanders of the twentieth century) could not have been higher.

In 1912 the Italians poured more troops into Libya and began to place intolerable diplomatic pressure on the Young Turk government in Istanbul. Threatened with an invasion of the Aegean, the Turks were forced to evacuate Libya. Some face was saved by retaining the religious leadership of the country through the sultan's position as caliph and by granting the country autonomy first, rather than directly surrendering it to the Italians.

TRIPOLITANIAN AND CYRENAICAN RESISTANCE

Given their long history of separation, it was not surprising that resistance to Italian colonization in Tripolitania and Cyrenaica differed substantially. In Cyrenaica it was believed that the Ottoman sultan had bestowed the leadership of Libya upon the Senussi brotherhood. From autumn 1912 the Senussi sheikh Sayyid Ahmad al-Sharif was known as emir of Cyrenaica. Although deprived of military supplies by the British blockade of the Egyptian frontier, Senussi-led resistance denied the Italians control of the Cyrenaican countryside. With the outbreak of the First World War the Libyan tribes were once again assisted by the Ottoman Empire. A joint Senussi-Turkish force of 3,000 men attacked British positions in the Egyptian desert, but when a British counter-offensive shattered this desert army Emir Sayyid Ahmad was deposed and replaced by his pro-British cousin, Sayyid Mohammed Idris.

In 1917 both the British and Italian authorities agreed to confirm the old privileges of the Senussi brotherhood, who remained the effective rulers of a vast desert region. In 1919 Cyrenaica signed a statute granting full Italian citizenship and an elected parliament. The Senussi emir Sayyid Idris was confirmed in his government of the interior.

In Tripolitania the brotherhood had never exercised any influence and leadership rested with tribal leaders. By 1914 the Italians had secured control of the coastal plain, but remained unable to enforce their authority over the steppe and desert. For a while an Ottoman prince attempted to create an alternative administration in the unconquered interior, but he was hampered by the bitter rivalries of the tribal chiefs. In 1918 a leading Arab nationalist from Egypt, Abdul-Rahman Azzam, used his personal standing to create a brief Tripolitanian Republic. Although incapable of government this paper republic did allow Azzam to negotiate with the Italians. In June 1919 the Tripolitania Statute was signed. This remarkably enlightened document would have allowed Libyans access to the full dignity of Italian citizenship while an elected parliament would have advised the Italian governor.

In 1921 the Senussi Sayyid Idris was placed in an impossible position when a delegation of Tripolitanian notables offered him the emirate. To decline the offer was to betray this golden opportunity of uniting Cyrenaica and Tripolitania and forging the Libyan nation, while to accept it was to betray the recent peace he had signed with the Italians. He accepted the offer at the same time as disappearing into exile, delegating his authority as emir of Cyrenaica to his brother Mohammed al-Rida and that as emir of Tripolitania to a cousin. These scrupulous moral dispositions came to nothing, for in October 1922 the fascist leader, Benito Mussolini, assumed the leadership of Italy.

OMAR AL-MUKHTAR, 1922–32

By the spring of 1923 the statutes had been torn up by fascist governors who were determined to proceed with the military conquest of the country. The whole frightful new technology of twentieth-century warfare, aerial bombardment, barbed wire, machine gun posts, minefields and armoured cars, was imported into North Africa for the subjugation of the Libyan tribes. By the end of 1923 effective resistance in Tripolitania had ceased whilst all the old Senussi *zaouia* in Cyrenaica had been occupied and their leaders expelled.

However, the Cyrenaican people continued to wage a heroic war of

Omar al-Mukhtar, leader of the resistance movement

resistance led by Omar al-Mukhtar, the sheikh of a small Senussi *zaouia*. Omar was a saintly figure of austere personal habits and an absolute moral integrity. He had a quiet, scholarly demeanour accentuated by his age and the small round spectacles beneath which hid incredible physical stamina. Collecting a Koranic tithe, he paid for the acquisition of military supplies which were smuggled into Cyrenaica through the Sahara desert. Omar was personally in command of his own band of warriors (*minifa*), which seldom exceeded 500 men. This band provided the core of the resistance, but one of the great successes of the Cyrenaican resistance was the diffusion of its authority. Each tribe marshalled its own *minifa*, led by its own commander, which could at a moment's notice melt back into the tribal population, hiding their weapons and picking up their customary farmers' or shepherds' tools. Omar's genius directed these scattered forces in simultaneous operations, engaging the occupying army on a dozen disparate fronts at once, ambushing the relief column and evaporating in the face of larger concentrations of the enemy. After seven years of counter-insurgency campaigns the Italian army still only ruled Cyrenaica by day. By night it was the domain of Omar al-Mukhtar.

In 1930 the appointment of Marshal Graziani resulted in a new escalation of this war of conquest. If the guerilla fighters could swim like fishes through the lake of people, Marshal Graziani determined to drain the lake. He constructed a chain of concentration camps along the coast into which the population of Cyrenaica was herded. Deprived of their traditional leaders and placed under constant supervision, the population was decimated by a combination of disease, malnutrition and the harsh, alien prison enviroment. On the eastern frontier a 300 kilometre-long barbed wire fence had meanwhile been constructed to cut off Omar al-Mukhtar's Saharan supply line. Native auxiliary troops were dismissed from service in case they continued to leak intelligence and munitions to the resistance. At the same time other native regiments (raised in Eritrea and Somalia) assisted the Italian army in ruthless manhunts that criss-crossed the now empty Cyrenaican countryside. On 11 September 1931 Omar al-Mukhtar's *minifa* seemed to be on the point of once again frustrating their pursuers by dispersing in different directions, but at a critical moment Omar's horse stumbled and crushed his leg. Omar was seized and after a fascist show trial, was executed five days later in the centre of the principal concentration camp. He maintained his dignity to the end, taking personal responsibility for all the Italian prisoners who had been executed during the war. His death was a critical blow to the doomed resistance and within four months the fighting had ceased.

THE FOURTH SHORE: COLONIAL SETTLEMENT IN 1930s LIBYA

In Tripolitania and the Fezzan the Italians had been careful not to offend native society by dispossessing occupants from the land. What colonial settlement did occur was restricted to land confiscated from the Turks and to new agricultural zones created by irrigation. After the victory in Cyrenaica however, the empty land and cowed native population in the concentration camps presented the Italian fascists with an irresistible opportunity. By 1934 over 500,000 hectares of the fertile middle belt of the Cyrenaican uplands had been confiscated from the powerless tribes and made available in small lots to Italian peasant cultivators at a nominal cost. This policy of state-directed settlement continued, with a further 20,000 peasant cultivators settled in 1938 and another 12,000 in 1939. Mussolini envisaged that this 'second period' of Roman colonization would, by 1960, create a population of half a million Italians in Libya. The tribal people, liberated from the camps, were directed to the less fertile southern and northern foothills where they were supervised by colonial officers.

Alongside this wholesale land expropriation there was a more constructive policy of state-directed public works. A 5,200 kilometre-long road network and 400 kilometres of rail track were laid down within a spectacularly short time, and showpiece constructions such as the monumental Arch of the Philameni, in the middle of the Sirte desert, were erected. The fascist state also assumed responsibility for the maintenance of mosques and shrines (apart from the tombs and *zaouai* of the Senussi which had been flattened), assisted in the organization of the pilgrimage to Mecca and even officially banned the sale of alcohol during Ramadan. In 1939 Libya was formally annexed to Italy as its 'fourth shore' with a special civic status created to preserve the religious traditions of the new Muslim citizens of predominately Catholic Italy. Whether the 120,000 Italians resident in Libya could, unlike the French, have forged an equal relationship with the indigenous population was never to be seen. The brief period of Italian rule was soon destroyed in the Second World War.

CHAPTER NINETEEN

The Struggle for Independence, 1934–62

In 1930, France's dominance of North Africa looked triumphantly assured. Yet a generation later, by 1962, Tunisia, Morocco and Algeria had all won their independence. Despite decades of talk about administrative reforms and constitutional adjustments, independence ultimately was secured only by the machine gun and the terrorist bomb. Although Tunisia led the way in political agitation, followed by Morocco after the exile of Sultan Mohammed V in 1953, it was the Algerian Insurrection from 1956 to 62 that was to be the crucial testing ground of power. Here, in one of the decisive battles of the twentieth century, the long legacy of European imperialism finally was drowned in blood.

The background changes that allowed this rapid reversal to occur require some explanation. On one side of the equation is the rising population of the Maghreb led by an articulate local leadership inspired by the rebirth of political confidence throughout the wider Arab and Muslim world. On the other side, France had been weakened and humbled by the Second World War (1939–45). Despite these testing circumstances, France's grip over North Africa had not loosened and in the 1950s she was still immeasurably superior to the Maghreb in terms of resources. Although the new world powers, the United States and the USSR, both clearly favoured Maghrebi independence, they were never more than interested well-wishers. Independence would have to be fought for in a passionate armed struggle, which was to claim hundreds of thousands of lives.

The Colonial Edifice Complete

In 1930 in Algiers, the *pied-noir* settlers celebrated 100 years of French conquest: statues were raised to generals, a celebration was held at the first landing point of Sidi Faraj and a monument raised to the unknown colonist at Bufarik. In Tunisia an Eucharistic conference was held in the prominent new cathedral in Carthage, where Catholic delegates dreamed aloud of a revival of North African Christianity. In the following years the last corners of native resistance were subdued with the aid of aerial bombing, armoured cars, minefields and machine guns. In 1931 resistance in Cyrenaica collapsed, in 1932 the tribes of the Anti Atlas and the western Sahara made their peace, while in 1934 the last faction of the Ait Atta of southern Morocco, besieged in Jebel Bou Gafer, made its submission. In countless articles and travelogues misinformed European writers praised the settlers and administrators who had brought peace and civilization to North Africa. Their role was compared nostalgically to that of the Roman Empire while the achievements of Islam and Arabic literature were either patronized or ignored.

Politicization Before 1939

In Algeria the revival of national awareness was led by a handful of traditional Islamic scholars who had studied in Cairo, Mecca and Damascus. The Salafiya brotherhood, a late-nineteenth-century Egyptian reform group, was of particular influence. The Salafiya argued that it was permissible to use European inventions as tools in the return to the progressive faith of the Islamic *salaf*, forefathers. On their return to Algeria these scholars established the Association of Reforming Ulama, which set up independent schools (some 200 by 1954) and printing presses, as well as educating adults. They produced the first ever Arabic histories of Algeria, such as Sheikh al-Madani's *Kitab al-Jazair*, which proudly carried on its cover the future battle cry 'Islam is our religion, Algeria is our country, Arabic is our language'.

In France, thousands of Algerian migrant workers were initially politicized by the Communist party who set up the Etoile Nord-

Africaine (ENA), the North African Star, in 1926. A year later Messali Hadj, a charismatic orator, took over the organization, which looked increasingly to the nationalist parties of the Middle East for inspiration.

In Algeria, the francophile Young Algerian movement led by Farhat Abbas continued to press for complete assimiliation with France. Their hopes had been disappointed in 1927 when the *pied-noir* deputies in Paris brought about the fall of Violette, a sympathetic governor-general. Violette, having had himself elected a deputy, returned to the attack in 1930 and tabled a private bill in parliament for a modest extension of the franchise to French-educated, middle-class Muslim Algerians. It was defeated. A year later Violette published his prophetic pamphlet *Will Algeria Survive?* in which he argued that France had now reached a political crossroads. If she failed to create allies of some of her North African subjects the colonial edifice would be overthrown in 20 years' time. Much of his argument rested on simple Malthusian arithmetic. In 1830 it had been possible for France, with a population of 30 million, to conquer Algeria with its population of 2 million. By 1950 Algeria's Muslim population would have risen to 8 million.

In 1936 the election of a left-wing government, the Popular Front, gave Violette a chance to continue with the peaceful reform of Algeria. The Blum-Violette Bill was a mild enough measure, for it only proposed enfranchising 20,000 of Algeria's élite, but even this proposal was defeated. This savage rejection of assimilation slammed the door closed. A new militancy entered the Algerian political arena, with Farhat Abbas' foundation of the Union Populaire Algérienne and Messadi's Parti du Peuple Algérien.

TUNISIA

In Tunisia there had been an even greater intensification of political activity during the late 1930s. It began in 1934 when the radical wing of the Destour Party, the political heir of Kherredine and the Young Tunisians, broke away to form the militant Neo-Destour party, which established underground cells throughout the nation, especially in the hitherto neglected provincial cities of the south. Cadres were trained patiently to reiterate the watchwords of the leadership and to politicize the masses. In the following years Tunisia, like western Europe, was rocked by a series of organized street demonstrations. Police repression resulted in hundreds of deaths, thousands of arrests and the imprison-ment of the party leadership. In the process the Neo-Destour and its leader Habib Bourguiba were firmly established as the political vanguard of the nation.

MOROCCO

In Morocco political development remained in its infancy. It was restricted to a small group of intellectuals from Fez and Rabat who had first met in secret in 1925 to discuss the prospect of independence if Abdel Krim's Rif rebellion succeeded. The scholars from Fez tended to be Salafi-influenced *ulema*, those from Rabat, French-educated, liberal members of the professional class. It was not until after the 1936 labour disputes (in which both French and Moroccan workers protested) and the drought of 1937, that this rarefied group emerged as a political party supported by 7,000 members. As the disturbances heated up during 1937, the French authorities clamped down on the nascent independence party and sent such leading figures as Allal al-Fassi into exile.

The Effects of the Second World War

Viewed from a Maghrebi perspective, the 1939–45 war loses its moral imperative and looks like another episode in the fight for European dominance between France, Britain and Germany. Had it not been that fighting spilled over into the Maghreb, it would have made little impact. For France never faltered in her rule over Morocco and Algeria, and even the six-month interregnum in Tunisia was swiftly crushed. American support for the right of self-determination encouraged the French to take a liberal attitude towards the nationalist parties during the war years, but this ended the moment the war had been won.

If the short-term effect was slight, the long-term effect of the 1939–45 war was of immense importance. France and Britain only emerged on the winning side thanks to their dependent alliance with the much greater powers of the United States and the USSR. Without doubt this broke the spell of authority cast by 100 years of European military superiority in the Maghreb. Perhaps of equal importance, but much more difficult to quantify, is the collective experience of the hundreds of thousands of Maghrebi men, recruited from Algeria, Morocco and Tunisia, who slowly fought their way across Europe in the service of the French army. At Monte Cassino and the crossing of the Rhine they proved themselves more than equal to any European soldier.

The Second World War in North Africa

The democratic republic of France was destroyed by the German invasion of 1940. All her overseas possessions passed seamlessly into the hands of Marshal Pétain's autocratic Vichy regime, which ruled the unoccupied rump of south-eastern France. In North Africa there was no support for General de Gaulle's Free French movement with its embarassing dependence on Britain. Indeed the regime of Pétain, the general who had subdued Abdel Krim's Rif rebellion, with its strident nationalism and anti-semitism, received the enthusiastic support of the French settlers.

The Second World War first spilled over into North Africa in the eastern desert in September 1940 when Italy, which had entered the war as an ally of Germany, launched an attack on British positions in Egypt from Cyrenaica. This offensive failed and by February 1941 the British counter-attack had seized control of Cyrenaica. The Italians were reinforced by the German Afrikakorps under General Erwin Rommel, which recaptured Cyrenaica in the spring although his advance was halted by the obstinate British defence of such key Libyan ports as Tobruk.

To North Africans the Germans seemed more like potential liberators than an evil empire. Britain, on the other hand, was known to have suppressed a series of nationalist uprisings in the Middle East and had gone on to occupy Syria, Lebanon and Iran to complete her stranglehold over the Middle East.

In 1942 a renewed offensive led by Rommel finally cleared the British from Cyrenaica and in June German tanks crossed the Egyptian frontier and sped east across the desert towards the Nile. But an over-extended supply line made the Afrikakorps halt at the El Alamein depression, giving the British army time to reorganize. In October 1942, under the command of General Montgomery, the British Eighth Army launched their bloody counter-attack. By November Rommel's Afrikakorps had been driven right back and the British were once again in possession of Cyrenaica.

At the same time a second Allied front was being opened with the landing of British and American troops on the Moroccan and Algerian coasts. This, the famous Casablanca Landings against the troops of Vichy France, was masterminded by US General Eisenhower. Its success had been guaranteed in advance by a number of secret agreements with senior French generals, and was confirmed by the armistice signed with the Allies by Admiral Darlan, the senior military commander in French North Africa, on 12 November. A month later the Allies assassinated Darlan on Christmas Eve, as he was setting out to visit his son in hospital. He was replaced promptly by the more amenable General Giraud.

The Germans responded by rushing troops in to occupy both Vichy France and Tunisia. That December the British First Army, advancing east from Algeria, clashed with the German army on the strategic hills of northern Tunisia around the town of Medjez el Bab. Meanwhile Montgomery's Eighth Army, having completed the conquest of Libya, advanced into southern Tunisia and gave battle at Mareth.

The German Afrikakorps was now faced with war on two fronts, and General Rommel decided on a daring offensive strategy. In February 1943 his tanks launched a surprise attack against the inexperienced American forces advancing across central Tunisia. The US Second Corps was decimated and fled back into Algeria through Tunisia's Kasserine pass. A second German offensive against the British First Army in the north became a vicious struggle in the winter mud. Rommel's third assault, against Montgomery's Eighth Army in the south, proved a costly defeat and destroyed his strategic reserve of tanks.

This destruction was decisive, for the combined British and US fleet and airforce had severed the supply lines to North Africa from Italy by sinking merchant ships as they attempted to dart across the Sicilian straits and by the saturation bombing of the principal Tunisian ports. By April 1943 the German–Italian army was neither receiving adequate supplies nor capable of evacuating its positions. Montgomery's Eighth Army (aided by the Free-French army of General Leclerc, which had completed a heroic march right across the Sahara from Chad) fought its way up the Tunisian coast to Enfida. In May a massive attack on all fronts broke through the German–Italian defences and the Allies occupied Tunis and Bizerte. On 13 May 1943 the 250,000 strong German–Italian army of Africa surrendered formally. Coming so soon after similar German losses on the Russian front, it marked a decisive turning point in the Second World War. Yet this momentous turning point in European history was an irrelevance to the average North African. Of much greater importance was the now almost forgotten example set by Moncef Bey.

MONCEF BEY, THE FORGOTTEN LIBERATOR

The Husseinite beys of Tunisia had long seemed almost complicit partners in French rule. It was therefore a surprise to everyone to find that in the middle of the Second World War (June 1942) a reform-minded prince, Moncef Bey (1942–3), had succeeded to the Tunisian throne. He abandoned court etiquette, mixed freely with his people, received politicans from every party and started supervising the work of his provincial caids. By August he had begun to transform the administration into something recognizably Tunisian, and had initiated plans for an elected assembly. When German–Italian troops occupied Tunisia in November 1942 and displaced the Vichy-French, he moved quickly to exploit the situation and appointed his own cabinet. For six months Tunisia, albeit bombed, mined and fought over by five foreign armies, recovered her independence. Just a week after the Axis surrender Moncef Bey was deposed by the Free French army, ostensibly as a collaborator, but in reality as a national liberator.

THE FOUR FREEDOMS?

At the end of 1941 the United States had entered the war against Germany. Its war aims had been defined by President Roosevelt in his Four Freedoms proclamation, and included a denouncement of territorial aggrandizement and support for self-determination. After the success of the Casablanca Landings, the US special representative in North Africa, Robert Murphy, put pressure on the French colonial administration to liberate the many North African politicians still in exile or in jail. In Morocco nationalist politicians like Ahmed Balafrej returned home. By the end of 1943 the Istiqlâl Party had been formed and members recruited, and in 1944 an independence manifesto was issued. Although the famous Casablanca Conference of January 1943 between Winston Churchill and Franklin Roosevelt did not much concern itself with Maghrebi affairs, the US President gave private encouragement to Sultan Mohammed V (1927–62) to work towards national self-determination.

In Algeria Robert Murphy was in direct touch with the moderate Farhat Abbas who was encouraged to try to negotiate a complete settlement with General Catroux, De Gaulle's new Free-French governor-general. In 1944 De Gaulle bowed a little to world opinion by enacting the old Blum-Violette bill. It was too little and much too late, however, for political expectations had risen to new heights. Even at Farhat Abbas' moderate party congress held in March 1945 the delegates no longer talked of assimiliation, but demanded the formation of an Algerian parliament and government. The moment the war was won and France was free of US pressures, she lost no time in showing what she thought of the Four Freedoms.

Postwar Algeria 1945–54: the Return of Colonial Night

In May 1945 a victory procession in Sitif escalated into a spontaneous, ill-organized insurrection, which spread to the coast. The French colonial authorities reacted with a speed and severity that many reckon to have been pre-planned. In a brutal wave of terror against the whole population of Sitif, as many as 10,000 civilians were killed in a few days. This deliberate expression of naked power left no one in any doubt that the old order had returned. The administration went on to arrest 4,560 leading Muslim Algerians of whom 99 were promptly executed. The colonial night had returned to Algeria and a chill wind blew right across the Maghreb.

Political repression was followed by a paternalistic programme of soil-conservation campaigns, the creation of new Muslim town centres

President Ben Bella en route for his first visit to the United Nations

and constitutional window dressing, which was designed to hide France's mailed fist behind democratic velvet. The Algerian constituent assembly of 1946 gave birth to two elected assemblies: one for the *pieds-noirs* and one for Algerian Muslims. Elections to the former were free and fair while the latter operated with a restricted franchise and were rigged by the authorities. No Muslim Algerian of any political standing allowed himself to be caught up in these deceptions.

The future of the nation was being forged elsewhere. In 1948 a team of revolutionary fighters formed the Organisation Sécrète and plotted the violent overthrow of colonial rule. The following year one of their leaders, Ben Bella, provided the financial backing for the organization by robbing an Oran bank of 3 million francs. Their first operation, an attempted strike, failed and by 1950 most members of the organization were either in jail or in exile. Another spark at a more propitious time was needed before the Algerian revolt would burst into flame.

The ingredients of the revolution were already there. By 1954 the native population of Algeria stood at 8.7 million, half of whom were under 20. Two-thirds of the population were locked into a subsistence economy (assessed at US$66 a year) on ever-diminishing and impoverished lands. There were at least a million under- or unemployed in the country, whilst migration into the native quarters and shanty suburbs of the old towns had produced an explosive density of unemployed young men with no future prospects. At least 90 per cent of the population were functionally illiterate. In 1954 there were only 589 Muslims attending any form of higher education, 165 qualified doctors and 185 secondary school teachers. In contrast 560,000 of the *pieds-noirs* could be defined as middle class, the bulk of whom dwelt in the privileged environment of Algiers and Oran. Within the 900,000-strong *pieds-noirs* there was a propertied élite of 6,385 who owned 87 per cent of all colonial estates. Algerian agro-industry was valued at 600 billion francs with a 93 billion franc annual turnover. The Algerian people had nothing to lose but their chains.

From the UN with Love: Freedom for Libya

After their military victory over the Italians in 1943, the British gradually replaced the Italian administration of Libya with their own officials. By the end of the war they were the dominant European power in Tripolitania and Cyrenaica while the French ruled over the Fezzan desert region. In Cyrenaica the Senussi, with British assistance, resumed their leadership of the region. There was impassioned local debate as to whether Cyrenaica should aspire to independence or opt for an association with either Egypt or Tripolitania.

In 1949 Britain, France and Italy made a joint proposal to the United Nations that France be given the trusteeship of the Fezzan, Italy that of Tripolitania and Britain that of Cyrenaica. This subdivision of the country was denounced vehemently by Arab nationalists and on 17 May 1949 the proposal was rejected by a majority of the UN General Assembly. As a corollary of this rejection the independence of Libya was recognized six months later in a second vote. A commissioner was appointed (assisted by an international council) and instructed to oversee the creation of an independent Libya by 1 January 1952.

At first sight this appears to have been a slap in the face for the colonial powers, but on further examination there is a suspicion that the whole affair was orchestrated secretly by Britain in collusion with the United States. The composition of the Libyan National Assembly that drafted the new national constitution was vigorously denounced by both Egypt and the Arab League. Certainly the federal state that finally emerged, the United Kingdom of Libya, with Sayyid Idris, the old, exiled sheikh of the Senussi transformed into King Idris I, had recognizable parallels with British ways. The new kingdom's most enthusiastic supporters, in terms of foreign loans, administrative assistance and help in economic development, were Britain and the United States. King Idris I allowed Britain and the United States to lease military bases in his kingdom, where they stationed their very latest aircraft and tanks. In due course it was British and American geologists who first discovered and helped exploit Libya's enormous petroleum deposits. Yet even if Libya was a classic example of neo-colonialism hiding beneath the djellaba of a traditional patriarchal leadership, it also represented an enormous and peaceful advance. For the first time in 500 years a native Libyan ruled over the united nation.

Mohammed V and the Moroccan Independence Struggle, 1946–56

In Morocco the political liberalization of the war years was allowed to continue, in part because it was still restricted to an educated minority. In 1946 Allal al-Fasi returned home after nine year's exile to assume leadership of the Istiqlâl Party, which grew to number 15,000 members a year later. That the sultan, Mohammed V, was working towards the same ends became clear in a speech he made on 10 April 1947 in the comparative freedom of international Tangier. From this date the sultan directed the pace of Moroccan political agitation. As an indication of this Allal al-Fassi left Morocco in 1947 to join the pan-Arabic movement based on Cairo.

Alerted to the new mood, the French appointed a tough resident-general, the ex-General Juin, to keep an eye on internal security while

Sultan Mohammed V flanked by his two sons with resident-general Juin

also granting more authority to Moroccans in the protectorate administration. An elective Council of Government was created to advise the resident-general, but the 1951 budget made clear that French colonial interests would continue to dominate. The Moroccan representatives on the Council showed their disgust by resigning and received the support of the sultan.

General Juin now determined on a show of force and called upon France's political allies within Morocco, such as the Sufi Sheikh al-Kittani and the Berber lord Thami al-Glaoui, to mount a counter-demonstration against the sultan. They managed to fill the cities of Rabat and Fez with Berbers who had been trained to call for a sultan of Morocco, not a sultan of the urban-based Istiqlâl Party. In February 1951 Sultan Mohammed V publicly renounced his Istiqlâl allies, but just a year later, in March 1952, he returned to the political fray and in a public letter demanded an end to the protectorate. Later that year, in December, the first mass demonstrations against French rule erupted across the breadth of North Africa, a spontaneous reaction to the assassination of Farhat Hached, the Tunisian trade unionist. This marked a critical threshold in the political evolution of the Maghreb. The battle lines were now drawn.

The French response in Morocco was to get their local allies to organize another counter-demonstration. Its success led to the sultan's deposition and exile to Madagascar in August 1953. But this was a disastrous miscalculation by the French, for it gave the Istiqlâl Party a cause behind which to unite the entire nation. The populace struck back against the new puppet-sultan (Mohammed ibn Arafa), against colonial settlers in their fields and in cafés, and against the even more vulnerable native agents of French rule. After two years of escalating terror and French counter-terror the hitherto peaceful Protectorate of Morocco seemed on the point of dissolving into open insurrection. In 1955 a newly formed 'Liberation Army' started military operations against the French in the Middle Atlas and Saharan regions.

Faced with the Algerian insurrection, which had erupted in November 1954, the French government decided on a sudden reversal of policy. In October 1955 Mohammed V was flown to Paris and began negotiations that led to the formal recognition of Moroccan independence on 2 March 1956.

The Struggle for Tunisian Independence, 1942–56

Although exiled and placed under house arrest in Marseille, the Neo-Destour leader Habib Bourguiba (1957–87) had supported De Gaulle's Free-French government loyally throughout the war years. From 1943 to 1945 Bourguiba was back in Tunisia, but he refused to authorize political agitation until the war had been won.

When no tangible reward from France for this political stance was forthcoming, Bourguiba left Tunisia in 1945 and spent two years trying to drum up international support for Tunisian independence. In his absence political agitation was directed by such militants as Salih ibn Youssef, secretary general of the Neo-Destour party, and Farhat Hached, the UGTT trade union leader. The French tried to wean moderate Tunisians to their side. From 1950 a Tunisian prime minister was appointed to lead a cabinet with equal numbers of French and Tunisian ministers, although real power remained firmly in the hands of the resident-general, who could also count on the support of the settler-dominated consultative councils. This did little to diffuse the clamour for independence, however. As Tunis was rocked by demonstrations in early 1952, the resident-general arrested the Neo-Destour including Bourguiba, and jailed the Tunisian prime minister.

Leadership of the struggle devolved on the trade unionist Farhat Hached, who was assassinated on 5 December 1952. He was murdered ostensibly by the Red Hand, a settler terrorist organization, but few doubted that the French government was directly responsible for his death. Spontaneous protests swept across the whole of North Africa and created a renewed determination to end French rule. Farhat's death was also taken as a declaration of war in Tunisia, and the following year there were around 3,000 Tunisian *fellagha* (bandit freedom-fighters) operating out of the mountains. Faced with a fast-escalating spiral of *fellagha* terror and colonial counter-terror the French government began to reconsider its options. It could either wage total war on the Tunisian people or attempt to salvage its investments by granting some form of autonomy. Half-hearted negotiations began in the summer of 1954, but were renewed with greater commitment after the *fellagha* escalated their armed struggle. The Algerian insurrection, which erupted in November 1954, and the fast deteriorating situation in Morocco further concentrated the minds of the negotiators. Bourguiba decided to accept the French offer of autonomy and returned to a hero's welcome in June 1955. He saw it as the first tactical step towards full independence, but his action was bitterly denounced by the two most prominent left-wing politicians, Salih ibn Youssef (secretary-general of Neo-Destour) and Ahmad ibn Salih (Farhat Hached's successor at the UGTT). At a crucial Neo-Destour party meeting that November Bourguiba's tactics were endorsed, Ahmad ibn Salih was won over and Salih ibn Youssef expelled.

In January 1956 the party was purged of Salih ibn Youssef's supporters, most of whom came from the urban lower classes, rural communities (especially those in the south) and from amongst the young Islamic students. To the latter in particular Salih ibn Youssef was a hero. Symbolically he had launched his first attack on Bourguiba during a Friday sermon in the Zitouna mosque.

After the January 1956 purge ibn Youssef fled to Tripoli where he organized an armed revolt in the south. Bourguiba was only able to crush this insurrection with the assistance of French troops, and in the process he became marked as a moderate in French eyes. He used this new *rapprochement* to press for the complete independence of Tunisia, which was granted on 20 March 1956.

The Algerian Insurrection, 1954–62

Muslim Algeria had seemed almost unnaturally quiet during the early 1950s as neighbouring Morocco and Tunisia limbered up towards open insurrection. In the summer of 1954 the success of the Tunisian *fellagha* was capped by the news from Indochina, where on 7 May a French army had been defeated by nationalist guerillas at the battle of Dien Bien Phu. On 22 July, 22 former members of the Organisation Sécrète met in Algiers and formed themselves into the Front de Libération Nationale (FLN), which would lead the revolutionary insurrection. Although many of the FLN members had once been supporters of Messali's nationalist movement there was no attempt to create a mass political party. The time for demonstrations and petitions was over and it was the turn of the machine gun. During the autumn the FLN leadership concentrated on the recruitment of 3,000 fighters for the Armée de Libération Nationale (ALN). Arms were supplied by Egypt, which looked to the Soviet Union for support.

The insurrection, which was launched simultaneously across Algeria on 1 November, took the French by surprise. They rounded up the usual suspects and reinforced their 80,000-strong garrison with another 50,000 men. It was not until January 1955 that they became aware of the scale and commitment of the insurrection. The new governor, Jacques Soustelle, revived the military government of the *bureau arabe* and recruited mobile rural police groups (GMPR), native irregulars, from rival tribal groups.

In the first year of fighting the ALN suffered heavy losses, but the indiscriminate repression and routine harassment of native Muslims by the French army soon began to produce a political dividend. From a few thousand hill fighters (principally concentrated in the Aurès mountains) the ALN evolved into a national movement with over-whelming popular support. They were increasingly referred to as *mujahidin* (fighters of a holy war). Fighting spread to the Constantine region and the Kabylie Mountains, and attacks were made on *pied-noir* settlements. From the radio came the passionate oratory of the FLN leadership and the support of the entire Arab world was felt through Cairo's Voice of the Arabs station. In September 1955 Algeria's right to independence was debated in the UN and even such moderate Algerian politicians as Farhat Abbas offered unconditional support to the FLN.

In January 1956 the new French socialist premier Guy Mollet tried to conciliate, but to the *pieds-noirs* the independence he was then offering to Morocco and Tunisia branded him a traitor. On a fact-finding mission to Algiers Mollet was abused and denounced by a *pied-noir* mob and withdrew Catroux, the newly appointed governor. It was a weak and foolish decision that served only to encourage the *pieds-noirs* into more and more politically assertive actions.

The new governor, Robert Lacoste, surrendered all political consid-erations to that of military victory, and brought the French army in Algeria up to 400,000 men. In March the execution of two FLN members brought a further escalation in the struggle as the ALN responded with urban terrorism and the *pieds-noirs* took to making violent reprisals in the native quarters. In August the ALN military commanders met in secret congress to try and place the FLN under their control. Similarly, on the French side the generals began to overawe their political bosses. This was demonstrated graphically in October 1956 when a French military jet intercepted a Moroccan plane carrying four of the senior FLN leaders, who were engaged in delicate peace negotiations with France. The French political leadership acquiesced meekly to this coup. By the end of 1956 Algeria was totally polarized, with the ALN accepted everywhere as the leader of the Muslims.

In January 1957 Governor-General Lacoste handed over command of Algiers to General Massu and his Tenth Parachute Regiment. The resulting campaign of torture, brutality and intimidation has been vividly chronicled in *The Battle of Algiers*, an epic film quite without equal. In it Massu's pursuit of Ali la Pointe and Ramdane Abbane, the Kabylie Berber in charge of Algiers terrorism, serves as a metaphor for the whole war. The construction of the so-called Morice Line (a fixed frontier of minefields, barbed wire and machine gun posts) along the Algerian-Tunisian border cut the ALN off from further military supplies and reinforcements. They were faced with near anihiliation in 1958 as General Challe took the state terrorism developed by Massu in Algiers and applied it methodically to the different regions of the country. By the end of 1958 most of the original leadership was dead and the surviving commanders were forced to abandon their military structure and return to the small terrorist cells of 1954. To deny the ALN support, over two million Algerian peasants were moved into new settlements controlled by paramilitary guards.

In this depressing military situation the FLN were able to resume control of the insurrection. Faced with crippling casualties at every attempted crossing of the Morice Line, the FLN concentrated on training up a new army in the refugee camps of Tunisia and Morocco in the hope of helpful political developments. Both King Mohammed V and President Bourguiba were dedicated to the Algerian struggle, but began to grow increasingly wary of the loss of authority on their borders. On 8 February 1958 the French airforce attacked the Algerian refugee camp at Sakiet Sidi Youssef, deep inside Tunisian territory. In the process they also destroyed the neighbouring Tunisian village, maiming hundreds and killing 69 civilians. Although this may have been a deliberate attempt by the French military to scupper a negotiated peace, the resulting international outcry provided President Bourguiba with the perfect opportunity to broker a peace. Sagely he called upon Britain and the United States to arbitrate. Robert Murphy once again returned to North Africa and was successful in sorting out French and Tunisian differences, but it was also clear that his remit was much wider.

The French generals and the *pieds-noirs* began to fear that their military success within Algeria was about to be undermined by a political settlement. The discovery of massive oil deposits in the central Sahara helped fuel their paranoia about the motives of Britain and the United States in involving themselves in Algerian affairs. As right-wing members of the French cabinet began to resign, their suspicion of a political 'betrayal' intensified. On 10 May Governor-General Lacoste gave tacit encouragement to the *pied-noir* mob of Algiers who occupied government offices and proclaimed the Algiers Committee of Public Safety, which received the public support of such charismatic generals as Massu and Salan. As the tension mounted in France, with fears of a military coup on the mainland, French politicians sought to avoid civil war by investing all the powers of the French Republic upon ex-General De Gaulle, who became a virtual dictator, albeit democratically appointed.

GENERAL DE GAULLE

Once in power De Gaulle launched an energetic campaign to create a political middle ground between the *pieds-noirs* and the FLN. A massive public works programme in Algeria aimed to create 400,000 new jobs in industry, while agricultural reform and the construction of thousands of new Muslim villages and urban suburbs pushed living standards up by a third. It was a dramatic demonstration of state power, but was of course far, far too late. At the same time De Gaulle toured the army camps, carefully explaining his policies whilst quietly removing dissident officers from their commands. However, his carefully orchestrated elections in Algeria that November were widely boycotted. The people of Algeria continued to put their faith in the FLN, who announced a provisional government of Algeria drawn from a wide political spectrum, including such respected moderate figures as Farhat Abbas.

In January 1960 General Massu was dismissed after he criticized De Gaulle's policy publicly. A *pied-noir* mob (led by the café owner Ortiz) took to the streets of Algiers, but De Gaulle was unmoved. Throughout the rest of the year he attempted to negotiate, but the FLN would not agree to surrender their arms before negotiation. Meanwhile the counter-terror launched by *pied-noir* gangs against Muslim Algerians, such as the Belcourt Massacre of December 1960, only helped strengthen the FLN's determination. In 1961 De Gaulle started to negotiate with the provisional Algerian government after a French referendum approved this action with a 75 per cent vote.

The army's reaction came in the form of the 'generals' insurrection' of 22 April 1961, which once more seemed to threaten France with a civil war over the Algerian situation. Although the bulk of the regular army backed the insurrection, De Gaulle retained the support of the navy, the police, most of the populace of France and the airforce. The support of the latter ensured that the troubles, and particularly the brutal and much feared paratroopers, remained in Algeria. De Gaulle then appealed directly to the army rank and file (now mostly conscripts longing to return home) in a series of radio broadcasts, and the movement crumpled. His rhetorical victory removed the last obstruction to the peace negotiations.

However, the *pied-noir* mob were determined to fight to the end and had made use of this anarchic situation to arm themselves and establish the Organisation de l'Armée Sécrète (OAS). In the face of an inevitable settlement, their terror campaign and scorched earth policy only served to close any remaining chance of an equable peace. The negotiations were inaugurated at Evian on 20 May 1961, but quickly reached two stumbling blocks: the future role of the *pieds-noirs*, and the oil fields of the central Sahara. The former issue solved itself, for as the end neared the *pieds-noirs* accepted the inevitable and swarmed back across the sea to France rather than face the expected vengeance of the Algerian people. The vast Saharan oil reserves were a different matter. De Gaulle planned to hold on to the Saharan region, allowing France to continue to dominate North Africa via the so-called 'invisible protectorate', a network of economic and financial strangleholds on the region. It would take a further year of negotiation, punctured by terrorist outrages, threats and counter-threats before the French gave up this position. An independence agreement was at last reached on 18 March 1962, fulfilling the 1841 prophecy of an Algerian tribal chief surrendering to the French:

> This land is the land of the Arabs. You are no more than passing guests. Even if you stay here for 300 years, like the Turks, you will still have to leave.

CHAPTER TWENTY

Kings, Colonels and Presidents

The leaders of the various independence struggles moved quickly to consolidate their hold over power. Despite the apparent contrasts between them, a desert sheikh, a highly educated lawyer, a peasant revolutionary and a hereditary monarch, they all assumed control of the same instruments of central state power. The Maghreb continued to be ruled with the traditional tools of the protectorates – the bureaucracy, the police force and the military. Multi-party democratic institutions, genuine elections, an independent judiciary and a free media have all been imported to some extent into the Maghreb's culture since independence. However, they are still weak-rooted saplings in the political soil of North Africa. What is much more important to an Islamic-based political culture is the process of consultation, which is pursued to this day in private meetings between the various heads of state and their leading citizens.

On a more profound level the real political challenge has not been who has survived in power, but how the governments of the Maghreb have responded to the escalating socio-economic challenges of the late twentieth century. These are immense. The population has grown by around 3 per cent a year, which exceeds the countries' modest levels of economic growth. At least half the population is now under 18 and prospects for future employment, whether at home or by migration into Europe, seem to diminish with each passing year. By contrast the very real successes in post-independence education have produced ever larger numbers of university graduates with high expectations.

King Mohammed V and King Hassan II of Morocco, 1956–87

Upon independence King Mohammed V (1927–61) was keen to emphasize his position as a modern constitutional monarch. In the first three euphoric years of independence he presided over a national government dominated by members of the Istiqlâl Party, which established schools and brand new universities, directed volunteer labour battalions to build much-needed roads and dams, and established regional assemblies. At the same time orthodox Islam was reaffirmed, the Sufi brotherhoods were reformed and a puritanical public morality tidied up the brothels and bars of the corrupt, un-Islamic colonial order.

The king was determined that the monarchy would remain at the centre of political life. As the heroic national liberator, the imam of Moroccan religious life and heir to four centuries of dynastic authority he was in a uniquely strong position. To safeguard the future, he insisted on appointing his own candidates to run the ministries of interior and defence. Thus the key instruments of protectorate rule – police, provincial administration and military – remained directly answerable to the palace. King Mohammed V continued the millenial traditions of state by appointing his son commander of the Moroccan army. By recruiting veterans from the French and Spanish armies as well as elements of the guerilla Liberation Army, Crown Prince Hassan was able to create a standing army of 30,000 men. Between 1958 and 1959 it was soon put to the test quelling rebellions that broke out in the Rif Mountains, the Middle Atlas and the Sahara, all traditional areas of dissidence.

By 1959 strains had begun to show in the national government. The left wing of the Istiqlâl Party broke away to form the UNFP, which closely allied itself to the UMT trade union. The central rump of Istiqlâl formed its own trade union, the UGTM, in the same year. The rural, often Berber-speaking hinterland remained suspicious of the urban agenda of Istiqlâl and the UNFP, and with the discreet support of the palace, formed the conservative Mouvement Populaire.

The shock caused by the earthquake in Agadir in February 1960, in which 15,000 people were buried alive, called a halt to the political bickering. Twelve months later the nation was stunned by the death of King Mohammed V at the height of his powers.

The new king, Hassan II, formed his first government from an alliance between Istiqlâl and the Mouvement Populaire. With the assistance of the legally trained monarch, the cabinet settled down to prepare Morocco's first democratic constitution, which was approved in a referendum held in December 1962 despite a UNFP boycott. In March 1963 these new principles were put to the test in a general election. The Istiqlâl Party did best in the old cities and successful farming areas, the UNFP in the new cities on the coast – Rabat, Casablanca, Kenitra and Agadir – as well as in the Sous valley. The Mouvement Populaire was strongest in Marrakech, the Berber mountains and the hinterland. The electoral victory of the FDIC (a royal coalition based on the Mouvement Populaire) was widely ascribed to the heavy-handed influence of the minister of the interior. Electoral rigging was again suspected in the FDIC's 85 per cent victory in the local elections a few months later.

THE UNFP AND BEN BARKA

The socialist UNFP party was strident in its criticisms and cited the republics of Egypt and Algeria as fitting role models for Morocco. Obstructed at the election, they began to think in terms of revolutionary change. The king arrested 130 UNFP militants and drove their leader, Ben Barka, into exile in Paris. This political breach was further widened when Ben Barka called upon the Moroccan army not to resist in the 1963 border war with Algeria. It might have been better if Ben Barka had played a less antagonistic role, for within two years the royalist political party had proved itself both inept and corrupt in government. As student and worker riots rocked the coastal cities in March 1965 the king dissolved parliament, but continued to make use of leading politicians during this period of direct palace government. In August his principal opponent, Ben Barka, was assassinated by Moroccan agents. Despite this unhappy augury the king's direct rule proved suprisingly popular as he borrowed one of the UNFP's most popular programmes and started the nationalization of foreign-owned businesses and farms. The king now had at his disposal an immense new pool of economic resources with which to reward loyal servants and win over opponents.

FAILED COUPS

In August 1970 Hassan II prepared a second democratic constitution, which was once again approved by a well-orchestrated popular referendum. Once again, subsequent elections seem to have been determined in advance by the minister of the interior, who had assumed the role of the evil grand vizier who appears so frequently in Moroccan folk tales. The UNFP and Istiqlâl, supported by the trade unions, boycotted the elections and the parliament building was filled with loyal placemen. Once again corruption and inefficiency soon became manifest, although this time opposition took the form of two coup attempts, launched against the king from within the ranks of the military. In the first attempt, at the seaside palace Skhirat in July 1971, young cadets massacred the king's guests at a garden party although he survived and directed a successful counter-attack. In the second attempt in 1972, the king's aeroplane was strafed by airforce jets, but he was saved by his quick-witted pilot who congratulated the airmen for killing the tyrant with their first attack. The jets abandoned their attack and the plane returned the king safely to land. Subsequent investigations traced both plots back to puritanical generals determined to reform Morocco's political corruption, although it now seems that in both cases the trail ultimately led back to General Oufikir, then Minister of the Interior. King Hassan, now even more careful of who he could or could not trust, continued skilfully to manipulate the ruling cliques within Moroccan political life.

In 1975 the king buried past dissatisfaction in a surge of nationalism. He orchestrated the so-called 'Green March', a march of 350,000 unarmed Moroccan civilians south into the desert to reintegrate the old Spanish colony of Rio de Oro, the western Sahara, into greater Morocco. It was a brilliantly timed political gambit, which caught the Spanish government when they were paralysed by General Franco's lingering death. The resulting war against the Polisario, those indigenous western Saharan tribesmen who wished for an independent state, prolonged the spell of national unity. The support that the Polisario

Coinage showing on *left* Habib Bourguiba of Tunisia 1976 and on *right* Hassan II, King of Morocco 1987

received from such socialist republics as Algeria and Libya in turn helped Morocco secure the firm backing of such financially useful allies as the United States, Saudi Arabia and the Arab Gulf states. The war, although expensive, has also helped keep the army busy and content with their royal commander. A referendum in the western Sahara, overseen by the United Nations, is promised in the near future to try to bring this long war to a satisfactory conclusion.

ECONOMIC CRISIS

By 1979 the economic crisis caused by Morocco's enormous national debt, stagnant economy and fast-growing population was being felt on the streets. Wages were slipping behind inflation, there had been a series of bad harvests and there was a new militancy abroad, encouraged by the recent overthrow of the shah of Persia by mass street action. In Morocco trade union strikes and demonstrations were kept under control by police repression. In June 1981 and again in January 1984 the International Monetary Fund (IMF), which acts as a world policeman on government debts, enforced a cut in the state subsidy of basic food stuffs. This issue (which irresistibly conjured up the image of rich western bankers dictating a reduction in the diet of the Moroccan poor) created an explosion of popular unrest. A six-month long state of emergency was declared, but by the summer of 1984 the political temperature had cooled. A round of comparatively fair elections produced a moderate government with a technocratic cabinet committed to economic and structural reform. There was much to be done. The internal tax situation was in an anarchic state, for all the heavy earners like farming, tourism and property speculation enjoyed an official tax holiday. The state phosphate industry, which bestrode the national economy like a giant, ran at a paper loss while a black economy, covering much of the same ground, turned over US$5 billion a year.

Since then a privatization campaign has attempted to reduce the enormous state sector, a stock exchange has developed and statutory accounting for businesses and VAT have been introduced. Political parties, trade unions and newspapers are free to address any issue providing it does not touch on the central position of the monarchy. Public debate is kept off the television and off the streets and is restrictedto newspapers and the convention halls of party conferences.★ If debate is limited it is also lively compared to other Muslim countries. The government is actively involved in improving roads and pushing forward with an ambitious policy of dams, irrigation schemes and house construction.

President Habib Bourguiba of Tunisia, 1956–87

A week after Tunisian independence had been celebrated on 20 March 1956, Habib Bourguiba inaugurated a Constituent Assembly to draft the new constitution of Tunisia. This assembly, like his cabinet, was entirely dominated by the Neo-Destour party. Debate was restricted to within the party and the democratic apparatus was used to present a monolithic unity of national purpose to the world. Bourguiba used this concentration of power to create a modern secular state such as Tunisian reformers had dreamed of for over 100 years. A universal adult franchise was declared with equal rights for women and a provision for universal education. The traditional practices of Islam were overturned as polygamy was abolished and women could officially contract their own marriages, sue for their own divorce and marry non-Muslims. The Sufi

★ The recent general election, held on 14 November 1997, seems to have been genuinely free as born out by the 58% turn-out of voters. The left of centre Koutla (a coalition of USFP and Istiglal) gained 102 of the 325 seats in the lower house to become the biggest single party.

brotherhoods were suppressed, for even if they had not been in tacit alliance with the French Protectorate, their quietism was seen as an attack on the new cult of civic consciousness. The administration of mosques was once more brought under government control and the *habous* lands annexed. In due course these would be gradually sold off by Neo-Destour commissioners to reward party loyalists.

The following year Bourguiba moved quickly to remove his political rivals. The last of the Husseinite beys was deposed and a republic established. To drive this point home Crown Prince Chadli Bey, members of the old regime and the moderate Destour party were all convicted of corruption and treason in a series of show trials held during 1958. In the same year another 50 Youssefites were convicted of conspiring to overthrow the state in collusion with Egypt and Libya. Their exiled leader Salih ibn Youssef was eventually assassinated by Tunisian agents who tracked him down in Frankfurt in 1961. In June 1959 Bourguiba's complete command of the state was demonstrated when the new constitution gave the president of the republic enormous executive powers. His relationship with France was fraught with difficulties while the struggle over Algeria continued. In 1961 Tunisian and French troops clashed in tussles over the Saharan border and Bizerte, which had remained an important French military base. After Algeria recovered its independence in 1962 the Franco-Tunisian relationship quickly found a new balance. France agreed to evacuate its bases, compensation for nationalized French businesses was agreed upon and France offered generous foreign aid and technical assistance.

In July 1961 Bourguiba followed prevailing world trends and pushed the ship of state in the direction of the socialist horizon. Ahmad ibn Salih was appointed head of a supreme Planning Ministry. By 1964 the nationalization of land (largely from big colonial landowners) had brought 400,000 acres of prime farmland under the Ministry of Agriculture. This achievement was celebrated by the Neo-Destour, which changed its name to the Socialist Destourian Party. In the following five years the Planning Ministry created a brand new tourist industry, a fishing fleet tied to an effective conservation policy and tried to relocate heavy industry to cities other than the capital of Tunis. A push to nationalize Tunisian-owned farms and olive orchards ran into determined opposition. The government backed down even before it was proved that the Agricultural Ministry had made a mess of its existing holdings. In 1969 Habib Bourguiba neatly side-stepped responsibility by dismissing Ahmad ibn Salih, whose disgrace was completed with legal prosecution.

The 1970s saw a return to a mixed economy with government revenue boosted by a run of good harvests and the discovery of some small oil fields. The drift to autocracy was marked in 1974 when Habib Bourguiba foolishly allowed himself to be elected as president for life. In 1978 the UGTT union (the historic partner of the Neo-Destour) called a strike against this growing personal dictatorship and its corrupt practices. It was only quelled after hundreds of deaths, mass detentions and the show trials of union leaders. On the second anniversary of the strike, an insurrection was attempted at the Saharan town of Gafsa by a guerilla band operating out of Libya. It failed, and although this incident is still shrouded in mystery it marked a threshold beyond which the domestic opposition (as opposed to the Youssefite exiles) was not prepared to go. In 1981 and 1984 Tunisia was rocked by mass disturbances following the IMF-enforced cut in food subsidies. In the same way as in Morocco, a state of emergency was declared and the cuts were later abandoned. In a nation that could not yet contemplate either the social insurance, health service or old-age pensions that functioned in Europe, the subsidy on basic foods was the one great service that the government afforded to the poor. As the 1980s progressed it became increasingly apparent that the very successes of the Tunisian Republic, particularly in the field of education, were producing a new generation whose high expectations were bitterly frustrated by the lack of work and political voice. The 1986 election was effectively boycotted by a population resentful of the Neo-Destour's grip on power and their tedious and unconvincing string of 99 per cent election victories.

As always in North Africa, the poor and the deprived have looked to Islam for their salvation, both in quiet prayer and in order to return to the near-perfect polity established by the Prophet Mohammed. The secular reforms of the republic, particularly in the field of female rights, were an area which troubled the more earnest and politically active Muslims grouped together in the Mouvement de la Tendance Islamique (MTI). Bourguiba for his part was passionately proud of Tunisia's educational programme. In 1956 only 70,000 girls had received an education while by 1961 200,000 were at school, many of whom went on to reach the apex of the system, the University of Tunis. But his suppression of the MTI, involving the imprisonment of 3,000 of its activists, went beyond reason. Bourguiba had lost his political touch, and rather than endanger the whole regime his closest allies reluctantly decided to remove their chief. On the evening of 7 November 1987 seven doctors visited Bourguiba's palace in Carthage and declared the president for life senile.

In accordance with the constitution the prime minister, Zine el-Abidine ben Ali was sworn in as president. Ben Ali, like Bourguiba, comes from a prosperous family with traditions of government service. He had made his way to the top of the Tunisian army, including periods at military academies in France and the United States. His political career had taken off with his efficient suppression of the IMF bread riots in 1981 and 1984 after which, in 1986, he was made minister of the interior.

Libya: the Senussi Kingdom, 1952–69

From the outset, King Idris I (1952–69) had to step warily to safeguard his new throne. Secure though he was in Cyrenaica, the larger population of Tripolitania held him in no such regard. In the first elections held after independence in 1952, government candidates won 44 out of the available 55 seats. The National Congress Party protested at electoral fraud but in truth their support, based on the towns of Tripolitania, was outnumbered by rural and nomadic countrymen who comprised 80 per cent of the population. At the elections the rural population followed the advice of their tribal leaders who preferred a traditionalist Senussi king to a party of urban pan-Arabists. With the backing of Nasser's Egypt the National Congress Party organized a series of demonstrations, but King Idris struck back and exiled the leadership. His command of the country remained unquestioned over the next decade, for he understood the need to include all the tribal chiefs in his deliberations. The latter, whether elected or not, served as reasonably effective representatives of Libya's tribal population.

Balancing the economy was a more difficult matter, for Libya was then a poor desert realm which imported three times as much as it exported. The deficit was covered by foreign aid from Britain and the United States, who had established military bases and assumed responsibility for the training of the Libyan army.

This economic dependency was to be dramatically reversed by oil. The first discovery, made by an American prospector in 1956, occurred when King Idris' government disposed of just £12 million a year. Nine years later the Libyan treasury received US$351 million in oil royalties, a sum that doubled the following year. The government had little idea how to manage this torrent of money and yet the population was set alight with feverish expectations. Farmers migrated to the oil terminals in search of work, but the jobs could only be performed by qualified foreigners employed by the British and American oil companies whose wire-fenced enclosures looked remarkably similar to their military bases. Food production dropped, prices shot up and a building boom, which only seemed to profit Libya's richest families, erupted.

At the same time the rising generation of young Libyans had become estranged from traditional society. They had been educated by Arab teachers recruited from the Middle East by King Idris' government. These teachers had no loyalty to their paymaster, but tended to act as apostles for the new creed of pan-Arabic socialism espoused in Egypt, Syria and Iraq. The older generation, meanwhile, was mostly illiterate, wary of towns, suspicious of politics and placed their faith only in local relationships. They had good cause for suspicion, for they had collectively witnessed much suffering. It has been estimated that between the Italian invasion of 1911 and 1943, the population of Libya dropped by a third, from 750,00 to 500,000. When listening to loose talk about 'western democracy' or European culture it is as well to remember that the generation-long period of European dominance in Libya was demographically more brutal than the Black Death.

A row in 1964 over the British and US military bases served only to prove how isolated old King Idris had become. His personal pro-Western disposition was in headlong collision with the national mood. The king dissolved the assembly elected in October 1964 and used the government machinery to fix the May 1965 elections. By then he longed to retire from the poisonous world of politics, although even his opponents were worried about what would become of Libyan unity without him. For it was he, as the young Senussi sheikh of Cyrenaica, who had first united the country in 1921 when he had accepted the Tripolitanian Emirate. No one doubted his personal integrity, for despite the millions of oil dollars he kept to his traditional clothes and a frugal diet of milk, dates and camel meat. In 1969 there were at least four coups being plotted against King Idris, one of which was apparently sponsored by the king himself. He had no faith in his heirs and so while all his attempts to abdicate failed he gave private encouragement to his army chief-of-staff, Abdul Azzi el-Shehli, to seize power in a palace coup.

The Libyan Revolution

In the event it was a young army officer, a captain in the signal corps called Muammar al-Qaddafi, who seized power in September 1969. Muammar was born in 1942, the child of a semi-nomadic shepherd of the Qadhaff tribe whose flocks had grazed Libya's central Sirtic desert for centuries. Muammar was clever enough to attend the new school established in the little town of Sirta between 1956 and 1959. His family then moved south into the Sahara, but he was expelled from the province by the local governor because of his political activity. Despite this black mark his educational qualifications enabled him to enroll in the military academy, where he qualified as an officer in 1963. Within a year of his graduation he was actively planning a coup. He formed the Central Committee of the Free Unionist Officers and deliberately encouraged old school friends with a similar political outlook, such as Abdul-Salam Jallud, to join the army.

The coup was originally planned for 21 March 1969 but it was cancelled so as not to interrupt the PLO charity concert given by the celebrated Egyptian singer, Oum Khalthoum. Instead the conspirators struck on 2 September and achieved a bloodless *coup d'état*. There were no executions, summary or otherwise, although members of the old regime were sent off to prison in conditions that ex-prime minister Baboush described as luxurious. The old constitution was overturned and power concentrated in the Revolutionary Command Council (RCC), which was composed of 12 of Qaddafi's closest conspirators amongst the Free Unionist Officers. It was a heady time, for not one of the 12 officers was over 30 as they set about the purification of Libya. Alcohol was banned, all Roman script on signposts and advertising billboards was torn down and replaced by Arabic, nightclubs were closed and the remaining Jews, as well as the last 30,000 Italians, were expelled. The British and American governments were politely but firmly told to pack up their military bases, which they did without any confrontation. The bases were handed back to the Libyan government within five months.

After coming to an agreement with Algeria, the other main oil producer in the Maghreb, the RCC was in a position to take on the big oil companies. A series of negotiations culminated in the nationalization of those oilfields whose owners refused to surrender a controlling 51 per cent stake to the Libyan National Oil Corporation. The lack of unity amongst the rival oil companies and the integrity of the Libyan negotiators who remained indifferent to the usual oil industry backhanders, assisted this victory. Libya had at last become truly independent, the master of her own economy and her own defences.

THE CULTURAL REVOLUTION

By 1973 Qaddafi had become disillusioned by the creeping corruption in Libya's oil-rich economy and the conspicuous wealth of its leading citizens. In the Zwara Declaration of 15 August he inaugurated the Libyan Cultural Revolution. The legal system was replaced by Islamic law, while all remnants of political allegiance to foreign parties, Communist, Ba'athist or Islamic, were to be eliminated. The people were to be armed to safeguard the revolution, the power of the bureaucrats was to be returned to the people and the existing ruling class was purged, from lawyers to merchants and intellectuals. On 7 May Qaddafi called for the creation of popular committees in every town and village, and a week later at a youth rally in Tripoli he unveiled his Third Universal

Theory. It was a brave attempt to find a middle-ground between the two antagonistic creeds of capitalist materialism and communist atheism. It was inspired by the ideals of early Islam fused with the communal practices of the Libyan nomads. Qaddafi was searching for a constitutional framework in which the bedouin tribal council, with its lack of formality, its integrity, its strong respect for personal sovereignty and the high value it placed on receiving advice and refusing orders might be incorporated into government. It was a quixotic endeavour for a Maghrebi government, for it sought to encourage those indigenous traditions that all the other rulers had been determined to suppress.

Eventually 187 people's committees were formed and by January 1976 each had dispatched three members to attend the first General Congress of the Socialist Popular Libyan Arab Jamahiriya. The latter word, coined by Qaddafi, translates as 'rule of the masses'. Profit sharing was to replace wages, multiple property ownership was prohibited, and the main import dealerships, larger retail shops and grocery distribution were all nationalized. What flawed the system was the RCC's undisputed control of all vital concerns such as the oil industry, the army and internal security. By now the RCC had been whittled down to four of Qaddafi's staunchest supporters: Colonel Jalloud (economy), Colonel Mustafa Kharroubi (intelligence), Colonel Khweldi Homeidi (people's militia) and Colonel Abu Bakr Younis (army).

Keeping the whole political experiment afloat was the enormous revenue from oil, estimated at US$20 billion a year, which had reversed the usual relationship between the governed and the governors. Where money normally flows from the people to the central government in the form of tax, in Libya it now flowed from the government to the people. In 1979 the average income was around US$8,000 and the Libyan people, for the most part, luxuriated in the care of the state, driving their cars on excellent roads, playing cards with friends in cafés or watching television, football or imported films. Demeaning physical labour was, and still is, largely performed by migrant workers from the Sudan or Chad while skilled jobs are performed by Palestinians, Egyptians, Moroccans, Tunisians, Koreans and East Europeans.

However, the blow delivered to the existing power structures by

Qaddafi's popular committees had begun to unwind the coherent direction of the state. A series of army coup attempts, in 1975, 1977 and especially that of 1978, resulted in the first executions in Libya for 23 years. Qaddafi's intemperance with opposition from the traditional Islamic leadership was to become just as marked. In 1980 the venerable mufti of Tripoli, Sheikh Mohammed al-Bushti, was dragged from his mosque and executed, while the ancient Zliten Mosque and the Beida Islamic University were demolished. Four years later the venerated founders of the Senussi brotherhood were disinterred from their tombs at the pilgrimage centre of Jaghbub. Qaddafi's opponents were also hunted down abroad. Between 1980 and 1985 at least five Libyans were murdered in Europe and 46 in the Middle East. These operations were resented as infringements of sovereignty, but none went so disastrously wrong as that in London when a Libyan Embassy official was filmed firing a machine-gun at random into a crowd of protestors and killed a young British policewomen, Yvonne Fletcher, in St James's Square.

QADDAFI'S FOREIGN POLICY

Qaddafi has always had a stormy relationship with the outside world. Right from the beginning he gave military backing to the Muslim side in the Chad civil war, and occupied the 3,700 square miles of the disputed Aouzou strip in the process. In this war Libya was indirectly ranged against France, which gave its support to the black Christian-Animists of southern Chad. By 1980 the Libyan army had emerged the sole victor in this confusing multi-factional civil war. However, in 1981 Qaddafi's proposal of a merger between Libya and Chad destroyed the fruits of ten years of struggle. His action was internationally condemned and it was said that in Chad even the dogs turned against the Libyans, who were driven clean out of the country.

In his first years in power Qaddafi also attempted to create a grand Arabic council to co-ordinate strategic policy against Israel, although this floundered in the face of the complexity of Middle East politics. The other leaders of the Arab world found Qaddafi worryingly sincere, intense and naive, while his fearless honesty alarmed them. On 12 February 1973 the destruction by an Israeli jet of flight LN 114, a Libyan Airlines' Boeing 727, after it had inadvertently strayed over Israeli territory during a sandstorm, proved to be a turning point in Qaddafi's foreign policy. His fiery rhetoric was henceforth increasingly matched by practical support for any revolutionary struggle, whether in Northern Ireland, Nicaragua, Palestine or Japan.

By the late 1980s Qaddafi's policy of murdering members of the Libyan opposition abroad and his long record of backing revolutionary causes, had turned him into an international pariah. However, it was not so much Libya's covert operations overseas as Qaddafi's lack of hypocrisy about them that condemned him. Dozens of countries routinely practise state terror overseas to a much greater extent, but they also consistently deny any such activity. Whether Libya was actually involved in the destruction of a PanAm airliner, blown up by a bomb over Scotland, or in the death of two US soldiers blown up by a bomb in a Berlin nightclub, has never been independently established. In the eyes of the US president of the day, Qaddafi was personally responsible. In April 1986 the US airforce brushed their way past the elaborate Libyan air defences and bombed Qaddafi's residence in the Aziziya barracks, two miles from the centre of Tripoli. Qaddafi survived the attack, outraged at the death of an adopted daughter, but the muted world response to this flagrant US breach of sovereignty revealed to him exactly how isolated Libya had become. As further proof of this the United States has also succeeded in getting the UN to place a partial trade embargo on Libya due to its support of international terrorism.

Military Dictatorship and One-Party Government in Algeria, 1962–88

Peace and independence on 18 March 1962 brought with them the release of the old FLN leaders, such as Ben Bella, who had been captured by the French during the war. His stormy arrival at the provisional government's congress in Tripoli in June 1962 split the fragile political coalition, which had been held together by the pressure of war. Ben Khedda, head of the provisional government, rushed to Algiers to assume command of the capital amidst the wild acclamation of the Algerian people, while Ben Bella moved to the old western capital of Tlemcen. The ALN commander in the Kabylie Mountains, Belkacem

Krim, emerged as a third potential leader. One of Ben Khedda's first actions was to order the dismissal of Colonel Boumedienne, the chief of staff who had trained up the new ALN in the Moroccan and Tunisian refugee camps. In the country at large the bloodshed of the independence struggle continued as old scores were settled. As well as lynching thousands of Europeans who had decided to brave it out, ex-militia men, seemingly pro-French government servants and the studiously apolitical all met their deaths. The extent of this purge has never been assessed, but it completely paralysed what was left of the economy and government after the exodus of the *pieds-noirs*.

By late August the country seemed on the verge of civil war as it lined up behind the three contenders. Peace was brokered by one of the few surviving founders of the FLN, which allowed Ben Bella (assisted by Colonel Boumedienne) to occupy Algiers. On 25 September 1962 the newly elected Constituent National Assembly proclaimed the birth of the 'Democratic and Popular Algerian Republic', to be led by Ben Bella. This was passed by 159 votes to 1. Not one member of Ben Khedda's broad-based provisional government was given office while all the key posts were filled by ALN officers trained by Colonel Boumedienne. By the time the September 1963 constitution had been approved in a referendum, the FLN had been proclaimed the only party of progress. Even Algeria's long established Communist and Socialist parties were banned.

SOCIALIST REVOLUTION

The FLN was committed to agrarian reform, socialist revolution and the 'Algerization' of the nation. All remaining *pieds-noirs* were driven from their land and businesses. The estate or factory workers were invited to form new management committees. Ben Bella's relationship with his immediate neighbours was equally authoritarian. In 1963 Bourguiba recalled the Tunisian ambassador after Ben Bella was caught backing a coup attempt in Tunisia. The long-standing FLN agreement with Morocco to redraw France's arbitrary Saharan frontiers brought about the Oujda Conference in early October 1963. By the end of the month the conference had given way to a border war.

At the FLN party conference in April 1964 Ben Bella launched an attack on the class enemies of the revolution, the *ulema*, state officials and army officers. The latter proved an imprudent target for a revolution backed by military power. On 19 June 1965 Colonel Boumedienne had Ben Bella arrested just before he was due to make the inaugural speech at the great Afro-Asian Conference, which he had assembled at Algiers.

The Algerian revolution had found its Bonaparte. The Algerian army now emerged as the true master of the nation. Colonel Boumedienne, like the true staff-officer he was, turned his back on revolutionary rhetoric and started to create a bureaucracy suitable for a socialist republic. Algeria was divided into regions (wilayas), which were to be composed of local communes. The worker management committees were placed under the direction of ONRA (National Office for Agrarian Reform) and ONACO (the state controlled organ for foreign trade) whose enormous powers were matched only by their collective ignorance. Officials were appointed on the basis of their revolutionary credentials and their absolute loyalty to the leadership. Valiant attempts were made to find new trading partners from the Russian-dominated Eastern block, fellow Third World countries and socialist or communist nations, but they all failed. Only the continued and generous foreign aid given by France (resented by both the Algerian and French populace) kept the once booming agricultural economy of Algeria from total collapse. Nothing was done for the unemployed, so emigration to France to find work increased dramatically after independence. It was a hideous irony after the great expectations nurtured during the heroic independence struggle. By 1981 the number of Algerian migrant workers in France rose to a million. Further irony was provided by the government's fervent championing of literary Arabic. This was like a foreign language to most Algerians, who continued to use a mixture of French and local Maghrebi Arabic in their business dealings.

THE ALGERIAN ECONOMY

It was only the exploitation of oil and gas from the central Sahara by foreign companies that saved the young socialist republic from complete economic collapse. By 1967 substantial revenues were flowing into the treasury, and in 1971 Algeria, in alliance with Libya, felt confident enough to nationalize this vital resource. After nationalization there was no shortage of money for the great four-year plans with which Algeria was to be transformed into an industrial nation. In common with other socialist economies there was always money to pay the salaries of the privileged state employees and the military, but never enough to ensure land, work, adequate housing or even water supply for the populace. Instead vast resources were dedicated to show-piece projects like the vast iron and steel mill at El Hadjar. The prevailing socialist orthodoxy never allowed the colonial estates to be distributed to the peasants, and there was no encouragement for small businesses, markets, or new irrigation schemes or to enhance local trade. It is little wonder that the planned Algerian economic take-off never quite occurred.

By the late 1970s it was clear that Algerian independence had spawned two societies, a privileged inner circle composed of the army and the bureaucracy, and an outer circle comprising the rest of the country. Beneath this crude division there were further tensions between urban workers, agriculture workers on the co-operatives and peasants. There was also a general envy of the northern coastal cities by the deprived and forgotten people of the steppe and desert. There were also tensions between the emerging language groups, between those who used literary Arabic and those who spoke crude Maghrebi, French or Berber. None of these issues were addressed by the FLN or their four-year plans.

The death of Colonel Boumedienne in December 1978 was followed by the election of President Chedli Bendjedid in February 1979. It was a time of hope when both the FLN and the four-year plan aspired to create 'a social decade' and 'a better life' rather than just a further leap forward in steel production. This led to the Berber Spring, when the tribes of the Kabylie Mountains forcibly rejected any further attempt at the arabization of their ancient cultural traditions.

However, the 1980s saw a fall in oil production and oil prices, as well as the tailing off of remittances from Algerian migrant workers in Europe. Just as the expectations of the new generation were growing, the government's revenue began to tumble. Nor was there much room for financial manoeuvre, for the interest on Algeria's foreign debt, which stood at US $21 billion, was absorbing an ever-higher proportion of national income. In an attempt to escape their predicament the government tried a half-hearted conversion to a capitalist economy. The planning ministry was abolished in 1987, the Chamber of Commerce re-opened and some attempt was made to encourage the moribund private sector and the foreign business community. But while the army and the FLN political élite continued to enjoy their conspicuous consumption of imported whisky and Mercedes cars, the Algerian people could no longer endure the endless shortages, rising cost of living and the freezing of wages. Algeria erupted on to the street from 5–12 October 1988. The so-called bread riots were mingled with a longing for liberty and democracy, and were brutally crushed by the army at the cost of hundreds of lives. Opposition leaflets declared that 26 years of military dictatorship and one-party government had led Algeria to economic, social and political bankruptcy.

Hope and Horror

The Maghreb Union Treaty (UMA)

In the spring of 1989 all the countries of North-West Africa, Libya, Tunisia, Algeria, Morocco and Mauretania signed the Maghreb Union Treaty. Those interested in the history of Maghreb were inspired by this turn of events, which with five peaceful strokes of the pen seemed to create a modern political entity capable of exceeding all past glories: of Carthage, Caliphial Ifriqiya or the great Fatamid, Almoravid and Almohad Empires.

The Union was a direct result of current political difficulties. Libya wished to break its diplomatic isolation, Algeria was running into economic troubles, Morocco wished to sever Libya and Algeria's support for the Polisario while Tunisia hoped for an expansion of cross-border trade with both of its comparatively oil-rich neighbours. They all also recognized the advantage to be gained by creating a united front in negotiations with the European Union, which had now created a monolithic block out of the disparate Christian nations on the northern shore of the Mediterranean.

On a popular level the move was greeted enthusiastically, for the modern national frontiers of the Maghreb had cut across all manner of cultural, economic and social links. As an example of these potent cross currents it is as well to recall that Habib Bourguiba's ancestors came from Tripoli, the Senussi moved from western Algeria to Cyrenaica in the nineteenth century while a good proportion of Algeria's FLN leadership started life as natives of the Moroccan city of Oujda.

The treaty became known as the UMA (Union de Maghreb Arabe) which has pleasing associations with the arabic word *umma*, which

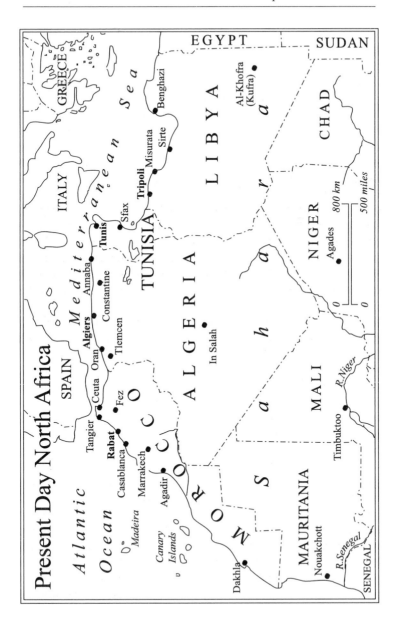

Present Day North Africa

means the world-wide community of Islam. The member states had particular satisfaction from receiving a diplomatic delegation from Egypt which expressed interest in joining this North African brotherhood of Islamic nations. It was also a time for some useful historical introspection, for while all the governments of the Maghreb insist on their primarily Arabic identity, they also had to acknowledge that what made them different from the rest of the Arab world was their common Berber heritage.

Civil Strife in Algeria

The effects of the treaty were, however, soon overshadowed by events in Algeria. After the suppression of the bread riots in October 1988, President Chedli amended the old FLN constitution to allow for multi-party elections. It was a brave decision, especially from such a figure as Chedli, who had only assumed the presidency after Boumedienne's death as a compromise candidate, because all the more ambitious generals could not trust each other. In his professional career as general of the Oran region from 1964 to 1979, Chedli had remained outside the faction struggles within the ruling élite. Chedli's wind of change did not extend to the commanding heights of the presidency, and he was re-elected as the sole candidate in December 1989 with 81 per cent of the vote. So in June 1990 Algeria went to the polls in its first free election. In an ebullient, exciting, but confusing contest over 136,00 candidates from a dozen different parties campaigned for office in the communes and wilaya (regions). A 65 per cent turnout of the population gave the Islamic Salvation Front (FIS) a landslide victory which gave them control of 45 of the 48 wilayas. This electoral victory represented a burning desire for efficient and responsible local government. It was also a desire to return to traditional Islamic moral values in a determined rejection of the corrupt ruling establishment. Our perception of this Algerian opposition has been coloured by its labelling as 'fundamentalist', a modern term coined to describe the desire to return to the ideal political entity established by the Prophet Mohammed. In the light of this survey of Maghreb history we can see that there is nothing new about 'fundamentalism', which has now been the principal political force in the Maghreb for well over 1,000 years. It would also seem to be a fact that although this reforming energy can often seize power it has proved less efficient at retaining power.

Throughout history we have seen that dominion falls back quickly from the hands of the reformers into the fists of generals. Such is the case of such fundamentalist reform movements as the Almoravids and Almohads; it was the commander of the army (Youssef ibn Tachfine and Abdel Moumen) not the charismatic founder-preachers of the movement (ibn Yasin and ibn Tumert) who established the ruling dynasty.

President Chedli planned to proceed with the next round of elections and either expose the new FIS leaders as isolated incompetents or co-opt them into the ruling circle. However, his confidence that he could work a deal with the FIS leadership was not shared by his fellow generals, who deposed him and cancelled the scheduled national elections. It appears to have been a drastic and misguided decision. In an attempt to deflect the storm of popular disapproval the generals proceeded to construct a government of national unity. This was to be led by Mohammed Boudiaf, a fearless and incorruptible old revolutionary of a Trotsky-like zeal and purity. Boudiaf also had unimpeachable credentials as one of the nine historic leaders of the Algerian revolution. In practice Boudiaf's authority was to be held in check by a council of state dominated by General Nezzar, the military strongman of the day.

The Algerian population was suprised by the sudden recall of Boudiaf from the political wilderness to centre stage, but they were not fooled. Street and political unrest against the generals' coup quickly escalated into a guerilla war waged between the militant wing of the Islamic opposition and government forces. The FIS leadership was arrested and the party was officially outlawed in March 1992. The strategy of either side has been difficult to follow, for it has been a cruel and merciless struggle which has claimed around 10,000 lives with every passing year. Most of the fighting has been concentrated around the northern cities and especially in the strategic hinterland of Algiers. Like almost every civil war it has borne forth a hideous catalogue of indiscriminate massacre as government militia and guerilla bands fight for control of hamlets, villages, districts and suburbs. Reports of throat-slitting, decapitation with axes, rape and inquisitorial torture have become routine and only the most outrageous crimes, execution by chainsaw, burning with petrol and the burning of children in ovens, has managed to capture the attention of the world's press. Nor is it an easy war for the media to cover. Right from the first, journalists, cameramen, aid workers, embassy officials and foreign merchants were targeted and have been murdered in sufficient numbers to deter all but the bravest and most well-connected of their comrades. Nor, apart from much dark talk about returning veterans of the Afghan war, is it at all certain exactly who is killing whom. The motivation of many of these crimes remains mysterious unless you bear in mind that alongside the central struggle there are other issues being settled. On one side the ruling clique of generals has been divided between hardline *éradicateurs* and moderate *dialogistes*. On the other the Armed Islamic Group (GIA), a loose coalition of bandits and passionate 'mujahideen' guerilla fighters, are rivals to the more disciplined FIS Islamic Salvation Army, which has its strongest bases in the west and east. Iran and Sudan have been publicly held responsible for the weapons and training of the various rebel groups while Britain and Germany have been accused of providing a safe haven for the financial and propaganda needs of the rebels.

President Mohammed Boudiaf was not content to remain a figurehead of the generals and began to dig into the corrupt practices (fueled by Algeria's enormous oil revenues) of the ruling establishment. His work was cut short when he was assassinated whilst giving a speech at Annaba (Bone) on 29 June 1992. His assassin was denounced as an 'Islamist fundamentalist' although few observers doubt that his death should be laid at the door of the powerful military élite. Ali Kafi, a revered ALN leader, served as an interim president for two years while the generals and their military factions jostled for dominance. On 30 January 1994, General Lamine Zeroual, a former general of the police, had formally assumed control of the government. In the same year the main opposition parties met in Rome and proposed a peace based on an 'enlightened Islamic' constitution. Zeroual rejected this and moved quickly to sever the government's association with the unpopular FLN party, and attempted to win allies from the middle ground. After a new constitution in 1996 had banned religion from politics,

President Zeroual's newly formed government party (the RCD) won the 1997 general election. He also entered into talks with two of the FIS leaders, Abassi Madani and Abdelkader Hachani, although nothing came of this.

The armed struggle continues regardless of these political manoeuvres. While the government manages to keep a secure hold over oil and gas installations it has little need to worry that it will lack for foreign allies or revenue with which to pay and equip its 120,000-strong police and army. It is estimated that Algeria currently earns around US$43 billion a year from its oil and gas exports. Except for the well guarded gas and oil pipelines that snake their way across the borders into Tunisia and Morocco (towards Italy and Spain) the frontiers of Algeria have slammed shut. The oil and gas fields all lie within the thinly populated Saharan provinces and are relatively easy to defend. One does not need to be too cynical to realize that these oilfields (although effectively excluded from the fighting) are also at the heart of the struggle. Algeria, despite all its past financial mismanagement and corruption is still a very rich country. The civil war is not only a battle for the hearts, minds and fear-driven loyalty of the nation, but also about possession of its vast resources. If it is now clear that mastery of Algeria is once more to be fought out in war, it is not at all clear what an outsider can do other than pity the nation that has suffered so much and suffers still more.

The situation, for all its attendant horrors, has helped to focus a constructive light on North Africa, on where it has got to and on what it hopes to achieve.

Past and Future

Even though the most recent centuries of North African history can read like a story of continuous decline there is no need for pessimism. In the fifteenth century North Africa could hold its head high with any of the world's great cultures, but the sixteenth and seventeenth centuries dealt a succession of near mortal body blows to its ancient economy. Firstly, the West African gold resources which fueled the trans-Saharan trade were drying up, and were to be superseded by the vast influx of American specie into the old world with all the attendant inflation.

Secondly, the opening of the Atlantic and Indian Ocean trade routes severed its ancient overland monopoly of African trade. Thirdly, the slave-worked plantations of America began to undercut and then destroy the hitherto lucrative Maghrebi export of such luxuries as sugarcane. By the early eighteenth century North Africa had been driven back to exporting its primary products, corn, olive oil and livestock assisted by the export of tanned leather and woven goods, the two dominant craft-industries of every major North African city.

Yet the Maghreb could still hold its own with Europe, and it is interesting that it was during the eighteenth century that the last European fortified outposts at Oran, El Jadida and Casablanca were expelled. Vitally, however, the Maghreb has no coal or iron-ore (with one or two inaccessible low-grade exceptions) and so it is impossible that the industrial revolution could ever have originated there or that it could have been a centre of power in the nineteenth century. For it was the possession of vast reserves of these two key resources (coal and iron) that distinguished all the great colonial powers; Britain, France, Germany and the United States. The flood of industrially produced imports from Europe during the nineteenth century also witnessed the mournful destruction of all the traditional Maghrebi industries, such as weaving, ceramics, or metal-work. Nor did the colonists and the European capitalists, when they finally seized power in North Africa, make any attempt to import the techniques of industrialization to the Maghreb. Instead they concentrated on exporting raw resources to feed their own economies, for instance esparto grass for European paper-mills, olive oil for the Marseilles soap makers or Algerian wine re-labelled in France.

There were, however, two exceptions, for in the late nineteenth and early twentieth century, the Maghreb's two new natural resources, phosphates (vital for fertilizers) and petro-carbons (oil and natural gas) were first discovered and exploited by European capitalists. These two brand new industries (Algeria and Libya have the petro-carbons, Morocco and Tunisia have phosphates) have done much to correct the enormous economic imbalance with Europe. The importance of these two industries cannot be over-emphasized; for Algeria and Libya oil and gas is responsible for at least 90 per cent of their GNP while phosphates in Tunisia and Morocco are responsible for between 30 and 50 per cent of foreign earnings.

Another adjustment in the economic balance has been made possible due to the Maghreb's greatest resource, the industry of its people. For well over a century now the Maghreb has been accustomed to send its young men over the Mediterranean to work in the factories of the European industrial towns. Due to the energy, dedication and careful parsimony of these migrants there has been a ceaseless flow of money south from Europe to North Africa. The North African governments usually have been able to tax this flow of cash, but it has also been a vital source of seed capital for small Maghrebi businesses as well as the basic resource that sustains thousands of poor villages and suburbs. It is difficult to quantify, but in any one year there might be five million North Africans sending remittances home. In recent decades this trade has diversified, there have been new opportunities, such as work in the oil-rich countries of the Middle East (as well as neighbouring Libya) and new restrictions into entering Europe.

MANUFACTURING

Migrant work has also served to provide the Maghreb with a disorganized, haphazard and yet invaluable industrial training programme. This in turn allowed for an exciting new trend as multinational companies have begun to establish factories and workshops in North Africa. This is especially true of the garment trade, which has identified North Africa as a rich source of disciplined, skilled labour. In order to achieve anything quickly in an office in North Africa (often hidden by drone-like layers of tea-sipping, newspaper-reading, cigarette-smoking, gossiping males) it is usually vital to find at least one hard-working, efficient female. Amongst the middle class women of the big cities and administrative towns, there is now no effective discrimination in educational opportunities although only the most determined and capable will be able to cope with a career in public life. In the countryside and the market towns the traditional patterns of male dominated life continue almost unaltered by the twentieth century, although at the same time all the Maghrebi Constitutions protect the political equality of the sexes. The young women of the Maghreb (particularly those saving up money for their marriage) have also been targeted as one the most productive sections of the populace. On the back of this, at times, degrading piece-work it is not hard to predict a revival in Maghrebi manufacturing, almost certainly spear-headed by Tunisia, which is the most far advanced in this aspect. For those who admire the old urban skills, the beautifully woven cloth with its delicate mixes of silk, linen, wool and cotton worked upon with gorgeous meticulous embroidery, or the woven mergoums and knotted carpets drawn from a millenial rural tradition, the future is far from certain. Perhaps they will survive as a luxury trade on the tide of a returning Maghrebi prosperity, as prototypes for a new creativity, or be exported to discerning purchasers abroad. However, the one watchword by which such a trade might survive (in the manner of say, Scottish tweed) is in a complete commitment to the finest quality. Yet at the moment one of the major impetuses behind these skills, tourism, tends to encourage cheap and shoddy workmanship.

TOURISM

Tourism is the third great source of hard European currency for North Africa, practised by those two countries (Morocco and Tunisia) who do not have oil. At its heart is a simple exchange that runs like a negative to the flow of Maghrebi migrant labour to the North, for in an opposite direction flow European workers seeking a week or two's break from their hard-working lives with a holiday at a beach somewhere in the hot sun. The vast majority of tourists are not capable or interested in getting to grips with the cuisine, let alone the realities of the Maghreb. Providing you are not expecting a cultural exchange to take place and are content with a financial exchange, this sort of tourism (one of the world's fastest growing industries) need not be culturally degrading to the host country. All that is needed is long-term investment sufficient to create a pretty-looking coastal resort insulated from normal life where the tourists feel free to holiday on the beach, in restaurants, bars and nightclubs and to return next year. Alongside this mainstream sun, sand and sea tourism, is a smaller market of visitors who wish to visit the monuments, cities, gorgeous landscapes and people of North Africa for themselves.

They may be rewarded with some fascinating insights. Perhaps they will be offered mint tea up in a traditional Berber kasbah in a High Atlas mountain valley and find themselves amongst an audience giggling at the antics of a British comic like Benny Hill on the satellite television. Or during the evening *passeo* on some town boulevard they may pass two sisters walking hand in hand, one heavily veiled, the other looking like a Californian. They may find themselves in a fish restaurant, having first parked their humble hire-car beside a line of gleaming Mercedes, and hear a well-heeled multilingual chatter that ranges freely between Bond Street, Madison Avenue, Beirut and Paris. Or perhaps they might find themselves taking a walk amongst the crumbling ruins of a government fortress in some obscure agricultural plain. Recently in just such a place I met a man who proudly showed me his collections: one dedicated to a jumble of discarded European objects such as old typewriters, ashtrays and hub caps, another a treasured bookcase of bound Arabic texts, while in a third room, the workshop, he inset carved bone and metal into wooden plaques to make Koranic story-boards.

There is no reason to worry about the overbearing influence of the Italian suit, the French language, the Japanese motor-car, Egyptian singers or American television soap operas on the culture of the Maghreb. As the triumph of Algerian Rai music has shown, the more influences the better. In all the more important matters: cooking, religion, festivals, language or personal honour and the family, North Africa remains inalienably true to itself. Absorption of the more attractive and useful elements of different cultures, whilst maintaining their own, has been a vital element of North African history.

Chronology of Major Events

533	Byzantine conquest by Belisaurius
622	Prophet Mohammed moves to Medina
632	Arabia united under Prophet's authority
642	First Muslim raid into Cyrenaica
647	Exarch Gregory killed at battle of Sbeitla
682	Oqba ben Nafi's half legendary campaign
697	Al-Kahina defeated at battle of Gabes
705–10	Musa ben Nasser completes conquest of Maghreb
711	Tariq's conquest of Spain
739	Mutiny of Muslim Berber soldiers at Tangier
742	Second Arab army destroyed at Sebou river
800	Aghlabid dynasty established in Kairouan
909	Fatamid armies subdue all of the Maghreb
943	Abu Yazid's revolt against Fatamids
969	Fatamids conquer Egypt and build Cairo
1051	Beni Hilal Arabs invade the Maghreb
1086	Almoravid Empire conquers Spain
1125	Almoravid army defeated at Arnisol in Spain
	Ibn Tumert establishes Tinmal mountain base
1147	Almohads seize Marrakech
1159	Almohads conquer Tunisia and Libya
1163–84	Ibn Rushd (Averroës) writes under patronage of Almohad Caliph Abu Yaqub Yusuf
1248	Almohad army destroyed at Moulouya
1270	Louis IX's Eighth Crusade against Hafsid Tunis
1354	Ibn Battuta dictates his travels in Merenid Fez
1364	Ibn Khaldoun starts writing his history
1415	Portuguese seize Ceuta
1492	Fall of Granada
1510	El-Uruj repels Spanish assault on Jerba
1518	Leo Africanus captured by Christian corsairs
1541	Saadians expel Portuguese from Agadir.
	Khayr al-Din (Barbarossa) repels third Spanish assault on Algiers led by Charles V
1551	Dragut expels Knights of St John from Tripoli
1560	Dragut destroys Spanish-Italian fleet at Jerba
1573	Uluç Ali expels Spanish garrisons from Tunisia
1578	Portuguese defeat at battle of Ksar el-Kebir
1591	Saadians conquer Timbuktoo
1603	Death of Ahmed al-Mansour
1668	Moulay Rachid establishes Alaouite rule
1671	Military republic of Algiers created
1672–1727	Reign of Moulay Ishmael of Morocco

1705	Hussein ibn Ali Turki defends Tunisia
1711	Ahmed Karamanlis massacre in Tripoli
1816	Lord Exmouth enforces an end to Barbary piracy
1830	French assault Algiers
1835	Libya placed under direct Ottoman rule
1848	Governor-general Bugeaud conquers Algeria
1877	Kherredine dismissed from power
1878	Congress of Berlin
1881	French invade Tunisia protectorate. Treaty of Bardo
1907	French troops first land in Morocco at Casablanca
1911	Italian army invades Libya
1912	Sultan Moulay Hafid concedes Treaty of Fez
1921	Foundation of Tunisian Destour (Constitution) party
1921–6	Abdel Krim's Rif rebellion
1922–32	Omar al-Mukhtar leads Cyrenaican resistance
1934	Ait Atta surrender at Jebel Bou Gafer
	French 'Berber Decrees'
	Neo-Destour party formed in Tunisia
1936	Blum-Violette Bill rejected by French Popular Front
1942	Casablanca landings
1943	Surrender of German army at Tunis
1945	Sitif insurrection and massacre
1947	Mohammed V of Morocco's Tangier speech
1952	Libyan independence at hands of UN
1952	Assassination of Farhat Hached
1953	French depose Mohammed V of Morocco
1954	Formation of Front de Libération Nationale (FLN)
1954	Algerian Insurrection
1955	Habib Bouguiba accepts autonomy for Tunisia
1955	Mohammed V returned to the throne
1956	Morocco recovers her independence
1956	Tunisia recovers complete independence
1956	French Army in Algeria increased to 400,000
1956	French airforce seize FLN leadership
1957	Massu and Challe destroy ALN within Algeria.
1958	*Pied-noir* settlers seize power in Algiers
1958–1960	De Gaulle's 'third force' campaign
1961	Generals' insurrection fails
1962	Algeria recovers her independence
1962	Ben Bella in command of Algerian Republic
1963	Border war between Morocco and Algeria
1965	Ben Bella arrested by Colonel Boumedienne
1969	King Idris deposed by al-Qaddafi

1973	Qaddafi unveils his Third Universal Theory
1975	Morocco recovers the western Sahara from Spain
1979	Chedli Bendjedid assumes power in Algeria
1981 & 1984	Morocco and Tunisia rocked by food riots
1986	US airforce bomb palace of Libyan president
1987	Habib Bourguiba deposed by Ben Ali
1988	Bread and liberty riots in Algeria
1989	Maghreb Union Treaty
1990	Islamic Salvation Front win local elections
1991	Cancellation of Algerian national elections
1992–	Algerian civil war
1992	Assassination of Algerian President Boudiaf
1994	Accession of Alaouin President Zeroual
1997	Left centre 'Koutla' coalition
	Largest party in Moroccan elections

List of Rulers of North Africa

A list of monarchs, kings, emperors, exarchs, caliphs, emirs, imams, sultans, beys, deys, beylerbeys, pashas, sherifs, sheikhs and presidents who have ruled the Maghreb

Magonid dynasty of Carthage 550–396 BC

Carthage under a dynasty of priest-kings united the Phoenician cities of North Africa against aggressive Greek competition

Republic of Carthage 396–146 BC

(whose mixed constitution incorporating elements of monarchy, aristocracy and democracy was much admired by Aristotle)

Battiad kings of Cyrene 639–439 BC

'Eight generations of men shall rule over Cyrene, four called Battus and four called Arcesilaus' – Delphic oracle

Aristoteles, Battus I *639–599*
Arcesilaus I *599–583*
Battus II the fortunate *583–554*
Arcesilaus II the cruel *554–550*
Battus III the lame *550–526*
Arcesilaus III *526–515*
Battus IV the handsome *515–470*
Arcesilaus IV *470–439*

Massyli kings of Numidia and Mauretania 201 BC – AD 42

E. Algeria, W. Tunisia, W. Libya

Masinissa, son of Gaia of the Massyli *201–148 BC*
In 148 Scipio as executor divides Masinissa's kingdom between three sons,
Gulusa, Mastanbal and Micipsa
Micipsa, son of Masinissa *148–118 BC*
Hiempsal I, son of Micipsa *118–117 BC*
Adherbal, son of Micipsa *118–112 BC*
Jugurtha, nephew of Micipsa *118–105 BC*
Rome's Jugurthine war *112–106*
Gauda (Jugurtha's half-brother) *105–81 BC*
Hiempsal II and Hiarbas, sons of Gauda *81–62 BC*
Juba I, son of Hiempsal II *62–46 BC*
Juba II, son of Juba I *25 BC – AD 23*
Ptolemy, son of Juba II *AD 23–42*

Roman emperors

ruled Libya, Tunisia, Algeria and N. Morocco through governors

Julius Caesar *49–44 BC*
Octavian–Augustus *30 BC – AD 14*
Tiberius *14–37*
Caligula *37–41*
Claudius *41–54*
Nero *54–68*
Galba, Otho, Vitellius *68–9*
Vespasian *69–79*
Titus *79–81*
Domitian *81–96*
Nerva *96–8*
Trajan *98–117*
Hadrian *117–38*
Antoninus Pius *138–61*
Marcus Aurelius *161–80*
Commodus *180–93*
Pertinax, Didius Julianus *193*
Septimius Severus *193–211*
Caracalla *211–17*
Macrinus *217–18*

Heliogabalus *218–22*
Alexander Severus *222–35*
Maximinus *235–8*
Gordian I and Gordian II *238*
Gordian III *238–44*
Twenty soldier emperors *238–84*
Diocletian and Maximian *284–305*
Constantine the Great *306–37*
Constantine II *337–61*
Julian the Apostate *361–3*
Valentinian I *364–75*
Gratianus *367–83*
Valentinian II *375–92*
Theodosius I *379–95*
Honorius *395–423*
Valentinian III *425–55*

Vandal kings of Carthage 429–534

ruled Tunisia and E. Algeria

Genseric *429–77*
Huneric *477–84*
Gunthamund *484–523*
Thrasamund *484–96*
Hilderic *523–30*
Gelimer *530–4*

Byzantine emperors of Constantinople 527–698

whose exarch of Carthage ruled Tunisia and W. Libya

Justinian *527–65*
Justin II *565–78*
Tiberius II Constantine *578–82*
Maurice-Maurikios *582–602*
Phocas *602–10*
Heraclius *610–41*
Constans II *641–68*
Constantine IV *668–85*

Justinian II *685–95*
Leontius *695–8*

Ommayad caliphs of Damascus 661–750

whose emir of Ifriqia ruled Tunisia, Algeria, Morocco and Spain

Muawiya I *661–80*
Yazid I *680–3*
Muawiya II *683–4*
Marwan I *684–5*
Abdul Malik *685–705*
Al-Walid I *705–15*
Sulayman *715–17*
Umar II *717–20*
Yazid II *720–4*
Hisham *724–43*
Al-Walid II *743–4*
Marwan II *744–50*

Abbasid caliphs of Baghdad 749–809

who appointed military governors over Tunisia and Libya

As-Saffah *749–54*
Al-Mansur *754–75*
Al-Mahdi *775–85*
Al-Hadi *785–6*
Harun al-Rashid *786–809*

Rustamid imams of Tahert 777–909

Central Algeria

Abdul-Rahman ibn Rustam *777–84*
Abdul-Wahhab *784–823*
Abu Said Aflah *823–72*
Abu Bakr *872–?*
Abul Yaqzan Mohammed *?–894*
Abu Hatim Yusuf *894–907*

Yaqub *897–901*
Yaqzan *907–9*

Midrarid imams of Sigilmassa 757–976

S. Morocco

Midrar Abu Qasim Samghun ibn Wasul *757–83*
Abu Wizir Ilyas *783–90*
Al Yasa ibn Midrar *790–823*
Midrar al-Mustansir *823–67*
Abdulrahman Mamun *867*
Mohammed I *877–84*
Ilyasa al-Mustansir *884–909*
(Fatamid governor) *909–11*
Al-Fath Wasul *911*
Ahmad *912–22*
Mohammed II *922–33*
Abu Mustansir Mohammed III *933*
Mohammed IV ash Shakir *933–58*
Abu Mohammed al-Mutaz *963–76*

Idrissid sherifs of Fez 789–920

Central Morocco

Idris I ibn Abdullah *789–91*
Regent Rashid *791–802*
Idris II *803–28*
Mohammed al-Muntasir *828–36*
Ali I *836–49*
Yahya I *849–63*
Yahya II *863–66*
Ali II ibn Umar *866–?*
Yahya III al-Miqdam *?–905*
Yahya IV *905–23*
Hasan al-Hajjam *925–7*
Al-Qasim Gannun (Rif Mountains) *937–48*
Abdul Aish Ahmad (Rif Mountains) *948–54*
Hasan II (Rif Mountains) *954–74*

Maghrowa emirs of Fez 972–1069

Central Morocco

Ziri ibn Atiya *972–1001*
Al-Muizz *1001–26*
Hamama *1026–40*
Dunas *1040–60*
Al-Futuh *1060–3*
Muansar *1063–8*
Tammim *1068–9*

Aghlabid emirs of Kairouan 800–909

Tunisia and E. Algeria

Ibrahim ibn al-Aghlab *800–12*
Abdullah I *812–17*
Ziyadat Allah I *817–38*
Abu Iqal al-Aghlab *838–41*
Mohammed I *841–56*
Ahmed *856–63*
Ziyadat Allah II *863*
Mohammed II *864–75*
Ibrahim II *875–902*
Abdullah II *902–3*
Ziyadat Allah III *903–9*

Fatamid caliphs of Mahdia 910–69

Tunisia, Algeria and part of Morocco

Al-Mahdi (Ubaydallah Said) *909–34*
Al-Qaim *934–46*
Al-Mansur *946–53*
Al-Muizz (moved to Cairo 972) *953–75*

Zirid emirs of Kairouan 972–1148

Tunisia

Yusuf Buluggin ibn Ziri *972–84*
Al-Mansur *984–96*
Nasir ud Dawlah Badis *996–1016*
Sharaf ud Dawlah al-Muizz *1016–62*
Abu Tahir Temim *1062–1108*
Abu Tahir Yahya *1108–16*
Ali *1116–21*
Abu Yahya Hassan *1121–48*

Beni Hammad emirs 1015–1152

Algeria

Hammad ibn Buluggin *1015–28*
Al-Qaid *1028–54*
Muhsin *1054–5*
Buluggin *1055–62*
Al-Nasir *1062–88*
Al-Mansur *1088–1105*
Badis *1105*
Al-Aziz *1105–21*
Yhaya *1121–52*

Almoravid (Murabiti) emirs of Marrakech 1061–1147

Morocco, W. Algeria, Sahara and Spain

(Ibn Yasin *1042–59*)
(Abu Bekr ibn Umar *1056–87*)
Youssef ibn Tachfine *1061–1106*
Ali ben Youssef *1106–42*
Tachfine *1143–5*
Ibrahim *1146*
Ishaq *1147*

Almohad (Muwahhidun) caliphs of Marrakech 1147–1248

North Africa and S. Spain

(Ibn Tumert *1125–30*)
Abdel Moumen *1130–63*
Abu Yaqub Yusuf *1163–84*
Yaqub al-Mansour *1184–99*
Mohammed en Nasir *1199–1214*
Youssef al-Mustansir *1214–24*
Abdul Wahid *1224*
Al-Adid *1224–7*
Al-Mamun *1229–32*
Abdul Wahid *1232–42*
Abu Said *1242–8*
Umar al-Murtada *1248–66*
Abul Ula al-Wathiq *1266–9*
Ishaq (at Tinmal) *1269–76*

Hafsid caliphs of Tunis 1228–1574

Tunisia and E. Algeria

(Abdul Wahid ibn Abu Hafs Omar *1207–21*)
Abu Zakariya Yahya I *1228–49*
Al-Mustansir *1249–77*
Yahya al-Wathiq *1277–9*
Abu Ishaq Ibrahim *1279–82*
Ahmad ibn Abu Umara *1282*
Abu Hafs Omar (Tunisia) *1284–95*
Abou Zakariya Yahya III (Algeria) *1285–99*
Al-Mustansir II *1295–1309*
Abu Bekr ash Shadid *1309*
Khalid an Nasir *1309–11*
Al-Lihyani *1311–17*
Al-Mustansir III *1317–18*
Abu Bekr *1318–46*
Abu Hafs Omar II *1346–8*
Ahmad al-Fadl *1349*
Ibrahim al-Mustansir *1350–69*
Abou Baqa Khalid *1369–70*
Ahmad al-Mustansir II *1370–94*

Abdul Aziz al-Mutawakkil *1394–1434*
Al-Mustansir IV *1434*
Abou Omar Uthman *1435–88*
Abu Zakariya Yahya IV *1488–9*
Abu Yahya Zakariya II *1490–4*
Abu Abdullah Mohammad V *1494–1526*
Mohammed Hassan *1526–43*
Ahmad III *1543–69*
Abu Abdullah Mohammed VI *1573–4*

Merinid sultans (Beni Merin) of Fez 1245–1465

Morocco

Abou Yahya *1245–58*
Abou Yusuf Yaqub *1259–86*
Abou Yaqub Yusuf *1286–1307*
Abou Thabit *1307–8*
Abou Rabi Sulayman *1308–10*
Abou Said Uthman *1310–31*
Abou Hassan *1331–48*
Abou Inan Faris *1348–59*
Mohammed as Said *1359*
Abou Salim *1359–61*
Abou Omar Tashufin *1361*
Abou Halim *1361*
Abou Zayyan III *1361–2*
Abou Faris Abdul Aziz *1366–72*
Abou Zayyan IV *1372–4*
Abou Abbas Ahmad *1374–84*
Musa *1384–6*
Abou Zayyan V *1386*
Abou Zayyan VI *1386*
Abou Abbas Ahmad II *1387–93*
Abou Faris *1393–7*
Abdul Aziz *1397–8*
Abdullah *1398*
Abou Said Uthman III *1399–1420*
Abdul Haqq *1428–65*

Wattasid sultans (Beni Wattas) of Fez 1472–1554

Morocco

Mohammed al-Shaykh *1472–1505*
Al-Burtuqali *1505–26*
Ahmed al-Wattasi *1526–45*
Mohammed al-Qasri *1545–7*
Ahmed al-Wattasi (again) *1547–9*
Ali Abu Hassun (Ottoman backed) *1554*

Zayyanid sultans of Tlemcen 1236–1553

W. Algeria

Yaghmurasan ibn Zayan *1236–82*
Abu Said Uthman *1282–1303*
Abu Zayyan Mohammed *1303–7*
Abu Hammu I *1308–18*
Abu Tashufin *1318–37*
Abu Said Uthman II and Abu Thabit *1348–52*
Abu Hammu II *1359–89*
Abu Tashufin II *1389–93*
Abu Thabit Yusuf I *1393*
Abu Zayyan Mohammed II *1394–9*
Abu Mohammed Abdullah *1399–1401*
Abu Abdullah Mohammed *1401–11*
Abdul Rahman III *1411*
Abu Malik *1411–27*
Ahmad al-Mutasim *1430–61*
Mohammed V *1461–8*
Mohammed VI al-Thabiti *1468–1505*
Abu Abdullah Mohammed VII *1505–16*
Abu Hammu III *1516–27*
Abu Mohammed Abdullah II *1526–40*
Abu Abdullah Mohammed VIII *1540*
Abu Zayyan Ahmed *1540–50*
Hassan ibn Abdullah *1550–3*

Saadian sherifs of Marrakech 1510–1659

Morocco and W. Sahara

Mohammed al-Qaim *1510–17*
Al-Araj *1517–40*
Mohammed al-Shaykh *1540–57*
Abdullah al-Ghalib *1557–74*
Mohammed al-Mutawakkil *1574–6*
Abdul Malik *1576–8*
Ahmad al-Mansour *1578–1603*
Zaidan *1603–28*
Al-Mamun (in Fez) *1610–13*
Abdul Malik II *1623–31*
Abdullah (in Fez) *1613–24*
Al-Walid *1631–6*
Al-Asghar *1636–54*
Ahmad III *1654–9*

The Alaouite or Sherifian dynasty of Morocco 1668–

(Moulay al-Sharif, Mohammed I *?–1631*)
(Mohammed II *1631–64*)
Moulay Rachid *1664–72*
Moulay Ishmael *1672–1727*
Succession war *1727–43*
Moulay Abdullah *1743–50*
Sidi Mohammed III *1750–90*
Yazid *1790–2*
Moulay Sliman *1792–1822*
Abdul-Rahman *1822–59*
Mohammed (IV) ibn Abdul-Rahman *1859–73*
Moulay Hassan I *1873–94*
Abdul Aziz *1894–1908*
Moulay Hafid *1908–12*
Youssef *1912–27*
Mohammed V (king from 1957) *1927–62*
(Mohammed VI *1953–7*)
Hassan II *1962–*

Muradid beys of Tunis 1628–1705

Tunisia

(Youssef Dey *1610–37*)
Murad Osta *1628–31*
Mohammed I *1631–62*
Murad II *1662–75*
Year of five rulers *1675*
Ali *1676–88*
Mohammed II *1688–95*
Ramadan *1695–8*
Murad III *1698–1702*
Ibrahim ash-Sharif *1702–5*

Husseinite beys of Tunis 1705–1957

Tunisia

Hussein ibn Ali Turki *1705–35*
Ali I *1735–56*
Mohammed I *1756–9*
Ali II *1756–82*
Hammuda Pasha *1782–1814*
Uthman *1814*
Mahmud *1814–24*
Hussein II *1824–35*
Mustafa *1835–7*
Ahmed I *1837–55*
Mohammed II *1855–9*
Mohammed as Sadiq III *1859–82*
Ali Muddat *1882–1902*
Mohammed IV al-Hadi *1902–6*
Mohammed V an-Nasir *1906–22*
Mohammed VI al-Habib *1922–9*
Ahmed II *1929–42*
Mohammed VII al-Moncef *1942–3*
Mohammed VIII al-Amin *1943–57*
Republic proclaimed *1957*

Presidents of Tunisia

Habib Bourguiba *1957–87*
Ben Ali *1987–*

Beylerbeys of Algiers 1516–1671

Algeria
El-Uruj *1516–19*
Khayr al-Din Barbarossa *1520–44*
Agha Hasan Qusru *1544–52*
Salah Rais *1552–7*
Agha Hasan Qusru (again) *1557–67*
Uluç Kiliç Ali Pasha *1567–80*
Ottoman governors, triennially *1580–1659*
Three aghas *1659–64*
Agha Ali *1664–71*

Deys of Algiers 1671–1830

Algeria

Mohammed I *1671–82*
Hassan I *1682–3*
Hussein I *1683–9*
Shaban *1689–95*
Ahmed I *1695–8*
Hassan II *1698–1700*
Mustafa I *1700–5*
Hussein II Khoja *1705–7*
Mohammed II Bektash *1707–10*
Ibrahim I *1710*
Ali I *1710–18*
Kurd Abdi *1724–32*
Ibrahim II *1732–45*
Kuchuk Ibrahim III *1745–8*
Mohammed IV *1748–54*
Ali II *1754–66*
Hassan III *1791–8*
Mustafa II *1798–1805*
Ahmad II *1805–8*

Ali ar-Rasul III *1808–9*
Ali IV *1809–15*
Mohammed VI *1815*
Umar *1815–17*
Ali Khoja V *1817*
Hussein III *1818–30*

Presidents of the republic of Algeria

Algeria

Ben Bella *1962–5*
Houari Boumedienne *1965–78*
Chedli Bendjedid *1979–91*
Mohammed Boudiaf *1991–2*
Ali Kafi *1992–4*
Lamine Zeroual *1994–*

Karamanlis pashas of Tripoli 1711–1835

Libya

Ahmed I *1711–45*
Mohammed *1745–54*
Ali I *1754–93*
Ahmed II *1795*
Yusuf *1795–1832*
Ali II *1832–5*

Senussi sheikhs of Cyrenaica

Libya

Sayyid Mohammed ibn Ali al-Senussi *1837–59*
Sayyid al-Mahdi *1859–1902*
Sayyid Ahmad al-Sharif *1902–18*
Sayyid Mohammed Idris *1918–69*
(ruling as King Idris of Libya *1952–69*)

Leader of Libyan Arab Republic

Colonel Muammar Qaddafi *1969–*

Further Reading

ABUN-NASR, J. *A History of the Maghrib in the Islamic period* (Cambridge, 1987)

AGERON, C.-R. (translated and edited by Michael Brett), *Modern Algeria, A History from 1830 to the Present* (London, Hurst & Co, 1991)

BRETT, M. and FENTRESS, E. *The Berbers* (Blackwells, 1996)

JULIEN, C. *A History of North Africa from the Arab Conquest to 1830* (London, 1970)

PICARD, G. and C. *The Life and Death of Carthage* (Sidgwick & Jackson, 1968)

RAVEN, S. *Rome in North Africa* (London, Longmans, 1993)

A highly personal selection of half a dozen books on more specific subjects, but still written for a general audience:

BOVILL, E. W. *The Golden Trade of the Moors* (London, 1958)

DAVIS, J. *Libyan Politics, Tribe and Revolution* (London, I.B. Tauris, 1987)

HORNE, A. *A Savage War of Peace 1954–1962* (London, 1977)

MAXWELL, G. *Lords of the Atlas* (London, 1966)

PORCH, D. *The Conquest of the Sahara* (London, 1985)

RABINOW, P. *Reflections on Fieldwork in Morocco* (California, 1977)

Historical Gazetteer

Numbers in bold refer to main text

Agadir, Morocco. The chief port of the Sous valley and chief city of southern Morocco, perhaps on the site of Punic Rusaddir. The Portuguese occupied the fortified trading post of Santa Cruz de Cap de Gue from 1505 until expelled by Saadian siege in 1541. The port closed in 1760, and was a centre of German intrigue. The city was destroyed by the 1960 earthquake. There is a small anthropological museum, and the ruins of a Saadian hilltop kasbah. **241, 243, 250, 310**

Ait Benhaddou, Morocco. A celebrated village of kasbahs (traditional fortified farmsteads of the pre-Saharan region) on an old High Atlas trading route.

Ajdabiyah, Libya. A medieval trading town on an internal caravan route, where excavations have revealed the 10th-century Fatamid palace and mosque. **160**

Algiers/El Djezair, Algeria. The national capital since the 16th century, it was the Punic foundation of Ikosim 'seagull island', the Roman Icosium. It was re-founded in the 10th century by the Zirid emir as El Djezair Beni Mezranna. In 1509 the Spanish turned the offshore island Penon into a fortress. The city, defended by Barbarossa in 1516 and 1541 against Spanish attacks, grew into the centre of Ottoman power until seized by the French army in 1830. Massu's 1957 counter-insurgency campaign known as the battle of Algiers, was followed by two Algiers-based coups in January 1960 and April 1961. Aside from the 18th-century monuments in the kasbah quarter the city was rebuilt in the 19th century by the French. There are important historical collections in the Bardo and Beaux Arts museums. **178, 203, 215–16, 218, 221, 222–8**

Al Hoceima (Villa Sanjurjo) Morocco. The centre of the 10th-century emirate of Nokour, and in the 20th century of the Beni Ouriaghel tribe who led the Rif rising of 1921–6. A small offshore island (Penon de Alhumecas/Hadjirat Nokour) was occupied by the English Admiral Lawson in 1661, then by the French and by Spain from 1673 to the present.

Ain Madhi, Algeria. The birthplace and first *zaouia* of Abou al-Abbas Tidjani (1737–1815) founder of the influential Tidjania brotherhood. It was besieged by Abdel Kader in 1838.

4km east is Kourdane, the 19th-century home of Sidi Ahmed Tidjani and his French wife, Aurélie Picard.

Ain Sefra, Algeria. The centre of the Ksour Mountain region of the Saharan Atlas with 2,000 examples of *gravures rupestres*. A flash flood in 1904 drowned the charismatic writer Isabelle Eberhardt.

Annaba (Bone), Algeria. 2km south of the modern port-city are the ruins of *Hippo Regius*, the Roman city on an old Punic site made famous by St Augustine, who died during the Vandal siege of 430. Revived as an important Byzantine base it declined after the 7th century into the village of Medina Zaoui. By the 11th century the new site of Bona El Hadida just 2km north, was defended by walls. Seized by Barbarossa in 1522, it was briefly held by the Spanish from 1535 to 1540, but then it was renamed Annaba. **183, 210, 258, 259, 332**

Apollonia, Libya. An excavated antique Cyrenaican city beside the modern village of Susa. Initially the port of Cyrene, it grew into greater prominence in the Byzantine period from which survive the palace of Dux and half a dozen basilica churches. **160**

Arzew, Algeria. A 12th-century Almohad naval base that declined into a fishing port, but now enjoys a vital strategic position as the chief port for the exportation of gas.

Asilah, Morocco. An attractive walled town on the Atlantic coast, it is on a Punic site (sacked by Norman Viking raids in the 10th century). It was held by Portugal from 1473 until reconquered by Sultan Moulay Ishmael in 1691. **212, 240, 241, 246, 254**

Aurès, Algeria. An arid, austere, pre-Saharan mountain region famous for its resistance to foreign conquest whether against Rome, Byzantium, the Arab Caliphate or the French under such leaders as Mazippa, Tacfarinas, Kosaila, Kahena or Mostefa ben Boulaid (1917–56), one of the six historic leaders of the FLN. **54–5, 111, 148, 151, 304–5**

Azrou, Morocco. A hill town of the middle Atlas, site of a fortress built by Moulay Ismael in 1684 and a 20th-century French military academy which trains Berber recruits. **253, 280**

Azzemour/Moulay Bou Chaib, Morocco. A walled port that slips down the banks of the Oum er Rbia river, known to the Carthaginians and home to an ancient Jewish community. It was seized by Portugal (1502–45). **212, 241, 243**

Banassa, Morocco. There are excavations into the city of Julia Valentia Banasa (with pre-Roman levels) which stood above the banks of the Sebou river between the 3rd century BC and the 3rd century AD. **87**

Al-Beida/Al-Bayda, Libya. The site of the first Senussi *zaouia* established in Cyrenaica in 1843 and the 20th-century palace of King Idris. **283, 284, 322**

Beja (Vaga), Tunisia. A millenial urban centre for the rich grainlands of the Mejerda valley, overlooked by its still-garrisoned ancient fortress. In 109 BC this Numidian market town massacred its Roman garrison in a famous incident during the Jugurthine Wars. **233**

Bejaia, Algeria. The strategic port of eastern Algeria. A Punic foundation known in the Roman period as

Saldae, it was the chief port of the Beni Hammad emirs and their capital after 1090. Assaulted by Genoa in 1136 it fell to the Almohads in 1152. The second city of the Hafsid state (after Tunis) in 1509 it fell to the Spanish who were besieged in 1512 and 1514 before the city was recaptured in 1556. Thereafter it fell into decline. **208, 210, 214, 245**

Benghazi, Libya. The chief port and modern city of Cyrenaica was re-established after construction of the Ottoman fort beside the tomb of Ben Ghazi in 1650. Excavations have revealed elements of the ancient cities of Euspherides, founded in the 6th century BC, and Berenice from the 3rd century BC.

Biskra, Algeria. The centre of the Ziban oasis valley south of the Aurès Mountains, it was known as Vescera to the Romans. Sidi Oqba, revered burial place of the 7th-century Arab general Oqba ben Nafi, is 17km to the SE. **160**

Bizerte (Hippo Diarrhytus), Tunisia. A strategic Punic and Roman city-port embellished with a Hafsid palace in the 13th century. A key corsair harbour-fortress much fought over during the Hapsburg-Ottoman wars, it was settled by Moorish refugees *c.* 1600. **60, 124, 228, 229, 296, 315**

Boujad, Morocco. The spiritual centre of the Tadla plains, it was founded in the 16th century by Sidi Mohammed ech Chergui, the 'master of the horsemen'.

Boulaouane, Morocco. A hilltop kasbah planted in the coils of Oum er Rbia by Moulay Ismael in 1710 to dominate the Doukkala region.

Bulla Regia, Tunisia. The Numidian royal capital, which grew into a rich Roman city where St Augustine preached a sermon in 399. It is famous for Roman villas with underground apartments.

Carthage, Tunisia. The Punic foundation in 814 BC rapidly grew to become the dominant city of the Phoenician west. It was the capital of the North African Empire from 650 BC until its destruction by Rome in 146 BC. Re-founded in 39 BC it grew into the second city of the Western Empire until destroyed in AD 698. Substantial excavated remains (such as the Punic *tophet* and harbour, Roman baths, houses and Byzantine churches) are scattered amongst prosperous 20th-century suburban housing. There is an excellent museum beside the ex-colonial cathedral on Byrsa Hill. **10–26, 43–7, 53, 60, 65, 78, 104, 109–13, 123–4**

Casablanca, Morocco. The Punic port of Anfa was the capital of the Berghouata heresy from the 8th to the 12th century. The corsair port was attacked by the Portuguese in 1486 and 1515 and held by them from 1575 until the Lisbon earthquake of 1755. Rebuilt in 1770 by Sultan Sidi Mohammed, it supplants Tangier as the principal port. The 1906 Casablanca 'massacre'– of nine French dockers – was the pretext for the first French military landing. Over the 20th century it has grown into the national economic centre with a population of 3.5 million. **255, 275, 277, 295, 297, 334**

Ceuta/Sebta (Septem), Morocco. One of the pillars of Hercules guarding the straits of Gibraltar. Punic, Roman, Byzantine (whose governor Julian traditionally incited the Muslim invasion of Visigothic Spain) and medieval Islamic (it was the birthplace of geographer El Idrissi) remains lie beneath the modern port-town. It was Portuguese from 1415 to 1578, thereafter held by Spain as a sovereign enclave in North Africa. **88, 150, 204, 210–11, 240, 247**

Chechaouen/Chaouen/Xaouen, Morocco. A beautiful Moorish town on a mountain slope established in 1471 by refugees from Andalucia led by Moulay Ali ben Rachid, sheikh of Jebel Alam. It was the centre of an independent emirate until the Saadian capture in 1561. **241, 245**

Chemtou, Tunisia. These famous marble quarries are surrounded by the ruins of a Roman city on Numidian foundations. There is a good new museum on the site.

Chenini and Douriat, Tunisia. Two neighbouring hilltop Berber trading villages of the pre-Sahara (now deserted) preserve such traditional architectural structures as the *ksar* (communal granary) constructed from a hive-like arrangement of *ghorfa* (storage chambers).

Cherchel, Algerian coastal town. The Punic port of Iol was embellished by King Juba II of Numidia and renamed Caesarea in honour of his patron Augustus. It served as the capital of the Roman province of Mauretania Caeserensis. The museum displays fine classical mosaics and sculptures.

Constantine/Cirta, Algeria. A dramatically sited regional centre with a striking continuity of settlement allied to a recurringly violent history. The citadel was the capital of such famous Numidian kings as Syphax, Masinissa, Micipsa and Jugurtha. The Roman Colonia Cirta, it was the rich centre of the league of four cities. Destroyed in 311 by Maxentius, it was refounded and named after the Emperor Constantine. For 1,000 years from the 8th century it served as a Muslim citadel of the interior (after Kairouan). It was the centre of Haj Ahmed Bey's resistance to the French from 1830. **42, 49, 74, 90, 222, 231, 259–60, 305**

Cyrene, Libya. These hauntingly beautiful Romano-Greek ruins (temples, theatres, villas, tombs, agora and nympheum) are of an ancient hilltop city, which dominated Cyrenaica for 1,000 years from its foundation in the 7th century BC until the Arab conquest. It was the seat of the Battiad dynasty (639–439 BC). **15–16, 22–3, 82, 99–101**

Dellys, Algeria. This millenial port of the Kabylie was built over Punic Rusucurru and Roman Cissi.

Derna, Libya. A Greek colonized port, this was not part of the Cyrenaican pentapolis. Its fortunes revived in the late 16th century with Ottoman rule and the settlement of Moorish refugees. **87, 237, 238, 285**

Djemila, Algeria. 'The pretty'. Roman Cuicul was founded as a colony by the Emperor Nerva at the end of the 1st century AD. Celebrated monuments include the new forum with its Severan temple, the arch of Caracalla and a basilica. There are also a theatre, great baths, market and temple of Venus by the old forum and a baptistery in the Christian quarter.

Dougga (Thugga), Tunisia. A Punic-Numidian citadel which grew into a graceful Roman town. The well-preserved classical buildings (including a Carthaginian mausoleum from which Punic was first translated) spread over a hillside amidst olives and fine views make it one of the most beloved ruins of the ancient world.

Draa, Morocco. An oasis valley stretching from the southern foothills of High Atlas for 200km into the Sahara desert. There is a rich legacy of traditional kasbah architecture, and the ruins of the 11th-century Almoravid city beneath Jebel Zagora. It was the homeland of the Saadian dynasty, and an important trans-Saharan trade route.

Ech Cheliff/Chlef, Algeria. This city, founded as Orleansville in 1843 by General Bugeaud on the site of the Roman ruins of Castellum Tingitanum, is also known as El Asnam, 'the idols'.

El Haouaria, Tunisia. These coastal sandstone quarries were used in the construction of both Punic and Roman Carthage.

El Jadida (Mazagan), Morocco. This is the site of Punic Rubisis, the Portuguese fort of El Brija el Jedida (with its famous 'cistern') which was held from 1502 to 1769 by the Portuguese, and was restored by Sultan Moulay Abdul-Rahman in the 1820s. **241, 251, 255, 334**

El Jem (Thysdrus), Tunisia. The celebrated Roman amphitheatre was built just before this wealthy city (a Punic foundation) was destroyed in 238 for its central role in the Gordian revolt. There is an excellent mosaic museum beside the villa excavations. **50, 78, 124**

Essaouira (Mogador), Morocco. After Punic and Roman occupation of the isle of Mogador, the medieval port on the bay, it was occupied by the Portuguese from 1506 to 1545. The port was re-founded in its present elegant shape by Sultan Sidi Mohammed in 1760. **241, 255, 275**

Fez, Morocco. One of the world's most important medieval monuments, Fez traditionally was founded by Moulay Idris, but definitely was established by 809 by Idris II as his capital. It was soon filled by Arab refugees from Kairouan and Andalucia who established two rival quarters. It was the capital of Merenid and Wattasid states from 1248 until the Saadians seized the city in 1554, and the Alaouites made it their co-capital from 1727 to 1912. The architecural glories include the Dar Batha museum, the 14th-century Bou Inania and Attarin *medersas* and the ancient great mosque. **134, 150, 160, 178, 193, 199, 222, 243, 252**

Fezzan, Libya. A Saharan region with scattered oasis systems populated in antiquity by Garamantians. There are excavations at Garama and Zinchecra near the modern town of Germa. **283, 288, 299**

Gabes (Tacapa), Tunisia. A strategic coastal oasis guarding the Saharan-Sahel frontier. It is the site of numerous battles, such as Al-Kahina's victory over Hassan ibn Numan in 694, which was reversed in 697. **124, 142, 156, 182, 183, 217**

Gafsa (Capsa), Tunisia. First findspot of stone tools of Capsian culture this strategic oasis town guards the frontier between the steppe and the pre-Sahara. Sacked by the Roman general Marius in a famous incident during the Jugurthan War, this centre of Christian Berber resistance to the Arab conquest was sacked in 668 by Oqba ben Nafi. There is an archaeological museum beside a Roman spring-fed pool. **217, 316**

Gasr al Libya, Libya. There is a well-preserved fort here and Byzantine church mosaics.

Ghadames, Libya. A strategic oasis settlement on the first leg of the trans-Saharan trade route, it was first fortified by the Romans in 19 BC, when it was known as Cydaus. A superb example of traditional urban Berber architecture in the Sahara. **162, 236**

Ghar el Melh (Porto Farina), Tunisia. This was a fortified corsair port in a sheltered bay between the 15th and 18th centuries. It was attacked by Charles V in 1541 and Admiral Blake in 1654, but is now all but silted up. **229**

Ghat, Libya. This small but strategic Tuareg oasis town between the Acacus Mountains to the east and Tassili to the west, was a key stage on the trans-Saharan trade route. It makes a good base from which to see Saharan rock paintings. **162, 236**

Haidra (Ammaedara), Tunisia. The monumental ruins of a Byzantine fortress above the Roman city was itself built over the site of a 1st century AD military camp of the III Augusta Legion. **104, 111**

Hammamet, Tunisia. A charming traditional Islamic walled town overlooked by the 15th-century kasbah is now the centre of a substantial beach tourist industry. It is the site of the Punic-Roman city of Pupput.

Hassi-Messaoud, Algeria. A large sprawling centre of the petroleum industry where oil was first discovered on 15 July 1956.

Jebel Nafusa, Libya. A crescent-shaped mountain range that encircles and defines Tripolitania, occupied by bellicose Berber tribes specializing in dry farming techniques who in the 8th century supported the Ibadite creed. It is Libya's principal area for traditional Berber architecture. **283**

Jebel Oust, Tunisia. There are ruins of Roman and Byzantine natural baths and it was a cult centre.

Jerba, Tunisia. An extensive low offshore island connected to the mainland by causeway. The legendary location of the lotus eaters, it held four Punic trading cities known in the Roman period as Meninx, Girba, Haribus and Tipasa. Conquered by Arabs in 667 it became a centre of, and later a refuge for, Ibadite Muslims. It was a chief point of contention in the corsair war until Dragut's definitive victory in 1560. The museum is in the principal town of Houmt Souk, outside which stands a medieval fortress. **183, 209, 210, 214, 216, 217, 234, 235, 238**

Jerid, Tunisia. A string of a fertile oasis palmeries on the northern shore of the extensive Chott el Jerid salt lake, chief of which are the towns of Tozeur (Thusorus), Nefta (Aggasel Nepte) and Kriz (Thagis). **151**

Jijel, Algeria. The Punic and Roman port of Igilgili where General Theodosius landed in 373 to suppress

Firmus' rebellion. An important port for trade with Sicily and Italy, which became Barbarossa's principal corsair base from 1520 to 1525. It won a notable victory against the French assault of 1664.

Kabylie/Djurjura, Algeria. This is a distinctive and strategic Berber mountain region stretching between Algiers and Skikda. The name comes from an 18th-century European derivation from *kbayl*, Arabic for tribe. Older descriptions include Zouaoua tribal region or *tamourt*, Berber for homeland. It was an important centre (wilaya 3) of the independence struggle led by such Kabylie heroes as Abbane Ramdane, Colonel Amirouche and Krim Belkacem. **147, 148, 153, 261, 263, 305, 326**

Kairouan, Tunisia. The celebrated great mosque was founded by Oqba ben Nafi in 670 (Muslim year 50). It was the capital of the caliphial governor of Ifriqiya, and of the Aghlabid and Zirid dynasties of Tunisia until the Hilalian invasion of 1057, thereafter surviving as a pilgrimage centre. **121–6, 139–43, 149, 153–4, 156, 217, 232**

Kalaa des Beni Hammad, Algeria. The ruins of the capital of the Beni Hammad emirs was founded in 1007 and abandoned due to the Hilalian invasion by 1090.

Kasserine (Cilium), Tunisia. The ruins of the Romano-Byzantine city include 'Pliny's' theatre and two mausolea. It was the site of the defeat of the Byzantine general, Solomon in 543 and of the US II corps in 1943. **112**

Kelibia (Clupea), Tunisia. There are Punic, Roman, Byzantine, Islamic

and Spanish levels of occupation on this key fortress and harbour town of the Cap Bon peninsula, which was occupied by every invader.

Kerkennah/Kerkenah Isles, Tunisia. A flat offshore archipelago settled by the Phoenicians, known to the Greeks as Kyrannis and as Cercina to the Romans, it was the last departure point of Hannibal. Much contested by Christian and Muslim corsairs, it was only finally repopulated in the 18th century. **209**

Kerkouane, Tunisia. An excavated Punic walled town (*c.* 450–150 BC) perched on the Cap Bon coast, its site museum exhibits important finds from necropoli.

Khroumirie, Tunisia. A forested range of mountains in north-western Tunisia, it is a traditional centre of tribal dissidence.

Ksar el Kebir, Morocco. This probably occupies the site of the Roman Oppidum Novum, an important walled medieval town outside which was fought the battle of Ksar el Kebir or Three Kings (1578) where the Saadian army destroyed the Portuguese army of invasion led by Sebastian I.

Ksar es Seghir, Morocco. An Almohad castle built by Yacoub el-Mansour in 1192 to guard one of the shortest crossing places to Spain. It was seized and rebuilt by the Portuguese who held it from 1458 to 1550. **211, 240**

Kufra, Libya. This principal historic centre of Libya's south-eastern desert is composed of a cluster of oasis settlements. It was the central *zaouia* of the Senussi brotherhood from 1895 and the centre of resistance to the Italian invasion, and was not finally captured until 1931. **284**

Laghouat, Algeria. 'El Aghouat', the garden, was an important Saharan trading post between the 10th and 17th centuries.

Lakhdar, Jebel, (Lakhdar Mountains), Algeria. An important collection of Berber royal tombs from the late Roman period. **107**

Larache, Morocco. The Muslim port of El Araich was founded in the 7th century by the Arab general, Beni Arous, on the opposite bank of the Loukkos river to Lixus. It was sacked by the Portuguese in 1471, although their new base of Graciosa in turn was destroyed in 1489 by Wattasids who refortified Larache as a corsair base. Ceded to Spain by the Saadian prince Zaidan in 1610, it was recaptured by Moulay Ismael in 1689. **212, 240, 246, 249, 254, 279**

Le Kef (Sicca Veneria), Tunisia. This was a much fought over Punic military base and cult centre, a Roman provincial town, a Byzantine fortress and the government centre of the Tell throughout the Islamic period. A dozen historical monuments and two museums are found in this attractive hillside town.

Leptis Magna, Libya. Magnificent Roman ruins stand east of the port of Al-Khums, founded in the Islamic period. Leptis, brought to its apogee by the native Severan dynasty, is one of the most astonishingly well-preserved classical sites in the world (theatre, amphitheatre, old and new Severan forum, port, circus track, villas, triumphal arches, processional

way with nympheum, two baths, markets, temples) now assisted by an extensive and elegant new museum. **58, 59, 60, 68, 75, 77, 111, 112, 120**

Les Andalouses, Algeria. This Oran beach resort is on an important archaeological site.

Lixus, Morocco. The Punic port of Makom Shemesh was founded in 1100 BC, absorbed into the Mauretanian kingdom after the fall of Carthage, and conquered by Rome in AD 45. It was relinquished by Diocletian at the end of the 3rd century and survived into the Muslim period. Excavations have revealed the port, theatre, baths and acropolis.

Madaure, Algeria. These are the ruins of Madauros, an old Numidian town partly colonized by the Romans in the 1st century. It is the birthplace of Apuleius and the town where St Augustine was educated. **73, 101**

Mahdia, Tunisia. This rocky promontory of Cap Afrique was turned into the 10th-century citadel fortress of the Fatamid caliphs. Only the gatehouse, harbour and great mosque survived later sieges and occupations such as that of Roger II of Sicily (1148–60) and of the Spanish in the mid-16th century. **149, 152, 153, 156, 158, 181, 183, 210, 228**

Maktar (Mactaris), Tunisia. These imposing classical ruins on a hilltop crown the Tell. It was a Punic-Numidian site that grew into a rich Roman city. **62**

Mareth, Tunisia. In 1938 the French built the 'Mareth Line' against the threat from the Italian army in Libya. It was defended for 40 days in 1943 by

Rommel against the British 8th army. **295**

Marrakech, Morocco. This red-walled medieval city overlooked by High Atlas peaks, was founded by Youssef ibn Tachfine between 1070 and 1073 as the new Almoravid capital. Captured by the Almohads on 23 March 1147, they ruled from the city until their fall in 1269, when it became the provincial capital of the Merenids. It was occupied by the Saadians from 1521 and was their capital from 1554 to 1668. There is a rich architectural legacy from the 12th to the 20th century including half a dozen museum collections. **167, 170, 171, 173, 177, 178, 185, 186, 187, 188, 197, 243, 248, 251, 252, 255, 277, 279**

Mascara/Mouasker, Algeria. A traditional Berber hill town used as the capital of the western beylik from 1710 to 1790 (before the recapture of Oran from the Spanish) and the first seat of Abdel Kader's emirate in 1832. At Sidi Kada Bel Mokhtar, some 32km west, are the ruins of the *zaouia* founded by Abdel Kader's father, Sidi Mahyieddine, while Abdel Kader's tomb and birthplace are at El Guethna.

Matmata, Tunisia. A village at the centre of the pre-Saharan hill district, famous for its traditional underground houses.

Mazouna, Algeria. A traditional Berber hill town, which served as the 17th-century capital of the western beylik of Algeria. The birthplace and first *zaouia* in 1837 of Mohammed ibn Ali al-Senussi (1787–1859), founder of the Senussi brotherhood.

Medea/Lemdiya, Algeria. An important medieval town founded by Ziri, a Berber tribal chief, in the 10th century near the Roman ruins of Lambdia. The capital of the beylik of Titteri from the 16th to the 19th century.

Medeina (Althiburos), Tunisia. Excavations into this Romano–Byzantine city (abandoned in the Islamic period) uncovered some fine mosaics.

Mehdia/Mehdiya kasbah, Morocco. This is the site of a Punic port, the Almohad naval base of El Mamora and a much assaulted corsair anchorage. The Portuguese attempt at occupation ended after a dramatic siege in 1515, and it was held by Spain from 1614 to 1664. The present kasbah was built by Moulay Ismael. **251, 254**

Meknes, Morocco. One of two cities founded by the Berber Meknassa tribe in the 8th century, it was captured and embellished by the Almoravids (1069) and Almohads (1145). Its apogee was as the chosen capital of Sultan Moulay Ismael (1672–1727) followed by its reversion to a provincial destiny by the mid-18th century. Amongst the vast edifices are a fine 14th-century *medersa* and a 19th-century palace-museum. **150, 160, 241, 248, 250, 253, 254, 255, 279**

Melilla/Miliya/Tamlit, Morocco. A sovereign Spanish enclave on the site of the Punic Russadir, it was a wealthy medieval port. Seized by Spain in 1497 it has been under intermittent siege ever since. It contains the 16th-century fortress of Medina Sidonia. **150, 213, 214, 279**

Mers El Kebir, Algeria. The port suburb of Oran and a naval base. It was

368 of A Traveller's History of North Africa

an Andalucian-settled corsair base until seized by the Portuguese (1415-37, 1471-7) and the Spanish (1509). The French navy was attacked in the harbour by the British fleet on 3 July 1940, but the naval base was not surrendered to Algeria until 1968.

Miliana/Meylyana, Algeria. A strategic medieval trading town established on the Roman ruins of Succhabar by a Berber tribal chief in the 10th century.

Mohammedia, Morocco. A medieval port on the fertile Atlantic coast, it was known as Fedala, and was occupied by the Portuguese *c.* 1480-1545. **268**

Monastir, Tunisia. A traditional walled Sahel city, over the site of the Punic Rous penna and Roman Ruspina, with an ancient coastal *ribat* (fortress for *jihad*). The great mosque is now over-embellished with monuments as it is the birthplace of Habib Bourguiba. **142**

Mostaganem/Mestghanem, Algeria. The Punic port of Moristaga was transformed into Roman Cartenna. Possession of El Mehal citadel was much fought over in the medieval period. It was occupied by the Spanish until they were defeated by Barbarossa in 1558.

Moulay Idriss, Morocco. An elegant pilgrimage village draped over two hills, which guards the tomb of Idris I (789-91) founder of the Idrissid dynasty and lineage.

Murzuk, Libya. The principal centre of the Fezzan desert region (which numbered 101 different settlements in 1798) in the modern period. It was the seat of an emirate whose castle houses a small museum. **107, 236, 237, 281**

Mustis, Tunisia. The Romano-Byzantine ruins of a market town on the major crossroads of the principal Carthage-Theveste road.

Mzab, Algeria. This solated Saharan oasis was settled by Ibadi Berbers escaping Fatamid persecution in the 10th century. Between 1012 and 1048 the five architecturally distinctive Mozabite towns were established, the chief of which is Ghardaia. **163**

Nabeul, Tunisia. The site of Punic-Roman Neapolis to the north of whose ruins grew the Jewish and Muslim town of Nabeul. This was settled by Moorish artisans in the late 16th century and became an important centre of ceramic production. There is a small archaeological museum with fine mosaics.

Nedrama, Algeria. The ancient centre of the Traras Mountains was dominated by the Koumia tribe of Abdel Moumen, 12th-century founder of the Almohad Empire.

Oran/Wahran, Algeria. Founded as Ouahran in 937 by Andalucian merchants it first emerged into pre-eminence as the favoured port for the Zayyanid dynasty of Tlemcen. It was seized by the Spanish in 1509 and held until 1708. They returned in 1732, but left in 1792 after the city was shattered by the 1790 earthquake. Seat of the western beys until the French conquest, it had a 200,000 *pied-noir* population before independence. There is an important prehistoric collection in the Demaeght museum. **171, 177, 202, 208, 210, 214, 222, 227, 245, 259, 298, 299, 334**

Ouargla/Wargla, Algeria. This was the first refuge of Yakoub, last Rustamid imam of Ibadite Tiaret in 909 before the community moved further south to Mzab. Until the late 19th century it was the seat of the independent sherifian dynasty of Alahoum. **163**

Oudna, Tunisia. This Berber village was transformed into the Roman colony of Uthina by Octavian settlement. There are ruins of baths and cisterns, an amphitheatre and richly mosaic-decorated villas.

Ouezzane, Morocco. A market town in the western Rif Mountains founded as a spiritual centre by Cherif Moulay Abdallah, sheikh of the Sufi Taibia brotherhood, in 1727.

Oujda, Morocco. This much fought over citadel-capital of the eastern plains of Morocco was founded in 994 by the Berber chief Ziri ben Atiya, first emir of the Maghrowa dynasty. It played a key role in the 14th-century Merenid-Zayyanid wars and the 16th-century Saadian-Ottoman rivalry. **252, 324, 328**

Ouled Mimoun, Algeria. At Hadjar Roum/Altava there is an important series of post-Roman inscriptions from the Berber Masuna/Massonas kingdom.

Rabat, Morocco. The capital city since 1912. The Punic and Roman port of Sala has been partly excavated in the Chellah necropolis. Rabat emerged in the 10th century as a fortress on the headland, and became the central military base of the Almohads during the 1146–8 campaign against the Berghouata heretics. It served briefly as the capital of Yaqub al-Mansour (1184–99), but declined in the 13th century. In 1609 it was

re-founded by Moorish refugees who established an independent corsair base until 1666. The modest but elegant 18th- and 19th-century port was chosen as administrative capital by the French in 1912. It has a rich architectural heritage, with a central archaeological museum. The 17th-century Oudaia palace houses a good anthropological museum. **132, 180, 185, 186, 241, 245–50, 251, 252, 254, 255, 293, 301**

Rachgoun, Algeria. This offshore island and sandy beach lie beside the ruins of Siga, a Punic foundation that grew into the twin capital of King Syphax (ally of Hannibal and chief of the Numidian Masaesyli tribe). It was known as Portus Sigensis in the Roman period.

Rif, Morocco. This politically influential northern mountain range runs like a rampart along the Moroccan Mediterranean shore, occupied by famously bellicose and particular Berber tribes. It is culturally divided between the western third known as Ghomara in the medieval period and Djebella in modern times, and the eastern two-thirds of the range. The latter is the Rif proper, which was led by Abdel Krim in the celebrated 1921–6 Rif rebellion. **191, 310**

Sabratha, Libya. These extensive excavated ruins of the wealthy Romano-Byzantine port-city (one of the three cities of Tripolitania that passed almost peacefully from Carthage to Masinissa's kingdom and on to Rome) are on Punic foundations. There is an impressive theatre, forum area, temple of Isis and celebrated reconstruction of a Punic tomb, with a museum on site. **111, 120**

Safi, Morocco. This Atlantic port was known in the Punic period as Mysokaras, and in the early medieval period as Asfi. It was occupied by the Portuguese from 1508 to 1541. The largest port in the early 18th century, it declined in relation to Essaouira, but revived in the 20th century with the export of phosphates and sardines. **241, 243, 255**

Salé, Morocco. A citadel of the Berber Beni Ifren tribe, it was conquered by the Almoravids in 1058 and grew into a walled medieval port-city. Although sacked by Alfonso X of Castile in 1260, it has a continuity of settlement and culture in contrast to its mercurial neighbour, Rabat, which stands on the opposite bank of the Bou Regreg river. **132, 211, 241, 249–50, 251, 252, 253, 254**

Sbeitla (Sufetula), Tunisia. The monumental ruins (a magnificent triple temple capitolium) of this Roman city perfectly express the prosperity of the Golden Age. The site of the defeat of the Byzantine exarch Gregory by the Arab cavalry army of Abdallah ibn Saad in 647. **120–1**

Sefrou, Morocco. This walled medieval market town on the southern foothills of the Middle Atlas was founded by the Berber Ahel Sefrou tribe who converted to Judaism between the 1st and 7th century AD. **135, 253**

Setif, Algeria. The ancient and modern centre of the high plateau region that stretches between the Atlas and Aurès Mountains. The Punic settlement of Esedif (black) grew into

Roman Sitifis, made capital of the province of Mauretania Sitifiennis in the reforms of the 3rd century AD. It is the site of the 1152 Almohad victory against Hilalian Arabs, and of the notorious French massacre of 8 May 1945. **142**

Sfax (Tapaura), Tunisia. A busy commercial centre for Tunisian phosphates and olive oil beside the walled medina with its central Fatamid great mosque and covered bazaar. There are three collections: the kasbah, the 18th-century Dar Jallouli mansion and the archaeological museum in the town hall. **143, 183, 217, 272**

Sidi Bel Abbes, Algeria. This traditional Berber market town is dominated by the Beni Ameur tribe. It was the headquarters of the French Foreign Legion from 1847 to 1962.

Sidi Bou Said, Tunisia. A beautiful clifftop traditional village that has inspired poets, painters and artists. The colonial mansion of the conservationist, Baron D'Erlanger (1872–1932) serves as a cultural museum.

Sigilmassa, Morocco. The ancient trading city of the Tafilalet oasis, which dominated trans-Saharan trade from its foundation in 757 to its destruction in 1395. The seat of the Ibadite Benin Midrar dynasty 772–976. Although now in total ruin, in the medieval period it was of an importance to match Fez and Marrakech. **132, 148, 149, 160, 163, 164, 165, 167, 204, 250, 252**

Skikda (Philippeville), Algeria. The port for inland Cirta/Constantine known in Punic as *Rus Ikada* and by the Romans as *Rusicadae*. The new town of Philippeville was founded in

1838 by the French and named after Orleanist King Louis-Philippe. The name became notorious after the thousands massacred on 20 August 1955 in retaliation for the 71 French soldiers and settlers killed by the FLN.

Slonta, Libya. A small pagan Berber sanctuary carved into the living rock above a Cyrenaican village.

Souk Ahras (Thagaste), Algeria. The birthplace of St Augustine (354–430) and his mother St Monica (331–87). **97, 101, 102**

Sousse (Hadrumentum), Tunisia. The second city of Tunisia from time immemorial (President Ben Ali's birthplace). The capital of the Sahel region, it has been continuously occupied from the Punic period to the present day. It retains old walls, the ancient great mosque and ribat as well as a fine archeological collection in the kasbah. **18, 38, 47, 50, 142, 143, 152**

Tabarka (Thabraca), Tunisia. A Punic-Roman port and town, which has revealed some important Christian mosaics. The offshore island fortress was surrendered to the Genoese Lomellini family (who held it for 200 years) by Barbarossa in 1541 in exchange for the release of Dragut.

Tadla, Morocco. The central nomadic plain dividing southern and northern Morocco, it was the site of many battles such as that between the Wattasids and Saadians in 1536. Tadla town has grown around the kasbah erected by Moulay Ismael on the banks of the Oum er Rbia river in 1687.

Tafilalet, Morocco. A strategic southern oasis formed from the Ziz and Gheris rivers, dominated by the city of Sigilmassa (see above) which fragmented into rival villages from 1395. It was the 17th-century Sherifian arbitrator of these rival oasis communities, Moulay Ali Cherif's sons Moulay Rachid (1664–72) and Moulay Ismael (1672–1727) who established the rule of the present Alaouite dynasty. **125, 252**

Tahart / Tiaret / Tihert / Tiharet, Algeria. The capital of the Ibadi Rustamid imams from 770 to 911. There are no remains, not even the mosque admired by el-Bekri or from the older Roman settlement of Tingartia. The variant spellings are all versions of the Berber word for 'lion'. **137–9, 146, 148, 151, 160, 163**

Tamanrasset / Tamenghest, Algeria. The centre of the Hoggar and Tefedest regions of the central Sahara is populated by the Touareg tribes who speak the Tamaheq Berber dialect, which alone preserves a written form, the Tifinagh.

Tangier, Morocco. This is the oldest continuously inhabited city in Morocco. A Phoenician foundation of 1000 BC, it was the important Roman port-city of Tingis. Only the medieval circuit of city walls survived English destruction in 1668. The great mosque, the palace of the governor in the kasbah quarter and the city gates are all 17th-century reconstructions by Moulay Ismael. There are Punic tombs on the cliffs west of the city. Museums include Dar el Makhzen (ethnography and archaeology), the American Legation and Contemporary art. **82, 88, 125, 129–30, 132, 150, 211–12, 240, 251, 254, 256, 275, 278, 300**

Taoughzout, Algeria. A small village outside of which ibn Khaldoun took refuge in a tent in 1374 and wrote *Introduction to the History of the Berbers*.

Tarfaya, Morocco. This anchorage on the coast of the western Sahara was named Fort Victoria by Mackenzie, a British trader who traded with Saharan tribes from 1876 to 1885. It was known as Villa Bens during the Spanish occupation of 1920 to 1958.

Taroudant, Morocco. This walled market town of the Sous valley, was the first capital of the Saadian dynasty from 1520 to 1541, and the base of a rival Alaouite nephew (1672–87) to Moulay Ishmail's reign and El Hiba, the 'blue sultan' 1912–13. **248, 253, 279**

Tassili N'Ajjer, Algeria. A high plateau east of Djanet, which contains the most splendid examples of prehistoric Saharan paintings.

Taza, Morocco. This citadel-city guards the Taza gap between the Rif and the Middle Atlas mountain ranges and the eastern entry to Fez. Founded in the 8th century by the Berber Meknassa tribe, it served as the first capital of the Almohads from 1132 to 1147. It was much embellished by the Merenid dynasty (who originated nearby), and was the military base of Moulay Rachid during his 1664–8 conquest of Morocco, of the Alaouite pretender Bou Hamara from 1902 to 1908 and of the French for their subjugation of the Middle Atlas tribes from 1914 to 1928. **185, 252, 253**

Tazoult-Lambaesis, Algeria. The ruins of a Roman military camp built by the III Augusta Legion between the 1st and 3rd centuries for the defence of the Numidian frontier.

Tebessa, Algeria. The site of a Punic citadel known by the Romans as Theveste, these famous ruins were later used by the III Augusta Legion as their headquarters after they had advanced east from Ammaedara. A colony of Trajan's in the 2nd century, it was turned back into a military fortress by the Byzantine general, Solomon in 535 before declining into an isolated garrison post. **108, 111, 112**

Telouet, Morocco. The mountain kasbah of the Glaoui, an influential Berber clan who controlled the summit of the Tiz n Tichka pass across the High Atlas Mountains. It was developed into a palace-fortress during the mercurial rise to power of the brothers Madani and especially of Thami el-Glaoui (1875–1956), chief ally of the French.

Tenes, Algeria. This was the Punic foundation of Cartenae, settled by Augustan colonists in the 1st century and by refugees from Andalucia in the 9th. An eastern outpost of the Almoravid Empire, it was infamous as the site of French atrocities in 1845.

Tetouan, Morocco. An elegant walled Moorish city founded in 1484 by refugees from Granada, it grew rich from trade and the corsair war. It was embellished in the 20th century as capital of the Spanish Protectorate. There is a small archaeological collection, and a larger ethnographic museum in Bab Saidin. **241, 251, 254, 275, 279**

Teuchira (Tocra), Libya. This excavated Greek port-city established in 510 BC was renamed Arsinoe (after the wife of Ptolemy II) and Cleopatris (after the daughter of Mark Anthony and Cleopatra). **119**

Thuburbo Majus, Tunisia. The impressive ruins of a wealthy provincial Roman city with a population of around 10,000 stand over an old Punic-Numidian site.

Tiddis, Algeria. The Roman ruins of the small town of Castellum Tidditanorum, celebrated for its hilltop position and intimate fusion of Berber and classical culture. 30km NW of Constantine.

Timgad, Algeria. One of the most celebrated ruins of antiquity is the Roman colony of Thamugadi founded by Trajan in 100 AD with its triumphal arch, five baths, forum, library, theatre, markets, temples, Catholic and Donatist cathedrals, Byzantine fort and intact streets.

Tinmal, Morocco. The distinguished ruins of the great mosque (built in 1153–4) alone mark the city built beneath the summits of the High Atlas Mountains. It was established by the founder of the Almohads, ibn Tumert in 1121 and destroyed by the Merenids in 1276. **175, 177, 179, 188**

Tipasa, Algeria. These famous Roman ruins are from a coastal city on a Punic site. There are remains of a temple, a theatre, forum, baths and an important Christian church associated with St Salsa. **82**

Tiznit, Morocco. This walled city was established by Sultan Moulay Hassan in 1882 as the new administrative centre for the Anti Atlas Mountains.

Tlemcen, Algeria. The spiritual and architectural centre of Algeria has such important medieval sites as the Grand Mosque, the Sidi Bel Hassen mosque, the Hadar quarter, the Mechouar citadel, El Eubbad and the Merenid Mansourah. On the site of the Roman camp of Pomaria, Idris I founded the citadel of Agadir, which served as the capital of the Beni Khazar and Beni Yala emirs. Refounded as Tagart by Almoravid Youssef ibn Tachfine in the 11th century it emerged as the chief city of the central Maghreb. It was the capital of the Zayyanid dynasty from 1236 to 1555 although subjected to countless sieges from rival dynasties. A vital centre of national consciousness during the French period, it produced many leaders of the independence struggle. **125, 137, 150, 160, 177, 185, 191, 193, 199, 202, 203, 222, 242, 244, 245, 323**

Tolmeita (Ptolemais), Libya. The port for the city of Barce (possibly beneath the town of Al-Marj) it was renamed after Ptolemy II in the 3rd century BC, when it grew into a large city. Extensive Hellenistic and Roman remains include a palace, cisterns, a gatehouse and a church associated with Bishop Synesius. **87, 99, 100, 160**

Touat, Algeria. A group of Saharan oasis communities that stretch for 20km between the towns of Adrar and El Mansour. A vital supply post halfway between Sigilmassa and Timbuktoo that historically centred on the Tamentit *ksar*. **162**

Tripoli/Tarablus al-Gharb, Libya. The Punic port of Oea, the central city of a league of three cities (including Sabratha and Leptis) which became known as Tripolitania. Oea alone survived the change into the Muslim era and its continous history of settlement is reflected in the Roman remains amongst the old mosques of the city. The principal urban centre for Hafsid rule, it was captured by Spain in 1510 and passed into the hands of the Knights of St John. They were expelled in 1551 by Dragut, who made it the centre of the new Ottoman province. The seat of the Karamanlis dynasty, of Ottoman and Italian governors, it remains the *de facto* centre of modern Libya. There is a superb archaeological collection in the recently redesigned museum within the old castle. **74, 120, 142, 183, 214, 217, 222, 236–9, 323**

Tunis, Tunisia. An ancient suburb of Carthage, Tunis was much used as a base for foreign armies besieging the city. It was re-founded as an Islamic city by Hassan ibn Numan after the slighting of Carthage at the end of the 7th century. The seat of the Khorassid emirate from 1059 to 1160, after which it emerged as capital of Tunisia. The old city remains one of the most beautiful Islamic cities in the world with its 9th-century great mosque, covered bazaar and distinguished collection of 17th- and 18th-century architecture. The archaeological collection housed in the old Bardo palace of the beys is one of the finest museums in the Mediterranean.

Utique/Uticca, Tunisia. There are excavated but sparse ruins (plus a small site museum) of an important Punic and Roman harbour-city now completely silted up. It was founded by Tyrians in 1101 BC so is 287 years older than Carthage. **11, 24, 38, 44, 47, 48**

Volubilis/walila, Morocco. A Punic-influenced Mauretanian city, this was perhaps Juba II's (25BC– AD24) western capital that grew into the elegant administrative centre of the Roman province of Mauretania Tingitana, AD 45–283. Although much diminished, it remained an urban centre for Christian Berbers, the site where Idris I was acclaimed imam in 799. **54, 56, 60, 88, 133–4**

Zaghouan, Tunisia. An elegant, hillside town on the site of Roman Ziqua. 2km uphill stands Hadrian's water temple, the starting point of the aqueduct to Carthage. **59, 66**

Index

Please also see the Historical Gazetteer for further references to places.

A TRAVELLER'S HISTORY OF FRANCE

Robert Cole

"Undoubtedly the best way to prepare for a trip to France is to bone up on some history. The Traveller's History of France by Robert Cole is concise and gives the essential facts in a very readable form" **The Independent on Sunday**

"Hundreds of thousands of travellers, visit France each year. The glories of the French countryside, the essential harmony of much of French architecture, the wealth of historical remains and associations, the enormous variety of experience that France offers, act as a perennial and irresistible attraction. For these visitors this lively and useful guide provides the essential clues to an understanding of France's past, and present, in entertaining and sometimes surprising detail"
From the Preface by the Series Editor, Denis Judd.

In *A Traveller's History of France* the reader is provided with a comprehensive and yet very enjoyable, general history of France, from earliest times to the present day.

An extensive Gazetteer which is cross-referenced with the main text pinpoints the historical importance of sites and towns. Illustrated with maps and line drawings *A Traveller's History of France* will add to the enjoyment of every holidaymaker who likes to do more than lie on a beach.

A TRAVELLER'S HISTORY OF PARIS

Robert Cole

"…an excellent resource…Robert Cole presents a complete picture of this historic city…" **Small Press**

Paris, in many people's thoughts, is the epitome of the perfect city – beautiful, romantic and imbued with vitality and culture. It is a wonderful place to visit and to live in.

Packed with fact, anecdote and insight. *A Traveller's History of Paris* offers a complete history of Paris and the people who have shaped its destiny, from its earliest settlement as the Roman village of *Lutetia Parisiorum* with a few hundred inhabitants, to 20 centuries later when Paris is a city of well over 2 million – nearly one-fifth of the population of France.

This handy paperback is fully indexed and includes a Chronology of Major Events, a section on Notre-Dame and historic churches. Modernism. Paris parks, bridges, cemeteries, museums and galleries, the Metro and The Environs. Illustrated with line drawings and historical maps, this is an invaluable book for all visitors to read and enjoy.

A TRAVELLER'S HISTORY OF ENGLAND

Christopher Daniell

A Traveller's History of England gives a comprehensive and enjoyable survey of England's past from prehistoric times right through to the 1990s.

All the major periods of English history are dealt with, including the Roman occupation, and the invasions of the Anglo-Saxons, Vikings and Normans, and the power struggles of the medieval kings. The Reformation, the Renaissance and the Civil War are discussed, as well as the consequences of the Industrial Revolution and urbanism, and the establishment of an Empire which encompassed a quarter of the human race. In this century the Empire has been transformed into the Commonwealth, two victorious, but costly, World Wars have been fought, the Welfare State was established, and membership of the European Economic Community was finally achieved.

Illustrated throughout with maps and line drawings, *A Traveller's History of England* offers an insight into the country's past and present and is an invaluable companion for all those who want to know more about a nation whose impact upon the rest of the world has been profound.

A TRAVELLER'S HISTORY OF LONDON

Richard Tames

A full and comprehensive historical background to the capital's past which covers the period from London's first beginnings, right up to the present day – from *Londinium* and *Ludenwic* to Docklands' development. London has always been an international city and visitors from all over the world have recorded their impressions and these views have been drawn on extensively throughout this book.

At different points in London's 2000-year history, it has been praised for its elegance and civility and damned for its riots, rudeness, fogs and squalor. Visitors and London's own residents will enjoy discovering more about the city from this fascinating book.

There are special sections on the Cathedrals, Royal Palaces, Parks and Gardens, Railway Termini, The Underground, Bridges, Cemeteries, Museums and Galleries, The London Year as well as a full Chronology of Major Events, Maps and Index.

A TRAVELLER'S HISTORY OF GREECE

Timothy Boatswain and Colin Nicholson

The many facets of Greece as presented in this unique book.

In *A Traveller's History of Greece*, the reader is provided with an authoritative general history of Greece from its earliest beginnings down to the present day. It covers in a clear and comprehensive manner the classical past, the conflict with Persia, the conquest by the Romans, the Byzantine era and the occupation by the Turks; the struggle for Independence and the turbulence of recent years, right up to current events.

This history will help the visitor make sense of modern Greece against the background of its diverse heritage. A Gazetteer, cross-referenced with the main text highlights the importance of sites, towns and ancient battlefields. A Chronology details the significant dates and a brief survey of the artistic styles of each period is given. Illustrated with maps and line drawings *A Traveller's History of Greece* is an invaluable companion for your holiday.

A TRAVELLER'S HISTORY OF ITALY

Valerio Lintner

In *A Traveller's History of Italy* the author analyses the development of the Italian people from pre-historic times right through to the imaginative, resourceful and fiercely independent Italians we know today.

All of the major periods of Italian history are dealt with, including the Etruscans, the Romans, the communes and the city states which spawned the glories of the Renaissance. In more modern times, Unification and the development and regeneration of the Liberal state into Fascism are covered, as well as the rise of Italy to the position it currently enjoys as a leading member of the European Community.

The Gazetteer, which is cross-referenced to the main text, highlights sites, towns, churches and cathedrals of historical importance for the visitor.

A TRAVELLER'S HISTORY OF SPAIN

Juan Lalaguna

Spain's vibrant and colourful past is as exciting to discover as is taking a fresh look at the tumultuous upheavals of the twentieth century. *A Traveller's History of Spain* will unlock the secrets of the country, its people and culture for the interested traveller.

Juan Lalaguna takes you on a journey from the earliest settlements on the Iberian peninsula, through the influences of the Romans, the Goths and the Muslims, the traumas of expansion and the end of Empire, the surge for national identity – right up to the current dilemmas that face post-Franco Spain.

A Traveller's History of Spain is an essential companion for your trip to Spain.

A TRAVELLER'S HISTORY OF RUSSIA and the USSR

Peter Neville

A Traveller's History of Russia gives a comprehensive survey of that country's past from the earliest times to the era of perestroika and glasnost. The reader first learns about prehistoric Russia and its nomadic invaders, then the story of the city state of Kiev is traced up to the crucial year of 1237 when the Mongol invasion took place. The rise of Muscovy with its colourful panoply of rulers from Ivan Moneybags to Ivan the Terrible, the despotism of the Romanovs and the Russian Revolution are dealt with in depth. The book concludes with an account of the rise of the Soviet state, its world role and current metamorphosis.

There is an A–Z Gazeteer for the visitor which is cross-referenced to the main text and highlights sites, towns and places of historical importance.

Illustrated throughout with maps and line drawings, *A Traveller's History of Russia and the USSR* encapsulates the nation's past and present and is a unique cultural and historical guidebook to that intriguing land.

A TRAVELLER'S HISTORY OF SCOTLAND

Andrew Fisher

A Traveller's History of Scotland begins with Scotland's first people and their culture, which remained uncrushed by the Roman invasions. Before the Vikings in 900 it was a land of romantic kingdoms and saints, gradually overtaken by more pragmatic struggles for power between the great families of Bruce, Balliol and Stewart. Centuries of strife led up to the turbulent years of Mary Queen of Scots, and Calvinistic legacy of Knox, and the bitterness of final defeat.

The dreams of the Jacobites are contrasted with the cruel reality of the end of the Stuarts and the Act of Union with England. Scotland now saw an age of building, industry and despoliation of their land. The result was much emigration and an obsession fostered by Walter Scott and Burns with the nation's past which glorified the legends of the Highlander and the Clans. In this century, a loss of identity and a drift to the south has been followed by a new surge of national pride with higher aspirations for the future.

A Traveller's History of Scotland explains the roots of Scottish history and is an excellent handbook for visitors.

A TRAVELLER'S HISTORY OF IRELAND

Peter Neville

The many thousands of visitors to Ireland are drawn by the landscape, the people and the underlying atmosphere created by its rich heritage.

The story of *A Traveller's History of Ireland* opens with mysterious early Celtic Ireland, where no Roman stood, through St Patrick's mission and the legendary High King Brian Boru. The Normans came in the twelfth century and this period also marks the beginnings of the difficult and tragic Anglo-Irish relationship. Reading the book helps one understand the complexities of the current political situation.

Its appendices include an A–Z Gazateer, a Chronology of Major Events, a list of Kings and Queens, Prime Ministers and Presidents, Famous Battles, a full Bibliography and Index. There are Historical Maps and line drawings to accompany the text.

A TRAVELLER'S HISTORY OF CHINA

Stephen G. Haw

"Haw manages to get 2 million years in 300 pages – and he does it without gimmicks or colour pictures. An excellent addition to a series which is already invaluable. Whether you're travelling or not." **The Guardian (London)**

A Traveller's History of China provides a concise but fascinating journey from the country's earliest beginnings right up to the creation of the economic powerhouse that is today's China. Stephen Haw carries the reader back in time to the prehistoric civilizations of 4,000 years ago, and from there to the centuries of China's silk trade with the less-developed countries of Europe. Some of the most significant inventions of the pre-modern world, including paper, gunpowder and the magnetic compass originated in China and were then transmitted to the West. The author describes the glories of the Tang and Song dynasties which saw the creation of the great Chinese cities to the period of its decline and the efforts of Europe to conquer and subdue this giant land. It covers the tumult and triumphs of the Chinese revolution and the dramatic changes in political policies since the late 1970s which have now made it one of the world's fastest-developing countries.

A TRAVELLER'S HISTORY OF INDIA

SinhaRaja Tammita-Delgoda

"For anyone…planning a trip to India, the latest in the excellent Traveller's History series…provides a useful grounding for those whose curiosity exceeds the time available for research." **The London Evening Standard**

India is heir to one of the world's oldest and richest civilizations and the origin of many of the ideas, philosophies and movements which have shaped the destiny of humankind.

For the traveller, India is both an inspiration and a challenge. The sheer wealth of Indian culture has fascinated generations of visitors. We see the sweeping panorama of Indian history, from the ancient origins of Hinduism, Jainism, Buddhism, and the other great religions, through the tumultuous political history of India's epic struggle against colonialism, to the ravages of Partition, Non-Alignment, and finally the emergence of India as a powerful modern state still grounded in the literature and culture of an ancient land. *A Traveller's History of India* covers the whole scope of India's past and present history and allows the reader to make sense of what they see in a way that no other guide book can.

A TRAVELLER'S HISTORY OF JAPAN

Richard Tames

Whether you are going to Japan on business, to study, to teach or simply on holiday, you know that you are going to a country which really does merit the title 'unique'. A century ago the first modern guidebook to Japan warned the visitor that 'he…who should essay to travel without having learnt a word concerning Japan's past, would still run the risk of forming opinions ludicrously erroneous.' This is still sound advise.

A Traveller's History of Japan not only offers the reader a chronological outline of the nation's development but also provides an invaluable introduction to its language, literature and arts, from *kabuki to karaoke*. Political, social and industrial history and economics are also well covered; this clearly written history explains how a country embedded in the traditions of Shinto, Shoguns and Samurai has achieved stupendous economic growth and dominance in the twentieth century.

There is a Historical Gazetteer, cross-referenced to the main text and particular attention is paid to the classic historical sites which feature on any visitor's itinerary. Special emphasis is given to the writings and reactions of travellers through the centuries.

A TRAVELLER'S HISTORY OF TURKEY

Richard Stoneman

A Traveller's History of Turkey offers a full and accurate portrait of the region from Prehistory right up to the present day. Particular emphasis is given to those aspects of history which have left their mark in the sites and monuments that are still visible today.

Moden Turkey is the creation of the present century, but at least seven ancient civilisations had their homes in the region. Turkey has also formed a significant part of several empires – those of Persia, Rome and Byzantium, before becoming the centre of the opulent Ottoman Empire. All of these great cultures have left their marks on the landscape, architecture and art of Turkey – a place of bewildering facets where East meets West with a flourish.

Richard Stoneman's concise and readable account covers everything including the legendary Flood of Noah, the early civilisation of Çatal Hüyük seven thousand years before Christ, the treasures of Troy, Alexander the Great, the Romans, Selcuks, Byzantines and the Golden Age of the Sultans to the twentieth century's great changes wrought by Kemal Atatürk and the strong position Turkey now holds in the world community.

To order your free 32-page full color
Interlink catalog specializing in world travel, world literature
in translation, and world history and politics, please call us at
1-800-238-LINK
or write to us at the following address:
Interlink Publishing
46 Crosby Street, Northampton, MA 01060
Tel: (413) 582-7054   Fax: (413) 582-7057
e-mail: interpg@aol.com